Coming Together in the Great Turning

Collective Liberation and Work That Reconnects

Aravinda Ananda • Molly Brown
Kurt A. Kuhwald

Copyright © 2026 by Aravinda Ananda, Molly Brown, Kurt A. Kuhwald.
All rights reserved.

Cover design by Diane McIntosh.
Cover image: ©iStock

Printed in Canada. First printing October 2025.

Inquiries regarding requests to reprint all or part of *Coming Together in the Great Turning* should be addressed to New Society Publishers at the address below. To order directly from the publishers, please call 250-247-9737 or order online at www.newsociety.com.

Any other inquiries can be directed by mail to:
New Society Publishers
P.O. Box 189, Gabriola Island, BC
V0R 1X0, Canada
info@newsociety.com

New Society Publishers is EU Compliant. See newsociety.com for more information.

LIBRARY AND ARCHIVES CANADA CATALOGUING IN PUBLICATION

Title: Coming together in the great turning : collective liberation and work that reconnects / Aravinda Ananda, Molly Brown, Kurt A. Kuhwald.

Names: Ananda, Aravinda, author, editor. | Brown, Molly Young, author, editor | Kuhwald, Kurt A., author, editor.

Description: Includes bibliographical references and index.

Identifiers: Canadiana (print) 20250263319 | Canadiana (ebook) 20250263386 | ISBN 9781774060131 (softcover) | ISBN 9781550928068 (PDF) | ISBN 9781771424028 (EPUB)

Subjects: LCSH: Activism. | LCSH: Social action. | LCSH: Social movements. | LCSH: Social justice.

Classification: LCC HN18.3 .C66 2025 | DDC 361.2—dc23

New Society Publishers' mission is to publish books that contribute in fundamental ways to building an ecologically sustainable and just society, and to do so with the least possible impact on the environment, in a manner that models this vision.

Praise for *Coming Together in the Great Turning*

While Joanna Macy's foresight in naming The Great Turning was prophetic, the beautiful work she created in the Work That Reconnects was in need of an update—so much has changed, evolving so rapidly in these past few years. For anyone who's been drawn to the beauty and power of the Work That Reconnects, this book is a timely adjunct, providing tools, practices, framing, and facilitation tips to help make the Work more accessible to people of many ages and identities. Given the genius of Joanna's work, it merits all the care, framing, and insight that may be readily accessed in these pages.

—Nina Simons, author, and Co-Founder and Chief Relationship Officer, Bioneers

I'd place this book next to *Coming Back to Life* on the shelf, not as a replacement but as a companion that brings the work into this new era with clearer eyes and a wider web. It remembers that forests fall when people are devalued, and that people fall when forests are cut down. It treats liberation not as a metaphor, but as the ground we plant in.

—John Seed, founder, Rainforest Information Centre, and long-time facilitator, Deep Ecology and the Work That Reconnects

Brilliant, helpful, and kind. The authors lovingly guide us through difficult truths on the path towards collective liberation. They provide diverse historic, cultural, and practical examples for growing the capacity of the Work That Reconnects to be more effective in creating deeply interconnected, just, and inclusive spaces. This book is a valuable resource for anyone working with groups to co-create a flourishing world for all.

—Constance Washburn, Founding Weaver of the Work That Reconnects Network, and Co-director, Spiral Journey Facilitator Programs

Coming Together in the Great Turning is an extraordinary, exquisitely articulated manifesto and guidebook for community and cultural transformation. Written by a vibrant assemblage of noted contributors from the collective liberation community, this book crafts flesh on the bones of a wizened response to the polycrisis and the dissolution of industrial civilization. It skillfully and compassionately guides us from interlocking systems of toxicity to flourishing wellsprings of interconnected support.

—Carolyn Baker, Ph.D., Executive Coach and Mentor, and author, *Undaunted, Collapsing Consciously,* and *Savage Grace*

This book is a comprehensive, instructive, challenging, and eye/heart/mind-opening exploration into collective liberation and its necessity for the Work That Reconnects and the Great Turning. An essential read for all WTR facilitators and facilitators of group process, *Coming Together in the Great Turning* is an important resource for the ongoing evolution of the Work That Reconnects.

—Kathleen Rude, facilitator, the Work That Reconnects, and lineage tender, environmentalist, ceremonialist, activist, and author, *The Redemption of Red Fire Woman*

The Work That Reconnects has been an essential framework and toolbox in my journey facilitating groups of white people with wealth reckoning with ancestral harm and moving toward repair. Just as I support people in engaging with their own family legacies, *Coming Together in The Great Turning* offers a reckoning for the Work itself—carrying forward what is most vital while letting go of what no longer serves. I am deeply grateful for the generous labor of Aravinda, Molly, Kurt, and so many others. This book arrives right on time.

—Morgan Curtis, Ancestors & Money coach

A welcome step forward. The great prophets tell us we must work together to survive a collapsing world. But, as Earth's people recover from 500 years of domination, we've only begun to find understanding and inclusive ways to work across our differences. With deep gratitude to the range of authors who've woven this quilt of history, theory, stories, and practices to guide us all towards more loving connection.

—Louise Dunlap, author, *Inherited Silence*

Contents

Foreword vii
by Pat McCabe (Woman Stands Shining)

Welcome xi

PART I—Context and Overview

Chapter 1: Taking Heart at the Trailhead
By Aravinda Ananda, Molly Brown, and Kurt A. Kuhwald 3

Chapter 2: Updated Overview of the Evolving Work That Reconnects
By Molly Brown 23

Chapter 3: From Interlocking Systems of Oppression to Interconnected Systems of Support
By Sarah Nahar 47

Chapter 4: A Critical History of the Work That Reconnects—Phases of Development
By Marc Decitre 71

Chapter 5: The Work That Reconnects' Evolving Commitment to Social Justice
By Marc Decitre 87

PART II—Expanding the Frame and Shifting Oppression Dynamics

Chapter 6: Freeing Ourselves from Systems of Oppression
By Aravinda Ananda 99

Chapter 7: Seeing and Addressing Oppression Dynamics: Part 1
By Aravinda Ananda 121

Chapter 8: Seeing and Addressing Oppression Dynamics: Part 2
By Aravinda Ananda 135

Chapter 9: Queering the Work That Reconnects: Embracing the Wild Fluidity of Life
By Ian Goh 155

PART III—Anti-Oppressive Facilitation

Chapter 10: Anti-Oppressive Facilitation
By Aravinda Ananda with Kurt A. Kuhwald 179

Chapter 11: Trauma Awareness and Approaches for Group Facilitation
By Aravinda Ananda, Margaret Babbott, and Janna Diamond 205

Chapter 12: Inner Work for Collective Liberation
By Aravinda Ananda and Molly Brown..................................... 223

PART IV—Cultural Contexts

Chapter 13: Culture and the Work That Reconnects
By Aravinda Ananda, Molly Brown, Rukmini Iyer, and Mayuree........ 247

Chapter 14: Re-Conectando: Weaving the Mycelium of the Soul for Peace in Colombia
By Helena ter Ellen, Héctor Aristizábal, and Liliana Moreno........... 267

PART V—Going Forth in Today's World

Chapter 15: Up Against the Limits: *Shifting* Towards a New Human Compact with Mother Earth
By Gopal Dayaneni and Brooke Anderson of Movement Generation... 297

Chapter 16: Whose World Is Ending? Resisting the Climate Apocalypse Narrative
By AJ Hudson... 323

Afterword
by Kurt A. Kuhwald.. 331

Appendices
A. Giving and Receiving Feedback About Harm 340
B. Community Agreements 349
C. Why Share Gender Pronouns.. 354
D. Reconsidering the Practice Called "Reporting to Chief Seattle"....356
E. Facilitator Assessment Guide... 358
F. Recommended Resources... 364

Acknowledgments.. 369
Endnotes... 376
Index.. 394
About the Authors and Contributors 404
About New Society Publishers 410

Foreword

by Pat McCabe (Woman Stands Shining)

Time keeping, histories, the age of human role and presence, are held differently by many Indigenous Peoples than by modern scientific views. Perhaps you have heard Indigenous People say that we are now in the Fifth World or the Sixth World; this implies that we have moved through other worlds than the one we occupy presently. One of my elders recounted that before we lost the world to the Great Flood, Dragonfly came to the People and warned them of what was arriving. Dragonfly counseled that if the Human Beings were to climb into the hollow reeds that perhaps they might survive the coming deluge. Some of the People were able to receive this counsel. They climbed into the reeds and waited. The flood waters rose higher and higher, but they did not go over the top of the hollow reeds. The waters subsided. The People emerged, and they say that these are the few Human Beings who lived to begin the Next World.

I think about those people often. I imagine them walking out into that new world with nearly nothing at all. People, places, structures, tools, gardens, societies, landmarks; all gone. While there are many "practical" and "pragmatic" logistics to consider, I find myself much more concerned with their inner resource. How did they steady themselves? What were they able to hold in the way of ethics, of spiritual bearing, of relational commitment? Just what was it that they reached for inside of themselves in such a moment?

Through ceremonial experience and through following the counsel and directives of guidance beyond human, I move in my life with the orientation that everything begins in the energetic, the "non-material realm;" everything begins in the intention, the belief, coupled with feeling, before it ever arrives in the physical realm. When I picture this Next World scenario, I think about how my words, thoughts, actions, willingness, and especially my relational capacities, might serve these Emergents. How can I fortify their inner resources from here, their ability to imagine, to intend a New World of *Hozho*—a Diné word, concept, Life Way, that might translate to beauty, harmony, thriving? A key aspect of my people's worldview is the foundational premise that we come from Original Beauty, or, Original Harmony - *Hozho*. This view holds that if we ever depart from that origin, that baseline, there are methods of restoration always available.

I consider Einstein's premise that we "cannot simultaneously prevent and prepare for war." It seems to me that that is exactly what we are called to do. The "war" being to stand my ground for Life, Light, and Love, for upholding the Honor of being a Human Being. I must understand and employ my powerful, sacred Gift of Consent by declaring "this I do not consent to," and "to this I give my consent." I must use all of my spiritual endowment to be willing to receive and assist my former opponents, as all new willingnesses arise in the most unlikely of places, as earth changes, political antics, fictional economies, and malformed narratives play themselves out. This is what the ceremonies are for: to give me a spirit fierce, soft, wise enough, to be able to receive my former enemies in their devastations/revelations to the degree in which I can, while maintaining my own well-being. Here, the spiritual principles of Radical Self-Love and Radical Self-Trust serve deeply (some will call this "trauma healing").

I am moving now from this logic. I am most interested in endeavors that bring about consciousness shift—which necessarily bring changes in belief, in willingness, and in feeling, too. I am interested in possibilities and movements of Radical Bridging. Who and where are the willing hearts, minds, and spirits that can risk opening to the "other," inquiring of the opposite or opposing, who can risk the vulnerability of receiving the tentative regret, confusion, pain, and fear of the beginnings of apology and reparation? Who can allow the relational landscape to sincerely shift?

I have a growing sense that it isn't all for me to "make happen." My part often is to declare my willingness and make myself available, to allow all of Life, this Mother Earth, Spirit, to lead me to the people, places, and events where my growing, transforming heart can hold and practice its nascent Radical Willingness. I release the twisted logics, the narratives, the fear, and sorrows of the Death Way, even as my body, my nervous system, is only beginning to unbend and unfurl from its miscreant adaptations. This allows vistas of new logics, methodologies, possibilities to come into play. Obstacles embedded in old narratives dissolve in front of my wide and tearing eyes.

For example: Land is being returned to Indigenous Peoples—the "Land Back" movement. Most Indigenous People I know never thought we would ever see such a thing happen in our lifetime. Sometimes land is freely given by private owners, sometimes it is public land return or joint use, and other times it is by purchase with the coming together of unlikely allies. But here's the thing, in every instance, as soon as the land "transfers" to Indigenous holding/care/stewardship, all the rules about "deeded land" suddenly come into question. It is not a principle of this grouping of humanity (Indigenous Peoples) to believe that it is possible to "own land." And yet, in order for them to have a sovereign relationship to place, modern-world paradigm insists that you must "hold the deed." This stunning event is interrupting foundational narratives: narratives of law, real estate, money/economy, ownership, traditional opponents, of siloed communities. I have come to believe that it is a genius strategy on the part of Mother Earth herself. I don't believe any of us could have contrived such a beautiful, *relational,* interruption of so many primary narratives that would seek to hold us onto paths of destruction. My part in this newness, often, was to recognize: If you can't give a full yes, just try not to say no.

Another is a Radical Bridging with Catholic nuns in the US. After some years of conversation and Radical Willingness on the part of all parties, we come to the moment where many of these nuns are declaring themselves "complicit no more with the doctrine of discovery." Sisters from five communities traveled to the deep desert in southern Arizona to stand with our Apache relatives at Oak Flat, a profoundly holy site to the Apache people proposed to be given to Resolute Coppermine by the US government in trade for other lands. We prayed together, we danced together, and the nuns held signs declaring that they stood for the religious freedom of Indigenous Peoples. A few months ago, one of the nuns' communities that we work with returned land to their neighboring Indigenous community. Unheard of.

While I do have a sense that at this moment, we are on the precipice of a Change of Worlds once again, I do not pretend to know what that looks like or what it means in any detail. It might very well be that many or all of us will step over that new threshold, or that the earth remains intact. Yet, I frequently engage with that image of a small group of humanity setting out upon the journey into the Next World somewhere in the near-ish future. It serves. I have no attachment to the thought that I might be, or must be, one of them. That seems beside the point. Instead, I find myself asking: How can my actions, my efforts, my life, right here and right now, be of service to those Ones Who Begin that Next World?

These instances I name are the source of my resilience. These shifts of the heart and in relations are what I live for, and are my offering to those Holy Emergents. Whoever they are, whenever their emergence occurs, what I would have kindling in their hearts, glowing in their minds eye, is the knowledge, the experience, of Radical Forgivenesses, of the most Unlikely of Allies finding their way together, in a Guidance beyond any of them, to participate in Beauties we only vaguely remember, or believed are possible.

Yes. I say yes. To the risk, to the excruciating vulnerability, to the breathtaking intimacy of the Work That Reconnects. It is now, in this time of transition and transmutation, that we, the youngers of the elder living world, find ourselves in a great school of UnLearning, and though it will no doubt be bewildering, Spirit has also said that its other name is to be: Joy House. With this work of willingness and refinement and reflection, *Coming Together in the Great Turning,* let us continue to make our beginning of finding the way for our participation in the very highest possibility for Life, Light, and Love. In my loving memory of dear matriarch and ally, Joanna Macy, with all of my heart, I say yes.

In deepest consent to the Authority of the Law of the Heart of the Mother Earth,

Weyakpa Najin Win
Woman Stands Shining
Pat McCabe

Welcome

Welcome to *Coming Together in the Great Turning: Collective Liberation and Work That Reconnects*

We authors/editors of this book are so honored to welcome you as a reader and global community member. We welcome you wherever you live in the world and whatever languages you speak.

We welcome you if you facilitate the Work That Reconnects. We welcome you if you are familiar with the Work. We welcome you if you are new to the Work.

We welcome your feelings as you pick up this book, whether they are curiosity or trepidation. We welcome your open hearts and your skepticism.

We welcome your culture and ethnic origins, your food preferences, music, cultural rituals, and all of the complexities that make up your cultural identity.

We welcome your race and your skin tone.

We welcome you with all of the relationships you bring with you: siblings, parents or caregivers, partners, children, animals, lands and bioregions, your ancestors and spiritual allies, and other loved ones. All your relationships are welcome here.

We welcome your spiritual practice, your religious affiliation, your walk with meaning—however you hold that aspect of your life.

Your love is welcome here. How you love, who you love, and your understanding of what love is are all welcome. We welcome you in all of the ways your sexuality is unfolding.

We welcome your gender identity and gender expression.

We welcome you wherever you are on your learning journey towards collective liberation.

We welcome you whatever your socially assigned privilege and proximity to power. We welcome you if you have been harmed by oppressive systems and we welcome you if you have harmed others. We welcome the complexity of feelings that may arise for you, your grief, guilt, or shame.

Your quirks and ambiguities are welcome. We welcome your humor and your solemnity. We welcome your affinities for silence or for boisterous expression.

We welcome the parts of yourself that you're still figuring out.

We welcome you in your roles as activists, healers, feelers, intuitives, parents, caretakers, students, artists, witches, diviners, change agents, magicians, educators, warriors, and peacemakers.

We welcome you whatever your range of mental, emotional, and physical abilities. We welcome your introversion and your extroversion. Your emotions, *all* of them, are welcome as well.

We welcome your wounds and scars. We welcome the experiences that led you to this moment.

We welcome your wise ancestors. *Ancestors, please be with us, collaborating with us to anchor the healing and what is most needed in these times.*

We welcome your sacred connections to the lands of your ancestors, the lands that hosted your birth, and the lands that you are currently standing upon.

We welcome all the life that came before you—the Indigenous peoples and ecosystems of the land you are now on.

We invite you to let your roots sink into this nutrient-dense soil, intertwining with the roots of everyone else reading this book and connecting to the root systems of all of the other living beings as we collectively build our power to create a healing community across continents and around our blessed Earth.

Welcome.

(Inspired by Training for Change's Diversity Welcome,[1] adapted by Spiral Journey Facilitator Development Program and further tailored by our team for this book.)

PART I

Context and Overview

1

Taking Heart at the Trailhead

By Aravinda Ananda, Molly Brown, and Kurt A. Kuhwald

You hold in your hands heartbreak and hope.

Coming Together in the Great Turning is the result of over seven years of labor to clarify and transform the generous and wise, challenging, and sometimes harmful, sometimes life-saving processes of the Work That Reconnects (WTR). The author/editors have undertaken this work so that concrete and viable practices, and sensitive, informed, compassionate understanding can illuminate ways of doing the Work That Reconnects that will reduce harm and strengthen authentic and just transformation for all participants, as well as facilitators. To do so is to undertake a direct path toward a profound realization: the full Gaian mandate in our times calls us to the collective liberation of *all* life and the flourishing of *all* ecosystems.

We want to emphasize that the opening line of this book does not read "heartbreak and *optimism*." It is rather *hope*, in tandem with the heartbreak that many too often experience in the world as well as in the

Work That Reconnects. Vaclav Havel's words on hope secure the path: "Hope is not the conviction that something will turn out well, but the certainty that something makes sense, regardless of how it turns out." It is, then, *hope* coupled with restorative processes that we want to lift up and engage.

And it is hope of a unique and actionable form that, instead of optimism, is both more relevant, and more attuned to the social realities of our difficult times. It is from this kind of hope that a committed, redemptive, and corrective understanding and facilitation of the Work That Reconnects may truly begin to emerge and flourish.

Here at the beginning, we take heart and support from the words of Dr. Cornel West:

> As a Black man in America, I am in no way optimistic about racism, but I do have hope. Hope looks at the evidence and says, "It doesn't look good at all. Doesn't look good at all. Gonna go beyond the evidence to create new possibilities based on visions that become contagious to allow people to engage in heroic actions always against the odds, no guarantee whatsoever." That's hope.

May this book offer that same sensibility and contagious visioning. We invite you to join us on this journey.

The Peril and Possibility of These Times

We are all bound together in this life on earth, and our collective behaviors shape our continued existence here.
  —Prentis Hemphill

Today's world faces a "polycrisis" comprised of interrelated, mutually amplifying horrors that threaten life on Earth from all sides. As humans, the need is great to come together to create a Great Turning to a life-sustaining human presence that works for everyone and all the living systems of Earth. As a species, we will not survive if systems continue that elevate the short-term material benefit of a few people over the health and welfare of the rest of humanity and the biosphere on which life on Earth depends. To come together in the Great Turning, we must recognize these systems of oppression and work to transform them into systems of mutual support. The lives of current and future generations depend on our coming together in collective liberation from systems of domination.

The creation of life-sustaining civilizations calls us to the centrality of collective liberation. Collective engagement in service to addressing the oppression of one group of people by another group of people is critical in order to move toward an authentically life-sustaining civilization.

Such collective action involves a varied spectrum of means and ends. The work of the WTR has flourished in its focus on the domination by humans of the web of life that is their home. What is further and crucially needed, however, in order to truly move toward a life-sustaining, global civilization, is to focus as well on the oppression of human beings by one another. Humans, after all, are embedded in the web of life, and the ranking and subsequent domination by human beings of life forms other than themselves is indivisible from the same mindset that ranks and dominates one group of humans over another. Addressing and changing this mindset is fundamental to the collective liberation of all life.

Further, the forces of othering, ranking, domination, and exploitation are interlocked and are the very roots of both ecosystem destruction and white supremacy. And because of their interlocking nature, it is impossible to adequately address ecosystem destruction without addressing white supremacy as well. Key to contending with how oppressions are interlocked is clarifying the fact of anthropocentrism as a dynamic that binds human agency to a destructively limited understanding of humankind's place in the web of life.

The results of the 2024 presidential election in the United States, and the ascension to power by the 47th president, have laid bare the racism, bigotry, misogyny, and unhinged impunity of the billionaire class and the right-wing ideologues who have assumed governmental power—they are alive and well as the bedrock of the American empire, which fully denies human integrity and the preciousness of all life—even as ferocious climate crises engulf the planet.

Advances in equity and justice face rollbacks on many fronts. Recent efforts to be more inclusive and respectful of the human rights of all humans are being met with resistance and active efforts to undo these gains. Some of us find ourselves in the midst of a tragic backlash: in the United States, the state of Texas recently banned the use of certain words in schools, like diversity, oppression, and gender identity. When the new presidential administration took office in January 2025, one of its first acts was to renounce and dismantle Diversity, Equity and Inclusion (DEI) programs in all government agencies.

What this abusive power further profoundly reveals is that moving forward to a just transition is only possible if we address the rigid and destructive hierarchies of human oppression. It is our hope that this book will be a meaningful and vital contribution to that transition.

As things fall apart, the need grows ever stronger to turn towards one another instead of turning on one another.

We need spaces to process the horrors of these times, to heal, replenish, and fortify for the work ahead. We need each other to be able to face and move through these feelings so that we may access something bigger than our fear—our love, passion for justice, trust, and space for the new. Being real with what is supports us to clarify and strengthen our empowered action and ways we can contribute to the healing of our world. Something quite magical is possible in groups that is not possible in isolation as we transcend dominant ideologies of separation. Belonging is medicine in today's fragmented world. We need spaces where we can heal our broken connections with each other and the web of life, our gaps in belonging with one another.

This is sacred work. This is a time when we need skillful holding and tending of group spaces such that we can receive nourishment, healing, unlearning, growth, empowerment, and transformation. We need spaces that connect us with each other, our inner power, our collective power, ancestors and future generations, and the healing powers in the web of life. We need spaces true to the name of work that reconnects.

The Work That Reconnects already has some decolonial approaches within it: connecting with the web of life, listening to life, and connecting with ancestors and future beings. It has helped to heal some of the worldviews and consequent relationships that got us into this mess, and yet a deepening is needed to more fully realize its promise.

While this book has a lot of content geared to people facilitating the Work That Reconnects, much of it is also more broadly applicable to anyone doing group work aimed at reconnecting people with themselves, each other, and the web of life, in order to support powerful action on behalf of the community of life. As such, it may be useful to more than just workshop facilitators, but to anyone seeking to facilitate group spaces that support collective liberation.

Why This Book, Why the Work Needs to Expand

In the years since *Coming Back to Life: The Updated Guide to the Work That Reconnects* by Joanna Macy and Molly Brown was published in 2014, numerous facilitators of the Work have become more acutely aware of and vocal about patterns of oppressive harm that have been showing up in workshop spaces.

Whenever we gather in groups, we bring all of our conditioning from the dominant culture, which, unless consciously interrupted, will lead to further ruptures in safety, dignity, and belonging. As Sage Crump writes in *Holding Change*, "Every time people are gathered together, the hegemony of dominant culture is playing out unless there is an intention to be/do otherwise."[1]

To confront this painful reality, we author/editors offer this book in order to address those patterns of harm—and the systems of oppression behind them—and to offer ways to replace them with "interconnected systems of support," to use Sarah Nahar's phrase in Chapter 3. We want to bring more attention to interpersonal and group dynamics in workshops.

People within the Work That Reconnects community, including editors and contributors to this book, have been advocating for an explicit inclusion of a commitment to collective liberation within the core assumptions/starting places of the work (theory), and how the work is conducted (practice). We author/editors and our contributors suggest ways to support deeper work, lessen harm, and respond compassionately to harm when it occurs. As adrienne maree brown teaches, "Any meeting or gathering is a space to practice the future together in the most tangible ways."[2]

Much of expanding the Work That Reconnects with a robust undoing oppression commitment is not specific to particular practices and teachings, but rather more generally relates to the anti-oppression awareness and praxis of the people engaging with this kind of work.

Joanna Macy's Central Contributions to the Work That Reconnects

Many of us whose lives have been profoundly transformed by the Work That Reconnects feel deeply grateful to Joanna Macy for her central contributions to its development and her extraordinary brilliance, generosity, and inspiration. We are grateful for her choice to keep this work open source so that many people can continue to benefit from it. In so many ways, Joanna has been one of the exemplary wise elders of this time. Yet, such a powerful contribution can also elicit aspects of celebrity culture and guru worshiping.

For all of Joanna's truly extraordinary contributions to the healing of our world, she is human like the rest of us, and was conditioned in many ways by dominant society. As a white, middle class, highly educated scholar, U.S. citizen, and daughter of a Protestant minister, Joanna carried her own social identities and social locations that influence the way she perceived and navigated the world, just as each of us do. Some of this was embedded in the work.

Some people have seen efforts to address these areas as an attack on the Work or an attack on Joanna, rather than being sincere, thoughtful, and necessary feedback about areas where the Work can grow and expand to have even greater positive impact. Joanna has made an enormous contribution in her lifetime, and this current effort of growing and expanding the Work That Reconnects needs the wisdom of a community. While this undertaking was not Joanna's to complete in her lifetime, we are grateful for her encouragement and support for this work:

> It is a good and necessary thing to take steps now to "decolonize" the Work That Reconnects. Midwifed by a white woman, it inevitably carries the limitations and distortions of white blindness. It is high time that clear and specific efforts are undertaken to correct for them—for the sake of us all in the Great Turning. (Letter, August 30, 2016)

About the Author/Editors of This Book

This book has contributions from many wonderful different people; please see About the Authors and Contributors at the end of the book to learn more about the contributors. The final form of this book was shepherded by three primary author/editors: Aravinda Ananda, Molly Brown, and Kurt A. Kuhwald. We have each written sections of this book and gathered chapters and sections of chapters from the wider community, curating them into the current collection.

The team organizing this book began with a fourth person, who, although we would like to publicly acknowledge and thank them for their positive contributions, has asked for us not to mention their name. We each gave many hours to this project (some considerably more than others) and as we did so, we experienced some great difficulties in working with one another, including disagreements about the purpose of the book and the use of AI.

Our work together, and these two disagreements in particular, brought up each of our respective life wounds, social locations, and conditioning. Many of the topics explored in this book were very much alive in our interactions: habits of whiteness and white supremacy, microaggressions, not speaking up after microaggressions happened, invalidations, defensiveness, empathy gaps, disproportionate divisions of labor, people not owning responsibility for the impact of their actions, people taking too much responsibility, and a lack of capacity to generatively navigate high levels of reactivity and triggering.

During the summer of 2024, we found ourselves spinning in meetings and unable to more skillfully address the dynamics arising among us. It became very confusing to sort out what members of our team were responsible for in current time and what may have been projections of previous life experiences. Despite concerted efforts, and faced with time and capacity constraints, we found ourselves at an impasse where dynamics were taking too high of a toll and we were no longer productively working together as a team. Completing the book we had initially agreed upon was in serious question. Three of us—Aravinda, Molly, and Kurt—who shared a more similar vision for the book and felt committed to the tremendous amount of work that had already been completed by contributors, decided to continue on as a smaller team with what would become this particular book. While some aspects of this juncture were a healthy splitting into what would become different book projects, the circumstances surrounding it have also caused deep pain.

Several months after the split in our team, a conflict transformation consultant recommended to us some more structured processes for equitable decision making as well as navigating moments of high activation/triggering. (Would that we had received and acted upon guidance such as this sooner!) Generatively navigating conflict and harm (two distinct things) are capacities that take a while to build, and developing greater capacity with this is something that is asked of each of us who are committed to a path of collective liberation. Even with years of experience and learning on the topics explored in this book, we three remaining author/editors still have particular learning and work to do to more deeply embody the work of collective liberation.

All three of us remaining author/editors are from the United States, and write and edit mostly from that perspective. Many of the things we share may be translatable in different cultural/historical/political contexts and some things may simply be different. To our readers in the many contexts outside of the United States, we hope there are useful lessons and parallels to your own context, even if the particulars are different.

We acknowledge the racial and other privileges present within this author/editor team and the power dynamics and limitations our collective lived experience presents. We are grateful for colleagues of the Global Majority who have joined us in this endeavor as contributors and acknowledge the ways in which we have not centered certain identities within our team structure.

Each of the three of us have been on a path committed to justice for many years, have much to share, and much still to learn. It is our sincere hope that this imperfect offering is still a helpful resource for moving more deeply and powerfully towards collective liberation.

Depending on where you are in your learning journey, some of what we share here may require more explanation and feel too advanced. For others of you, it may feel too basic, surface-level, or not decolonial enough. Where your understanding surpasses what is shared here, we hope you will contribute to the efforts to shape this evolution as a community. We don't consider ourselves experts on transforming systems of oppression; we care a lot and we don't have all of the answers. We know that we do not have to know everything in advance to commit to a north star of collective liberation, and know that we will discover and grow more on the journey.

While we three organizers of this book may be able to point in some directions for collective liberation, it certainly does not mean we are able to fully embody these approaches, most of which require life-long effort. Some of you will likely notice places where we are still operating from colonized thinking and perpetuating Business as Usual. It takes a lot to truly get free of these death-dealing systems. We need each other on this journey of learning, unlearning, and deep transformation in order for collective liberation to become more possible.

We have each put countless hours, dedication, and energy into writing and editing this book, and realize there are still shortcomings. Here are statements from our editorial team to share some about who we are and why we committed to this project.

Aravinda Ananda

At the time of this writing, I am a 41-year-old social ecologist living on Massachusett land in the northeast United States. I use she or they pronouns. While I come from a family of mixed European and African ancestry and identify as mixed race, I present as white to a lot of people and carry many of the advantages that affords.

Growing up in rural western Massachusetts where my mother and darker-skinned sisters were the only visible people of color, I witnessed from an early age how I was treated differently than my other family members because of the color of my skin. I have a mixed class background, having grown up without a lot of access to financial resources, but currently am in a comfortable middle-class household that I share with my partner Joseph and child Raphael. While part of my identity is nonbinary and queer, I present to many as being cisfemale and in a heterosexual relationship. Having attended several elite schools, I have a significant amount of education privilege, and find myself to be generally able-bodied and neurotypical. Having substantial access to opportunities and resources, I hold a deep value that with great privileges come great responsibilities. I have received so much in my life, and feel it is my duty to give back what I can.

For many years I called my life's work "Living rEvolution," which is helping to facilitate a shift in human relationships with the web of life to be more life-affirming and sustaining. I was working on a book of that title when I first encountered Joanna Macy's writing and the Work That Reconnects in 2008 as part of my research. I immediately fell in love with the Work and felt deeply nourished by it and started facilitating the Work That Reconnects around 2010.

In 2014 my relationship with facilitation of this work shifted when I was on the co-facilitation team for a program called the Earth Leadership Cohort (ELC) which is an immersion in the Work That Reconnects for people ages 18–30. To date, there have been five of these cohorts, and while the format for each has varied to some extent, each program has included the cohort joining a larger intergenerational group for a workshop as well as a separate retreat just for the cohort. In 2014 we brought the first cohort to a larger intergenerational workshop of

80 people facilitated by Joanna Macy. Of the 15 ELC participants, the only person who identified as a person of color withdrew after the first meeting. This was a real wake-up call for me.

While the participant had numerous reasons for withdrawing, some of the reasons had to do with how unwelcoming it was for them to be in such a white-dominant space—white dominant both in terms of who was in the room as well as who was being centered. One factor was that during the Harvesting the Gifts of the Ancestors practice, this participant experienced the way the practice was shared as speaking more to the European experience than to their family's experience, and thus they felt written out of the work. I knew at that moment that if I was going to be in integrity with facilitating something true to the name of Work That Reconnects, I needed to be able to grow in my facilitation of this Work to be more inclusive of everyone in the room.

Since 2014 I have been exploring how to facilitate the Work That Reconnects in ways that better address how systems of oppression show up. Whenever possible, I have sought to work with others in this exploration whether as the lead convenor of the Anti-Oppression Resource Group (a community of practice focused on anti-oppression approaches to WTR facilitation), or as one of the guest editors of the August 2017 special issue of *Deep Times* journal focused on the impact of race and culture on the Work That Reconnects, or as one of the co-authors of a document entitled "De-escalating patterns of harm in white dominant spaces," or as one of the editors of this book.

One of the most difficult things I have ever done has been persevering with the content and the dynamics of the team working on this book, while parenting a child under the age of two and a half years, and amidst a host of other responsibilities. I offer it with humility and love, and I hope that this is of service to healing in the world. May we each be part of the medicine needed in this planet time.

Molly Brown

I am an 83-year-old white middle-class EuroAmerican neurotypical straight cisgendered woman, descended from Northern European (mostly Swiss) and some Greek ancestors. I've been married for over 60 years to Jim Brown. I grew up in Los Alamos, New Mexico, and have lived in both New Mexico and California most of my life. I was disabled as a child with hip dysplasia, but able-bodied as an adult until my older years, when I now have some hearing loss. Although my parents taught me to respect all races, the whole family was conditioned in a racist, colonial culture, and I have worked hard to overcome this conditioning—especially in the last ten years. Growing up in New Mexico, I certainly witnessed prejudice against—and oppression of—Hispanic and Indigenous peoples, as well as misogyny and various other forms of patriarchy.

I have been involved in the Work That Reconnects and related endeavors for 35 years. When Joanna Macy and I wrote the second edition of *Coming Back to Life* (published in 2014), we had become more keenly aware of the history of the transatlantic slave trade and slavery in the USA and its lasting impact in the USA and world-wide, including mass incarceration targeting black and brown people. We cited examples of injustice and oppression when describing the Great Unraveling and the state of the world. However, neither of us had grasped the full extent and impact of racism as a weapon in the class war that continues to concentrate wealth and power in the hands of a few while manipulating everyone else to blame other groups for the challenges they face. I realize now that as two older white EuroAmerican women, our perspective was (and is) understandably limited, although we didn't see that at the time.

Not so many years ago, I thought "white supremacy" referred only to neo-Nazis and other outspoken racists. Now I understand that the term also refers to a globally dominant political, economic, and cultural system in which white (or lighter-skinned) people control most of the power and material resources. White supremacy culture holds conscious and unconscious assumptions that the way that most white people think and act is the norm to which everyone else is expected to conform. Any deviation from that norm is seen as inferior or problematic—at best something to be merely tolerated—rather than an equally valid or possibly healthier way to think, act, and live.

Over the last ten years or more, many people in the Work That Reconnects community and beyond have worked to raise awareness of how unconscious white supremacist bias and assumptions have shaped the Work That Reconnects and played out in WTR spaces, so that what happens in workshops can be unwelcoming—and even harmful. When I found out that a group of WTR facilitators had formed to address this concern, I joined them. This group later came to be called the Anti-Oppression Resource Group (AORG), and the efforts of this group gave birth to this book project.

Rereading *Coming Back to Life* with this broader understanding, I see so much I would like to change! For example, Joanna Macy and I quite often used the plural possessive pronoun "we" when referring to humanity in the 21st century. We did so in order to express the belief that when it comes to the polycrisis now facing the planet, all of humankind is caught in what Rev. Martin Luther King, Jr. called an "inescapable network of mutuality."

I now realize that the use of "we" often actually—although unconsciously—referred to people like ourselves, rather than all people—that is, to those who live in modern industrialized countries where the government, the economy, and cultural norms directly benefit them and systemically exclude groups of others deemed less deserving. Simply put, our use of "we" often excluded most People of the Global Majority. I have been alert to correct that in writing and editing this book.

I have learned so much in the process of working on this book—and I'm still learning! I am learning about my own blindspots, my own unconscious biases and racist, ableist, classist assumptions. I am learning how to hear, comprehend, and acknowledge—without defensiveness—the harmful impacts of my speech and actions. I am learning how my relative position of power and authority impacts others in challenging ways, no matter what my intentions may be. And I keep learning more about multiple systems of oppression that are so deeply and tragically entrenched in the modern world and throughout its history.

I pray that the Work will continue to evolve to better support and inspire everyone working for a Great Turning to a loving, thriving, and peaceful future for all Earthly beings.

Kurt A. Kuhwald

At the outset of this bio I can say that, while the team-writing journey of this book has been one of the more difficult and challenging experiences I've had in these latter decades of my 81 years, it has, paradoxically, also been one of the most rewarding. I say this because for most white people raised in the United States, racial issues are among the hardest personal dynamics to see, accept, and to heal—at least for me they have been. In this book project, I have had to acknowledge that even as an elder person, the work—my work—for racial healing truly is life long. I feel blessed that sitting down to finish this bio on a clear, crisp, and cold Oakland morning, I have been brought, yet again, into the chastening, cleansing, and welcome arms of humility. Necessarily facing into my own white privilege from that sacred space, I know, yet again … I am simply human, doing my best to live honestly, fully, and with as much compassion, courage, and care as I can. Thanks to my team members, Aravinda and Molly, for their grit, honesty, resolve, and care—it has been more than an honor to work with them.

I came to the Work That Reconnects via the book, *Coming Back to Life*. It opened my heart-mind to the climate crises while on a silent retreat in Big Sur, California, in August of 2006. Under *Coming Back to Life*'s thrall, that September, I attended an intensive in the Work, led by Joanna Macy, seaside, at the mouth of the Salmon River in Oregon.

Those two experiences brought this white-identified, straight, cis-gendered male, and person-without-visible-disabilities, into a cauldron that contained enthusiasm, empowerment, community, loving friendship, intellectual enrichment, zealousness … and a deep dis-ease that grew over the years of my involvement and facilitation within the WTR community. That dis-ease, about the WTR's lack of presencing human trauma and oppression, is what brought me to this author/editor team.

Significant to the foundation of my dis-ease within the WTR was my father's influence on my psycho-social-spiritual development. His war-time-induced PTSD, incorrectly diagnosed in the waning years of the U.S. "police action" in Korea (1950–53), drove him over a 15-year arc of misery, violence, and alcoholism, to suicide. Addressing the deep wounds I received at his hands became a life-long project of inner liberation, and added fuel to my commitment to justice in the world. That inner liberative process was actively kick-started in my adolescence after my mother, bravely, and scandalously for the times, divorced my father and began the difficult life of a divorcée and single mother. Soon after the divorce, she entered a self-study process as a student of a small, esoteric psycho-spiritual program led by a brilliant, diminutive woman, Helen Craw. The Helen Craw Theosophical Foundation became the family religion. Based on the work of mid-20th century psychotherapists (chiefly C.G. Jung and Karen Horney), it established my life-long understanding that we are rooted in the divine, that there is fluidity, immensity, and sacredness at our core. It also taught me that the multiplicity of sacred and foundational qualities that make up our human personhood, when traumatized and/or consistently, negatively conditioned, take on defensive roles that are frozen in the past, restricting and distorting our true potential.

Ironically, when I was 78 years old, I was introduced to a similar work, Internal Family Systems (IFS) which has deeply supported my understanding of our human journey as well as of humankind's inner multiplicity. All these learnings illuminate, for me, the centrality of human liberation within the context of our current Gaian unraveling.

As a Special Education teacher with adolescents and young adults; as a psychotherapist in mental health clinics, adolescent drug rehab units, and individual practice; accompanying people living homeless in San Francisco's Tenderloin; as a Unitarian Universalist minister leading middle-class, predominately white congregations to face into their white privilege; as a Seminary Professor exploring personal Presence when speaking in public, and also plumbing the depths of the climate crises; and on the streets and in City Council meetings, working in coalitions for worker justice as Interfaith clergy; and sitting in rooms with individuals deeply exploring the sacred importance of what most deeply sources them on their passages into freedom ... in all of that ... the sanctity of the human person and the dignity of the human spirit have shown me that whatever oppresses that sacredness oppresses all of life and the Earth and that injury against the Earth, and the life that expresses its spirit in animal and plant form, is a poisoned arrow flying straight out of the traumatized human heart. Liberating Earth's processes, *along with the liberation of oppressed and exploited humankind*, which has been neglected within the WTR, is, for me, a vision and path into the future.

That vision and the trauma-informed, anti-oppressive analysis and practices offered in this book, offer the final resting ground for my disease. I pray it will be of benefit.

Considerations for Language in Writing This Book

What feels like respectful language to different identity groups changes over time. For example, "colored people" is no longer a used expression, and People of Color is also falling out of use by many people who would be categorized that way. While some people use the term BIPOC which expands the complexity of who is included (Black, Indigenous, and People of Color), others do not use it because it defines a group in reference to another dominant group. For this reason, and because numerically they are a majority, people who are not of European/white ancestry will be referenced as People of the Global Majority. Likewise, what feels like respectful language has also changed over time about ability, disability, sexual orientation, gender, and all kinds of social identities. The author/editors of this book have tried our best to use up-to-date language that is respectful, and offer our sincere apology if we use language to describe an identity group you are a part of that lands as disrespectful.

> *People use different terms to refer to the work explored in this book. Some terms used in this book include:*
>
> **Anti-oppression or undoing oppression** is the work of understanding how systems of oppression work and how to interrupt and transform those systems.
>
> **Liberation** is a framework of action guided by the premise that the only way to end systemic oppression is by dismantling

> the system itself, as opposed to only giving people equitable resources so they can exist under a system that doesn't naturally benefit them.
>
> **Collective liberation** recognizes that systemic oppressions are interconnected, and we are stronger if we work together to dismantle interlocking oppressions in concert with one another, and that our liberation is bound up with each others' liberation: none of us are truly free until all of us are free.

When "we" or "our" or "us" appears in this text, we author/editors have tried to indicate specifically to whom those terms refer. As Molly acknowledges in her biographical statement above, "we" statements such as "We are destroying the environment," act as if "we" included all people equally on the planet. And yet, every human on Earth is not equally responsible for the global polycrisis in all its facets. Individuals and communities contribute in different ways and are affected in very different ways.

Shared Beliefs, Values, and Commitments

While the author/editors of this book have varied perspectives and approaches, we share some beliefs, values, and commitments. While we may use different terms to describe our work, at its heart ours is the work of confronting and transforming mindsets, worldviews, and orientations and actions that disrespect and degrade life, with particular attention to the oppression of humans. Our pursuit is liberation from the many systems of domination, exploitation, extraction, and denigration that disrespect and harm life, that subjugate human bodies and the body of the wider living land to the engines of profit and power for the few.

We author/editors believe that everyone in the web of life belongs, everyone matters, and we want everyone to have basic safety and well-being and the opportunity to flourish, thrive, and realize much, if not all, of their full potential. Because we know that some people have been systematically denied safety, dignity, and belonging, we are committed to working to confront, dismantle, and transform human supremacy systems on all levels—internal, interpersonal, and systemic (institutional and cultural).

Therefore, we are all accountable for reducing and eliminating harm whenever and wherever we can. When people (ourselves included) stray from that ethic, we can call them up to a higher place of care and respect for all life, and we are committed to learning non-punitive ways of doing that. We may not be able to ensure safe spaces, but we can commit to creating brave spaces, where ruptures in safety, dignity, and belonging are not ignored, but are explored and, as far as is possible, transformed. It can take courage to confront these massive systems of violence that show up in both subtle and not so subtle ways in group spaces.

At its heart, a commitment to collective liberation isn't about being "right," "woke," or "one of the good ones," and it certainly isn't about perfection. This work requires humility because each of us will likely make many missteps on this journey. As we all often miss the mark, we can continually commit to certain values and work day by day to embody those values. Our values can be our compass.

This work also requires humility because it takes a lifetime, if not lifetimes, to undo toxic conditioning and get free of oppressive systems, so we can start where we are and take one step after another. All of us are collectively called to be in it for the long haul.

Ultimately, a commitment to collective liberation is not about policing people's behavior, but rather holding healthy boundaries and calling people towards a deeper manifestation of Beloved Community. We can choose to have care for ourselves and care for one another at the core of our relationships. A commitment to collective liberation means that attending to how we are together is an important part of what we do together, as we work to shift, dismantle, and transform recurring patterns of oppression.

A commitment to ongoing learning, accountability, and embodied solidarity is asked of us, and we don't have to do this alone. In truth, this work is aided by doing it together. Long-term learning communities that meet over time can be particularly supportive. We are each asked to commit to inner psychological and spiritual work so that our actions can go beyond performative to embodied and integrated understanding.

In the chapters ahead, we explore reframing and practical strategies to infuse these values and commitments into the Work That Reconnects and our work more generally in the Great Turning.

Overview of the Book

Coming Together in the Great Turning is organized in five parts:

> **Part I — Context and Overview** offers updated framing and concepts of the Work That Reconnects, Sarah Nahar's analysis of systems of oppression and support, and Marc Decitre's two chapters on the historical context of the Work That Reconnects.
>
> **Part II — Expanding the Frame and Shifting Oppression Dynamics** explores how to shift systems of oppression and patterns of harm that show up in workshops, and Ian Goh digs into "Queering the Work That Reconnects."
>
> **Part III — Anti-Oppressive Facilitation** offers specific approaches to liberating group facilitation, including trauma awareness and the inner work needed for collective liberation.
>
> **Part IV — Cultural Contexts** explores cultural competency and respect; Rukmini Iyer and Mayuree share their work in India; and Helena ter Ellen, Héctor Aristizábal, and Liliana Moreno describe Re-Conectando's powerful work in Colombia with the Truth Commission.
>
> **Part V — Going Forth in Today's World** includes two perspectives on today's polycrisis from Movement Generation and Afrofuturist AJ Hudson.

> The **Afterword** offers a poetic reflection on the book from the perspective of an elder activist.
>
> The **Appendices** are not to be skipped as they offer some useful opportunities for going deeper, including a list of recommended resources.

There is a lot presented in this book! We would like to bring in a caution from the fourth core assumption of the Work That Reconnects which states that: "Cognitive information about the social and ecological crises we face is generally insufficient to mobilize us. Only when we allow ourselves to experience our feelings of pain for our world, can these feelings reveal on a visceral level our mutual belonging in the web of life and free us to act on our moral authority."[3] This is some of the magic unleashed in the experiential practices of the Work That Reconnects. Systems of oppression shut down feeling—as a survival mechanism for those targeted by these systems and, substantially, as a means for people in positions of power to avoid both accountability as well as feeling the enormity of the pain inflicted upon the larger body of society. While we author/editors present a lot of cognitive information about systems of oppression in this book, some of the deeper work lies with allowing ourselves to feel the pain they cause.

Realizing a vision of the Beloved Community requires that we practice beloved community daily, contributing to greater safety, dignity, and belonging for everyone. It is imperative that we be compassionate with ourselves and each other, as well as rigorous in interrupting and transforming oppression whenever it rears its ugly head. We will not be perfect. We will make many mistakes along the way, and we can choose to keep going, keep growing, and keep learning. Our current capacity limitations may not match our ideals; the important thing is to keep building over the long term ways of being that liberate us all from systems of domination.

2

Updated Overview of the Evolving Work That Reconnects

By Molly Brown

Coming Back to Life: The Updated Guide to the Work That Reconnects (2014), authored by Joanna Macy and myself, shares the theory and practices of the Work That Reconnects. While many people have contributed to the Work That Reconnects over the years, Joanna Macy wove these threads into a coherent body of thought and practice that continues to evolve. (See Chapter 4 for more about Joanna's central role.) In this chapter I offer an overview of the essential assumptions and framing of the Work That Reconnects, incorporating some new and expanded concepts and understandings that have evolved in the last decade through the work of many dedicated facilitators.

Global Polycrisis and Global Transformation

The underlying intention of the Work That Reconnects is to assist people in fully reconnecting with the living Earth and all its lifeforms, including other humans, and with themselves as members of the Earth community. The Work supports people in responding more fully and effectively to the on-going polycrisis of our time, with its multiple interconnected threats to life. The Work offers tools and perspectives to help people all over the world to "sustain the gaze"—to see, acknowledge, and respond to these threats—according to their specific resources and life situations, as well as envision a flourishing future for people and planet.

The polycrisis has many facets: widespread human oppression and injustice, arising from deeply embedded racism, white supremacy, anti-semitism, Islamophobia, ableism, and other prejudices; ecological destruction and climate breakdown; dominance of the "military-industrial complex" with wars fomented for profit and political power; the erosion of civil liberties and human rights; and rising fascism and genocide. Many of these threats have become evermore deadly as technologies amplify their impact.

These crises are radically intertwined, arising as they do from a common root: the erroneous belief that individual humans exist separate from—and competitive with—the web of life and one another. As people come to realize the radical interconnectedness of all life, themselves included, they are more empowered to work for a Great Turning to a cooperative, life-sustaining society that is built on the health and well-being of all people and all beings.

The Work That Reconnects is based on a few core assumptions and concepts, many of which will already be familiar to anyone engaged in working for a more equitable, just, and sustainable world. Many will also be familiar to anyone who has been exposed to Buddhist teachings, which deeply inform the Work.

Core Assumptions of the Work That Reconnects

These are the core assumptions listed on the Work That Reconnects Network website, updated from the 2014 edition of *Coming Back to Life*:[1]

1. **Our Earth is alive.** It is not a supply house and sewer for the

Industrial Growth Society. As most Indigenous traditions teach, the Earth is our larger body.

2. **Our true nature is far more ancient and encompassing than the separate self defined by habit and Industrial Growth Society.** As a living system, the planet—having evolved us into self-reflexive consciousness—can now know and see itself through us, behold its own majesty, tell its own stories—and also respond to its own suffering.

3. **Our experience of moral pain for our world springs from our interconnectedness with all beings—including humans of all cultures—from which also arise our powers to act on their behalf.** When we block our pain for the world, by denying it or repressing it, or viewing it as a private pathology, our power to take part in the healing of our world is diminished.

4. **Unblocking occurs when our pain for the world is not only intellectually validated, but also experienced and expressed.** Cognitive information about the social and ecological crises we face is generally insufficient to mobilize us. Only when we allow ourselves to experience our feelings of pain for our world, can these feelings reveal on a visceral level our mutual belonging in the web of life and free us to act on our moral authority.

5. **When we reconnect with life, by willingly enduring our pain for it, the mind retrieves its natural clarity.** Not only do we experience our interconnectedness with the Earth community and the human community, but also mental eagerness to match this experience with new-paradigm thinking. Significant learnings occur as the individual re-orients to wider reaches of identity and self-interest.

6. **The experience of reconnection with the Earth community, human and other-than-human, arouses desire to act on its behalf.** As we experience our essential desire for the welfare of all beings, Earth's self-healing powers take hold within us. For these powers to function, they must be trusted and acted on. The steps we take can be modest ones, but they should

involve some risk to our mental and social comfort, lest we remain caught in old, safe limits. Courage is a great teacher and bringer of joy.

The author/editors of this book join with contributor Sarah Nahar and other members of the Anti-Oppression Resource Group to recommend yet another essential assumption:

7. **Collective liberation within our species is essential to the flourishing of the larger web of planetary life.** None of us are free until all of us are free. The Industrial Growth Society is founded on and perpetuates systemic inequalities. These structural power dynamics play out painfully in human relationships. When we address generational and contemporary oppressions as they manifest, we truly enact the Great Turning.

A beloved Work That Reconnects practice, **Open Sentences,** helps people get in touch with, and share, thoughts and feelings that may lie just under the surface of consciousness. Open Sentences are usually done in pairs, with one person speaking and the other listening silently, in turn. Here are a few Open Sentences that follow these core assumptions, as prompts to encourage reflection. To make use of an open sentence, simply repeat to yourself the opening words and let flow whatever comes forth from your mind and heart.

1. *When I think of myself as part of the living system of Earth, I feel ...*
2. *When I see the destruction happening in the world today, I feel ...*
3. *Some ways I try to avoid these feelings are ...*
4. *One way I feel called to act on behalf of life is ...*
5. *The possibility of collective liberation for all life stirs these feelings in me ...*

Additional Underpinnings of the Work That Reconnects

- **Moral imagination**

Joanna Macy describes the "moral imagination" as our capacity to imagine something different from what is now—for the good of the whole (community, humanity, or world). It is our human capacity to imagine and embody what it is like to be another person or another being. We use the moral imagination in many Work That Reconnects practices, such as the Council of All Beings, the Milling, and the Seventh Generation practice. It is one of our most powerful creative tools for personal and social transformation. Moral imagination also fuels the human capacity to enter the depths of fundamental goodness that exists in the center of the living world/universe.

- **Uncertainty**

With the polycrisis of today's world, humans now face the strong possibility that modern civilization will not survive, at least not in its present form. And if too much damage is done before modern civilization radically transforms, many fear that humans could be reduced to a few isolated groups of people scratching out a living on devastated lands.

Uncertainty is always part of life, especially in important transitions like birth, child rearing, rites of passage like adulthood, new relationships, marriage and divorce, new jobs and careers, and of course death. Uncertainty can bring us more fully awake and alert into the present moment, as we look for clues and guidance for how to respond. Rather than hold on to false guarantees, the Work That Reconnects supports us in embracing uncertainty in whatever endeavors we undertake. It is important to note that uncertainty is not the same as hopelessness.

As Botswana traditional healer and facilitator Lebogang Seitshiro observes, "There is no panacea, no guarantees. In contemplating impermanence, we become aware that everything is possible."[2]

- **Emergence**

In systems thinking (a crucial resource for the Work That Reconnects), emergent properties are those properties or behaviors of a newly forming system that were not predictable based on the characteristics of the subsystems or separate parts that make up the new system. If such properties cannot be predicted, then we humans must be constantly open to new possibilities emerging in every situation and every ecosystem or social system that we encounter or form. Rather than having a master plan that we doggedly follow, we tune into what is trying to emerge of a life-affirming nature, and step up to support it however we can. Intuition, meditation, receptivity (especially when out in natural settings), and moral imagination are all avenues for tuning into emergence. Many Work That Reconnects practices help us be open to and responsive to emergence.

> Open Sentences for these underpinnings:
> 1. *I tend to respond to uncertainty in my life and in the world by ...*
> 2. *Using my moral imagination, I can envision a world in which ...*
> 3. *I have experienced emergence in my life when ...*
> 4. *Some life-affirming trends emerging today that I want to support are ...*

Foundational Teachings from Related Disciplines

Joanna Macy and her colleagues wove many strands of scholarship into the Work That Reconnects, including systems thinking and Deep Ecology, as well as ancient and enduring spiritual traditions. In the process, the importance of a perspective emerged that includes human interconnectedness through time, with ancestors and future beings. Joanna calls this perspective Deep Time (a term geologists and philosophers have used to refer to geological time spanning billions of years). Practices were created to transform dominant relationships of power from "power-over" to "power-with." In more recent years, many facilitators of the Work have embraced a commitment to undoing oppression in all of its forms as being central to the Work.

The Three Stories

In addition to these theoretical and practical foundations, a central frame offered in the Work That Reconnects is "The Three Stories of Our Time." Since the 2014 edition of *Coming Back to Life*, many of us in the Work That Reconnects community have expanded our understanding of the scope of these stories and their relationship to one another. What follows is an updated revision/reframing/expansion that draws on suggestions and feedback from Patricia St. Onge, Kurt Kuhwald, Sarah Nahar, Aryeh Shell, and Joanna Macy.

A story is a version of reality, how someone sees and understands what is happening in the world. Often a story in a culture is largely unconscious and unquestioned by its members; therefore, people in that culture may assume it to be the only reality for the entirety of humanity, when in fact there are always multiple stories from many different cultures and worldviews.

The overstory that the Work That Reconnects offers about our current reality is that there are three stories relating to the industrialized world today: Business as Usual, the Great Unraveling, and the Great Turning. Each of these stories is intended to reveal a profoundly different lens through which people understand the world we all live in. Taken as a whole, they may assist people to make sense of what they see and experience, to navigate their own lives, as well as to engage in the work of change.

> The term "the Great Turning" is a cultural meme that appeared in the 1980s and 1990s to convey the revolutionary nature of the changes seen as necessary for the survival of life on Earth. Craig Shindler and Gary Lapin used it as the title of their 1989 book,[3] advocating a turn away from war and toward peace. The term arose again spontaneously from role plays in the Work That Reconnects, as people spoke for future beings in "deep time" practices.

While all three stories simplify vastly complex global realities, they can nevertheless offer fresh insights and clarify people's commitment to collective human liberation and the living web of Earth. Most of the stories that individuals, groups, and cultures hold as true have been formed and conditioned by their social, economic, and political location in society. Stories are tools for understanding reality, but they also shape—and even control—the picture of the world people believe they live in.

I offer this version of the three stories in the hope they will be helpful, but caution the reader about their inherent limitations. I suggest they can be seen as concentric circles of widening perspectives, the first being the most constricted and narrowly focused consciousness experienced by many people in today's world.

1. Business as Usual is the story of what has been called the "Industrial Growth Society" in Work That Reconnects circles—and it is also the story of the European-based colonial empires from which the Industrial Growth Society emerged. It is the dominant enforcing mechanism of a predatory, oppressive, imperialist, mostly capitalist, economic system (in other words, the corporate, colonial, financial, military-industrial complex) that perpetuates patriarchy and white supremacy for the profit and the power of a few.

The defining premise, which politicians, corporations, corporate-controlled media, and the military promote, is that there is little need to change the way we in the industrialized world live—and, in fact, there is no alternative! The central plot is about getting ahead by competing for profit and power by "growing the economy" and suppressing any deviant beliefs or practices. Economic recessions, extreme weather conditions, and civil uprisings and protests are seen as temporary difficulties from which mainstream society will soon recover and from which corporations and their wealthy owners can benefit. This story functions to maintain the power and privilege of a handful of ultra-wealthy people while legitimizing the impoverishment and disempowerment of the rest of humanity.

> There are always systemic forces at play, and a great many of them have to do with the core capitalist imperative to expand and grow by seeking out new frontiers to enclose.
> —Naomi Klein[1]

From its beginnings in England three centuries ago (and actually several centuries before that), the Industrial Revolution was funded by the enslaving and trafficking of Africans across the Atlantic Ocean, and built upon the colonial theft of land and life of Indigenous peoples in the Americas, Africa, Australia, and Asia. Business as Usual ignores or discredits the essential labor that enslaved and colonized peoples have contributed to the apparent success of the industrialized world, even as it has destroyed their lives, freedom, and cultures and suppressed the history of their oppression.

Most people caught up in the dominant socioeconomic system may assume this story to be the only possible reality.

> In my daily life, I see evidence of the Business as Usual story in …
>
> Business as Usual has affected my life in these ways …

We who live in settler colonial states like the United States, Canada, and Australia have, for the most part, never truly reckoned with the fact that our nations exist only because of the twin thefts of stolen land and stolen people, that slavery and genocide were the bloody subsidies that allowed colonists, many of whom were themselves in debt peonage, to engage in their self-making adventures. And neither have the European nations that launched those colonial crusades in the first place.

—Naomi Klein[2]

2. The Great Unraveling is the expanded story told by scientists, journalists, activists, and others attuned to the growing catastrophic dynamics caused by Business as Usual. Their accounts cite definitive evidence of the ongoing derangement and collapse of biological, ecological, economic, and social systems.

The Great Unraveling is becoming increasingly apparent today to people in the middle and upper classes largely due to the accelerating rate of change and technological advances in communication. In stark contrast, however, frontline communities and lower socioeconomic classes have for generations directly and disastrously experienced the historic and ongoing unraveling under colonial expansion and rule. People of the Global Majority and subjugated communities have carried the weight of the unraveling for centuries. Their land has been stolen and despoiled, their labor exploited, their human presence marginalized. They have been violently assaulted in multiple ways. The horrors they have been—and continue to be—subjected to are chillingly pinpointed in Raoul Peck's docuseries, Exterminate All the Brutes.[4] With unparalleled dramatic intensity the series lays bare the use of violence by colonizing powers to secure complete dominance over "the Other."

The climate itself, its massive complexity and power, is now unraveling world-wide and the sixth great extinction of species is devastating sentient life of all forms. Hurricanes, earthquakes, floods, wildfires—and wars—amplified by global warming, leave millions of people without shelter, food, or potable water. Whole ecosystems are being radically altered, even destroyed, causing devastation from the particular (the collapse of bee colonies whose plant pollination is essential to plant and animal life) to the global (the reshaping of major oceanic currents that profoundly affect continental weather as well as the teeming life of the seas).

Military operations and warfare, as well as famine and drought, drive staggering numbers of people to flee for their lives, turning them into refugees trying to cross borders, who all too often are blocked from entry, incarcerated, enslaved, and/or consigned to detention camps for years on end. Systemic racism, class struggles, and long-standing cultural and religious enmities, promoted and exacerbated by those in power, take an immeasurable toll in human suffering.

> *Some of the ways I see the Great Unraveling happening are ….*
> *Some of the ways the Great Unraveling is affecting me deeply are …*

3. The story of **the Great Turning** provides an even wider perspective that includes the Great Unraveling and goes beyond it to envision a transition to a just and sustainable future for all living beings. This possibility is based in part on ancient lifeways that existed all over the world in pre-colonial times and that thankfully continue today in pockets around the world. In this story, attitudes and practices shift from exploitation to respect, from extraction to regeneration, from

competition to cooperation. More and more people come to see how interwoven we are as humans and biological beings, and to recognize that solidarity with one another is the surest way through these crises. The Great Turning, therefore, moves at the speed of solidarity away from hierarchical, fear-based competitive thinking and towards a just transition to a Thriving Life Global Society[5] for everyone.

The story of the Great Turning includes the resurgence of sustainable Indigenous traditions that bear strong witness to the interconnectedness of all life and bring forward regenerative lifeways. It includes as well the emergence of creative new responses, and the expansion of science, in particular, and relevantly, the life sciences—as well as the evolving insights and development of systems thinking. The efficacy of this story can be amplified from the perspective of future generations, an imaginative practice that taps into the deep power of all life and the further reaches of consciousness. From the view of future generations, the Great Turning strongly increases in momentum, accelerated by the choices of countless individuals and groups as they band together in growing solidarity, forging effective networks and campaigns all over the world.

> To truly love we must learn to mix various ingredients — care, affection, recognition, respect, commitment, and trust, as well as honest and open communication ...
> —bell hooks[3]

> *I see the Great Turning happening in these ways ...*
> *What most gives me hope about the Great Turning is ...*

The Three/Four Dimensions of the Great Turning

In earlier writings about the Work That Reconnects, the Great Turning was generally described as dynamically and simultaneously unfolding in three mutually reinforcing dimensions: 1) holding actions to resist and slow down the damage to Earth and all its beings; 2) transformation of the socio-economic foundations of our common life to what are often called Gaian structures; and 3) a perceptual, cognitive, moral, and spiritual shift to biocentric values and worldviews that affirm our human responsibility to life, in all its richness and diversity, and to future generations. This shift is made real through our courage to take committed and purposeful action.

The Buddhist Peace Fellowship framework of "Block, Build, Be" echoes these three original dimensions. Block refers to resistance or holding actions; Build refers to the building Gaian structures; and Be evokes the shift in perception and consciousness. I find these shorter names quite appealing in their simplicity.

In 2020, ethnobotanist and Work That Reconnects facilitator Jolie Elan proposed a fourth dimension: nurturing life. She placed this dimension at the center of the Venn diagram of the Great Turning, because the other dimensions actually grow out of "nurturing life." Many facilitators agree with this idea and have started including Nurturing Life in their descriptions of the Great Turning.

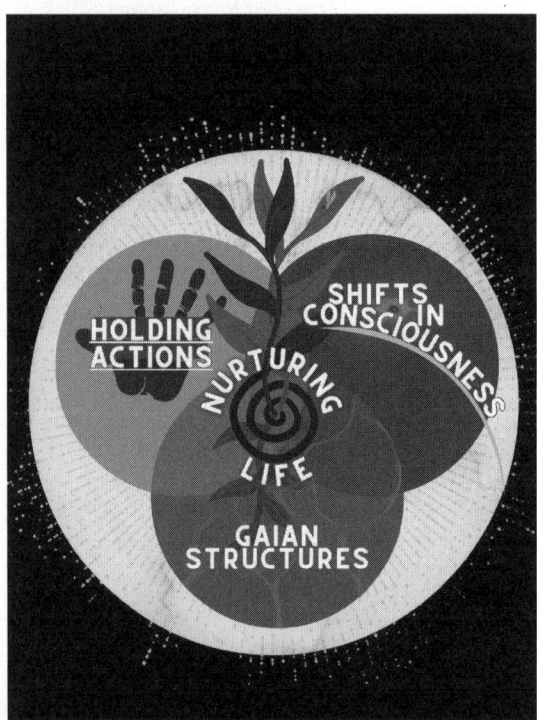

The four dimensions of the Great Turning.
Credit: Frieda Nixdorf

Nurturing Life

This newly named dimension of the Great Turning is so basic and essential that it can easily be taken for granted. Yet human life would not continue without people caring for one another and all of life in so many simple yet vital ways. Nurturing life includes caring for and educating children, growing healthy food for one's family and community, providing basic life-sustaining services for food, housing, health care, safety, and education in community, and caring for elders. It includes protecting the habitats of other species, along with wilderness, rivers, mountains, water, soil, and whole ecosystems—not only for the sake of humans, but for the sake of life itself.

Moreover, humans are embedded in, and integral to, the larger living world that is powerfully, sensitively, and intricately built on a deep natural ethic of care. From the responses of those species that protect their young and their collective, to the sharing of information and nutrients by trees to insure the health of the whole forest, to the great pulsating forces of survival that regulate overpopulation in a species—all these are examples of the deep care of Nature to maintain homeostasis—ensuring diversity, survival, and thriving for all life.

> The pervasive disconnection and alienation from Life that has resulted from centuries of colonization, imperialism, and industrialization has fortified a dominant society that distances itself from Life, imposes itself onto Life and is predicated on the illusion that humans are in charge.
>
> Humbling ourselves in service to Nurturing Life subverts this illusion and is a profound way to heal and repair this disconnection. By becoming intimate, once again, with the ways and the wisdom of the living world through providing care to living beings, ecosystems, and communities, we open ourselves—both personally and collectively—to the emergence of Life Sustaining guidance.
> —Jo delAmor[4]

I nurture life every day when I ....

One of the expressions of Gaia's care for life that most moves me is ...

Transformational Resistance/Holding Actions in Defense of Life ("Block")

Perhaps the most visible dimension of the Great Turning consists of the countless actions to creatively resist and slow down the destruction being wrought by the dominant predatory imperialist economic system. We refer to these efforts as "transformational resistance" because they also seek to transform destructive energies, policies, and behaviors, into more life-giving ones. They include political, legislative, and legal actions, as well as direct action to challenge oppression and exploitation.

In actions to defend life, solidarity is often key, for collective action helps generate and sustain the necessary courage, wisdom, and dynamism. Two examples of community actions are: 1) long-term protest camps, such as the more-or-less permanent reoccupation of portions of unceded Indigenous land in Canada, often to prevent mining and other industrial incursions; and 2) civil disobedience, including trespassing and symbolic sabotage on government or corporate property.

Historically and in today's world, protests and civil disobedience have been met with repression and brutality as law enforcement officers—and the laws themselves—treat activists as terrorists, repressing dissent, beating and arresting demonstrators, and punishing whistle-blowers. Police brutality is condoned, even encouraged. As the Business as Usual empire is exposed and threatened, the violence of its response becomes more naked and indifferent to public opinion.

I have taken part in active resistance to Business as Usual by ...

Building Gaian Structures ("Build")

This dimension of the Great Turning is essential in order to free ourselves and our planet from the damage inflicted by Business as Usual. It has two aspects: 1) understanding the dynamics of the dominant socioeconomic system, including the structures of law, economics, governance, and education that support it, and 2) generating structures based on the inherent authority and rights of all people to support the ecosystems on which life depends.

The savage reality of the dominant paradigm is very challenging to confront. It takes courage and confidence in our own intelligence to look at it clearly. People in ever greater numbers are discovering a plethora of resources that demystify the workings of this monstrous system. For all its apparent might, we also are increasingly able to see its fragility, dependent as it is on obedience, deception, secrecy, surveillance, and violence.

As we work to build Gaian Structures, we not only study the structural causes of the global polycrises, we also learn old and new ways to better serve the common good. All across the planet, people are banding together to take action in their own communities. Enslaved and oppressed peoples have struggled against colonizers and autocratic governments for centuries, leaving a legacy to inspire us today.

Some examples today include: the concept and practices of a "Gift Economy"; Black Lives Matter and related movements for liberation from white supremacy; Truth and Reconciliation Commissions, reparations, and other forms of restorative and transformation justice; retrieval and creation of laws to protect the commons from privatization and industrial harm; and so on.

> *Some Gaian structures emerging in my community are ....*

Shift in Perception and Consciousness ("Be")

Unfortunately, some holding actions or Gaian initiatives only tweak—or may even perpetuate—the dominant political economic system if they do not arise from a deep and broad understanding and experience of our radical interconnectedness and interdependence. This Shift in Perception and Consciousness, essential to the Great Turning, is underway now, as both cognitive revolution and spiritual awakening.

The insights and experiences that enable people to participate in this shift may arise from grief for our world that reveals the illusion of the separate and isolated self. Or they may arise through wisdom traditions of Indigenous peoples and mystical traditions in many religions. They may arise through psychological/spiritual work, such as meditation, spiritual guidance, entheogen-enhanced journeys, immersion in nature, or through life-threatening disease or injuries, or even spontaneously. These insights have led to scientific breakthroughs in quantum physics and systems theory, which then influence collective understandings and worldviews. These insights and experiences can free people from the grip of the neocolonial power-over paradigm, and lead to a redefining of wealth and worth, liberating them from illusions about what they need to own and what their place in the order of things should be.

Recent examples of efforts to shift perceptions and consciousness include: podcasts and articles that center voices of Indigenous, Black and Brown people; Aboriginal teachings for the protection of sacred sites put into writing for the development of an Earth jurisprudence; and grassroots educational efforts to transform attitudes, unconscious assumptions, habits, and behaviors that give rise to racism, patriarchy, heterosexism, misogyny, ableism, neuro-ableism, etc.

A shift in our collective sense of identity will be life saving in the face of the socio-political and ecological traumas that lie before us. The realizations arising within this dimension of the Great Turning can save us from succumbing to panic, paralysis, or violence. We join together with the living systems of Earth for healing and transformation, knowing that there is no individual salvation.

> *I have experienced a shift in consciousness when ...*

Beyond the "Industrial Growth Society"

The term commonly used in the Work That Reconnects for the overarching or underlying systems of Business as Usual is "Industrial Growth Society" (IGS). When I suggested finding a new term, Joanna Macy told me that she has used Industrial Growth Society for two reasons. 1) It is not inherently negative—so that people who believe in it, upon hearing the term, might say, "Yes, Industrial Growth Society, that's progress, that's a good thing!" and 2) The word "growth" is useful in naming the obsession with growth in profit margins and markets, which denies the biological limits to growth on a finite planet.

However, as my colleagues and I have discussed our expanding understanding of that dominant global political economy, "Industrial Growth Society" seems inadequate. For one thing, "Industrial" may evoke images of factories and material production, and only that. It doesn't include the complex predatory machinations of the global hegemonic financial system. What's more, the term doesn't even hint at the centuries of white supremacy and colonial expropriation of land, resources, and labor, enslavement and genocide, from which the IGS has risen.

Here's what I would like to be able to name in a few words: the overarching paradigm that dominates the industrialized and industrializing world today, that is committed to profit above all else, requiring ever-increasing extraction, consumption, and disposal of resources, that exploits the labor of most of Earth's people and/or drives them from their land, while using the Earth as supply house and sewer, demanding not only "growth," but rising *rates* of growth, control of markets, and widely disparate wealth accumulation. This approach to naming this overarching paradigm is similar to how Sarah Nahar names interlocking systems of oppression in Chapter 3.

So what shall we call it in the Work That Reconnects and elsewhere?

In the Business as Usual description above, I wrote about the "predatory, imperialist, mostly capitalist, economic system (in other words, the corporate, colonial, financial, military-industrial complex) that perpetuates patriarchy and white supremacy for the profit and the power of a few." I could also add "extractive, exploitative, oligarchic." That's hardly a few words!

I've heard the word "modernity" used by several current writers and thinkers, including Vanessa Machado de Oliveira and Bayo Akomolafe. Sometimes Bayo uses "white modernity," or even "whiteness," not referring to white people per se, but to the assumptions, beliefs, and social structures that comprise the Business as Usual/white supremacy/neocolonial world.

Vanessa Machado de Oliveira, in her book *Hospicing Modernity*, describes "modernity" this way:

> ... modernity is not a concept, label, or object of analysis. Rather, it is a worlding story, a complex adaptive living system that actually actively does things, including conditioning the habits of knowing and being of those whose lives and liveli-

hoods are intertwined with it.[6]

... Colonialism is identified as the constitutive underside of modernity: inherently extractive, relationally unethical, and ecologically unsustainable ...[7]

The complexity of our current dominant global systems of power is such that any one phrase or term risks omitting important history, groups, dynamics, and much more. So we author/editors have decided against using any one single term.

The Spiral of the Work

The practices of the Work That Reconnects have traditionally been organized around a spiral, mapping a journey through four successive movements or stages: Coming from Gratitude, Honoring Our Pain for the World, Seeing with New/Ancient Eyes, and Going Forth. These four movements support one another, and usually work best in sequence.

Although primarily used in workshops, these stages can also be incorporated into political and social movement work, providing opportunities for people to share their gratitude, to grieve and rage together, and to share insights and fresh perspectives that will support and enrich whatever actions the group undertakes.

The Spiral begins with **Gratitude**, because that quiets the mind and brings participants back to source, stimulating our empathy and confidence. Expressing our love for life on Earth, in brief and concrete terms, helps us to be more fully present and grounded for acknowledging the pain we carry for our world. Beginning with gratitude is not something unique to the Work That Reconnects but is common among many wisdom traditions and Indigenous cultures.

Honoring Our Pain for the World means allowing ourselves to experience and express grief, anger, fear, and other emotions when we witness or learn about harm happening to people and communities, creatures, places, or ecosystems (like rivers, mountains, forests, deserts). These emotional responses are real and healthy, arising as they do from our essential interconnectedness with all life. Honoring them helps us realize the essential meaning of compassion: to "suffer with." We rediscover the immensity of our belonging within Earthly life and our interconnectedness with people near and far, which can guide and sustain our actions.

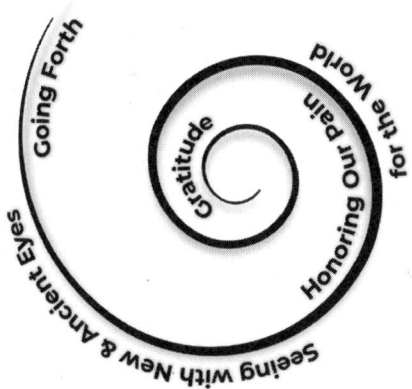

The Spiral of the Work That Reconnects
Credit: Frieda Nixdorf

Sensing the larger life within us lets people conditioned by modernity "see with new eyes," perceiving the world as many Indigenous peoples still do, and as most ancient human ancestors likely did as well. At this turning point of the work, we know more genuinely our relatedness to all that is. We taste our own power to change, and feel the texture of our living connections with past and future generations, and with our kin species. Many of us in the Work now call this stage of the Spiral, **"Seeing with New/Ancient Eyes"** to acknowledge that what is "new" to many people is not new to people still connected to their ancient Indigenous roots. For this reason, facilitator Jane Hera suggests calling this stage, "Seeing Anew with Ancient Eyes." To address concerns about ableism, some people no longer use the language of seeing, and instead use a phrase such as "Perceiving in New/Ancient Ways."

This stage includes **Deep Time**, connecting to and drawing upon the wisdom of ancestors and future beings; some facilitators consider this to be its own stage in the Spiral.

Then we **Go Forth** into the actions and lifeways that call each of us, in keeping with our life situation and gifts. We explore the synergistic power available to us as open systems and apply these understandings to our work for social change. We don't wait for a blueprint or fail-proof scheme, for each step will bring new perspectives and opportunities. Even when we don't succeed in a given venture, our efforts may have effects beyond what we can see, and we can nearly always learn from the experience.

And so the Spiral begins again. In the face of devastation and tragedy, gratitude can sustain us, especially when we're frightened or tired.

The Spiral sequence can repeat itself even within a particular stage. For example, the Seeing with New/Ancient Eyes stage may reveal to us with greater clarity the horrors being inflicted on the Earth community, bringing up fresh grief and outrage. We may need to honor that pain with a practice or ritual before moving on.

The Spiral can be discerned over the span of a lifetime or a project, and it can also happen in a day or an hour. Some counselors and life coaches have found the Spiral a helpful format for sessions with individuals and couples.

Many facilitators have realized that more preparation is needed to create a supportive and inclusive community container throughout the Spiral. Conscious attention to the diverse identities and social locations (see Chapter 6) present in the group can help build mutual respect, understanding, and compassion. These are so necessary for everyone to feel safer and more accepted. It is also essential to bring more attention to systemic oppression and power dynamics in the larger society—and the racist, sexist, ableist conditioning that so many of us carry (and act out) unconsciously.

In her work in the Spiral Journey Facilitator Development program, Mutima Imani has developed an "Decolonized Expanded Spiral" to address these needs. She adds two stages to the Spiral between Gratitude and Honoring Our Pain for the World: Self-awareness (also called Social Location), and Systems of Oppression (or Social Awareness). She adds a stage of Liberation following Seeing with New/Ancient Eyes and preceding Going Forth. To learn more about the expanded Spiral, see the webinar she offered through the Work That Reconnects Network (https://workthatreconnects.org/event/the-expanded-spiral-webinar/). Mutima has made huge contributions to the Work That Reconnects and I encourage you to check out her website. (https://mutimaimani.com).

> Here are four Open Sentences that can help the reader experience the four original stages:
>
> *Something I love about life is …*
>
> *When I see the suffering and destruction in today's world, I feel …*
>
> *A time I felt connected to something larger than myself was …*
>
> *Some ways I want to contribute to the Great Turning include …*

Practices of the Work That Reconnects

Practices and rituals form the core of the interactive body of the Work That Reconnects. Interactive practices help people to uncover and express both their gratitude and their pain for the world, to reframe and revitalize a deep and encompassing understanding of the world and their place in it, and to participate in the Great Turning with renewed focus and inspiration. Practices *do not tell people how they should think or feel;* they set the stage for the sharing and expression of what is already in the hearts and minds of participants (whether or not consciously) by virtue of everyone's essential interconnectedness in the web of life.

All the core practices, and many new ones, can be found on the Work That Reconnects Network website in their most current form (https://workthatreconnects.org). Many have been revised from the versions that appear in the 2014 edition of *Coming Back to Life* to be more inclusive and respectful of diverse human experiences and challenges. You are welcome to download and print out the practice descriptions for convenient use in workshops. (I have a binder to keep them in.) You are also invited to contribute your own new or adapted practices to help expand and evolve the body of the Work.

Some of the practices appear with "scripts" to help you guide them. It's best to use the scripts as a jumping off place, using your own words and examples according to your own experience and the needs of the group, to make them authentic to you and relevant to your group. Gradually, you may be able to dispense with the script altogether, or use it as an outline to remind you what needs to be covered in your directions.

Suggestions for guiding these practices: Try to make your comments non-prescriptive and in accordance with current issues and challenges. Use an ordinary tone of voice, without drama or sentimentality. And coming from someone with a hearing loss: remember to speak relatively slowly with sufficient volume so everyone can clearly hear.

In practices that involve people moving around, facilitators need to take into account mobility considerations by offering alternatives to walking around. Some participants may not be comfortable with physical touch or eye contact because of cultural norms or past trauma. Leave out the hand exploration section of the Milling if you have not had enough time to determine if there are people in the group for whom this may feel inaccessible. Avoid asking people to look directly into each other's eyes and offer alternative ways of regarding one another. You can invite people to close their eyes or lower their gaze whenever needed.

Three practices that have been particularly revised to address harmful impact now appear in the Resource section of the Work That Reconnects Network website: The Milling, Harvesting the Gifts of the Ancestors, and Accepting the Challenges and Gifts of This Lifetime (aka the Bodhisattva Check-in). Any of these practices can feel challenging, especially for people who have experienced trauma, abuse, or other difficult circumstances in their lives. Acknowledge at the beginning of each practice that this process might bring up pain. Suggest that participants hold themselves with gentleness; use trauma-release methods if needed; keep breathing. If possible, have a co-facilitator or other resource person available to accompany anyone needing support into another space, to be present and listen.

Let people know they are free to opt-out of any practice, using the time for reflection—meditation, walking outside, journaling, or art. Online, invite people to tell you privately in chat if they don't want to go into a break-out room; during the break-out room time, they can turn off their video and sound.

Note: Please see Appendix D for an exploration of concerns with the practice, "Reporting to Chief Seattle."

May these Work That Reconnects practices be of benefit for all who experience them as we facilitators deepen our skillfulness in offering them.

3

From Interlocking Systems of Oppression to Interconnected Systems of Support

By Sarah Nahar

Introduction

You are standing very close to a robin who is sitting in the middle of a small structure. You notice one wire, and that the robin is acting as if it perceives that this one wire is restricting its movement, making it unable to leave the structure. The bird chirps, and you recall the title of Maya Angelou's autobiography, *I Know Why the Caged Bird Sings*. But this robin could get out, you think. The wire only partially blocks your field of vision as you gaze at this rather attractive robin.

You eventually step back and other vertical wires come into view. You make eye contact with the robin. Your heart sinks, but you see the cage for what it is, an interlocking system of wires which surround the robin's space in such a way that escape is pretty much impossible. The mindset of deep ecology permits you to profoundly empathize; you put yourself in her place. Her pitch gets higher, her tweeting louder. Your mind rapidly runs scenarios. You think to hurl your robin-body against the wires hoping they will give way enough to break it slightly open; you wonder doubtfully if that will work. So you also try to calm your robin-self, gathering your energy in order to concentrate on creating a beautiful life within constriction. What song will you sing?

Black feminist author Patricia Hill Collins brought forth the term "interlocking systems of oppression."[1] Oppression is prolonged cruel, distressing, pressure and/or unjust treatment. Each type of oppression can be observed on multiple scales of life from the smallest to the largest (mono, micro, meso, macro, mondo). Different functional parts of society participate in perpetuating oppression, creating a system. Therefore oppression is systemic and systematic, rather than capricious; cruelty, pressure, and injustice are part of how a society operates and reproduces itself. Furthermore, each system of oppression (such as sexism, classism, racism, and ableism) interact and reinforce one another. While each type of oppression in and of itself has a devastating impact on everything a human does, the compounded intensity comes from the ways that systems of oppression interlock. Living life at the intersections of the interlocking systems creates additional invisibility and negative impact. It is the foundational aspect of intersectionality.[2]

Another aspect of intersectionality, according to Black feminist Kimberlé Crenshaw, who invented the term, is that challenging oppressions must take the interlocking nature of these systems into account. It is impossible to separate the various cage wires from one another as they come together to reinforce each other like steel beams, becoming stronger and inseparable as they do so. My identities, such as that of being Black and a ciswoman are interconnected in my body-mind-spirit. They cannot be arbitrarily separated from one another. This interconnection is positive and nourishing. My identity is neither a negative thing, nor the sum total of my existence—it is incorporated into the vessel through which I experience this life. However, in a society that privileges whiteness and maleness, the intersection of my identity results in the particular type of racism and sexism I and other Black women (trans and cis) experience—*misogynoir*.[3]

Therefore, any liberatory campaign addressing the sexism I face without paying attention to racism, or racism without paying attention to sexism—or both without attention to heterosexism and transphobia—will fall short in the long run.[4] This is especially true of environmentally related campaigns. All environmental subjects exist within interlocking systems of oppression and if we want to transition our societies from the current realities to liberatory, inclusive, and biodiverse community realities, we have to understand and take intersectionality seriously.

A disabled person who relies on electricity for medical support in their daily life is more likely to be impoverished because the healthcare system in the United States is not universally affordable. They may need to pay partially or entirely for life-preserving support systems that are tied into the grid. This is one way the system caters to able-bodied people whose employers pay for some or all health insurance. Disabled people also have less access to salaried jobs because the able-bodied are hired more often for them as they are perceived as more competent and capable than disabled people, even if job candidates' mental capabilities are similar.[5] This is one way ableism and classism interlock. Those systems further enmesh with racism, xenophobia, and carcerality (for example). If environmental liberation is envisioned *only* as reduced reliance on the grid, without accounting for medical or financial constraints or needs, then that vision perpetuates ableism, classism, and exclusion. For a disabled person in a Work That Reconnects (WTR) workshop in which the facilitator doesn't notice and/or carefully attend to the impacts of the interlocking systems of oppression, they may feel no relief from the "routine state violence and neglect" they experience elsewhere.[6]

Studying the Cage Wires

WTR Facilitators want people to feel relief in their workshops, so a growing number of us are rigorously studying obstacles to connection. As in the above example, they are assisted in their study by scholars such as David Naguib Pellow who are doing work with others putting critical environmental studies in conversation with disability justice. They theorize that climate change and "other environmental catastrophes, both swift and slowly unfolding, are mass disabling events for humans, nonhuman animals, and ecosystems."[7]

Their paper asks, "How can we develop a praxis of indispensability within our own communities as we face the impacts of climate change?" They begin to develop their praxis by sharing stories of networks of care "comprised of people with multiple marginalized identities ... who come together to explore how mutual aid can serve as an adaptive strategy for climate and environmental change by increasing community resilience."[8] This type of praxis requires that people speak their truth, and share their gratitude, sorrow, fear, anger, and other emotions and experiences. Praxis here is a combination of theory and practice, action and reflection, to obtain the best of both activism and scholarship. I see a WTR workshop as being ripe for participation in a praxis of indispensability.

This praxis is key now because the politics of *dispensability* are rampant, for example, eco-fascism, which advocates for policy based on the idea that only some people will make it out alive, and it's going to be *us* not *them* and so amasses resources only for the in-group's survival. As a facilitator, I feel empowered to draw on the scholarship of indispensability. One of the places within the WTR network where I brought this article is a space for discussion called the Anti-Oppression Resource Group (AORG). We began in 2017 as a group that wished to center an analysis of the interlocking systems of oppression within the context of WTR workshops. We collectively set our agendas in service of learning and co-metabolization of oppression. I say co-metabolization here because when we are together our organisms work together to digest the intensity of multisystem collapse; no one person has to do it alone.

We create space and time to put new information together with our lived experiences to expand our compassion and insight.[9]

Doing it together is helpful because analyzing interlocking systems of oppression is daunting. Things as they appear in any given society can be confusing. Cage wires not only travel vertically but horizontally—even diagonally—zig-zagging everywhere to make an enmeshment so intense it blocks out most of the light. Not only do caged birds sing, but they rage and ache, fantasize and dream—the bird's existence nearly circumscribed before we were born. Heartbreaking.

Group Agreements for When It's "The Work That Falls Apart"

When a facilitator is aware of how interlocking systems of oppression are functioning (both in macro-society and in the micro-society that is in their workshop) there is a much greater chance that a safe and cathartic experience for all attendees can occur. Building on awareness and theory, the AORG provides facilitators with opportunities to build their capacity, that is to practice responding to manifestations of oppressions (e.g. microaggressions, violations of consent, etc.). The more facilitators increase their tools to attend to the impacts of oppression in real time, and practice with those, the stronger our network gets and the higher the quality of workshops we can offer.

Addressing patterns of harm and oppression in real time doesn't necessarily mean "solving" an issue or doing something heroic. It means using the authority entrusted to the facilitator by the group to hold and craft the container even when ugly things happen. If a facilitator has rigorously studied how oppression functions, it supports them in responding in ways that enable everyone, (but especially those marginalized in macro-society) to be seen, heard, understood, and included in a way they are likely yearning for. The whole workshop does not necessarily need to change direction as a result of pausing to address and redress a painful moment. It may, but it doesn't *have* to. A facilitator is responsible for caring for the whole and providing leadership in that moment, strongly holding the container so that there is clarity of purpose, plans for care, and guidance for attendees with regards to their attention and energy moving forward. Attendees with lived experiences of structural violence are likely to feel more relaxed if they know that a facilitator understands the contours of societal and environmental oppression, embodies self-awareness, and has some competency with addressing patterns of harm as they arise, in a trauma-informed way.

I distinctly remember the moment at a WTR Facilitators' Intensive Gathering in 2017. After a series of major breakdowns during the intensive, the facilitation team (of which I was a young-adult member) was exhausted. We took a break to step out and regather ourselves. I offered to be the first speaker after the break and to share our process transparently with the group. It was a capable group of about 60 people, ranging in knowledge about the Spiral and basic assumptions of the WTR as well as other modalities. I was interested in leaning on their expertise for "where we go next." After the break when I began to speak, a young person's voice called out from the group, "You are the facilitation team, please do not simply hand it over to this whole group to decide where we want to go." I know from experience that group decision making can be exhausting, especially if that is not what people signed up to do together. This was the third day (maybe fourth day?) of an already intense intensive.

I knew that this person was not giving over their power of critical thinking or resisting an opportunity for self-governance. They were calling me and the rest of the facilitation team to recognize the power and position we were in to hold and craft the container so that participants could do what they signed up to do—go deep and be vulnerable in the context of their acute feelings of rupture. In what has become one of the most instructive facilitation events of my life thus far, I responded affirmatively to their plea. I read the diverse, disoriented room as best I could, and took the risk to offer strong guidance as to *what to do next*. Though marked by hurt, things flowed from there. Through this I learned that providing sufficient predictability and continuity is key to supporting flow, even as the torrent of chaos pulls at all of us constantly. A WTR facilitator is signing up to provide this for the group they gather.

As a facilitator who seeks to support a range of attendees, I recognize that the patterns inscribed by interlocking systems of oppression are always and already with us as any group gathers to do the WTR, whether or not the oppressions overtly present themselves. Workshops are not a space sealed from broader society, in fact *they are constituted by broader society*. Sometimes group agreements are written to address what to do "when harm happens" rather than recognizing that harm is *already* happening. Group agreements, then, can be commitments to stopping the flow of activity to give attention to a noticing of oppression that becomes glaringly obvious to someone, or to support re-focusing on something acutely hurtful in order to deepen in intimacy and clarity for the remainder of the workshop. In order to support the development of group agreements (without overwhelming a newly gathered group by asking them to make many decisions together), I provide a number of them.[10] I then ask the group to add, challenge, or raise questions about any of them with the purpose of establishing a set of agreements to which each person will commit. I use this activity as an exercise after I talk about the Great Turning and before going into the Spiral because in the Great Turning we will self-govern at multiple scales; group agreements are an opportunity to practice ways of being together with one another in a liberatory and life-sustaining way.

Other parts of this book speak to the negative impact of using the term "we" in a generalized way. Generalizations regarding humanity and "humanity's actions" toward the rest of the natural world are unhelpful and elitist. In that same vein, it is not sufficient to simply state in a workshop group that all humans "simply have different experiences," or that "everyone is oppressor and oppressed." While these generalizing statements are sometimes said with the intention of making space for the gathered group's diversity, the impact is that statements like these inadvertently reduce space. Explicit permission to name the interlocking systems of oppression, as it comes from the heart, is what I've found to create more space to grieve, rage, sigh, and breathe together.

From Interlocking Systems to Interconnected Support

This work of noticing, naming, strategizing, and dismantling interlocking systems of oppression together with others is often called "collective liberation." It is essential to the Great Turning. Collective liberation means that our ability to thrive is linked with the entire web of life and specifically, that no one can be truly free while others are oppressed. Everyone experiences oppression differently depending on their social position, and we take great care to not prescribe ways of challenging an interlocking system. Wherever people choose to intervene—through holding actions, transforming structures, or shifting consciousness—what matters is the commitment to choose to use one's capacity to challenge oppression in some way. What makes liberation *collective* is the recognition that no matter where you are in the scene, the caged bird's liberation is intrinsically bound up with the viewer's own liberation. One is not free while others are in cages.[11]

Since WTR workshop attendees carry such a yearning for life on planet Earth to thrive, in my workshops I make space for people to craft and share stories about ways they have participated in (or learned about) challenging interlocking systems of oppression meaningfully. For example, I adapted an exercise created by Beautiful Trouble called "The Museum of People Power".[12] Dividing the workshop attendees into groups large enough to make a meaningful still-life dramatic image (everyone striking a pose in a scene), they dramatize a story they know of people who resisted oppression in the past. One group holds their physical position as other groups come to visit the museum. The observers share what they see, naming the elements of resistance to injustice that are present. The museum-goers also imagine what came before and after these scenes to make them possible (e.g., meal provision and revolutionary after-care). The statues in the museum then get to shake out their position and share. They become the observers as others take their turn in the *tableau vivant*. Then we move to dramatizing stories of the present moment. Lastly, we gracefully offer these stories to future humans, and express gratitude, grief, curious questions, and inspirations from seeing it.

I began to collect and create dozens of exercises from anti-oppressive direct action trainings, conflict transformation, and restorative justice materials, plus dyad activities based on Miki Kashtan's approach to "weaving togetherness for nonviolent global liberation."[13] Building on her Nonviolent Communication training with Marshall Rosenberg, Kashtan's efforts seek to heal in many dimensions, including the dimension of time. Dwelling in Deep Time as a distinct stage of the Spiral emerged from all this collecting and creating.

It was 2014 when Dwelling in Deep Time emerged as a distinct stage. I had just participated in the second people of color facilitator cohort led by Joanna Macy, Patricia St. Onge, Adelaja Simon, and Anne Symens-Bucher. We soaked profoundly together in their wells of knowledge and genuine humanity. I shared about the stage's development with Joanna. She responded graciously, maintaining her general orientation to joyous intrigue when she hears about the ways in which her open source work has evolved and moved in one of her students. In response, she shared that while she had not originally imagined deep time as a distinct stage, it is crucial that the consciousness of it permeates the work in each stage. That made sense to me, and yet offering Dwelling in Deep Time as a differentiated stage resonated even more crucially as time went on.

When *Coming Back To Life: The Updated Guide to the Work That Reconnects* came out, I noticed that the Table of Contents had a section featuring Deep Time specifically. That section became the place from which I drew many exercises, as well as the ones from other modalities that I incorporated. Now when I facilitate, Dwelling in Deep Time comes after Perceiving in New/Ancient Ways and before Going Forth. In addition to placing oneself in the lineage of life-sustaining justice movements, restoring kinship networks with the past, present, and future beings has been a growing focus for this stage.

I focus on kinship networks because *interlocking systems of oppression* targeted them for destruction. Enactors of utilitarian, speciest, and Western Christian supremacist worldviews targeted kinship networks of Peoples who had meaningful relationships between them as humans and between them and other Beings with whom they shared

Place. Enslaved mothers were ripped from infants on the auction block. Indigenous fathers were told they must send their children to boarding school or face deadly consequences. Queer lovers were not allowed to partner and form families in imperial contexts. Children who bonded with animals, plants, and places constantly had their realities questioned. The bodies of plants and animals have been forcibly mated and crossed in order to increase production at a pace detrimental to their cycles and the rhythms of the earth. The interlocking systems of oppression continue to constrict the creation of kinship outside ones that benefit industrial production and reproduction.

Kinship—the broad and intimate relationships we are able to nurture—are the crucial *interconnected systems of support* we each need to be our full, cherished selves and live purposefully. The work of repair is often one of remaking kin—reconnecting broken bonds. Therefore, dedicated time to repair of kinship structures is vital as part of the WTR, and the Great Turning for which it advocates. This repair of kinship is happening all the time in the more-than-human world as plants and animals seek reconnection. It is crucial for me that humans catch up, dedicating time to conflict resolution.

At the most intense point of the Dwelling in Deep Time stage, I pose a question to participants: What one relationship do I want to repair based on the collective work we've done in this WTR workshop? They journal about this, and it often brings up a lot. If there is time I will have them share in dyads about it, just before I transition to Going Forth.

I invite this relationship to be as much in the present moment as with past or future ones. I think we are called to work within this present moment, and after so much has shifted for people in a workshop, to return to it with poignancy at this point can be potent. It is not okay to spiritually bypass the at-times chaotic and conflictual relationships we are experiencing presently, just because they are difficult. I don't insist that people have to choose the hardest fight, or the most fraught relationship, but I invite them to write about, visualize, and/or plan for how one *specific* relationship with a *specific person or being* will get an infusion of hope. I consider my workshop successful if participants use the increased resilience they feel as a result of being so deeply seen, heard, and understood at the workshop to strengthen them to go back to a relationship where they don't feel resourced. I wish to resource folks to lean into the kinship (re)making process—examining how aspects of the interlocking systems of oppression are working in that relationship, and what aspects of interconnected systems of support would be of assistance to bringing healing, peace, and flow in our relational work. Conflict can be generative, if we become more skilled and resourced at addressing it. The WTR is an ideal workshop space to practice these skills and resource participants.

Naming the Interlocking Systems

The more I learned about interlocking systems of oppression, the more I saw that they weren't reducible to just one terrible system or story, or even a human characteristic such as greed. It made these interlocking systems hard to name, because I noticed that each type of oppression had particular and differing impacts on workshop participants. I wanted attendees to feel seen for the cage wires that were most potently slicing their battered wings as they railed and sang against the harm and hardship these constructs caused. But it was also hard to remember them all! Inspired by scholar-activists like bell hooks, I wrote them down for a while, to name as many as I could. And that felt authentic. Yet in the end it was not just about specificity. It's the *way* they interact.

I began saying them in a long run-on sentence that serves the function of becoming a word cloud. The impact has been that *the quick and intense recitation* actually creates the *sensation* of mental and emotional severe weather coming from many directions at once, wrecking concentration on particular words and landing on and in the body affectively. Here it is: Say it as fast as you can: cisheteronormative Christian hegemonic classist settler-colonial white supremacist petrochemically ecocidal U.S.-centric ageist mono-amorist patriarchal corporate capitalist industrial growth society of premature death!

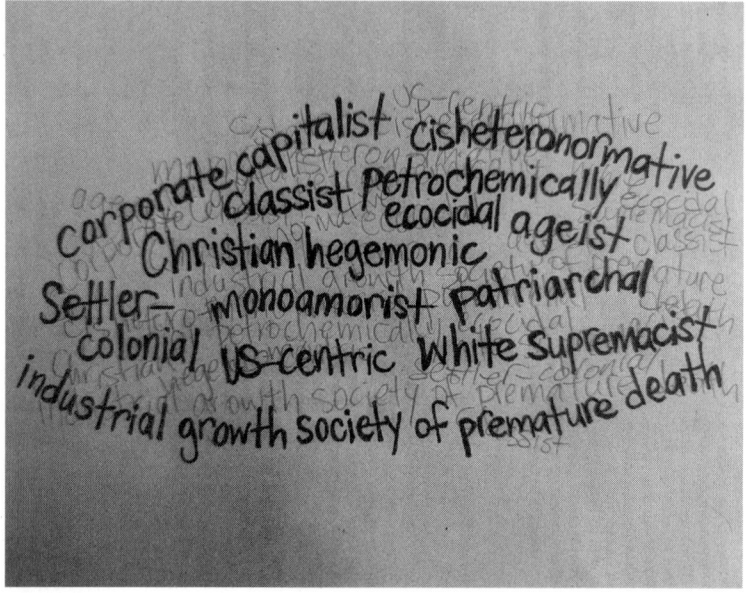

Word Cloud
Credit: Sarah Nahar

> That's what we live in!
> Sigh.
> Deep breath.

With the sensation comes a hope that it is clear that a rupture of the cage is needed. We need to clear the air. It is not so much whether or not participants agree that all of the systemic forces listed above are trying to contort our forms and oppress us. Rather it's about recognizing, really *feeling into*, the interlocking aspects of these systems, how their enmeshment in dominant lawmaking is what makes it so difficult to achieve collective liberation so we can follow the cosmic law of the clouds, which is a poetic way of saying being attuned and responsive to consequential natural laws and how they can structure society.[14]

Diné environmental justice policy expert and activist Jade Begay is familiar with the WTR. She shared an experience from a workshop where someone was mourning the loss of the whales in the Pacific Northwest. The grief was genuine, the rage at the impact on this species as a vital part of the web of life was palpable. But the person did not, in their mourning, mourn for the people who had cared for the whales since time immemorial. The loss of the whales is directly tied to the near genocide of the Coast Salish peoples who were an intact part of the ecosystem.[15] Ouch.

Without necessarily "correcting" the participant, a facilitator who is committed to collective liberation and who has educated themselves about how colonization impacted the area where the workshop is taking place will find a skillful way to articulate the connection and help all participants mourn what happened (and continues to happen) to the People(s) of that Place as well. I cannot *prescribe* how a facilitator would do this, but I am confident that if they have prepared themselves to take risks to enable collective liberation, they will find a way to address the gap. It may be more or less public; even if the facilitator doesn't know the specific history, pausing to notice the erasure in and of itself can open to new layers of mourning and teaching.

A pillar of U.S. imperialism and anti-Indigenous policies is that of erasing and invisiblizing Indigenous Peoples of Turtle Island/Abya Yala and their ways of being, doing, and conceptualizing. Therefore, not addressing erasure in a workshop directly perpetuates colonization.[16] A facilitator cannot and does not have to know everything, and should not speak about what they do not—that often results in intellectualism or over-explanation. However, finding a ritually meaningful and thoughtful way to push back on the false divide between environmental catastrophe and social catastrophes is essential to fostering the Great Turning.

Starting the Climate Clock in the 1400s

Environmental and social struggles can be perceived as different struggles *if the climate crisis* (aka Business as Usual) *is dated to begin with the Industrial Revolution.* This dating will center issues of carbon and its sequestration. In the mid-1700s in Europe there was a fierce increase in the mechanization of production of materials and transportation methods, among other things. The humans and institutions that crafted and promoted the mechanization process reinforced a trajectory that significantly impacted human migration patterns (from rural to urban), paid work rhythms (labor issues), and the construction of desire (consumerist acquisition). This also had a detrimental impact on the planet, as more material was demanded of local and global ecosystems than ever before, rendering some unable to regenerate sufficiently before another extraction.

Most tellings of the Industrial Revolution do not locate its origin in the Doctrine of Discovery and Domination (DoDD), or in the reason that so much textile material, for example, was available for processing. Slavery, genocide, and ecocide are all the conditions in which such a "Revolution" became possible. Because it wasn't a revolution at all, rather an acceleration and mechanization of the policies of environmental injustices to Peoples and Places colonized by Europe, where the Industrial Acceleration began. For this reason, I start the clock with the DoDD. The clock I am talking about is the "climate clock" that's now doing a countdown until midnight. This clock is a famous artivist installation created to remind humans in New York City, Seoul, Glasgow, and elsewhere where it is displayed that we are in the 11th hour—a climate emergency must be declared.[17]

When did it start counting? Herein lies a major issue, because how you define the crisis greatly influences how you address it. I timestamp the climate crisis to the ecclesial decrees of the 1400s: *Malleus Maleficarum* (the Witches' Hammer) and the bundle of Papal Bulls now known as the DoDD. The humans and institutions that crafted and promoted the process created the trajectory that significantly impacted the Earth via human migration patterns in the transatlantic, work rhythms that entrenched desecration, indentured and chattel servitude, and extraction via property law, plus they stratified desire—codifying Occidental racial science as part of a religious world construction that gave them a mandate to dominate all in the larger web of life. Sounds like another word cloud. Indeed it is, as it's the dense origin story for the interlocking systems of oppressions that Black feminists later help us collectively understand and transform.

The Doctrine of Discovery and Domination is a set of 15th-century Catholic Papal Bulls that condoned the invasion, capture, murder, kidnapping, and enslavement of anyone non-Christian.[18] Even before wreaking massive havoc on the peoples and ecosystems of the so-called Americas, the Doctrine of Discovery "justified" the Christian conquest over and mistreatment of Muslims (called Saracens in the documents) in Jerusalem and surrounding areas, and the invasion of the societies of African Peoples (called pagans in the documents) and all of their lands. The DoDD touched almost every area of life as European colonization moved worldwide. It was encoded into U.S. law in 1823, in a case called Johnson v. McIntosh concerning who was allowed to sell Indigenous land—Indigenous Peoples were barred.[19] Far from disappearing, the DoDD's claims were reinforced as recently as 2005 in Sherrill, New York vs. the Oneida Nation. In this case, Supreme Court Justice Ruth Bader Ginsburg wrote the majority opinion refusing to allow sovereign governance for Indigenous groups who bought back parcels of their historic homelands.[20] In additional to legal issues of land sovereignty, the DoDD influences educational, carceral, cultural, health care, and economic systems. It is the code of domination written to create and sustain the interlocking systems of oppression.

The oft-cited paragraph from 1452 *Dum Diversas* is central to this project. It instructs Christian explorers on what to do if they found land where no European Christians were living. They were to

> ... invade, search out, capture, vanquish, and subdue all Saracens and pagans whatsoever, and other enemies of Christ wheresoever placed, and the kingdoms, dukedoms, principalities, dominions, possessions, and all movable and immovable goods whatsoever held and possessed by them and to reduce their persons to perpetual slavery.[21]

"Movable and immovable goods" identifies "natural resources"—the more-than-human relatives of the Indigenous Peoples of a Place. The idea of "natural resources" was not yet conceived (because everything was still "natural"). In this church document's worldview, however, everything was also a commodifiable "good." Most Peoples in those Places saw themselves as not only People of a Place but totally interwoven with it, as People-Place, so observing colonizers violently separating life into moveable and immovable goods had immense epistemological and ontological consequences for Indigenous communities. Some of their relatives became classified as possessions, others were captured as endorsed by the doctrine, and then they themselves were forced to be possessions (chattel) through perpetual slavery. It was a complete apocalypse. The vanquishment endorsed by this doctrine led to the arbitrary worldview division between Peoples and Places becoming materially manifested in colonizer actions such as the burning of cultivated relatives (crops), wanton killing of animal relatives, and deforestation. Colonization targeted Peoples-Places together *and* People-as-Place.

This is not just a history lesson. It is important to the work of the Great Turning because how you define a problem informs how you solve it. If Business as Usual is viewed primarily as the way that neoliberal globalization functions to render climate catastrophes (made profitable by disaster capitalism), then we leverage government initiatives that center public efforts and oppose privatization. If the climate crisis is understood as deriving from Reaganomics or Trump, then that basically makes it a partisan issue in the United States, where green capitalism can continue as long as it's accompanied by some robust social programs. If we see it as solely a carbon issue, then we try to capture carbon, while leaving the market system intact. We cannot "cap and trade" our way to eco-peace while maintaining worldviews of individualism and doing practices that replicate current political and social inequities.

If we see its source as colonization, conceptualizing colonization as a series of environmental injustices against Peoples-Places, then decolonization becomes a central part of addressing climate change. Some start the climate clock with settled agriculture and the control of surplus at that point.[22] This prompts thinking about the depth of rewilding that is both possible and needed. If we see the climate crisis as connected to stories that come from particular worldview(s), which created and recreated manifestations of reality, then we seek to rout out that worldview in every institution, heart, and organization in which it exists. We offer a different worldview.

This is part of the genius of Joanna Macy's corpus: she identified that the climate crisis, no matter where you start the climate clock, is about stories. Each way of telling the story offers important insights to the layered experience we are living these days. What I am offering here is a look into the stories in ways that then allow us to grieve into the depths and refuse shortcuts and ways of addressing the crisis that are actually part of the crisis.[23] While we're all in this together in the Great Turning, we're all in it together *differently*.[24] Embracing those differences, rather than resenting them, offers a way through to being human together in a shared future.

An additional word about *Malleus Maleficarum* is important because so many white women-identified people find significant healing in the Work That Reconnects, making up the majority of its leadership and network participants. In 1484, when this Catholic document was written, the criminalization of "witches" intensified to the level of femicide in Europe. Any female-bodied person who was free thinking, a practitioner of traditional ecological knowledge, a midwife, or disliked for whatever reason could be accused of being a witch. This led to impunity for church-led physical, psychological, and sexual abuse against them—encouraging these violent acts as acts of faith. Communities divided amongst each other, women were pitted against other women.

Sara Jolena Wolcott writes in depth about the Witch Papal Bull, calling it one of the "most blatantly misogynist documents ever written."[25] This decree happens after *Dum Diversas* and closely precedes Columbus's 1492 encounter with the Caribbean and the Inquisition. The physical death of so many women and the dramatic loss of traditional ecological knowledge they held absolutely devastated Europe. The turning of women on other women in order to themselves avoid death enabled patriarchy's momentum. All this was happening as the enclosure of the commons accelerated, depriving the populace of land-based knowledge as they lost access to their ancestral and communally held land. Along with the new work rhythms and labor demands the enclosures created on those still alive, the stress was immense. It was Europe's devastated men, then, that went all around the world and committed horrific femicides, genocides, and ethnocides to other Peoples-Places as well. This key moment in history, which systematized and legitimized violence in the web of life is where I start the climate clock.

It may not feel "practical" to start the clock "back that long," but the WTR is not about "practicality" above all. Rather it prizes creating a container that can witness the ways our collective ego patterns have formed. If we don't grapple with the traumas that have targeted us, we can live them out again. For example, *Malleus Maleficarum* can show up in fear, jealousy, scarcity mindset, and feeling threatened when receiving feedback. Knowing these stories can help us ascertain why people behave in particular ways when gathered in a group. It has been powerful in mixed groups when I name the European pre-colonial femicides as part of all the oppression that is showing up in the room. I do not hesitate to note how horrific and impactful they've been on white women, just as I also make sure to note impacts of other aspects of the word cloud including ableism, racism, and imperialism.

When doing this, I notice there tends to be palpable relief in the room, because I have named a root of sexism without over-centering white women's experiences. Being seen for ancestral oppression experienced, and not only feeling guilty of contemporary oppression continued, allows for relaxation into the healing gift that opening to deep time offers. Then, if something else occurs where a pattern from *Malleus Maleficarum* is playing out, I'm able to intervene. Patterns include extreme oversharing, over-centering, inflexibility, refusal to follow directions, or othering. In these times I want folks to be seen, but also I don't want the group to veer into detrimental care-taking of privileged group members. This has helped, and I'm still working to get to the noncontroversial essence of it all:

> I see you sister. I see the history that has formed you. I see your witchy self being reclaimed and I see you wanting to also feel and act normally without worrying about how someone will interpret your actions. I see the concessions that you've made

to white male power structures in order to keep yourself safe. I see how you haven't wanted to give in to it, but you did, in order to receive safety and protection. I see how this makes you feel ashamed, shaky and confused, less resilient and without knowledge of what the next step of your liberation journey is. You are welcome regardless. When you thrive it's not a problem, and it takes skilling-up to figure out how to do this. You are not alone. We are here figuring it out together. I am inviting you to be attentive to how much space you're currently taking up, and why.

Without over-centering themselves, I want white women to have an understanding of their own power, how it functions, and how it can be used in the Great Turning. Given Joanna Macy's positionality as a European-American who grew up Calvinist, healing at these roots in particular honors who she is and what she saw as an important part of the story shift. Even as her positionality (like all of our positions) created limits in the facilitated work, there are immense gifts available in naming this root and start of the climate clock. It can move us deeper into our grief and wellspring of our power.

Integrating Interlocking Systems of Oppression into the Stories of Our Time

When I tell the Three Stories of Our Time near the beginning of each workshop I bring in education about *Malleus Maleficarum* and the Doctrine of Discovery and Domination. This sets me and the group up well to feel free to address the biggest range of suffering that we know how to name as we move through the spiral. In this way, the struggles of the People and the struggles of the Earth are articulated early on as interconnected. For example, I say that my grief is not *only* that enslavement was terrible for humans, it's that it solidified a system of monocropped agribusiness across an area where there used to be lush other ways of growing things. The trauma of how people were forcibly broken in order to forcibly break the land stays with us. The *Transit of Empire* as Jodi Byrd writes, impacts Black and Indigenous Peoples who were formerly enslaved, as well as enslaving and indentured populations—all social relations and our relationship with land today are formed by it.[26] Preceding the Industrial Acceleration, the exploitation of workers, racialized populations, and the Earth are shown to be intertwined. Racial capitalism doesn't *have* an environmental policy, it *is* an environmental policy. All this is based on a religious and patriarchally motivated femicide in Europe which drowned knowledge of local plants and lifeways. This femicide immediately preceded the deluge of lonely sea-faring men leading the European colonial era. In order to get to the Great Turning the WTR must grapple with the deepest roots of Business as Usual and the Great Unraveling—the stories of separation, scarcity, and powerlessness that propel it.[27]

This gives permission to participants to try—even if it feels awkward at first—to articulate the specific contours of the connections they see in their daily lives. Facilitators can create a sober but friendly atmosphere where they can be vulnerable and try to say things in a new way from the heart as it breaks open. An example of this happening within the WTR is the continual examination and refinement of the WTR's core assumptions over time. They were first listed in the original *Coming Back to Life* (1998) and in the updated version (2014). The book's co-author, Molly Brown, has been involved significantly with the intentional work of undoing oppressions in the WTR Network and beyond. Part of this work is through her work on the Weavers team, the group of people who weave threads of connection across the open-source WTR Network of facilitators and constituents. Together with others, she stewarded the process of clarifying and updating the core assumptions. Whereas before they sidelined questions of intense societal oppression, in 2014 they gave attention to it on the WTR website.[28] The AORG's work, as part of the constellation of efforts to undo oppression via *and* within the WTR, offered an additional Core Assumption in 2024. We wished to be even clearer about the inextricable connection of dynamics of societal power within the larger web of life. This can now be shared whenever the Core Assumptions are shared (e.g., at the beginning of the workshop where we make it transparent why we think these activities have power, and/or shared along with the foundational teachings, prinsiples, and aims of the WTR in a facilitator's training.) The additional Core Assumption is:

> *Collective liberation within our species is essential to the flourishing of the larger web of planetary life.*

By articulating that we assume our work in addressing the interlocking systems of oppression and transforming them into interconnected systems of support is essential (not an add-on) to any initiative for ecological flourishing, we can address any false split between the struggle for human flourishing and the struggle for environmental wellbeing that lingers in some enactments of the WTR. If humans find ways to live well with one another, we will learn the type of reciprocity, forbearance, restorative mannerisms, and balance that make us a beneficial presence in the larger web of life.

Too many people have experienced historic and ongoing collective trauma that leaves them nearly unable to be in a type of relationship with the larger web of life that benefits all beings. So, finding ways to live well with one another can happen in a workshop where there is time and space to shift consciousness, or in a holding action alongside marginalized people, or in the work of transforming the foundations of our common life. Uplifting collective liberation efforts on any scale strengthens the flow of energy that reconnects us to our true nature.

The AORG elaborated on this Core Assumption: "None of us are free until all of us are free. The Industrial Growth Society is founded on and perpetuates systemic inequalities. These structural power dynamics play out painfully in human relationships. When we address generational and contemporary oppressions as they manifest, we truly enact the Great Turning."[29]

Conclusion

It's been an honor to work within this corpus for over a decade. I write this chapter as a break from dissertation writing within the same academic department (Syracuse University Religion Department) where

Joanna Macy did her doctoral work nearly five decades before me. Writing on mutual causality in Buddhism and general systems theory, she brilliantly offered insights about the Dharma of natural systems. She was also influenced by Haudenosaunee power and presence in this region. A Confederacy that formed over a millennia ago through grief rituals, strategic hospitality, shuttle diplomacy, and grassroots mobilization, the Haudenosaunee (People of the Longhouse, formerly known as the Iroquois Confederacy) is a participatory democracy. It formed based on a story of original instructions given to humans about how to live in harmony with the larger web of life, and the impact on the Earth and human society when those were violated.[30]

Grounding in Gratitude is the first part of all Haudenosaunee meeting protocol. They are the words that come before all else.[31] The more I live in this region, the more I see the fingerprints of Haudenosaunee wisdom all over the WTR. I believe it honors the WTR for facilitators to give close attention to how Indigenous Peoples in the area where they live facilitate, and to lift up specifics about how Peoples-Places survived the interlocking systems of oppression. Three questions can guide this process: Who lived here before me? Where are they now? What happened?[32] And after these, a fourth question: What does that mean for my life?

Integrate what you learn into the Spiral, allowing it to break you open and share what is truest in your heart so that you can be witnessed in your remembering. The process of waking up and dismantling our conditioning around power and privilege is extremely demanding and ongoing—but it is an essential component of the Great Turning. The AORG encourages anyone who wishes to facilitate the WTR or other group modalities to approach the challenge with the same fierce determination, humility, and compassion with which we approach the WTR itself. Breathe through the pain that comes with recognizing our own complicity and the complexity of the problem. This is not just part of the Work, it is integral to the Work and our own wholeness and well-being. We are in it for the long haul.[33]

It can be very difficult to perceive and dismantle the often insidious ways we might be causing harm by replicating structures of oppression.

And yet, nothing brings greater joy, freedom, and intimacy with life than aligning our actions with our most life-enhancing values! We keep going because success in our mission is impossible without this shift. It is our commitment to *the Great Turning within our own consciousness* and our recognition that this is not separate from the transformation of the larger web of life that keeps us engaged with this difficult task. As AORG co-founder Belinda Griswold says:

> A key step in this process is a shift in consciousness among those with privileged identities: we can move from guilt and defensiveness into an understanding of how our complicity in systems of oppression devastates our siblings with less power, and also corrodes our own souls, making us fragile and disconnected from the truth of the interdependence that animates all life.[34]

When this shift occurs, everyone can become much more powerful in acting to dismantle interlocking systems of oppression. We find common cause in our bodies and solidarity in our actions; we are far more humble, flexible, and willing to experience the stress that comes from a non-individualist perception. We can create interconnected systems of support for sustaining life on planet Earth.

4

A Critical History of the Work That Reconnects— Phases of Development

By Marc Decitre

This chapter offers a critical reading of the history of the Work That Reconnects . It draws from research originally undertaken for a masters thesis in environmental humanities from 2020 to 2022, which included interviews with key historical and contemporary figures, archival work on early publications from the Interhelp Network, and socio-historical contextualization of the movements from which the work originally sprang. As with any history, it remains a partial and provisional reconstruction shaped by the material I had access to and the particular questions and biases I carried with me.

The chapter delineates major phases in the WTR's development: the emergence of its ancestors, Despair and Empowerment Work, from 1978 to 1983 within the U.S. peace movement, and Deep Ecology Work in Australia from 1985 to 1988; its international circulations and ramifications in the late 80s and 90s; the reforging of these different repertoires as the Work That Reconnects within the context of the rising alter-globalist movement, from 1998 to 2012; and finally the current efforts to intersectionalize its practices and language in the wake of a resurgence of racial justice movements.

Because these efforts have sometimes been contested within the broader WTR community, it is followed in the next chapter by a critical discussion of certain key factors that may shed more nuanced light on the link between the Work and a robust commitment to social justice.

1977–1983: Emergence and Elaboration Within the U.S. Peace Movement[1]

Joanna Macy's writings on the Work That Reconnects offer useful milestones to delineate the successive phases of its evolution. Her first article, *How to Deal with Despair*, appeared in the summer 1979 issue of the *New Age Journal*, three months after the nuclear accident at Three Mile Island that crystallized the apocalyptic ambiance of the time.

Two years earlier, Joanna had experienced an overwhelming sense of despair after attending a symposium on "Threats to the Biosphere." Her despair found a startling resolution in the wave of solidarity that arose when, several months later, she offered participants of a seminar on the "Prospect for Human Survival" an opportunity to share a personal image or story of how the planetary threats impinged on their own lives.[2]

The 1979 article laid bare the teachings of her "dark night of the soul," though only few concrete practices were outlined. The question of how to pragmatically facilitate the passage from despair to empowerment remained largely open.

And yet, the complete Despair and Empowerment Work handbook came out in 1983 (*Despair and Personal Power in the Nuclear Age*), a mere four years later. Complete with over 50 exercises, it laid out the theoretical foundations for the work, offered detailed instructions for how to organize a workshop, and outlined a three-stage structure that prefigured the WTR's four-step spiral ("Despair Work" for Honoring Our Pain; "the Turning" for Seeing with New Eyes; and "Empowerment" for Going forth).

How did things go so fast? A first answer lies in the names that populate the book's pages: Joseph Havens, Chellis Glendinning, Frances Peavey, John Steiner, David Hoffman, Carol Wolman, Tova Green, Sarah Pirtle, Barbara Hazard, Kevin McVeigh, Elissa Melamed, Paul Fink, and many others. All were members of the Interhelp Network that gave rise to these practices and refined its methodology.

But what made these people come together? And what made their endeavor seem so urgent that so many of them shifted the course of their lives to dedicate themselves to it? These questions bring us to the second answer: the Euromissile crisis and the Nuclear Freeze Campaign that arose in response to it.

If Joanna's first article had been informed by a sense of impending environmental catastrophe characteristic of the 1970s within industrialized countries, the Interhelp Network came together primarily in response to the heightened threat of nuclear war of the early 1980s. When NATO voted to deploy a new category of inter-ballistic missiles in Western Europe potentially targeting the Soviet Union, and the incumbent Reagan administration began speaking of a "winnable nuclear war," a mass movement took form across the United States and Western Europe calling for a freeze on the production of nuclear weapons. Marches, citizen forums, and ballot initiatives multiplied across the U.S., as well as more direct forms of action like women's peace encampments around the military bases of Seneca Falls in NY and Greenham Common in the UK (in which many Interhelpers participated).

The movement faced a paradox, however. Although fear of nuclear war was pervasive, the subject remained taboo, even for activists. And yet, the reactions of dissociation and avoidance it engendered prevented people from becoming engaged.

"How can we reclaim our power to act?" The Interhelp Network can be seen as the coming together of activists seeking to answer this question. Building on their experiences as therapists and teachers, activists and spiritual practitioners, they drew from multiple bodies of practice (Quaker and Buddhist, (eco)feminist and pacifist, humanistic psychology and personal growth) to cobble together a practical, creative, and experiential response to psychic numbing. As their experimentations grew public, invitations from the peace movement multiplied, validating how needed they were, and heightening the sense of urgency to develop and disseminate them.

The years spanning 1977 to 1983 thus mark a period of explosive experimentation and formalization in a context of a high-stake mobilization. Despair and Empowerment Work (D&E Work) emerged because it was desperately needed to serve a specific political movement. *Despair and Personal Power in the Nuclear Age* represents a repository of the Interhelp Network's collective explorations. With its publication, the Work can be seen as entering a second phase, one of international circulation and dissemination beyond this original matrix, leading to new ramifications in contact with other social worlds.

1983–1988: Dissemination and Ramification: Deep Ecology Work in Australia's "Rainbow Region"[3]

Carried through webs of personal connection woven by the peace movement, D&E Work quickly began to spread internationally. Interhelp chapters were set up in the UK and Australia, and the U.S. Interhelp conferences received delegations from Germany, Canada, Japan, Holland, and South Africa.

Like dandelion seeds cast out in the wind, its propagation proceeded organically from the ground up; the energy it unleashed in people inspired them to appropriate it for themselves and their communities. Activists could adapt it to their specific circumstances, hybridizing it with other artistic, ecological, therapeutic, and social change methodologies. The diversity of the forms these took is staggering and the subterranean transformations they catalyzed are too manifold to capture.

Among these circulations, one in particular marked an important milestone in the work's evolution. Joanna Macy's meeting with John Seed and other Australian rainforest activists in 1985 gave rise to a new repertoire of experiential practices that would become a new center of gravity for the next decade: Deep Ecology Work.

This meeting emerged from a specific social context: the "Rainbow Region" of New South Wales. Communes and intentional communities had been proliferating there for over a decade, in the wake of the Aquarius Festival—often remembered as the "Australian Woodstock"— contributing to build "a concentrated population of alternative lifestylers influenced by the environmental concerns, protest culture and counterculture of the 1960s".[4]

In the summer of 1979, the region had been the site of an intense mobilization to preserve Terania Creek, one of the last remaining primary rainforests of the region. The struggle, infused with a festive and nonviolent countercultural spirit, emphasized the activists' affective ties to the land and its intrinsic worth. It was during this time that John Seed, who played a central role in the mobilization, coined the phrase "I am the rainforest protecting myself" that became emblematic of this new outlook.

The struggle was ultimately successful in making the forest a national park. The activists, galvanized by this first victory, traveled to other sites of environmental struggle, spreading their new action style and sensibility: to safeguard the Franklin River in Tasmania in 1982, the Daintree Rainforest in Queensland, and Errinundra Forest in Victoria in 1983 and 1984.

So, when Joanna and other Interhelpers were invited to the region in 1985, the memory of these struggles was still fresh and the Australian environmental movement in full swing.

The invitation emerged from two intentional Buddhist communities near Terania Creek where copies of the 1983 D&E Work handbook had found their way. Bobbi Allen, one of the activists involved in the original blockade, organized the visit, enlisting the help of Pat Fleming, a British-Irish psychologist who had helped to co-found Interhelp UK. Together they organized several workshops before the tour, catalyzing a wide demand for the work before Joanna arrived.

When she met John Seed in Terania Creek, he had been turning to Arne Naess's deep ecology to articulate the insights emerging from these mobilizations. Advocating for a wider sense of identification, the philosophy seemed to herald the deeper change in consciousness John recognized as necessary to turn the tide of environmental destruction.

While Naess called for this "Ecological Self" to be fostered by forms of "community therapy," he offered no concrete steps for enacting them. D&E Work's experiential approach seemed to hold the key to answering this call, and the seed idea for the Council of All Beings was born. A few weeks later, Joanna and John co-led the first workshop, with input from Pat Fleming, which gathered 50 people north of Sydney. Whereas the name now refers to a specific practice within the WTR, at the time this was a four-day process, with numerous exercises leading up to and following the council. The reunion of the council's co-initiators at the 1987 Interhelp conference in San Francisco prompted them to publish its methodology in *Thinking Like a Mountain: Towards a Council of All Beings*.

1988–1998: Holding the Flame: The Work in Abeyance During the Rise of Corporate Globalization

The publication of *Thinking Like a Mountain* allowed Deep Ecology Work to begin its wider dissemination just as Despair and Empowerment Work had with its handbook. The U.S. Interhelp Network, meanwhile, held its last annual gathering that same year (1988).

Following this threshold, the carriers of the Work can be seen as entering a period of abeyance, a concept used by scholars in describing the shifting cadences of social movements. Phases of ascendance, of intense political activity, often give way to periods of retrenchment, either because the unifying goal holding diverging factions together is achieved, or because the broader political climate shifts. In these phases, recruitment tends to scale down and the most committed activists, facing a non-receptive political environment, perpetuate the movement's values and action repertoire within protected niches, tending the flame until the next phase of mobilization.

Indeed, after a mobilization peak in '82–'83, the peace movement had already begun to slow down, starting in '84–'85, when the Reagan administration began softening its tone regarding offensive nuclear war. The ratification of the Intermediate-Range Nuclear Forces Treaty in 1988, while far from ushering in total disarmament, constituted a form of limited resolution. Without a unified goal, many Interhelp members carried on their activism focused on different issues (environmental, educational, antiracist, social justice, staying armed conflicts), although various regional chapters continued to perpetuate D&E Work, including the northeast U.S. chapter that survives to this day.

Some, like Fran Peavey (and later Tova Green, her partner at the time), built long-lasting ties with the Interhelp chapter in New South Wales, whose annual Heart Politics Conferences recurred well into the early 2000s. Named after Fran's book, which sought to offer a heart-and-listening-centered approach to politics, these were places to deepen the "going forth" dimension of the Work and support activists at a deeper emotional level, sending ripples throughout change-making forums in Australia and New Zealand.

Building on this path, Bobbi Allen and Karina Shields co-founded the The Social Change Training & Resource Centre that equipped activists with strategic and facilitation skills and gave rise to a handbook on activist burnout prevention that remains a reference for activists today.

Joanna, meanwhile, shifted her center of gravity towards deep ecology and its broader networks, co-founding the U.S. Institute for Deep Ecology (along with Bill Devall, Stephanie Kaza, Elias Amidon, and Elizabeth Roberts) and promoting it within existing institutions, such as the Findhorn Foundation and Schumacher College. In parallel, she turned to the question of nuclear guardianship with a group of scholars and activists (including Fran Macy, Susan Griffin, Brian Swimme, and Molly Brown). From 1988 to 1994, the group co-developed another body of practice—Deep Time Work—to render palpable the bewildering time spans of vigilance and care that nuclear waste requires.

As previously mentioned, movements often enter abeyance due to unfavorable changes in the broader political climate. The late '80s and especially the '90s were particularly hostile decades for environmentalism (and progressive social movements more broadly).

Of course, many local and sectorial struggles did take hold, such as the Forest Wars in defense of old growth forests championed by groups like EarthFirst! (for whom the Council of All Beings, as disseminated by John Seed, constituted an important resource). And yet, however combative these movements were, they remained largely on the defensive faced with the rising tide of neoliberalism, ushered in by the conservative revolution that had brought Reagan and Thatcher to power, and corporate globalization that took the world by storm after the fall of the Berlin Wall.

Whereas the environmental movement of the '60s and '70s had called for a radical challenge to the status quo, arguing that the future of human survival on the planet required a total rethinking of growth-based economic structures and industrialized modes of life, a new countervailing discourse became increasingly hegemonic. Terms like "ecological modernization," "sustainable development," and "green growth" replaced the pessimism of earlier critique with an unshakeable optimism in the capacity of science, technological innovation, and the market-based instruments of big-money capitalism to overcome the opposition between the economy and the environment. Greenwashing, compromise, tech-fixes, and incremental solutions triumphed, while those who held the line of radical critique became increasingly inaudible and marginalized within broader public debate.

Those who carried the Work through this decade of abeyance held that critical line, nourished by and nourishing webs that would allow the alter-globalization movement to emerge in the late 1990s.

1998–2014: Reemergence and Reconsolidation: The Forging of the Work That Reconnects Within the Alter-Globalization Movement

By the late 1990s, Despair and Empowerment Work, Deep Ecology Work, and Deep Time Work existed as three separate bodies of practice. Each had been developed within a specific social container and had managed to persist past that container's life span, perpetuating itself within its own specialized (and sometimes overlapping) niches. This decade of abeyance raised new challenges, however.

Because the practices had originally been developed in specific movements, those who developed them shared a set of values and frames that gave them a common political orientation. In those earlier years, because the work of analysis and strategic goal setting was taken on by broader movements, it could be productively bracketed during a workshop to facilitate the emotional dimension of the Work.

Once the Work became free-floating, however, its political dimension depended entirely on the level of politicization of those who offered it and those who showed up. People deeply woven into existing activist networks would take cues from ongoing social developments and return to specific endeavors with renewed energy and creativity. These bodies of practices themselves, however, did not articulate an actualized political frame to help orient newcomers in their understanding of the structural drivers of the Great Unraveling and what to do about it, beyond the general notion of consciousness change.

When Joanna Macy and Molly Brown reforged these three bodies of practices within the Work That Reconnects as we know it today, the main innovation was the political container in which the practices were cast: the Great Turning, which later evolved into the Three Stories of Our Time under the impetus of Chris Johnstone, who co-wrote *Active Hope* with Joanna in 2012.

These stories offered a political baseline, identifying a political adversary (Business as Usual), connecting the myriad forms of social and environmental dislocation in a coherent tableau (the Great Unraveling), and pointing towards an inspirational destination allowing participants to inscribe their restorative actions within a wider, shared narrative (the Great Turning, and its three dimensions). Whereas the shift in consciousness dimension had been predominant in Joanna's writings heretofore, and holding actions had been implicit in much of Deep Ecology work's history, the building alternative systems framework brought in a more sharpened attention to structural issues.

This sharpening gaze reflected the influence of the nascent alter-globalization movement on the Deep Ecology milieu. The term refers to a loose coalition of actors revolted by corporate globalization's assault on the Earth and human rights, spanning from peasant and Indigenous struggles in the Global South to labor unions, environmental NGOs, and diverse leftist groups in the Global North.

After organizing through a series of "counter-summits," following the Rio Earth Summit of 1992, the movement erupted onto the public scene in the Global North with the dramatic Vancouver protests against APEC in 1997 and the Seattle protests against the World Trade Organization in 1999. These protests directly challenged the Washington Consensus and the dominance of neoliberalism. The International Forum on Globalization played a key role in forming a deep ecology or eco-spiritual wing within this nebulous coalition.

Starting in 1994, and funded by the Foundation for Deep Ecology, the forum brought together environmentalists from the Global South (Vandana Shiva, Sara Larraín), Indigenous leaders (Chief Oren Lyons, Victoria Tauli-Corpuz) and intellectuals from the Global North (David Korten, Helena Norberg-Hodge, and Jerry Mander). The meetings helped to articulate a common vision,[5] one that brought a more grounded structural understanding of how corporate globalization functioned within deep ecology circles, while also advocating an eco-spiritual path forward that gave voice to the sacredness of the Earth.

The rising threat of climate change offered a second driving force contributing to the resurgence of a political climate favorable to the Work. While it operated more slowly and subtly, the increasingly numerous and dramatic alerts concerning the scale and speed of climate catastrophe (conjoined with other alarms linked to peak oil, mass extinction, and the overshoot of planetary boundaries) began to increasingly delegitimize the capacity of existing institutions to solve these crises.

The widespread awareness of ecological destruction on one hand, coupled to a growing loss of faith in business as usual on the other, contributed to a rise of eco-anxiety that gave the WTR a renewed relevance. Books like *Active Hope* allowed the Work's key insights to reach a wider audience, while movements like Transition Towns and Permaculture Design integrated the practices within the inner transition dimension of their local change initiatives, and the climate justice movement ushered in a new generation of activists.

This generational renewal cut both ways, however. While it brought younger activists to the Work, they brought with them a sharpened attention to intersectional issues of power, privilege, and social location, to which they had been politicized by the environmental justice movement. Many (but not all) within the older generations found these new frames difficult to integrate, generating frictions which existing networks were unequipped to handle.

Indeed, as opposed to earlier phases of development, the Work was no longer held by a structured community of practice but became much more centered around specific individuals, including Joanna Macy. The *Work That Reconnects Network* and the *Deep Times* journal emerged much later (in the mid 2010s). For more than a decade, then, the Work lacked formal bodies to reflect on and reactualize its practices and frames in alignment with shifting social realities.

In particular, the tensions that had been building up around the integration of an intersectional frame were not finding a satisfying resolution. These ultimately opened a new phase of development: an "evolving edge" to include a more explicit "anti-oppression" approach to its practices and challenge its presumed universality to make it safer and more relevant to less dominant groups.

2012 and Beyond: Evolving Edge: The Intersectionalization of the Work That Reconnects in the Wake of the Black Lives Matter Movement

For most of its history, mainstream offerings of the Work That Reconnects attracted a largely homogeneous public, mirroring the social composition of the movements it was born of—white, middle and upper class, higher educated, able-bodied and cisgendered, with an overrepresentation of women and clergy. These biases also reflected broader patterns of differential access to the time, connections, and resources necessary to participate in residential workshops.

While this reality had been raised in the early years of Interhelp,[6] it had not been enough to inflect a more public grappling with the question of the Work's relevance beyond its social base. Of course, many practitioners *did* use the Work with minoritized demographic groups—including in the Global Souths—finding ways to translate and hybridize them to make them culturally appropriate. But in the absence of a space to share and uplift this pragmatic knowledge, the presumed universality of the Work remained largely unchallenged in the mainstream.

Multiple doorways were available to tackle these questions, but it is not surprising that they crystallized around race, nor that the issue came to the fore around 2012, when the BLM hashtag was first coined, following the killing of Trayvon Martin, pressuring the broader WTR network to reckon with issues that People of Color had been raising for years.

Racial ideology stands as one of the most foundational social constructs that structure and maintain the antagonistic social hierarchies of the United States, having both legitimized the settler colonial project of dispossessing Indigenous nations from their land and demarcating the political distinction between slaves and free persons foundational to the plantation system along a Black-White color line.[7] While racial categories shifted and complexified following waves of new immigration over the course of the country's history, they continue to elevate specific social groups at the expense of others.

The 1960s Civil Rights movement in the United States, which had overturned the more formal and most egregious forms of racial segregation (though its leaders were assassinated when they turned their eye towards economic justice) ushered in a contradictory era in U.S. racial relations, which scholars have referred to as "color-blind" racism.[8]

This paradigm held that racism was a thing of the past, that it no longer formally impeded the pursuit of economic and political opportunity by previously oppressed groups, and that the most progressive position one could embrace was to not see race. That tremendous racial disparities continued to exist, in terms of access to wealth, education, housing, and employment, in terms of exposure to police violence and criminalization, was largely downplayed, or explained by "cultural failures." The rise of a select Black economic and political elite was heralded as proof that those who failed to rise out of their condition must be themselves responsible for their dispossession. The elevation of the first Black man to the country's highest political office seemed to signal the triumph of this post-racial era.

As historian Keeanga-Yamahtta Taylor has argued, however, the Obama era paradoxically set the stage for the eruption of the Black Lives Matter movement in 2014. His failure to concretely address the social condition of disposability faced by the Black working class, which had been particularly hard hit by the 2008 financial crisis, signaled the failure of pushing for "Black faces in high places" as a strategy to advance Black liberation.

Two years after the highly publicized killing of Trayvon Martin in Florida, which had already begun to mobilize racial justice activists around the "BlackLivesMatter" hashtag, the summer of 2014 saw several egregious police killings of African-American boys and men (Michael Brown in Ferguson, Missouri, Eric Garner in New York, among others). Protests erupted across the country, fueled by decades of repressed outrage, bringing the pervasiveness of racial violence back to the forefront of the public stage.

This moment of reckoning reconfigured the parameters of the post-Civil Rights era: in the face of systemic racism, to claim colorblindness was to participate in its reproduction.

For a generation of white liberals who had lived through and supported the Civil Rights era, yet had subscribed without much question to the colorblind paradigm, the terms racist and racism brought up images of vitriolic defenders of segregation in the South. Knee-jerk refusal to be identified with such overt, reactionary figures made it difficult to hear what was at stake in the charge of complicity with structural racism.

Cultural historian Michael Rothberg offers a useful frame here—the notion of implicated subjects—to understand what this call to accountability (being actively antiracist), that collapsed the space of passive bystander, entailed:

> Implicated subjects occupy positions aligned with power and privilege without being themselves direct agents of harm; they contribute to, inhabit, inherit, or benefit from regimes of domination but do not originate or control such regimes. An implicated subject is neither a victim nor a perpetrator, but rather a participant in histories and social formations that generate the positions of victim and perpetrator, and yet in which most people do not occupy such clear-cut roles. Less "actively" involved than perpetrators, implicated subjects do not fit the mold of the "passive" bystander, either. Although indirect or belated, their actions and inactions help produce and reproduce the positions of victims and perpetrators.[9]

The implicated subject helps us touch on one of the most important stakes in intersectionalizing the Work That Reconnects : questioning its universalizing language to recognize the specific vulnerabilities and responsibilities that come from occupying different positions of power and privilege. As Sarah Nahar argued in her seminal article in *Deep Times*: "While we're all in this together in the Great Turning, we're all in it together differently [...] a waking up to the reality of the ecological self also includes a fearless analysis about one's social location."[10] (See also Chapter 3 by Sarah Nahar.)

Thus, as with all other phases of its evolution, the Evolving Edge stage of the Work followed and reflected broader social trends. This story is still being told and, as such, the following account should be taken as a provisional and incomplete introduction to some of the dynamics and actors at play. For the limited purposes of this chapter, the story can be broken down in two waves.

The first began with three People of Color (POC) cohorts between 2012 and 2014, organized by Anne Symens-Bucher, Joanna's executive assistant, and held at Canticle Farm, an intentional community based in the Work That Reconnects in Oakland, California, co-founded by Anne. These marked a first step in recognizing that the WTR was not sufficiently equipped to give space to the specific vulnerabilities faced by oppressed groups. The experience informed the "Learning with Communities of Color" chapter of the 2014 edition of *Coming Back To Life*, with contributions from many involved, including Patricia St. Onge, Adélájá Simon, Adrián Villaseñor Galarza, Andrés Thomas Conteris, and Andrea Avila.

For many, this chapter did not yet go far enough, however, and glossed over many of the tensions that had arisen in the experience— which was further emphasized by its placement at the back of the book. The issue was framed as a question of inclusion (how to bring previously marginalized publics into the fold), a sectorial add-on to the WTR that did not challenge its fundamental frames, nor the harmful behaviors that workshops often reproduced.

Embracing a resolute commitment to undoing oppression within the Work was the goal of a second wave of mobilization by a coalition of practitioners— including the authors of this book—who saw this work as increasingly necessary and urgent.

Following a first gathering of facilitators in September 2016, initiated by Belinda Griswold, Jade Begay, Aravinda Ananda, Sarah Nahar, and BJ Star, the idea for what would become the Anti-Oppression Resource Group emerged: a regular site to meet and discuss how to rewrite practices and create resources to interrupt patterns of harm within workshops. These efforts yielded several fruits over the years,[11] including the following:

- "The Impact of Race and Culture on the Work That Reconnects," a special issue of *Deep Times* journal (August, 2017), providing personal reflections, analysis, and guidance for facilitators, from a U.S.-based perspective.
- A joint statement, "Toward Greater Solidarity and Inclusion within the Work That Reconnects," (2018) that delves deeply into the context and way forward for undoing oppression within the Work That Reconnects.
- "De-escalating Patterns of Harm in White Dominant Spaces: A Guide for Work That Reconnects Facilitators and Participants"

by members of the Anti-Oppression Resource Group (originally created in 2018 and 2019, and opened for public comment in late 2021 and early 2022).

- "Quick Tips for Intersectionalizing the Work That Reconnects" by Sarah Nahar, a quick, practical reference for facilitators (excerpted from Sarah's article, "Intersectionalization of the Work That Reconnects" from the August 2017 issue of the *Deep Times* journal).

- "Reflections on Attending to Power, Privilege and Oppression Dynamics in Work That Reconnects Spaces" and "Going Deeper: Anti-Oppression for Facilitators," both by Aravinda Ananda, offering further guidance and reflection for facilitators and anyone wanting to support safer workshop spaces for folks in marginalized groups.

In many ways, the book you hold in your hands coalesces the fruits of these long years of learning, reflection, and struggle to establish Undoing Oppression as foundational to the Work.

This was not an easy task, and those who carried it encountered a range of negative reactions, from polite but unsupportive interest, to tepid indifference, to outright hostility and resistance.

Some of these reactions can be seen as symptoms of white U.S.-Americans' broader reticence to reckon with their colorblind racism in the wake of the Black Lives Matter movement, not to mention the resurgence of Indigenous resistance that arose at the same time. Yet one fear in particular arose again and again: the fear that too strong a focus on decolonization and social justice would dilute, distract, or decenter the Work.

Because these fears continue to hinder the work put forward in this volume, we continue the conversation raised by this historical presentation with some deeper reflections in the following chapter.

5

The Work That Reconnects' Evolving Commitment to Social Justice

By Marc Decitre

This chapter follows from the previous chapter on the history of the Work That Reconnects, turning to the past and present links between the WTR and issues of social justice, broadly understood as the commitment to human liberation from the manifold systems of domination that perpetuate social hierarchies and structural violence—capitalism, patriarchy, imperialism, and colonialism to name a few.

Many practitioners who tried to push for a greater inclusion of social justice in recent years have experienced varying degrees of friction, leading to the perception that this commitment was not foundational enough for the Work. The concept of "evolving edge" helped to reframe the issue within the evolutionary language of systems theory, presenting these frictions as a system-wide positive disintegration on the way to the "next level of intersectional decolonial struggle."[1]

Presenting the issue in this way risks making the intersectional and antiracist frames this book advocates for appear as latecomers: logical next steps in a linear evolutionary process. Doing so would sidestep a number of dimensions that complexify the story: the centrality of social justice to the pacifist political culture from which the Work arose; the presence, both at the Work's founding and over the years of its evolution, of minoritized voices who advocated for its greater integration; and early historical debates in which deep ecologists were challenged for their omission of these issues.

If social justice did not factor as a central concern to mainstream Work That Reconnects circles, this cannot be attributed to a lack of historical opportunities to make it so. We may ask, then, what did impede a greater integration?

This is an important question, and many of the actors involved will have their own answer, and may even contest the way it is formulated. This chapter aims to offer leads that appear important to consider from the insider-outsider position I adopted during my research. They are not meant as definitive last words, but as invitations to be discussed, refined, and contested as other perspectives weigh in on the issue. May they stimulate further conversations, facilitate recovery and repair where harm arose, and embolden those who carry this torch today.

A Hidden Root of the Work That Reconnects: Pacifist Political Culture

The Work That Reconnects did not come out of a vacuum, but emerged out of the much broader and older political culture of pacifism, specifically its post-Protestant strand.[2] Many of the Work's commitments can be seen as prolonging its key features: a mystique of interconnection, a commitment to radical transformation of both individual moral conscience and broader social structures, the elevation of the senses and the imagination, and the weaving together of spiritual practices and political engagement.

A broad commitment to social justice, and to antiracism more specifically, has also been a pillar of this tradition. The mass peace movement of the 1930s saw pacifists, inspired by the radical theology of the Social Gospel, expand opposition to war to include opposition to the causes of war, namely capitalism, racism, and imperialism. These social ills were understood to be deeply interwoven, their unmaking a necessary requisite to peace and justice.

The '60s was an important continuation of this spirit; one of its best illustrations, and most relevant for the history of the Work, is how it was taken up by the Movement for a New Society (MNS)—"a national network of feminist radical pacifist collectives that existed from 1971 to 1988."[3]

At a time when arguments over the primacy of class, gender, and race were the norm, this movement articulated a multi-issue political analysis which tied together different elements of leftist thought, including ecological issues and their relation to neo-colonial North-South relations, critiques of sexism and racism, and an advocacy of "decentralized socialism" and "participatory economics."

Building activist intentional communities was a key dimension of the movement—a way to free up more time for activism and to live in the present the values they sought to bring about. As such, undoing oppression took on an important role. Activists were encouraged to "work on their shit" in order to root out sexism, homophobia, classism, and racism within the movement through workshops and personal growth frameworks.

The Interhelp Network had numerous implicit ties with MNS. Joseph Havens, who was close to its central Philadelphia hub, hosted a number of their retreats at Temenos. Joanna Macy and her family participated in their macroanalysis seminars, prompting them to embrace communal living. Many Interhelpers in fact lived in one of their communities (including Fran Peavey), and a number of D&E workshops were held in them. Even after MNS ceased operations, the publishing house some members had founded—the very one publishing this book—also published works by Interhelp's founders.

A commitment to undoing oppression, though it may not have been framed in today's language, is thus neither new, nor was it foreign to those who originally built the Work. In fact, in the later years of Interhelp, as the urgency of the Nuclear Freeze campaign was subsiding, some in the network did seek to make it a more explicit focus, but were unable to make it a lasting inflection.

Part of this missed opportunity can be traced to personal disagreements between different members of the network, though in the absence of an open conversation, it is difficult to draw conclusions from these today. This chapter will thus seek to place the issue within a wider lens, focusing on two overlooked elements in the WTR's collective memory: the impact of the nuclear threat on understandings of social difference, and the early debates between deep and social ecology on these issues.

Blessings and Limitations of Anti-Nuclear Frames

For those of us who did not live through the nuclear arms race, it is difficult to apprehend how imminent and totalizing a threat this was. The first uses of atomic weapons ushered in a planetary horizon of responsibility in which the very survival of the Earth and its people was seen to be at stake. The frames developed to name and respond to this predicament durably marked both the peace and environmental movements, which were deeply intertwined at the time.

These frames allowed millions of people around the world to mobilize to limit the proliferation of nuclear weapons. Thanks to them, we have inherited a future in which the disaster of mutually assured destruction has thus far been avoided, and we should not forget that there were no assurances, at the time, that it would be so.

These foundational orienting principles served a sincere purpose in their time, yet find themselves at odds with contemporary frames championed by environmental justice movements, potentially fostering friction and misunderstandings across generations. Making them explicit may help soften resistances and allow generosity to arise.

A first dimension of the nuclear threat was its totalizing nature. Given the quantity and destructiveness of the weapons involved, their use guaranteed a catastrophe from which no one, regardless of their degree of power, would be sheltered. The predicament was understood as flattening social difference, stripping humans of their social roles to highlight, to quote Chellis Glendinning, "common experience, common vulnerability, common caring." In words that echo the sentiment of the time, she said, "This overwhelming threat is the greatest equalizer of all, and, as such, its presence offers us the ultimate opportunity to come together for common survival."[4]

Thus, the '80s peace movement, drawing on earlier anti-nuclear discourse, structured itself around a strong universalizing frame. This does not mean it was not challenged, nor that a certain degree of reflexivity around social location and the relative social homogeneity of the movement was absent, but it played only a marginal role.

This contrasts sharply with environmental justice frames, which highlight how class, racial, and gender divisions, far from being erased by the climate crisis (and related environmental breakdowns), are deepened and accentuated. Vulnerabilities are not equalized, but deeply dependent on geographical and geopolitical factors—with the Global South bearing the brunt of the impacts while having contributed the least to its causes. Even within the same region, differences in power and privilege can radically affect the capacity to evacuate, relocate, and/or rebuild in the face of disaster.

This first universalist frame opened to a second frame, which emphasized the recognition of our shared humanity as essential medicine. Because the arms race was rooted in bitter antagonisms between two warring blocks, where each side sought to dehumanize the other, the peace movement turned to a horizon of unification across lines of difference as a key to the conflict's resolution. This move echoed a much deeper sentiment prevalent within the internationalist peace movement since the end of World War II: that these great wars have been caused by "the lack of consciousness in the minds of individuals that they were related to the world community."[5] If humanity could only recognize the reality of its deep interconnection, then there would be no war.

One cannot overstate how ubiquitous this sentiment was within the mainstream peace movement, which may have contributed to forging an unreflexive aversion to discourses that forefront difference and (perceived) division. Environmental justice, by contrast, places differences in social location as a necessary starting point to conversations around differential responsibilities. As such, these frames highlight the dangers of invoking unification without justice, gesturing rather towards a horizon of reparation.[6]

Finally, the nuclear threat created an image of catastrophe as one singular event in the future that would mark an unmistakable rupture between before and after. The shadow it cast on the present eclipsed the multiplicity of smaller, local disasters and injustices, and risked minimizing them. So long as the Bomb had not again been dropped, the catastrophe had not yet happened.

In environmental terms, this translates to waiting for the moment of collapse as a big bang. Doing so turns attention away from the myriad forms of "slow violence" already unfolding in the present at the expense of the most dispossessed.[7] As a number of these voices are stressing, part of facing the present moment is recognizing how the catastrophe "has already happened"[8] with the onset of imperialism and genocide. (See Chapter 2 in this volume on different ways to think about the start of the Great Unraveling).

In short, environmental justice frames ask a question that was sidelined by the mainstream '80s peace movement: Where do you stand? Where do you stand in relation to the nexus of historical forces that are driving the Great Unraveling? Do you descend from people who have been selected as worthy recipients of the Industrial Growth Society's fruits, or from those who have been dehumanized, torn from their lands, put to work in the service of accumulation?[9]

To forefront this question logically leads to paying greater attention to the socio-historical roots of human oppression. Unfortunately, the philosophy that became the next step in the Work's development—deep ecology—sidelined the question even further. By identifying "Humans" as the single, monolithic driver of ecocide, it paid little regard to the fact that, in the wake of modernity, a great majority of this humanity was excluded from the very category of human. This omission gave rise to sharp critique by ecofeminists and social ecologists in the late 1980s, with which we conclude this chapter.

The Deep Ecology Versus Social Ecology Debate

Many Interhelpers came to deep ecology with prior commitments to feminism, social justice, or antiracism. Taken on its own, however, this philosophy offered little guidance to make these commitments central. As a consequence, new recruits who found there a first doorway to understanding ecological issues were not equipped to adequately name and counter structural social violence, or even understand these as key issues.

This was an important point of contention in the debates that pitted deep ecologists against social ecologists in the early years of the U.S. Green Party. Social ecology, championed by the eco-anarchist philosopher Murray Bookchin, found its roots in Marxist-inspired materialist analysis. As such, it forefronted the issue of systemic violence as a key to ecological problems, with the credo that the forces that drive the domination of humans over nature are the same forces that drive the domination of humans over other humans. This led him to formulate a polemical critique of deep ecology's omission of these questions:

> Deep ecology's philosophy ... does not highlight or systematically address the social roots of the ecological crisis. ... It presents no explanation of ... the highly graded social as well as ideological developments which are at the roots of the ecological problem. ... Thus, even when individual deep ecologists show concern for harmonizing relationships between races, genders, and classes, their concern does not stem from a coherent expression of deep ecology philosophy. ... Women, poor folks, and people of color are right, I think, to be very wary of a philosophy which interprets vital questions of human solidarity, democracy, and liberation as optional and secondary concerns ... Ecological philosophy, if it is to provide a solid basis for alliance-building, must be a social ecology that critiques and challenges all forms of hierarchy and domination, not just our civilization's attempt to dominate and plunder the natural world.[10]

This critique erupted with a high degree of vitriol in the summer of 1987 at the 2nd National Green Gathering at Amherst, Massachusetts. Over the next two years, a number of key figures, including Charlene Spretnak, Fritjof Capra, and Joanna Macy defended deep ecology and its more spiritual, holistic approach in various green publications—limiting the integration of this critique. While the issue gave rise to a much more productive and charitable debate in 1989 between Murray Bookchin and Dave Foreman (one of the founders of EarthFirst!), it never found a satisfying resolution, and contributed to the Green Party's fragmentation in the early '90s.[11]

What matters for our purposes is that these debates did occur. That they did confront deep ecology, and the environmental movement more broadly, on the issue of racism and social justice. In light of this road not taken, the tensions that the "evolving edge" has generated in recent years can be seen as a resurgence of the issues left unresolved by deep ecology's inability to integrate social ecology's critique.

What was, and still is, at stake?

The way we draw the line of antagonism through ecological questions matters because it determines how we think about the causes of ecological degradation and its remedies. Drawing the line, as deep ecology does, between humanity and nature, or the more than human world, has a number of implications.

As previously mentioned, it dissolves differences that exist within the category of the "human" in terms of power and responsibility. But more than that, it mutes the fact that the processes of exploitation and desecration which have reshaped the natural world have also been an assault on most of humanity. That the transitions to capitalism and industrialization were wars waged by the European bourgeoisie over and against women, the peasantry and working class, and the enslaved and colonized people to whom this war was exported.[12] Doing so, it assents to the dominant narrative that the forces driving these great upheavals—marketization, industrialization, endless capital accumulation—were pursued in the service of humanity, erasing the crucial concept of alienation: the fact that these forces have subjugated most of humanity rather than working for them.[13]

A focus on alienation places humans and nature on the same side of the line of conflict that pits the Industrial Growth Society or the Plantation System against the vitality of the Web of Life. From this perspective, the stake of ecological politics shifts from one of reconnection between two separate poles (humans/nature)—a frame that creates the temptation to consider social justice issues as internal to humans and thus unrelated to environmental protection—to one of co-liberation, where humans ally with each other and more than human powers to free themselves from the forces that threaten their lives and flourishing.

One can only wonder what direction the Work would have taken had these critiques been integrated much earlier in its development. Luckily, history is offering a new chance to place these issues at its heart, solidifying its critical and liberatory potential. Let us not miss this chance.

PART II

Expanding the Frame and Shifting Oppression Dynamics

6

Freeing Ourselves from Systems of Oppression

By Aravinda Ananda with Marc Decitre

Whenever we gather in groups, socially generated power differentials will be present and will give rise to dynamics within the group. Being on the receiving end of systemic oppression contributes to a lack of safety, dignity, and belonging. When instances of oppression arise and are not recognized, named, or addressed by leadership in the room, participants may feel that they are not valued, that their needs don't matter, and that they are not safe in the space. To free ourselves from systems of oppression, we must be able to recognize and address the adverse impacts of power differentials. Having a basic understanding of systems of oppression, understanding our places and roles in these systems, and committing to change are important places to start. We explore these three areas in this chapter.

Understanding Systems of Oppression

Many hierarchical social systems exist around the world today—classism, racism, sexism, ageism, cisheteropatriarchy, and ableism just to name a few. Depending on where you are located in the world, other prominent systems of oppression may be based on religion, citizenship, profession, or education.

These hierarchical social systems rank and systemically advantage or disadvantage certain social groups. In many places, prominent hierarchies rank and assign value according to one's distance from the "untamed" world. Those at the top of the hierarchy declare themselves as superior, and everyone else below them as inferior. The social hierarchy assigns who is considered most human, most godlike, and closest to the divine. It also ranks others as not even fully human, ranking who and what is considered worthless.

In the United States, the cluster of hierarchies generally looks something like this: At the top of the hierarchy are white, property-owning, Christian, rational, cisgender, able-bodied heterosexual men; below them are cisgender women, people of the Global Majority, LGBTQIA+, nonbinary and trans people, bodies and emotions; and below them are the body, emotions, animals, plants, ecosystems, and soil (believed by some to be just dirt!).

> Readers around the world: *Who is at the top of the hierarchy in your local context, who is in the middle, and who is at the bottom?*

These hierarchical systems, purposely constructed by dominant groups in order to maintain their own power, are recreated with each generation. Dominant groups use their power to develop specific ideologies that justify and uphold their role. People are forced to abide by the rules of the hierarchy whether they believe the ideology or not. By internalizing these ideologies, people then do the oppressors' work for them. A consequence of keeping so much attention on these ideologies of superiority and inferiority is that insufficient attention is directed towards dismantling the power of the groups that dominate. This can readily be seen in the 2024 United States presidential election, when billionaires stoked identity fears among the masses, thereby keeping attention away from the elite uber-wealthy class's further consolidation of wealth and political power.

The Co-Arising of Historical Process and Social Location: A Materialist Understanding of Systems of Oppression

By Marc Decitre

Intersectional analyses help us understand the "crossroads" effect of interlocking systems of oppression. They both complexify our understanding of individual social location and combat the temptation to focus on a single overarching struggle (whether it be anti-capitalist, feminist, or decolonial) to the detriment of minoritized positions within that struggle.

Historically, the thinkers who first developed intersectional analysis were rooted in the materialist Left, and saw their intervention as expanding and complexifying its Marxist lineage.[1] Over the decades, however, some of its iterations have become unmoored from this original matrix. One indication of this shift is the tendency to see *ideology* as the root driver of oppression: what generates systemic differences in access to resources, power, and recognition is, first and foremost, the process of valuing one group at the expense of others.

A materialist analysis, by contrast, places the control of land, resources, and labor at the center. In this vision, a system of domination appears first and foremost as an apparatus of power (economic, institutional, military) that organizes a systematic transfer of resources and labor from one group to another. Ideology and prejudice appear as *means* that uphold and facilitate this process, and as *outcomes* that allow the system to reproduce itself, but not the *goal* itself. The goal of a system of oppression is *the enclosure of wealth and power* (see Movement Generation featured in Chapter 15).

Prejudice appears secondary, not because it isn't necessary for a system to function, but because those who profit from it are quite indifferent as to which particular group fills subaltern roles. In this view, categories such as worker, slave, and even "Black" and "woman" arise from the social requirements of systems of domination (whether it be cisheteropatriarchy, racial capitalism, or settler colonialism). They do not pre-exist as fixed categories that these systems then exploit: they are actively produced by the systems themselves. In the language of systems theory, we can call this the co-arising of historical process and social location.

Let's take a few examples. The history of capitalism's emergence in Europe involved a complex web of processes that gradually reshaped the social categories of feudalism (serf, cleric, aristocrat). Some of these processes were economic; they contributed to the creation of a class of workers forced to sell their labor to a propertied bourgeoisie, including *commodification* (transforming nature and the product of human work into marketable products), *proletarianization* (stripping artisans and peasants of land and tools in favor of concentrated, mechanized industry), and *the enclosure of the commons*.[2] Other processes contributed to rigidifying gender roles: a male-centered *sphere of production* (wage labor, economic activity) was increasingly shuttered off from a devalorized *sphere of social reproduction* (domestic labor, child rearing, relational care) assigned to women and other minoritized subjects —a process coined *housewifization* by eco-feminist Maria Mies.[3] Still others participated in the creation of racial hierarchies: the contradictory requirements of a slave-based plantation system within a self-proclaimed "egalitarian democracy" in early U.S. colonies produced a rigid Black-White color line,[4] just as *imperial forms of land dispossession and un-*

equal exchange produced enduring global disparities between a so-called developed North and underdeveloped South.[5]

These historical processes were not happening side by side but were complexly interwoven. Distinguishing these processes from the social hierarchies they produced (class, race, and gender, to name a few), however, offers a number of crucial insights.

First, it helps us account for how these categories emerged in the first place. Thinking about systems of oppression through the lens of *processes* rather than through the lens of *identity* helps us move from intersectionality's image of a *crossroads* toward the image of a *confluence* (the place where rivers meet). Here, the different dimensions of oppression appear not as roads (static, fixed), but as rivers: dynamic processes subject to historical change.

Second, it sheds light on the dependent co-arising nature of systems of domination: although these were in part *produced by* certain historically social groups, they also attain a form of self-catalyzing autonomy, actively *producing* social subjects to occupy the roles required to reproduce themselves over generations.

Third, it points towards a path of transformation. These processes have a beginning, which can be examined: how do they operate *in the big picture*? And they can be reshaped, which requires collective action to produce counteracting processes *at the macro-level*. How do we change the very rules of the game that produce the very positions of oppressor, target, and all the nuances in between? How do we change the course of these hierarchical rivers to generate just, emancipatory, and life-affirming ones?

While this book focuses primarily on the internal and interpersonal aspects of oppression, to get free of systems of oppression, the political, economic, and legal arrangements that maintain the power of a dominant group, and the ideologies they create, must also change. Isabel Wilkerson in her book *Caste*,[6] explores the similarities between how oppression happens with caste in India, racism in the United States, and Nazi persecution of Jewish people and other groups in Germany. While the particular ideologies of superiority and inferiority differed, the mechanisms by which dominant groups maintained their advantage were similar.

While the creation of systems of oppression was and is intentional and conscious, much of the maintenance of systems of oppression is unconscious—norms, beliefs, and consequent modes of relating with one another have been socialized into people from the moment of birth, and so people often do not even realize they hold certain views. One way to begin to consciously interrupt these systems is by naming them and taking steps to understand how they are created and maintained.

> **Power, Prejudice, and Oppression**
>
> **Power** is the ability to act. There are different kinds of power, or ways power can be exerted, such as power over, power with, power to, and power within. In the Work That Reconnects, people most commonly distinguish between power-over and power-with. With this book, we are particularly focusing on how power-over is exerted in social systems.
>
> **Prejudice** is pre-judgment. Any of us can hold pre-judgment about others for any reason, but under systems of human oppression, socially constructed hierarchies systemically prejudice *for* (in favor of) some identities, while other identities are systemically prejudiced *against*. Not only is there a systemic assignment of value, but also a systemic arrangement of power enabling dominant groups to enforce prejudice in favor of their own group, or against members of any subordinate group.
>
> **Oppression** can be defined as prejudice plus the power to exert dominance in a systemic way. Sometimes people use a short-

hand of Oppression = prejudice + power. However, because there are many different kinds of power, it is important to note that oppression entails the systemic power to enforce advantage and disadvantage.

In systems of oppression, this prejudice does *not* just simply exist, but rather is manufactured (and recreated with each generation) by a dominant group in order to maintain advantage for their own group. An example in the United States is how racism was created by rich white male property owners to divide working-class and indentured Europeans from enslaved Africans. Because these male property owners had social power (economic, political, cultural, and judicial), they could create and then enforce ideological value judgments about "race"—a socially constructed concept not based on biology.

The *Four "I's" of Oppression* is a framework frequently used in the United States to help people understand how oppression operates on different reinforcing levels.[7] Once a group has amassed enough power, it can culturally reinforce the idea that their group is superior to another and thus has the right to control that other group. While there is nothing inherently true about these value assignments, they get encoded at the level of culture, norms, and beliefs as **Ideological Oppression**.

This ideological normalization that one group is better than another group and has the right to control the other is systemically embedded and re-embedded in the institutions and structures of society through laws, educational systems, etc. This is the second "I" of **Institutional Oppression**.

This systemic advantaging or disadvantaging of particular identity groups operates in interpersonal interactions through behavior such as microaggressions, forming the third "I" of **Interpersonal Oppression**. Finally, oppression becomes internalized within people as a self-understanding of either superiority or inferiority with **Internalized Oppression**. The Four "I's" form an interrelated system; each aspect reinforces the others as depicted in this image.

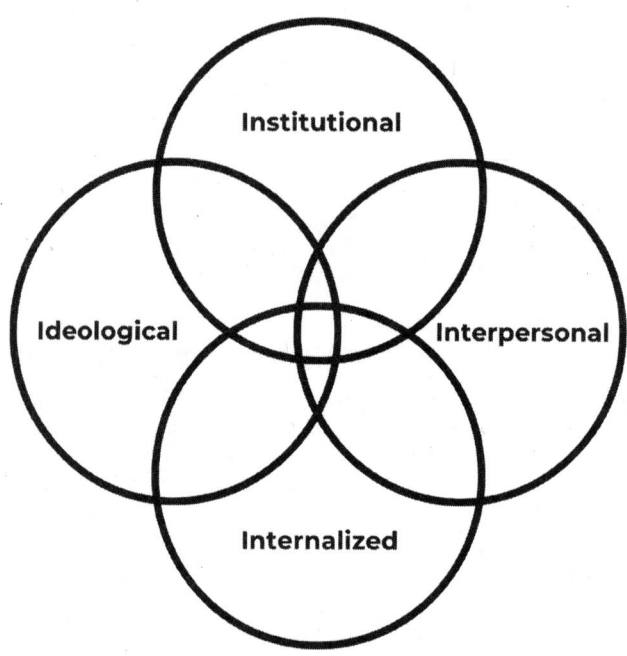

4 I's of Oppression
Credit: Frida Nixdorf based on a concept by John Bell

These four levels co-arise with one other, and thus it is essential that efforts are taken to dismantle supremacy hierarchies on all of these levels. Progress on shifting oppression on any one level will support movement on the other levels. For example, it can be difficult to believe in our inherent worth, or question our supposed inferiority or superiority, if all the other levels reinforce a contrasting message. Thus, shifting oppression on interpersonal, institutional, and ideological levels can support the internal reorganization of our felt sense of inherent worth and our knowing that we don't have (or lack) inherent dignity and worth because of a social identity. Rather we have fundamental inherent worth and dignity by virtue of being alive.

While sometimes ideological oppression—the idea that some identities are superior or inferior to others—is consciously intentional, it is often unconscious. **Implicit bias** is a term that describes this. Also known as implicit prejudice or implicit attitude, implicit bias is a positive or negative attitude, of which one is not consciously aware, towards a specific social group. Because perceptions, attitudes, and stereotypes can operate prior to conscious intention or endorsement, individuals' perceptions and behaviors can be influenced by implicit biases they hold, even if they are unaware they hold such biases.[8] What is so complicated about implicit bias is that it is embedded in our unconscious and thus shows up in our actions even if our conscious intention may be the opposite.

Understanding Socialization

How do these implicit biases get embedded in our unconscious? Bobbi Harro's Cycle of Socialization[9] is a useful tool that helps illustrate how bias can get conditioned into people throughout their lifetime. The cycle starts with "The Beginning" when someone is born into a world with all of the mechanics of oppressive systems already in place—all of the norms, beliefs, and institutionalized power arrangements. In the beginning, none of this is by conscious choice—we are babies! It didn't start with us, but we inherited it from the moment of birth and throughout our lives it will be reinforced over and over, often with no conscious thought.

In our early years we will receive our "First Socialization" through messages (verbal, nonverbal, and by what is modeled to us) from parents, caregivers, relatives, teachers, and all of the people who regularly interact with us. Upon reflection, we may come to realize that many of the messages received from our parents or other people in our early years did not start with them either, but were inherited beliefs and behaviors. For example, gender-normative messages heard early in life—such as "boys shouldn't cry" or "girls should wear dresses"—may often be messages that did not start with one's parents or caregivers, but were in fact beliefs they had also inherited in their early life as well.

"Institutional and Cultural Socialization" occurs as one gets older and begins to interact with more of the institutions of society—religious places of worship, schools, medical and mental health systems, television, etc.—and dominant messages are reinforced over and over. Cultural socialization is reinforced with song lyrics, language, customs and practices, and a broad array of media including television, the internet, and social media.

> *What are some of the messages you received in childhood about how and why "your people" were different, special, superior, or inferior?*

This repetitive bombardment of messages can lead you to believe that these dominant cultural beliefs and norms are reality, just the way things are. Throughout your life you will encounter many "Enforcements" whose purpose is to keep you in line with the status quo. These enforcements, which take the form of both punishments for deviation and rewards for adherence, occur along a range of severity, and manifest in both overt and covert ways. For example, in a workplace setting, punishments for deviation could range in severity from someone simply changing the subject when you try to raise an issue to being passed over for promotion or even fired.

> *How have superiority and inferiority valuations about identities you hold been enforced and reinforced throughout your life? This question is asked with care, knowing that it can be a painful reflection for those of us who have received messages of inferiority.*

Most often people will continue with the status quo, doing nothing to make waves, not through some deficiency in character, but because there is so much systemic inertia and reinforcement to do so. In addition, one may not have had an opportunity to see that there is a different option. Or, compliance may be a survival tactic because the cost of deviation is simply too high. At some point, however, one may encounter a dissonant event or experiences may accumulate that cause one to pause and generate the impetus to act for something different. Making conscious some of the unconscious beliefs we have been socialized to hold takes time, and shifting those beliefs and consequent behaviors takes even longer. Understanding and shifting our socialization is a lifelong endeavor.

Social Identities and Their Respective Locations

Social location refers to one's proximity to (or distance from) the ability to exert systemic power. An important step toward getting free of systems of oppression is understanding the social identities each of us carry and their respective locations within systems of oppression. Many of us will carry some identities that have been systemically prejudiced for (considered superior and afforded rights) and some identities that are systemically prejudiced against (considered inferior and denied rights).

Some major social identity categories include:
- Race
- Ethnicity
- Class (including factors such as income or accumulated financial assets, formal education, employment, housing, and access to transportation)
- Gender identity
- Sexual orientation
- Relationship status (e.g., single, married, divorced, widowed, monogamous, polyamorous) and family structure (e.g., have children or no children)
- Age
- Ability—both physical and mental ability including neurodiversity
- Body type
- Citizenship
- Language
- Religion

Often people with dominant identities may not even be conscious that they carry them, because their identity has been considered the norm. For example, in societies where the standard is "white" and only those who are not white carry a racial identity, many white people may not think much about their identity or the power and rights afforded to it.

Within each of these identity categories, there will be differences in the value that has been socially assigned—ranging from superior to inferior and including positions in between—because many of the identities are not a binary and occur on a spectrum. For example, with regard to wealth, there are not only rich *or* poor people, there is a whole middle class with its own stratifications. Or people's class experience may have shifted throughout their life, for example if they were born into a family with little financial wealth, but acquired it later in life.

Each socially assigned valuation is paired with access to or exclusion from the systemic power required to enforce advantage and disadvantage. Often people experience systemic advantage in some identities and systemic disadvantage in other identities. For example, in much of the world today, a white middle-class female with a physical disability will experience some systemic race and class advantages, while facing some systemic gender and ability disadvantages.

Each of us is much more than our identity boxes and their corresponding assigned value, and some of the identities most important to us may have nothing to do with major social identity categories. That said, being able to understand and name the way power is arranged in a society or a group, along with understanding which identities are afforded systemic power and which identities are denied that power, are important skills.

This Simplified Social Location Mapping Wheel is a smaller version (only six categories) of a fuller wheel with 16 categories that Kara Bender and I (Aravinda) developed for a U.S. context. Adapted from Tessa Watkins' Intersectionality Wheel of Privilege,[10] the fuller Social Location Mapping Wheel is available on the Interhelp Network website[11] in the resources section.

Freeing Ourselves from Systems of Oppression | 111

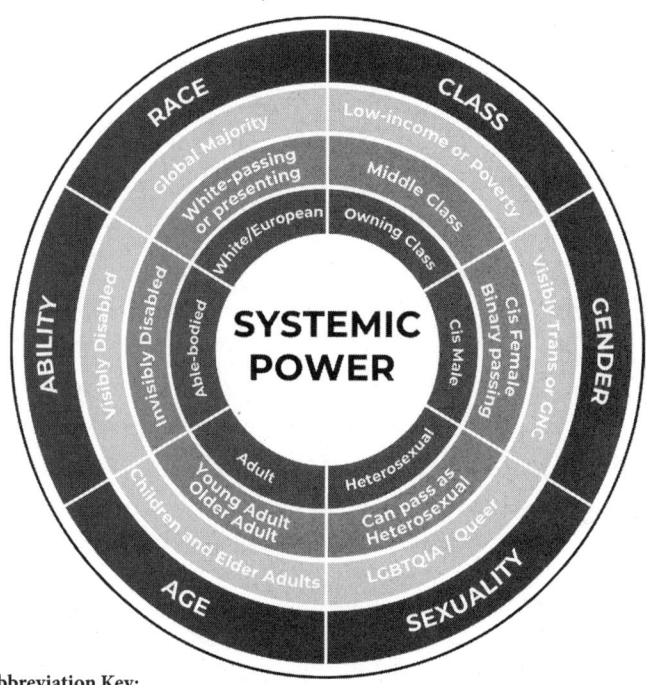

Abbreviation Key:
GNC: Gender Non-Conforming
Cis: Cisgender

Simplified Social Location Mapping Wheel
Credit: Aravinda Ananda

The wheel provides a graphic tool for locating the proximity of different social identities to systemic power. The closer one's identity is to the center of the wheel, the more the identity has been defined as superior and is systemically *prejudiced for*. The further out one's identity lies, the more one's identity has been defined as inferior and is systemically *prejudiced against*. Many of one's life experiences will have been greatly shaped by these social locations, and depending on one's identities, this can bring up a lot of painful memories of harm, exclusion, or guilt.

If or when used in different contexts, it is necessary to modify the wheel with appropriate local information (e.g., which religion has dominance will vary based on where you are in the world). Aysu Miskbay has adapted a social location mapping wheel with relevant categories and locations for a Turkish context.[12] Dr Amy Tan has created a similar Power and Privilege Graphic Tool for Canada.[13]

While the way the wheel is constructed gives the same graphic representation (same size wedge) to each of the identity categories, it is worth reflecting on whether certain identity categories carry considerably more weight than others; e.g., in the United States race is a major identity category along which advantage is afforded or denied, while in England class is particularly prominent.

> **Social Locations Inventory and Reflection**
>
> 1. *With gentleness, you are invited to do a social identities and social locations inventory. Depending on our identities, doing this inventory can bring up painful memories and feelings. While being able to do a power analysis is an important skill to develop, this inventory is not just an intellectual activity, and may bring much to light that is in need of healing.*
>
> 2. *Choose if you will use the simplified mapping wheel in this book, the fuller version (for a U.S. context) available online, or a new one you draw filled in with the particulars of your local context.*
>
> 3. *Circle or write in the appropriate location the identities you hold for each identity category (e.g., middle class, adult, able-bodied).*
>
> Reflect on:
>
> - *Where are the identities you hold located on the wheel—towards the center, middle ring, or periphery?*
> - *Do you have more identities located closer to the center or closer to the periphery?*
> - *What does the location of your social identities mean for the value you have been socially assigned (superior to inferior) and how you have been systemically prejudiced for or*

> *prejudiced against?*
>
> - *Is the systemic advantaging or oppression of particular identities more pronounced for some identities than others in your context? If so, what are the implications of this for the identities you hold?*
>
> - *Do you experience any oppression or systemic advantage that results from the intersection of different identities? (For example, as explained in Chapter 3, misogynoir is a particular manifestation of oppression that Black women face because of the intersection of race and gender.)*
>
> - *What feelings does doing this inventory bring up for you?*
>
> - *Is there any support you need as you transition out of this activity?*

Social Location in Group Settings

Being able to not only recognize differences in social location but also attend to the impacts of these differences is critical work for creating safer and more inclusive experiences for everyone present in a group.

What is noticed: The social location of facilitators will influence how an internalized sense of inferiority or superiority has been inculcated into them and the life experiences they have had. Often these factors influence what they will or will not notice. People who have been systemically disadvantaged by social systems will often have an acute sense of the lived impacts of this social location, having experienced it often on a daily basis throughout their lives. People who have been systemically advantaged have often been conditioned not to notice harmful impacts of these same systems.

The more work we can do to understand social location in general and our own particular social locations, the better prepared we will be to anticipate, notice, and engage with dynamics that arise within groups due to differences in social location.

Whose voice is heard: Social location can also influence who is more vocal in the group and who tends to remain silent. While factors influencing these different tendencies may include personality or life experience unrelated to social identity, social identity can be a large factor. People who grew up with repeated messages about their inferiority may struggle with believing their voice matters and have a difficult time speaking up, while people who grew up believing that their voice inherently mattered may be conditioned to speak up much more frequently than others in the room.

> *Have you noticed dynamics in groups you are a part of where people of certain social identities speak up much more than others?*

Chapter 10 shares some strategies for supporting greater equity in participation opportunities.

Empathy gaps: Empathy gaps present another place where people's experience in groups can be impacted according to social location. Empathy gaps occur because people raised under social systems of oppression have been conditioned to be able to more easily *empathize up* and not down on a hierarchy. People with dominant identities get treated as being deserving of empathy while empathy is frequently withheld from others. People with advantaged identities have often been socialized to not feel the pain of people being oppressed by their identity group. As a matter of survival, sometimes people with identities that have been systemically disadvantaged may also participate in this dynamic of empathizing up when, for example, being quicker to offer comfort to distressed people in advantaged identities than to people from their own identity group.

Empathy gaps add another layer of complexity to doing group work with people of different social locations because they make it less likely that everyone's pain is held with care. This is especially true of "Honoring Our Pain for the World" work. Because people in oppressor identity groups are often trained not to feel the pain of those being oppressed, this training can get in the way of being able to feel compassion for people in non-dominant groups, and especially about the pain of oppression.

While different from empathy gaps generated from conditioning to *empathize up*, people of oppressed identity groups can also feel challenged with relating to the pain of people from dominant groups, especially when said people have shown no understanding or empathy for people in the oppressed group.

Doing some identity exploration and social location work before moving more deeply into the "Honoring Our Pain for the World" phase of the spiral can offer an opportunity for people to deepen their self-awareness, learn more about each other's experience and humanity, and hopefully be able to relate more easily and respectfully across difference.

Doing Social Location Work with Groups

Awareness of one's own social location is an important foundation for being able to more respectfully relate across differences. Facilitators can take steps to support groups in this exploration. There are different options for this based on the time available. Explicitly naming social identities and social location towards the start of a program can help make different aspects of diversity more visible in the room. This could be done through a diversity welcome (more about this in Chapter 10), or in an introductions round where participants are invited to share an identity, with a prompt such as "Share your name, pronouns if you use them, and an identity that is important to you."

As a facilitator you can model sharing the social location of a particular identity you hold. For example, one way I (Aravinda) have responded to this prompt is by sharing that I come from a mixed-race background of European and African descent. While I present/pass as white to a lot of people, having family members with darker skin has allowed me to witness up close how differently I am treated based on the color of my skin, and has kindled a passion to work for justice not only for my family members, but also for all people adversely affected by racism. If you don't have time to include an explicit prompt about social identities and social locations during introductions, another way you can bring it in is by modeling it to the group with a statement about yourself that names your social identities, e.g., "As a white, able-bodied, cisgender woman, I ..."

Time permitting, facilitators can also provide some framing comments that offer broad strokes about social systems of oppression and then invite further exploration of participants' own identities and social locations. With longer time formats, two options for further exploration include:

> **1) Verbal sharing in pairs**: After sharing an overview of major social identities and what social location means, have people share with another person two to three of their identities that are important to them and have significantly shaped their life experience.
>
> Because people are often more conscious of the ways they have been persecuted or excluded because of identity and less conscious of the identities that give them systemic advantage, encourage people to share at least one identity that has afforded them systemic advantage.
>
> Also consider including prompts that help people reflect on the cultural experience of their upbringing, and their realization of difference.
>
> Because some of us have deeply painful experiences with social location, this is not just an intellectual exercise and requires sensitivity. The potential for vulnerable content and "ouches" can arise across differences in social location, so for this particular pair sharing it may be better for you to allow participants to choose their own partner rather than using techniques of random assignment such as "turn to the person next to you."
>
> **2) Exploration through self-reflection and writing**: Give people some writing prompts about their identities such as the ones

suggested above for verbal sharing in pairs, or develop your own prompts that guide people through some explicit aspects of their social location. Or, writing a poem or creating a free drawing can provide options that tap more of the right brain.

If group time is limited for exploring social location, facilitators could also consider inviting people to reflect on their social identity in advance of the workshop through reflection prompts, so they are arriving with more of this self-awareness.

Committing to Collective Liberation

Until an explicit commitment to equity, justice, and liberation is embraced and steps are taken to embody this commitment, dominant social norms from hierarchical systems will be the default in social spaces. This is true even in well-intentioned spaces, and it can be even more painful to encounter oppressive harm in these places, where the expectation and hope may have been to be treated with care and respect.

Under systems of oppression the default is to be held accountable (that is, answerable or responsible—please see Chapter 8 for more on accountability) only or primarily to people in positions of power. Adverse impacts to people deemed lower on socially constructed hierarchies are not even acknowledged. Committing to collective liberation requires a radically different accountability—it asks us to be answerable to the purpose of furthering collective liberation rather than upholding hierarchy and it asks us to take responsibility for harmful impacts. With the shift from allegiance to hierarchy to allegiance to collective liberation, comes a shift from authoritative answerability driven by fear, to equitable answerability driven by care for all. This shift does not happen overnight, and will take time. An important starting place is *making a conscious commitment,* and then taking steps over time for your actions to be in alignment with that commitment.

In making a conscious commitment to collective liberation, these questions can help make more visible *to whom and/or what* (values, purpose, ways of being) you as a particular individual or a group as a whole are accountable:

- Are you accountable only to people in dominant social positions? Or are you accountable to everyone?
- Are you accountable for upholding hierarchies? Or are you accountable for liberating people from hierarchies?
- Are you accountable to productivity and accomplishing a particular outcome without regard for process and what happens along the way? Or are you accountable to attending to dynamics as they arise and addressing harm when it happens? Do you affirm that *how* we are together is an integral part of *what* we do?
- Are you accountable to creating a Beloved Community, a place where everyone belongs, everyone matters, everyone's inherent dignity is valued and respected, and no one is disposable? Do you commit to reducing and mitigating harm as it happens, in a non-punitive way (please see below for more about non-punitive approaches to harm).

If you believe that you are accountable to everyone and to liberating people from human hierarchies of ranking and oppression, then it is essential to take steps to build anti-oppressive spaces. Chapters 7, 8, 10, 11, and 13 offer particular guidance for this. This commitment requires us to be willing to be disturbed and go outside of our comfort zones.

Once you've committed to collective liberation, you will need to practice that commitment moment by moment. Those of us on this path will face numerous pitfalls and challenges on the way. Earlier in our journeys some of us may be very quick to pass judgment, attempt to be a savior, come off as "woker" than thou, be quick to punish and dispose of transgressors, or may all too frequently (and unwittingly) do other oppressive acts in our earlier attempts to get free of those systems.

I have found Janet E. Helms' work on racial identity development (with similar parallels for other identity categories) helpful for thinking about that journey and holding ourselves with a little more grace. Helms' model of the stages of racial identity development describes this all-too-common trajectory: once people have woken up to the pain and injustice of systems of oppression, if they don't go back to sleep (and there are many pressures to go in this direction), their first steps toward greater equity and justice will likely be performative (surface level, not yet embodied) and clumsy. It can take considerable effort over years to integrate a skillful embodiment of a commitment to collective liberation.

Some of us may feel compelled to lash out at people who cause harm. While rage is justified when justice has been denied for far too long, if you have a commitment to transforming violence, you are not entitled to inflict violence in your responses to harm. As adrienne maree brown notes in *Holding Change: The Way of Emergent Strategy Facilitation and Mediation*, describing those of us who grew up in punitive cultures:

> We are socialized, trained, encouraged and given permission to punish each other. Punishment starts very early in most of our lives. Time-outs, spankings, detention, suspension, expulsion, juvenile detention, jail, prison, solitary confinement, death ... even when it isn't our politic or intention, we pass on these punitive behaviors to others who cause harm or challenge us. In this way, a cycle of punishment perpetuates.[14]

Adrienne then gives this directive to facilitators: "Your work is to break the cycle of punishment in any room you hold."[15]

Orienting to non-punitive responses to harm is essential, and the vision of Transformative Justice can inspire us. Transformative Justice seeks to transform the root causes of justice by supporting survivors in their healing, supporting people who have caused harm to take accountability, and engaging community members in the process. The goal is to transform the conditions that gave rise to the harm in the first place. Transformative Justice supports getting truly free of the systems of oppression that bind us, and offers us approaches for practicing non-punitive responses to harm. This vision of Transformative Justice informs the following chapters on exploring and addressing patterns of oppressive harm.

7

Seeing and Addressing Oppression Dynamics: Part 1

By Aravinda Ananda

While people on the receiving end of oppressive dynamics feel their impact acutely, people in more dominant positions often do not notice them at all, or do not recognize them as being harmful. Systems of oppression maintain themselves by hiding harmful impacts or otherwise desensitizing people in positions of power to the pain of these impacts. This chapter and the next cover some major oppressive dynamics that have surfaced in Work That Reconnects spaces (particularly in the United States) and offer some suggestions for how to address these dynamics.

In 2018, a group of Work That Reconnects facilitators gathered in Oakland, California, on Ohlone territory, to look at patterns of oppressive harm that had been happening in Work That Reconnects spaces. Members of the Anti-Oppression Resource Group subsequently created a document that described not only these repeated harms but also some suggestions for how facilitators could avoid or address these patterns. Principally authored by United States facilitators Aravinda Ananda and Carmen Rumbaut, this document was entitled "De-escalating patterns of harm in white dominant spaces." In 2023, Aravinda Ananda and Tamir Notovny substantively rewrote and expanded this into another document entitled "From Harm to Care: De-escalating patterns of harm in group facilitation." Chapters 7 and 8 are a further iteration of those two documents and include some sections excerpted from the document co-authored with Tamir.

While some of the patterns and especially some of the examples explored in these two chapters are specific to a particular context (local culture, politics, etc.), many of these patterns of harm share some similarities around the globe.

Many patterns of harm flow out of the unspoken rule of strict adherence to the established order of prevailing social hierarchies. Under systems of social hierarchy, there is an established order of who matters and who doesn't; who has power-over and who doesn't; whose needs are considered and whose are not; who deserves comfort and safety (two distinctly different things) and who doesn't; who deserves empathy and who doesn't; who has impunity and who doesn't; and whose labor can be extracted without compensation. Feedback that deviates from or challenges the established order is typically silenced swiftly. Four major oppression dynamics/patterns of harm that have repeatedly surfaced in workshop spaces (and indeed throughout much of society) are explored in this chapter and the next.

They include:
1. Centering
2. Not noticing, ignoring, or reinforcing oppressive harm
3. Avoiding accountability
4. Extraction

Pattern: Centering

Centering is the normalization and prioritization of the perspectives, experiences, comfort, leadership, and needs of people in dominant identity groups while ignoring, invalidating, or otherwise negating the needs, perspectives, experiences, comfort, and safety of people in non-dominant identity groups. In hierarchical societies, people with dominant identities are often treated as if they are the only ones that matter. They represent the norm, the standard of humanity, and everyone else is treated as if they either don't exist or are a deviation from that norm.

The United States has centuries of history in which dominant identities have been the only ones considered human, normal, or acceptable. Earlier in U.S. history, only white male property owners could be citizens, vote, sue in court, and make many personal and legal decisions. While laws have changed, culture hasn't completely evolved and manifestations of this dynamic continue to exist today, even though they may seem more subtle and are less apparent to people who are advantaged by these systems of oppression. For people who are on the receiving end of this power dynamic, the felt experience is obvious and often acute.

Much of centering is unspoken and unconscious. For example, there is no explicit rule in the United States that white cisgender men get to speak the most frequently in a group. Rather, this happens because of implicit cultural assumptions about whose voice is valued, and how this gets modeled to people throughout their lives and is thus embedded in their behavior. Unless it is pointed out, facilitators conditioned by dominant culture may not even notice if they or others in the room are centering dominant identities.

In the United States, dominant identities that frequently get centered include (but are not limited to): people that present as white, cisgender male, heterosexual, able-bodied, upper class, university educated, and (in some circles) Christian. People in countries and cultures with different histories may have different social groups that are the most dominant, but the dynamics of centering are often similar in any culture built on hierarchical arrangements of human value.

While people from dominant groups center themselves a lot, people from oppressed groups can center dominant groups as well. However, the latter group's reasons for doing so are typically about daily survival rather than maintaining any kind of individual or group advantage. Colluding in oppressive dynamics including centering can be an important survival strategy to avoid activating, or to soothe the already agitated, nervous systems of people of dominant identities. Not doing so has proven to have harsh consequences.

Examples

Normalization and prioritization of dominant identities can manifest in Work That Reconnects spaces in several ways. Here are some examples.

Framing: An older version of the Three Stories of Our Time framed the Great Unravelling as a phenomenon that had only begun recently, and as such centers people for whom this is a new phenomenon. While some dimensions of a Great Unraveling have reached global dimensions more recently, such as climate destabilization, peoples and ecosystems around the world have been experiencing unravelings and total destruction of life and lifeways for as long as empires have existed. Acting as if this is only a new phenomenon centers the people for whom this experience is new and writes everyone else out of the picture as if their experience didn't even exist.

Content: Often content is geared towards a dominant identity, as if only that identity exists in the world. For example, an older version of the practice Harvesting the Gifts of the Ancestors centered the experience of European-descended peoples.

We statements: "We" statements, especially ones made by people in dominant identity groups, can overgeneralize their experience as if it were true for everyone. This erases and makes invisible the experience of non-dominant groups.

Here's an example from *Coming Back to Life: The Updated Guide to the Work That Reconnects* (2014):[1] "The most remarkable feature of this historical moment on Earth is not that we are on our way to destroying the world—we've actually been on that way for quite a while. It is that we are beginning to wake up, as from a millennia-long sleep, to a whole new relationship to our world, to ourselves and each other." This statement omits acknowledging the fact that not everyone has been equally contributing to "destroying the world" nor has everyone been in a millennia-long sleep. Sweeping statements like these, which may be true for members of dominant groups, serve to erase people with different experiences. For example, Indigenous tribes in the Amazon have contributed almost nothing to current anthropogenic climate change. Even within industrialized countries that have contributed the most to climate change, corporations and the wealthy have contributed far more than the average person.

Participation: Often activities are offered in a way that centers the participation of dominant identities. Examples include:
- Offering an activity that requires walking with no alternative options given when there are participants present with mobility constraints.
- White men in a group dominating conversation and no one, and especially not the facilitator, says or does anything to bring attention to or change this dynamic. It perpetuates the same voices being heard while there is little or no room for other voices. This frequent dynamic in the United States may also arise with different dominant identity groups in other places in the world.
- Over-relying on rational and cognitive thought (preferred facets of intelligence for some dominant identities), and thereby excluding emotion, intuition, and body awareness.
- Defining active listening as only one speaker at a time, when some cultures have a more interactive style of back and forth communication.

Comfort: Dominant-group comfort frequently gets prioritized in general, and especially in times of conflict, tension, or harm. An example of this is after a Person of the Global Majority has named harm they have just experienced, facilitators and/or participants may move to comfort, defend (e.g., "I'm sure they didn't mean it that way") or educate the white person who caused the harm, rather than focusing on the person(s) who just experienced harm. All too often, the comfort and needs of the person(s) with positional power are centered, leaving the person(s) who have just been harmed with little or no support.

Empathy: Life-long conditioning in oppressive systems teaches people to more easily empathize up and not down on a hierarchy. Therefore empathy much more easily flows to dominant group people than it does to people of oppressed identities.

This can also be true within groups of people of oppressed identities. Here's an example of how an empathy gap operates within an oppressed group: During a shared pair practice called "Open Sentences," after a Black man shared about some racial pain he had experienced in his life, his open sentences partner who was a white woman started crying profusely. The man's conditioning was to comfort the woman and direct empathy first towards her rather than primarily to himself.

Social conditioning that leads people to empathize more readily with people of dominant identities shows up all the time in Work That Reconnects spaces and makes it more difficult for everyone's pain to be regarded with the care it deserves.

Shifting the Pattern of Centering Dominant Identities

As the examples above illustrate, centering people with dominant identities happens in many different ways, including in session design, framing, and how dominant group comfort, experience, and participation is prioritized. Because our systems have been imbalanced for so long, it is important to take steps to actively center the perspectives, needs, experience, and leadership of groups that face oppression.

While decentering is fundamentally about equity and *not* about casting aside or punishing people from dominant groups, it can feel disconcerting for a group that is used to being centered by default to no longer receive that treatment. Members of dominant groups may initiate some pushback that facilitators should be prepared for, while also considering the potential impacts of that pushback on people with targeted identities. Done well, decentering dominant identities is about affirming historically marginalized peoples and restoring balance and equity to the way we affirm and care for each other—not about marginalizing people with dominant identities.

Decentering dominant groups is also *not* about including people from oppressed identity groups in something that fundamentally still centers dominant groups. It's about shifting power dynamics so that people from marginalized groups are valued and their needs are attended to. This power shift is needed both in our facilitated group spaces and in the overarching systemic conditions that marginalize some groups. The rest of this chapter offers some recommendations for shifting the dynamic of centering dominant identities in group spaces.

Growing Anti-Oppressive and Cultural Awareness

For facilitators with dominant identities, simply being able to notice centering when it is happening is an essential first step, so continuing to engage in ongoing learning is important. Books, articles, trainings, and movies that expand awareness about the experience of different identity groups are a good place to start. While written particularly for people working in nonprofits, I have found the book *Embracing Cultural Competency: A Roadmap for Nonprofit Capacity Builders*[2] more broadly applicable and a helpful starting text to help people of dominant identities learn more about the experience of different identity groups. Because the centering of dominant identities is often widely apparent and acutely felt by people who are excluded by this dynamic, the work of people with oppressed identities lies less with being able to notice the dynamic, and more with not perpetuating or colluding in it.

Outside of workshop spaces, facilitators of dominant identities can take steps beyond book and other learning to expand their knowledge of different cultures and different identity groups' experiences by building more authentic relationships with people of diverse identities. Done respectfully, this can increase opportunities to learn about how different identity groups may experience a given topic. Within workshop spaces, facilitators can ask workshop participants how things are landing for them and what they need to feel genuinely included, rather than making assumptions on others' behalf. Increasing one's familiarity with some common needs of different identity groups can help them prepare to better include different needs.

If you have co-facilitators, you can support each other in paying attention to how things are landing for different identity groups. While not everyone within an identity group will feel the same way about something, you may come to notice, for example, if there are times when people from a dominant identity group seem to be resonating a lot more with what you are offering than participants from an oppressed group. Paying attention to body language can be helpful. You might notice if many of the white people (or people from another dominant identity group) in the room are engaging enthusiastically with an activity or content while multiple People of the Global Majority (or people from another oppressed identity) seem checked out, have their arms crossed and seem closed down, are anxiously tapping their foot, etc. A person's reasons for "checking out" or exhibiting distressed body language can be because of personal reasons rather than a dynamic in the group, so observations of distress in multiple people can be a better indicator than a single person.

Session Design and Content

Be sure to plan your content to be relevant to who will be in the room, particularly keeping in mind people with non-dominant identities. If you will be working with a group of people you do not know, you may want to get some demographic information in advance. This can give you a better sense of who will be in the room, so you can plan your content to relate to their experiences. For example, using quotes from people of the identities of those who are in the room can be helpful, so that the voices and perspectives of people in the room are seen as valued. For example, don't only quote white people in a multiracial space.

Facilitation Team Considerations

Having, for example, an all-white facilitation team in a multiracial group can perpetuate centering the leadership of a dominant identity. Whenever possible, have diverse facilitation teams that reflect who will be in the room. Having people of diverse backgrounds on a facilitation team increases the chances that a team member will have had some similar lived experiences to those of participants from marginalized groups. It is especially important for people from oppressed identities to see people who look like them in leadership positions.

In efforts to expand diversity in a facilitation team, care is needed with ensuring equitable power in decision making. Otherwise, it's easy to slip into tokenization, whereby people are included due to their marginalized identity but not allowed real decision-making power, and are furthermore somehow expected to represent their entire identity group. While a Person of the Global Majority will have daily lived experience with this identity and may have insights into how some other members of this group may think and feel, they do not represent or speak for their entire identity group. Expecting them to do so is harmful because it erases their humanity and their individuality and reduces them to an identity group label.

Be aware that early in the learning journey with anti-oppression work, it can be all too easy to employ other oppressive dynamics in one's efforts to avoid centering dominant identity leadership. Proceed with care.

Making Difference More Visible and Welcome

Naming social identities and social locations can help to address the dynamic of centering because it lessens the cultural assumption that dominant identities are the only ones, or the only ones worthy of consideration. It can sometimes be helpful to share a diversity welcome such as the one created by Training For Change,[3] or an adaptation thereof that feels relatable for your current audience. This is a way to normalize that this is a space for every identity present, and to set a welcoming and inclusive tone, rather than ignoring difference and assuming (or appearing to assume) that everyone is the same or should conform to the dominant norms.

If you incorporate a diversity welcome at the start of a group's time together, adapt the language to fit you and your group, and work to have your subsequent actions consistent with what you signal in the welcome itself. For example, if you say, "We welcome people of all genders" and then use gender binary language throughout your facilitation, that broken commitment to inclusion may feel even more harmful to genderqueer and nonbinary people than it would without having expressed that welcome at the start.

Inviting participants to introduce themselves with one or more of their identities can also be helpful. This can help to make difference visible and create more space for it. Going even deeper can involve inviting participants to reflect on and share not only their social identity, but also their social location—that is, their positions of power and degree of advantage or oppression within a given system of oppression. This can help surface unspoken power differentials present in the room. If your workshop context is such that it does not make sense to include social location in introductions (e.g., in a one-hour program with a lot on the agenda, there would not likely be time for this), there are ways as a facilitator to acknowledge and model social location when you speak about yourself. For example, "As a white passing, cishetero female, able-bodied, college-educated person, I ..." You can also acknowledge that your lived experience may be different based on your respective advantage or oppression.

Group Agreements or Guidelines and Facilitation Techniques for Inclusivity and Diverse Participation

Having explicit agreements through a community agreements or guidelines process offers an important opportunity to shift group behavior around centering dominant identities. One more common community agreement to address centering is the request for people to "Speak from personal experience and use I statements." If such an agreement is in place, then be sure to call attention to times when people make "we" statements that harmfully universalize the experience of one identity group. Naming and bringing awareness to it can help participants learn and change their behavior. For an environment conducive to learning and growing, it is helpful not to use a "gotcha" tone or engage with a policing attitude. Instead, hold (as best you are able and willing to) both compassion and rigor. A simple statement could be, "I'd like to bring our attention back to the community guideline about speaking from personal experience and using 'I statements.' Can you rephrase what you just said with an 'I statement'?"

Another group agreement that can help address whose voice is heard is "Make Space, Take Space." Some of you may be more familiar with the language of "step up, step back" which many people no longer use because of some ableist connotations. This guideline can encourage people who tend to talk a lot to hold back at times and really listen, and encourage people who tend to not speak a lot to consider sharing more.

If multiple people raise their hand at once, you can prioritize calling on people with non-dominant identities first. Or if the group would like to do this, you could even make an explicit group understanding that the first opportunity to speak, often (or always, depending on what works for your work and group) goes to people of non-dominant identities. You can also use facilitation techniques during group conversations such as "Let's hear from someone who hasn't spoken yet" as a way to create more space for less-heard voices.

Prioritizing the Needs of Impacted Persons After Harm Happens

Despite earnest intentions to reduce and eliminate oppressive harm, it will inevitably occur in group spaces. When this happens, one can make choices to prioritize the healing (or other needs) of the person who just experienced the harm, rather than perpetuating a frequent dynamic of centering the feelings, comfort, or learning of the person who just contributed to the harm. While one can make their best attempt to hold the needs of all people involved, one can also make conscious choices about what to prioritize in a given moment to address long-standing imbalances in whose needs get centered.

What a person will need to restabilize or heal after experiencing harmful impact will differ from person to person. To get a better sense of this, you could ask questions such as, "What would feel helpful now?" "Is there anything you need to feel ok with continuing in the group?" "Is there something that would feel helpful to hear?" Keep in mind that someone may not immediately know what they need, as it can take some people a while to process and integrate not only what has just happened, but also what their needs are. Being pressured or put on the spot in unwelcome ways can cause someone to shut down, so offering these questions with gentleness can be helpful. What is crucial is that this isn't about fixing, rushing to a resolution (that may be false), or pushing an agenda such as pressuring the person who just experienced harm to help other people feel ok about it. Rather it is about inquiry, curiosity, and willingness to actually support needs that are present.

Because sometimes people will not immediately know what they need, one way that facilitators may be able to help share some of the load of figuring that out is by first reflecting back something they heard the person say, and then asking if they would tell you more about it. Sometimes when openness to explore is supported, people can find the answers within themselves, or have more support to verbalize what they already know. Or, you could offer a guess about what the person may be feeling and needing in that moment, such as, "Would it feel helpful to have the impact on you acknowledged?" If the guess doesn't end up being accurate, it can sometimes still help clarify what would be helpful instead. For example, "Yes it would help for the impact to be acknowledged, but it's much more than that. It would also feel really helpful for me to know if they regret that impact and are willing to grow and learn so they don't do this again in the future."

Use of Affinity or Identity Caucus Spaces

Sometimes it can be helpful to have separate concurrent spaces (affinity groups or identity caucuses) for different identity groups so that different needs can be prioritized simultaneously. Dominant identity groups can benefit from having spaces that prioritize their learning, and doing this in a caucus space allows this need to be met without centering it as the activity for an entire group. Groups that have been historically marginalized can benefit from having spaces to talk and just be without having to navigate some of the dynamics present with dominant identities.

Following the Leadership of Those Most Impacted

In addressing the dynamic of centering, people in dominant identity groups may need to do some inner work to help them relinquish some of the control and comfort they have become accustomed to, and follow the lead of people most impacted. As Work That Reconnects facilitator Sarah Nahar shared in her seminal *Deep Times* journal article entitled "Intersectionalizing the Work That Reconnects":[4]

> I think it's best to follow the leadership of those most impacted by colonial, racist, sexist violence—in the sense that they know most what is needed for their reality. It is only through a different kind of movement (one not white-led or white-dominated) that we can shift from what we have now to the world we all want to see. Not white-led or white-dominated ***does not*** mean that white folks and settlers-of-color aren't involved. ***Rather it's an invitation to get involved in a way without being in control of the direction or managing the situation to suit (y)our comfort.***

In the book *Emergent Strategy: Shaping Change, Changing Worlds*,[5] adrienne maree brown describes an adaptation of a privilege walk exercise, which many people no longer use because having some people so far in the back can serve to only reinforce painful life experiences of being left behind and excluded. In the adaptation, rather than starting in a line and asking people to step forwards or backwards based on life experiences of privilege or adversity, people start in a big circle, shoulder to shoulder, and take steps forward for life experiences of oppression and take steps back for experiences of privilege. Those most impacted by oppression end up towards the center while those with most privilege are furthest out.

A facilitator can then suggest that people in the room follow the lead of those at the center, so that this embodied way of seeing differences in social location also affirms those most impacted by systems of oppression. As adrienne maree brown writes, "Those in the center are those whose lead we should be following—they know the truth of oppressive impact and they know the brilliance of survival against numerous odds."[6] Affirming and supporting the leadership of people most impacted by systems of oppression in the struggle to get free of these systems is an important step. And as mentioned above, to embody this commitment may require some deep inner work from people with dominant identities.

In summary, centering of dominant identities occurs all too often in social spaces, in both obvious and subtle ways. Fortunately facilitators can take specific steps to stop perpetuating this dynamic. In the next chapter, we continue exploring several other oppression dynamics and how to shift them.

8

Seeing and Addressing Oppression Dynamics: Part 2

By Aravinda Ananda

In this chapter we explore three more major oppression dynamics/patterns of oppressive harm:

1. Not noticing, ignoring, or reinforcing oppressive harm
2. Avoiding accountability
3. Extraction

Not Noticing, Ignoring, or Reinforcing Oppressive Harm

If people from dominant groups fully empathized with the impacts of oppression, the status quo would become intolerable and collapse. Therefore, systems of oppression, in order to preserve themselves, condition those in power to be oblivious or insensitive to the harm experienced by marginalized groups. As a result, many forms of oppressive harm are not apparent to people from dominant groups until they are examined more closely. All too often people from dominant identity groups do not even notice the impacts of oppressive harm except in its most overt forms.

The oppressive harm that occurs in workshop spaces can be missed entirely by people who have been conditioned their whole life by societal norms not to notice it. These societal norms did not start with any of us, but once we are consciously aware of them, we may be able to build more choice in how not to perpetuate them.

Unfortunately, even if people do notice oppressive harm, all too often the tendency is to not do anything about it. There is a range of reasons for this: from thinking it is no big deal, to not knowing what to do, to feeling nervous about making anyone in positions of power uncomfortable, to fear of pushback and other reprisal if it is named.

All too often people do not acknowledge or respond to oppressive harm at all; when they actually do, they may respond in a way that further reinforces harm. A prominent example is the dynamic of centering the comfort and needs of a person who has caused harm, rather than attending to the needs of the person who was harmfully impacted.

Another prominent example of this major dynamic is not addressing microaggressions. We turn to this topic now in some length.

Understanding Microaggressions

Microaggressions are a common form of oppressive harm in workshop spaces (and, in truth, in most social spaces) that frequently go unaddressed. Microaggressions, as defined by Derald Wing Sue and colleagues, are "commonplace daily verbal, behavioral, or environmental indignities, whether intended or unintended, that communicate hostile, derogatory, or negative slights and insults towards members of oppressed groups."[1] They can be committed by facilitators or by participants.

"Micro" refers to the scale at which aggressions can occur. They are usually interpersonal, but can also be environmental—e.g., meeting in a public building named after someone who committed atrocities against members of a particular identity group—as opposed to macro or systemic/structural aggressions. Micro in no way refers to the magnitude of harm resulting from these behaviors.

Often people not targeted by these microaggressions will not recognize them as hurtful, and don't see them as a problem, e.g., "It was just a joke." But for people on the receiving end of microaggressions, they are deeply hurtful. Because they can unfold in rapid succession, the cumulative load is considerable, sending the message that some people aren't valued, don't belong, and are considered less human.

These behaviors fundamentally undermine safety, dignity, and belonging—which are core human needs. Not naming, acknowledging, or addressing microaggressions adds a double layer of harm, because doing nothing signals that other people present condone them. It can be destabilizing not only for the person directly targeted by the microaggression, but also for other bystanders who notice and observe that nothing was done about it.

Microaggressions
a poem by Carmen Rumbaut

Microaggressions sound tiny
as though they wouldn't hurt
as they pass through
without an obvious trace.

They go by so fast!
Hidden in a normal conversation,
hard to notice in real time.

As tiny as a female mosquito's proboscis,
inserted between living skin cells
sucking blood
leaving behind saliva
that creates an angry red welt,

keeping us up at night,
unconsciously scratching
at an invisible intruder.
We are lucky if we don't get malaria.

Maybe a better analogy is radiation poisoning,
invisible to the eye
destroying the peaceful functioning of the body
each malignant ion burning quietly
undermining health
causing cancer.
Is there medicine I can take?
Are there preventive measures?
Can I escape exposure?

Should I organize a brigade
to take out the cause?
Can I somehow increase awareness
of the harm caused?

Will I get communal help
in clearing out the pollution?

Two common forms of microaggressions are microinsults and microinvalidations. Both happen frequently in workshop spaces (and in society at large). A microinsult is "characterized by communications that convey rudeness and insensitivity and demean a person's ... heritage or identity. Microinsults represent subtle snubs, frequently unknown to the perpetrator, but clearly convey a hidden insulting message to the recipient."[2] An example of a racial microinsult all too common in the United States is when a white person refers to a Black person as "articulate," implying that Black people are not typically articulate, as if this person is "a credit to their race."

Microinvalidations are "characterized by communications that exclude, negate, or nullify the psychological thoughts, feelings, or experiential reality of a person."[3] Microinvalidations can include comments like "I don't care if you're Black, white, or purple," and can even involve invalidating someone's experience of other microaggressions through statements such as, "I'm sure they didn't mean that," or "they were probably having a bad day."

As Marc Decitre explored in Chapter 5, progressive communities in the United States went through a period of time in which some people believed that being "color blind" (acting as if one doesn't see differences in skin color) was a way to be antiracist. While seeing people for who they are and not just their race is important, to claim one doesn't see race ignores a whole set of social realities and experiences and, as such, can be a painful microinvalidation.

Some other common examples of microaggressions that happen in the United States include: repeatedly misgendering people (using pronouns to refer to someone that are other than the ones that he, she, they, ze, etc. use for self reference); treating someone's name as exotic and asking what it means; or asking a Person of the Global Majority where they are from, and then when they respond with a geographic location in the United States (e.g., "Boston"), persisting with "No, where are you really from?" which is a veiled demand for someone's racial or ethnic identity to be named.

While this section on microaggressions contains many examples relating to race in a U.S. context, microaggressions happen to members of every non-dominant identity group, and will accordingly look different based on the identity and the context.

> *For readers around the world, what are some common microaggressions that happen in your context, and are there any parallels with the examples here that feel applicable to other identities in your context?*

Keep in mind as you read the next section that different approaches may be needed depending on the local culture and context.

Addressing Microaggressions

Microaggressions all too often go unaddressed for a number of reasons. People from dominant identities may not even notice them, or if they do, they may not know what to do and so do nothing. People on the receiving end may choose to say and do nothing about them because the added labor of naming them and the risk of subjecting oneself to all-too-likely pushback or other reprisals carries too high a cost.

Backlash from people of dominant identities against accountability for microaggressions can be so strong that it can create a chilling effect on naming them at all. In many spaces, naming microaggressions or other forms of identity-based harm is viewed as rude and a violation of the established order.

If you hold dominant identities and have trusted relationships with people from identity groups facing oppression, you may or may not have already heard many stories of their experiences with microaggressions. Because the pushback from people with dominant identities for daring to speak up about a microaggression can be so harsh, it is possible they have not been mentioned even if you have trusting relationships with each other.

> If first-hand stories of microaggressions have been shared with you, it can be helpful to reflect on how you have responded. *Have you affirmed the person or people sharing their experiences, or have you explained their stories away?*

In some circumstances, it may be helpful to ask people from marginalized groups about their experiences with microaggressions, but it is essential to exercise discernment about when and whether this is an appropriate ask. These questions can put the person you're asking in the awkward position of either having to do the emotional labor of educating you (and possibly retriggering themselves or risking reprisal from you in the process) or risking conflict by saying no.

For people of dominant identities, articles such as the above referenced "Racial Microaggressions in Everyday Life" by Derald Wing Sue et al. can help with recognizing and understanding the dynamics of microaggressions. The more you learn on your own, the less you will need to depend on people who have been targeted to share with you on this vulnerable topic.

Deepening your ability to notice unfolding dynamics in the room is also important. No one person will know everything that can be experienced as a microaggression in advance, but one can pay attention to what is happening in the room and be alert for signs that harm was just experienced. This can include things such as noticing if the energy in the room shifts (this can be an indication that nervous system state changes have occurred); noticing people's body language such as clenched hands, a participant anxiously tapping their feet, or a pained expression on someone's face; or a feeling in your gut. Reading the room in this way is a skill that may be more developed for some than for others. From an early age, people from oppressed identities have very often had to perceive subtle changes in affect as a survival necessity, while others have not developed a sensitivity to notice this at all.

Even if a facilitator does not cognitively recognize something that happened as a microaggression, noticing changes in emotion and body ease can be possible clues that something painful or otherwise off may have just occurred. However, it is possible that a person's mood shifted not because of harm experienced directly in the moment, but because a present moment event reminded them of pain experienced in the past. Sometimes the only way to know if someone has just experienced some form of harm such as a microaggression is by checking in with them. Sometimes there are tactful ways to do this in real time in the whole group and sometimes it is helpful to wait until a more private moment such as a break so as not to put someone on the spot in an unwelcome way.

Once a microaggression has been noticed or named, a facilitator has lots of choices of how to respond. If the facilitator is the person who just committed the microaggression, and they either realize it or have been told about it, it is important that they acknowledge it. This can be a valuable opportunity to model receiving feedback without defensiveness. Useful steps are acknowledging impact, apologizing if that feels genuine, and consciously changing behavior. These steps echo Mia Mingus' work on "The Four Parts of Accountability and How to Give A Genuine Apology."[4] It may require some self-reflection to be able to engage with these steps authentically.

Because defensiveness can be a default tendency for many of us, it can take considerable inner work to be able to respond more non-defensively to feedback about harm you have caused (please see Chapter 12 on Inner Work for more about this). Shifting patterns of defensiveness can be aided by work with a therapist, conversation with a trusted friend, or through journaling, among other means. Practicing receiving feedback about harmful impact when you are not facilitating, including doing roleplays with co-facilitators or other colleagues, can help to strengthen that capacity. Please see Appendix A on Giving and Receiving Feedback about Harm for some recommended steps for acknowledging feedback about harm you have caused.

Because the consequences of speaking up for people being targeted by microaggressions can be so high, and because that is a tall ask at a time when people may be reeling and needing to restabilize or otherwise focus on their own healing, it can be particularly important for other people to intervene. Bystanders—people not being directly targeted—can play a critical role in intervening when microaggressions happen. Because of their positional power, people from dominant identity groups can interrupt without risking the same level of targeting and reprisal. This is not to say that they will not experience any pushback or consequences, but the magnitude will not be of the same severity as it would be for a person from a targeted identity. Because of their assumed credibility, individuals from non-targeted groups can also sometimes use that to more effectively get through to the person committing the microaggression.

Once you make the decision to speak up, how you speak up or otherwise intervene matters. Here are a few cautions:

- Consider if and how your intervention might bring unwanted attention or blowback on the person being targeted.
- Interventions done with a savior attitude or orientation actually

decrease the agency of the person who was just targeted by the microaggression.
- Some of us may have an urge to come down extra hard on the person committing the microaggression in a way that ends up being more about demonstrating how woke we are than about mitigating harm.
- Hypervigilance in watching for microaggressions can put you on edge, and it can encourage hypervigilance in the group. This can change the energy in the group, and it can be triggering for participants of marginalized identities to be in such a space.

This may feel like a lot to keep in mind, and it could be easy for some of us to get tripped up with trying to get our interventions perfect. There is no such thing as perfection, and there is no cookie-cutter approach for the "right" intervention because what is needed will vary based on the context and the people involved. If we are committed to harm reduction, what we can do is strengthen our muscles of intervening in ways that center care for the people who have been targeted.

So, taking all of this into account, how might one practically respond after a microaggression has just happened? Some factors to assess when determining whether and how to intervene include:
- Given how many microaggressions typically unfold in social spaces, you will have to discern which ones to address. You can ask yourself: How big an impact did the microaggression just have? Sometimes you may be able to assess this through body language, etc., sometimes not.
- Does your intuition say you need to pause now to address this, and if yes, how forcefully? How will the group's energy be impacted if this is addressed in real time? If you do nothing or respond later?
- What intervention, if any, would most honor the agency and dignity of the person or people who were targeted or impacted?
- Can you respond in a way that upholds accountability and dignity for all?

The most helpful interventions will typically center the person or people being targeted. If you are able to, check with the person who was just impacted about what would be helpful in the moment. They may or may not be able to answer. It isn't always possible to ascertain in real time what would best meet their needs, and you may not have the opportunity or relationship needed to determine that. As a facilitator you can also make best guesses based on things like body language.

One quick intervention that centers the person being targeted is to directly counteract the slight or invalidation with a positive statement and then move on, without putting any more attention on the person who did the microaggression. This is a quick way to acknowledge and address the rupture in dignity without taking the time to check in with the impacted person or directly engage the person who did the microaggression.

If you do choose to engage a person who just did a microaggression, make a conscious choice about whether your goal is to set a hard boundary, help them learn, or both. Addressing them in as non-accusatory a way as possible may help them be more receptive to learning and changing behavior. You may want to follow up at a later time and suggest some resources for further learning or other accountability actions.

You might choose to use the microaggression as an example of a pattern that's been playing out in the space, and invite all participants (especially those with systemic advantage) to commit to interrupting that pattern. Here's a construction you could use: "I'm hearing some language like X, and as I'm sure many of us are aware, that language can carry hidden meanings like Y. Let's try to be aware of that going forward."

Here's an application of that construction: "I've been hearing some gender binary language like he or she, when the gender identity spectrum is much larger than that. Going forward, let's try to use more gender inclusive language to include nonbinary and gender fluid people." This is a quick way to name things in the moment and take steps for participants to understand what is being lifted up without otherwise taking a lot of time on it. Another option would be to engage in deeper exploration on the topic at hand in real time, or to suggest ways for people to do that at a future time. Taking time in real time means facilitators need to assess if there is capacity in the group to do this deeper exploration at this time, and also be able to adjust what comes next to fit the available time.

Interrupting this dynamic of not noticing, ignoring, or reinforcing oppressive harm can go a long way toward making workshop spaces safer for everyone in the room. This dynamic also relates to the next pattern explored here: avoiding accountability. Once harm has been recognized as such and named, calls for accountability can meet stiff resistance, pushback, and deflection. We turn now to an exploration of addressing the pattern of avoiding accountability.

Avoiding Accountability

An important part of accountability is taking responsibility for one's actions and their impact. Under systems of oppression, people in positions of power are not accountable to anyone deemed lower on the hierarchy, and are certainly not accountable for any harmful impact. In truth, harm frequently is not even registered as such by people in positions of power because it is seen as just the way things are.

Systems of oppression are constructed such that people in positions of power are the authority and maintain themselves as such through control and threat-imposition. They get to make the rules and are only accountable to others in positions of power and to upholding the hierarchical system. This default system of accountability in systems of oppression is actually a system of non-accountability for people in positions of power.

As explored in Chapter 6, a commitment to collective liberation asks us to shift our allegiance regarding who we are accountable to—everyone; and what we are accountable to—collective liberation. For workshop facilitators, explicitly sharing an anti-oppression intention upfront, building that expectation into community agreements (see Appendix B for more on this), and addressing instances when people deviate from this are important steps in building healthier structures for accountability.

However, when we ask people in positions of power to be accountable for harmful impact, we may encounter a vast array of accountability deflection tactics. We turn next to exploring how accountability deflection can manifest and then look at ways to address this.

Accountability Deflection

Often when people deemed higher up on a hierarchy are asked to be accountable for harmful impact to people deemed lower down on a hierarchy, the request is ignored or rebuffed. The person asking for it may even be silenced, demonized, or treated with suspicion for challenging the established social order that gives unquestioned authority and impunity to those in positions of power. Note that accountability deflection is not unique to people with social identities that afford them systemic power. However, systemic power affords people in positions of social power enhanced ability to deny responsibility for their actions.

When called to account (and particularly when called to account for oppressive harm), people in dominant positions all too frequently become defensive and can act to shut down the person or people providing feedback by:

- Maintaining innocence
- Turning all attention to their intentions or otherwise offering no acknowledgment of impact
- Interrogating or cross-examining the person who provided the feedback
- Tone policing the person who provided the feedback (making it only about the person sharing the feedback in an unacceptable way, e.g., too angry, and thereby ignoring the content of the feedback)
- Deflecting responsibility for the issue onto the person providing the feedback
- Gaslighting the person who provided the feedback by denying their experience as though it never happened

- Giving a non-apology (e.g., "I'm sorry you feel that way")
- Punishing the person who provided the feedback
- Otherwise invalidating the experience, validity, and feedback of the person naming harm

Sadly, this kind of deflection only adds further harm to the initial injury. It can be particularly fatiguing and painful to have dared to have spoken up about something, and then have it deflected in one of these ways.

Because hierarchical social systems such as white supremacy define people with dominant identities as good by default, this absolves them of the impact of their actions. People from dominant groups can often get away with harm by defending, or having others defend, their intentions. They couldn't possibly have done a bad thing if their intentions were good, and of course their intentions were good because they are a good person. Thus, calls for accountability can be met with robust defense of one's character and intentions, rather than genuine reflection about impact and consequent acknowledgment. This defensiveness to feedback about harm serves to keep oppressive behaviors unexamined and unchanged.

So, one layer of complexity in coming to healthy accountability is this challenge with cultural assumptions about worth and guilt—you are bad if you do a bad thing, which gets people caught up in denying their "guilt" so they can maintain their essential goodness. A distinction between shame, guilt, and healthy remorse is helpful here. Shame is the feeling that you are a bad person. Guilt is the feeling that you did a bad thing. Healthy remorse is the awareness that you did something with harmful impact that you regret and may even want to make amends for. The problem is that guilt and shame can get in the way of healthy remorse and a desire to be accountable.

Punitive cultures add another layer of difficulty with coming to healthy accountability. Punitive cultures punish people who are found responsible for having done "bad" things. Prentis Hempill has a brilliant exploration of the dangers of the innocence/guilt binary in their book *What It Takes to Heal: How Transforming Ourselves Can Change the World.*[5] As Hemphill explains, fear of punishment or expulsion may keep people focused on defending a false innocence rather than genuinely showing up for accountability. If all of our energy goes into proving our innocence, no energy is left for honestly understanding our roles in causing harm. The work of collective liberation, of truly getting free from hierarchical systems of human supremacy, asks us to leave behind guilt and innocence, as well as good/bad binaries, and to show up for an honest accounting of harmful impact and commitment to whatever healing and repair is possible.

Accountability deflection also shows up when after someone has caused harm, rather than denying responsibility, they fall apart or over-perform guilt when confronted with the impact of their actions. This can force others into a caregiving role, pressuring people to affirm that the person who caused harm is good rather than focusing on addressing the harm that was experienced.

Accountability deflection also manifests when onlookers turn towards punitive responses that dismiss and dispose of people who cause harm. This deflects true accountability because it denies those who cause harm the opportunity to learn and grow and avoid causing the same harm in the future.

Causing harm does not mean we are bad people. However, deflecting responsibility for the harm we cause exacerbates the original harm and leaves conditions of oppression in place, thwarting our movement toward collective liberation.

Building Healthy Accountability

Healthy accountability is an internal and external commitment to aligning one's actions with certain values, and willingly making efforts to take reparative steps when one's actions are out of alignment with those values. When working to transform systems of oppression, accepting responsibility for our role in harm and committing to reparative action is particularly important.

Genuine behavioral change takes more than simply making a cognitive commitment. Staci K. Haines' book *The Politics of Trauma: Somatics, Healing and Social Justice*[6] is a valuable resource to aid shifting one's behavior. Haines also offers a helpful frame of "centered accountability" whereby we acknowledge our responsibility for harm (intended or not) without either trying to avoid or deflect responsibility (under-accountability) or taking on fault or blame automatically (over-accountability). As Haines writes, "centered accountability seeks to hold complexity, to both be accountable and know what is not our responsibility, and to stay connected in relationships."

> Try on this approach: *My actions caused harmful impact, and that does not cancel out my inherent dignity. I can acknowledge what my responsibility is, and take steps to address ruptures in safety, dignity, and belonging with others.*

In *Healing Resistance: A Radically Different Approach to Harm*,[7] Kazu Haga shares that the critical word in the phrase "holding people accountable" is the word "holding." You can't force anyone to take accountability—that is, to get to an internal understanding and recognition that you had a harmful impact that you regret and you want to take responsibility for; to offer whatever repair is possible; and not do it again. But you can support people in that process. Most of us could use this support.

Even if we are eagerly showing up for accountability work, many of us often don't know how to do it well on our own because healthy accountability was never modeled to us in the dominant society. Having learning partners, teachers, coaches, and accountability buddies can offer critical support on our learning journeys. Accountability buddies can be particularly helpful because we can't necessarily see everything on our own; having an outside perspective can be really helpful. If you have a co-facilitator, you can make it a part of how you facilitate together to watch for impact when the other person is facilitating and debrief with one another afterwards.

It may take many of us years, if not decades, of learning and unlearning to get to embodied healthy accountability, and each of us can take steps along the way. Abolitionist leaders working for non-punitive responses to harm—including Mariame Kaba, Shira Hassan, adrienne maree brown, Mia Mingus, and Prentis Hemphill, to name just a few—have offered many teachings about accountability. Their work is a great place to deepen your engagement with this topic (please see the section on non-punitive responses to harm in Appendix F: Recommended Resources).

A great tool for facilitators to strengthen a culture of healthy accountability is to have a community agreement about impact vs. intention which encourages people to acknowledge harmful impacts. With such a community agreement in place, facilitators can refer people to the agreement if defensiveness arises. For example, "I hear that it was not your intention to cause harm, and can you acknowledge the impact?"

Because healthy accountability is a new learned behavior for so many of us, it can require coaching, practice, and long-term inner work in order to be able to do it well. We can start with a commitment to healthy accountability, and then take steps over time to more fully embody that commitment in our actions.

We turn next to the final pattern explored in these two chapters: Extraction.

Extraction

In accordance with the systemic rule of strict adherence to the established order, human supremacy systems deem that those higher up on the hierarchy are entitled to extract whatever they want from people deemed lower on the hierarchy, with no need for consent, compensation, equitable exchange, respectful relationship, or even acknowledgment . We can see this clearly with anthropocentrism, whereby some humans view themselves as entitled to extract whatever they want from the Earth and other species. It happens within the human species as well.

Extraction from humans by other humans has been seen in the United States with theft of land from Indigenous nations and theft of life and labor from Africans enslaved in chattel slavery. Around the world under patriarchy, women's care work is frequently uncompensated and under-valued. Some aspects of contemporary extraction may be less overt, but they are deeply painful nevertheless.

Whatever form extraction takes, it perpetuates the same core dynamic: people of dominant identities act out conscious or unconscious entitlement to the free or poorly compensated labor and resources of people deemed lower on the hierarchy with no regard for their needs, dignity, and self-sovereignty. This dynamic is deeply rooted in internalized and institutionalized supremacy (e.g., capitalism) and must be consciously interrupted through learning, self-reflection, behavioral change, and institutional change.

Some common ways extraction can occur in workshop spaces involve emotional labor, educational labor, unfair compensation, and cultural appropriation (see Chapter 13 for more about cultural appropriation).

A prominent form of emotional labor extraction happens when people of oppressed identities are expected to tend to the comfort and psychological well-being of people from dominant groups, without regard for their own well-being. This can include maintaining dominant group comfort, soothing people's distress when they are confronted about their privilege, or being forced to listen to triggering stories or anecdotes that are shared in order to educate people from dominant groups.

Emotional labor extraction is not reciprocal. People with marginalized identities, such as People of the Global Majority, women, and femmes, are expected to offer this labor without regard for their boundaries, needs, or safety. After an oppressive dynamic has been named, all too often, people with oppressed identities are expected to center the comfort and learning of people with dominant identities. People declining to provide this kind of emotional labor may be cast as heartless, angry, or aggressive, or as the cause of the negative feelings they are refusing to triage.

In facilitated spaces in the United States, this is a consistent pattern between white people and People of the Global Majority. All of the empathy in the room will typically go to the people of dominant identities who have caused the harm. Meanwhile, people who have just been harmed by the dynamic are expected to not only comfort the people who have just harmed them, but also to provide educational labor about why what just happened was harmful.

Many forms of "invisible work" such as emotional labor, educational labor, and other forms of care work are often by default assigned to people from oppressed groups such as People of the Global Majority, women, and femmes. This dynamic can show up on co-facilitation teams where people with dominant identities may be compensated more while people with less positional power are expected to volunteer, or less desirable tasks are relegated to people with less positional power.

Shifting the Pattern of Extraction

How does one shift these patterns of extraction? Making these often unconscious and invisible dynamics visible is an important place to start. Another step is seeking out existing resources (books, articles, trainings, etc.) where work has already been done to explain things rather than making demands on people from oppressed identity groups to provide information. Peer accountability spaces with people of similar social location who are also committed to anti-oppression could help you unpack and learn from incidents that come up in workshops or daily life. Over time, facilitators can work to grow their ability to notice and anticipate extractive dynamics and lessen the frequency with which they extract other people's labor.

Co-facilitators could decide how to allocate emotional labor so that it is distributed more equitably. For example, a facilitation duo of a white person and a Person of the Global Majority can make an arrangement that the white facilitator will address disruptive or problematic behavior from white participants. This can help to avoid the default dynamic of this labor falling on the people most adversely impacted.

It is essential for facilitators with more systemic power to do their own inner work. Facilitators get to be human, have feelings, and make mistakes. We do not get to impose a burden of care on people with less systemic power than we have, without their consent. Practices in this area could include:

- Holding (and, when appropriate, naming) our own discomfort rather than forcing a group to hold it
- Working with a coach, therapist, accountability partner, or other healing practitioner, outside of our spaces, to help us prepare our nervous systems for discomfort and trigger responses, and/or
- Developing practices for self-management when challenged or called in/out/on/up in a space we're facilitating

In order to directly counter patterns of entitlement, facilitators can build the expectation that consent in general, and more specifically consent about labor, in all the forms we have discussed, is a bedrock principle that everyone is requested to follow. This could be part of a community agreement process with special encouragement to people from marginalized groups to practice choiceful emotional labor in this space, choosing if and when they offer care to someone else.

In summary here are some key steps for facilitators to shift a dominant pattern of extraction:

- If you have dominant identities, grow your awareness of the work you are asking others to do, especially emotional and educational labor.
- Grow your capacity to track who is being expected to do different kinds of labor, and implement ways to rebalance the load so that consent is honored and historical inequities are not reinforced.
- Have transparent conversations within your co-facilitation teams about fairness in compensation and distribution of labor, particularly invisible forms of labor that have been demanded of certain identity groups.

Taking steps to address the oppression dynamics explored in these two chapters—and the harm they cause—goes a long way to making workshop spaces safer and more welcoming for everyone in the room. It may take considerable time to be able to skillfully address these dynamics; however, this investment makes a significant contribution to collective liberation.

9

Queering the Work That Reconnects: Embracing the Wild Fluidity of Life

By Ian Goh

What is queerness if not another word for wild? That untamable part of us that is determined to grow no matter what. To thrive, despite the environment that it's in. To adapt and change, and grow and evolve and to be itself.[1]
—Willow Defebaugh, editor-in-chief of *Atmos*

Imagine a world where the boundaries we've drawn between ourselves and everything else dissolve. A world where our sense of identity and self can flow as freely as a river, adapting and changing course as it encounters new landscapes.

For me, such a world gives the impression of being disorienting and liberating at the same time. Disorienting because I am used to conventional ways of referring to myself and have to unlearn a lot of social scripts that I've internalized as a cisgender man. But this mode of being is also liberating since it enables me to truly embrace my queerness and live in alignment with Nature itself.

I also believe that this is the world that ultimately emerges when we begin to live in the Great Turning. And perhaps it is already happening, albeit slowly. Which is why there is a huge need to queer the Work That Reconnects.

But why queer the Work? How would queering transform our current understanding of the Work?

The answer lies in the nature of life itself. Life, in its essence, is queer. It defies categorization, breaks down barriers, and thrives in diversity. Queer is the fluidity and dynamism of life itself. As living beings embedded in the natural world, we are all queer to a certain extent. However, we often fail to realize this because the existing rigid structures imposed by dominant, capitalist social structures obscure this innate queerness. They constrain us within narrow, illusory notions of static, independent selves and fixed, binary identities.

By queering the Work That Reconnects, we're not just making space for LGBTQ+ perspectives—we're opening up new possibilities for understanding our relationship with the Earth and with each other.

> Heteronormative—believing that heterosexuality is normal and anything other than that is not.
> Cisgender—when a person's gender aligns with the sex they were assigned at birth.

Understanding Queerness

To queer is to challenge binaries in all forms. It's not just about disrupting heteronormative and cisgender assumptions; it's about questioning the very way we categorize and separate our experiences.

Think about the term "queer" itself. It's simultaneously a noun, an adjective, and a verb.[2] This fluidity mirrors the adaptability of nature, the interconnectedness of ecosystems, and the complexity of our own identities.

When we apply this queerness to the Work That Reconnects, we begin to see that the rigid categories we've created—man and woman, human and nature, self and other—are just that: psychological and linguistic constructions of the mind.[3] They have been conceived through performances we've been enacting, often without realizing it.

While the Work That Reconnects has provided a basis for understanding these concepts within a larger context of interconnectedness, diversity, and systemic thinking, the framework has not explicitly explored the queer aspects of nature, ecology, and being. This is a missed opportunity because there is so much to learn about life and nature through the lens of queerness. In fact, there's an entire field of study dedicated to exploring this work: queer ecology!

Queering the Three Dimensions of the Great Turning

Based on the three dimensions of the Great Turning, there are three possible ways in which we can queer the Work That Reconnects:

1. Queering actions in defense of life
2. Queering the foundations of our common life
3. Queering perception and values

Queering Actions in Defense of Life

When we queer our actions in defense of life, we recognize that defending queerness is defending life itself. This means acting to slow down the damage caused by heteronormativity and cisgender bias in all forms, knowing that such actions will also slow down the damage towards Earth. This is because fighting for ecological justice and liberation naturally involves fighting for gender and sexual justice and liberation.[4]

Ecological crises disproportionately affect women, LGBTQ+ peoples, and systemically excluded communities, creating overlapping vulnerabilities that cannot be addressed in isolation. These struggles share common roots in confronting systems of oppression that prioritise profit and power over the wellbeing of all earthkin.

The Problem with Heteronormativity

Heteronormativity is a lie that has propagated harm in the form of violence, discrimination, and systemic inequality, especially towards those who identify as women as well as transgender and gender nonconforming (TGNC). It restricts people's freedom to pursue their interests and make life choices, often pressuring LGBTQ+ people to conform to heteronormative expectations like opposite-sex marriage. This limitation of opportunities extends to various aspects of life, from personal relationships to professional aspirations.[5]

Perhaps most alarmingly, rigid gender roles and unequal power dynamics have contributed to high rates of violence[6] against queer individuals. Transgender women, especially trans women of color, are facing an epidemic of violence motivated by transphobia and toxic masculinity.[7]

We need to be aware that heteronormativity has socialized most of us into conforming to either "male" or "female" gender roles. Such binaries are restrictive, arbitrary classifications that have largely been shaped by a white, cisgender, and Eurocentric bias.[8]

Even how we perceive biological sex and what is deemed "natural" has been constructed through language and cultural meanings inscribed on bodies, not by an absolute reality. Biological sex is not a simple binary of male and female, but rather a spectrum. The existence of intersex people—individuals born with reproductive or sexual anatomy that doesn't fit binary definitions of male or female—who constitute around 1.7% of the world population,[9] has proven that this notion of a rigid biological sex binary and other heteronormative assumptions are untrue.

Another significant problem with heteronormativity is that it interacts with and enables other systems of oppression,[10] including but not limited to racism, ableism, and especially patriarchy. By promoting an illusory dichotomy that confines people into binary categories, it reinforces and sustains existing structures that thrive on this way of thinking.

In the case of patriarchy, heteronormativity promotes a binary view of gender that aligns biological sex, gender identity, and sexual orientation within rigid male-female categories. This justifies patriarchal narratives of men being "naturally dominant" and women being submissive.

Not to mention how heteronormativity can compound other forms of discrimination for LGBTQ+ peoples who are also part of other systemically excluded groups like those who identify as Black and/or as a woman.

Heteronormativity in all forms not only harms LGBTQ+ people but also reinforces restrictive and oppressive norms that force everyone to conform. Therefore, the healing of heteronormativity through queering is not just the fight for queer liberation or female liberation; it is working towards the liberation of all beings, all intersecting identities.

Politicizing Our Practice

To queer our actions in defense of life, we need to politicize our practice. This involves recognizing queering as a form of counterculture that challenges the dominant narratives that separate us from nature and each other.

Dr. Jennifer Mullan, clinical psychologist and author of *Decolonizing Therapy*, describes this process as "an internal process of re-educating, reclaiming and re-membering your True Self and that of your Ancestors."[11] It's about acknowledging the inseparability of our personal/spiritual work, social justice, and ecological crises.

In the context of queering the Work That Reconnects , politicizing our practice means:

1. Challenging business as usual: Queering becomes an act of rebellion against narratives that separate us from nature, that put binary and heteronormative oppression over queer inclusion, and that value conformity over diversity.
2. Connecting personal transformation to wider social change: The Work That Reconnects is already doing this to some

extent through practices that link individual growth to collective action. By explicitly incorporating queer perspectives, we can deepen this connection and make it more inclusive.

3. Transforming despair into "inspired, collaborative action":[12] Tools within the Work That Reconnects that help us move from despair to action can be enhanced by considering the unique experiences and perspectives of LGBTQ+ peoples and communities. In later sections of this chapter, we explore this by introducing variations of WTR practices that have been adapted to include queer ecological perspectives.

4. Raising awareness of oppressive systems: As we engage in the Work, we must consistently highlight and challenge the systems and structures that perpetuate oppression, including those that enforce heteronormativity and cisnormativity.

5. Embracing interconnected systems: Recognizing that the paths to collective liberation and embracing queerness are one and the same. To live in the Great Turning means to be queer—to challenge binaries, embrace fluidity, and recognize the interconnectedness of all struggles for justice.

Here are just some of the many oppressive heteronormative practices, policies, and institutions[13] at which we can target our queering actions:

- Binary gendered spaces and activities
- Heteronormative media representation
- Cisnormative dress codes and appearance standards
- Binary gendered options on forms and documentation
- Marriage institutions that do not recognize same-sex marriage
- Heteronormative education, especially sex-ed curriculums focused only on heterosexuality
- Discriminatory healthcare practices like intersex genital mutilations
- Conversion therapy
- Organizations lacking inclusive policies for LGBTQ+ employees

- Religious exemption laws that justify LGBTQ+ discrimination on the grounds of religious beliefs
- Family planning policies that promote a nuclear, heteronormative ideal
- Lack of LGBTQ+ representation in all aspects of society

By queering our actions in defense of life through politicizing our practice, we not only make the Work That Reconnects more inclusive and effective, but we also contribute to the broader movement for social and ecological justice.

We recognize that to truly reconnect with the Earth and each other, we must challenge the binary thinking and heteronormative assumptions that have contributed to the current ecological crisis.

Queering the Foundations of Our Common Life

In *Coming Back to Life,* Joanna Macy and Molly Brown highlighted working towards the "cultural recognition and legal definition of the rights of LGBTQ+"[14] as a crucial aspect of building life-sustaining societies. After all, a life-sustaining society is one that embraces the diversity and inclusion of all living experiences. In other words, it is a heteronormative-free and queer-affirming society.

A World Without Heteronormativity

With that in mind, I'd like to invite you to imagine a world without the social norms and assumptions associated with heteronormativity. What would it be like? Take a minute or two to reflect on this before continuing to read.

Here are some ways I imagine what a world without heteronormativity would be like:

- Perhaps the concept of gender wouldn't exist at all since everyone does not differentiate themselves in that way in that world.

- Diverse representations across all levels. Media, literature, and popular culture would feature a wide range of relationships, family structures, expressions of love and care without privileging one narrative over another.
- Expanded definitions of family. There would be recognition and legal protection for diverse family structures, including same-sex parents, polyamorous families, and chosen families. Any legal constructs of what constitutes a family would be based on who you choose to be with.
- Freedom and liberation. People would feel more comfortable expressing however they would like to express without fear of judgment or repercussions. There would be flexible social expectations and people won't be pressured to follow a specific life path.
- Gender equality in all forms. There would be no patriarchy as there would be no norms and expectations based on one's gender in that world.
- People would have an intersectional awareness and a fluid sense of identity. If people of that world were asked to explain themselves in detail, they would probably say that there are fluid, ongoing, mutually-influencing intersectional processes that make up who they are.
- No othering, only tolerance and acceptance since people of that world do not think predominantly in binaries and are probably able to hold paradoxes better.

> *How do you feel when you read this? What do you experience in your body?*

To generate queer-affirming structures that are life-giving and protect the grounds of our common life, here are some possible strategies:
- Ensure facilitators are trained in queer-affirming language, including using gender-inclusive terms like "folks" or "folx," "spouse," "parents" and avoiding heteronormative assumptions like "ladies and gentlemen."

- Actively seek out and amplify the voices of LGBTQ+ leaders within the WTR community.
- Embrace the diversity of responses in WTR practices, including those that may not align with expected responses typically found in the work.
- Provide specific spaces or workshops for queer individuals to explore their unique experiences within the context of environmental and social justice work (e.g., LGBTQ+-only WTR workshops as queer affinity spaces).
- Create queer-affirming media and content.
- Organize intersectional environmental justice workshops that explore the relations between LGBTQ+ rights, racial equity, and ecological sustainability.
- Facilitate LGBTQ+ wilderness retreats and nature education programs focused on building connections between queer communities and the natural world (similar to the work of organizations like Queer Nature).[15]
- Organize workshops on traditional ecological knowledge led by Two-Spirit and LGBTQ+ Indigenous educators, bridging together queer identities with ancestral environmental practices.
- Form queer ecology study groups exploring texts on ecological philosophy through the lens of queer theory.

By creating spaces that allow queer perspectives and experiences to thrive, we align our practice more closely with the fluid, diverse reality of life on Earth.

The Council of All Beings: Tapping into Queer, Natural Wisdom

The Council of All Beings has been a cornerstone ritual for those who are familiar with the Work. The practice invites participants to step outside their human identity and speak on behalf of other life forms. A typical format often involves introductions, sharing of pain and challenges, followed by offering of gifts and guidance. We can further expand this practice to focus discussions around social justice issues.

Setting a specific agenda for hosting a Council of All Beings not only creates a novel experience for those familiar to the practice but also generates life-giving insights that are informed by the more-than-human world.

This is a variation of the Council of All Beings that specifically explores gender issues. Here are some ways to incorporate this:

1. Invite life-forms that are known to engage in queer behavior. Researchers have reported that there are at least 1,500 such species.[16] You may want to learn more about these life-forms—and share with your participants—before holding such a council. Here are some beings that have been commonly known for their queer behavior, ranging from raising young ones as a same-sex couple to transitioning by changing their gonadal structures:

    - Mammals such as bonobos,[17] bottlenose dolphins[18]
    - Birds such as penguins,[19] Laysan albatrosses,[20] flamingos[21]
    - Fish such as clownfish[22] and wrasse[23]
    - Insects such as fruit flies[24] and dragonflies[25]

2. Set an agenda that specifically explores gender issues in human societies. If you're wondering what you could have conversations about, you can refer to the list of oppressive heteronormative practices, policies, and institutions highlighted earlier in the previous section.
3. Participants can express their concerns through these voices of the more-than-human beings, perhaps by commenting on how the existing binary heteronormative structures in human societies are peculiar and unnatural. Towards the end of the practice, participants can offer validation, support, and encouragement through tapping the inherent strengths and gifts of each life-form.

Here are two examples you can adapt in your practice:

"I, Bottlenose Dolphin, present you with my capacity for lifelong same-sex bonds. Draw upon this gift to form deep, lasting relationships beyond traditional partnerships. Let it remind you that love and companionship come in many forms."

"I, Penguin, offer you my ability to form loving families in unexpected ways. Draw upon this power to create homes filled with love and care, remembering that what truly matters is the devotion you share, not the traditional roles you fill."

Holding a Council of All Beings that examines gender issues would benefit from recognizing this diversity and complexity of sexual and gender expressions in nature. This variation clearly demonstrates that same-sex and queer behaviors are a natural part of the biological world. Through this practice, we can foster greater acceptance of diversity and fluidity in gender and sexual expression across species, including humans.

Queering Perception and Values

The Work That Reconnects (WTR) has long been a powerful framework for transforming our perception and values, drawing inspiration from systems theory and Indigenous and Buddhist ecological perspectives. Despite that, we can further enrich and expand this Work through queering, creating a more inclusive and nuanced approach to ecological and social transformation.

Queering Mindsets

The personal layer of queering perception and values involves the transition from a rigid, binary, heteronormative dualistic mindset to a nuanced, fluid queer mindset. This shift is crucial for practitioners to embrace complexity and paradoxes as natural parts of life, rather than simplifying them into binary oppositions.

A rigid binary mindset often fuels a narrative of separation,[26] viewing individuals as independent entities disconnected from one another and their environment. In contrast, a fluid queer mindset nourishes the narrative of interbeing,[27] recognizing the interdependence of all life forms and embracing the complexity of existence.

By critically examining societal norms and power structures, a queer mindset can reveal how apparent paradoxes may be rooted in restrictive or artificial social constructs. This is not a simple binary shift from one mindset to another. Rather, it is an invitation to expand one's understanding to recognize the complexity and nuances of life itself and transcend rigid categories to appreciate the diverse spectrum of Nature.

Moving Beyond Binaries

Queering Language

Besides the use of inclusive gender pronouns, we can start by examining how we frame certain concepts with the terms we use.

Instead of using rigid binary categories like "natural vs. unnatural" or "male vs. female," we can use more inclusive language that acknowledges the spectrum and fluidity found in nature. This applies to binaries in all forms, not just gender.

For instance, "more-than-human" or "earthly beings" would be more inclusive terms than "nonhuman beings." This is because the framing of "nonhuman being" implies a binary opposition between humans and other beings. Furthermore, "more-than-human" subtly challenges the notion of human exceptionalism by implying that other beings may possess qualities or capacities that exceed human ones.

Also, we could avoid the use of certain terms that assume heterosexuality as the default in nature. While some Indigenous cultures embrace concepts like "Mother Earth"[28] (Pachamama) alongside fluid gender identities such as two-spirit, issues can arise when we uncritically pair gendered concepts like "Mother Earth" and "Father Sky" together, as this can reinforce heteronormative assumptions. The key is to recognize the cultural context and avoid automatically imposing binary gender roles onto natural phenomena.

Transcending Either/Or Thinking

Queering perception means embracing and holding apparent paradoxes with both/and thinking,[29] working towards synthesis and integration rather than opposition. An easy way to tap into both/and thinking is to add the magic word *and* to connect all your options whenever you are trying to solve a problem or making a choice.[30]

If you are engaged with other practitioners of the Work, I highly encourage you to try the collective practice called *Wicked Questions* from the Liberating Structures toolkit[31] to explore and confront the paradoxical challenges you face in your practice. It involves working together to formulate questions that frame challenges as both/and rather than either/or, typically in the format "How can we address X while simultaneously addressing Y?" Engaging with *Wicked Questions* allows practitioners of the Work to explore messy realities and become more adaptable in response to uncertain complexity, rather than settling for reductive, simplified narratives.

Exploring Margins and Intersections

Queer approaches often focus on perspectives that have been excluded and erased from dominant systems. This also involves amplifying diverse voices to help prevent the danger of relying on a "single story"[32] to represent entire groups.

Based on my personal experience, the more you read and learn from the works and living experiences of authors whose intersectional identities have been systemically excluded, the more likely you will discover hidden perspectives that can shed light on specific issues associated with living under systemic oppression.

Queering the Self

The Work That Reconnects recognizes that our sense of self is not isolated, but deeply interconnected with the world around us. This understanding aligns beautifully with the practice of queering, which challenges rigid categories and embraces fluidity. When we queer our notion of self, we expand beyond limiting labels and fixed identities, opening up to a more fluid and interconnected way of being.

Just as ecosystems are diverse and ever-changing, our inner landscapes are equally complex. According to psychosynthesis, which is the psychological approach to integrating parts of one's psyche, we contain multitudes. Some of these aspects of ourselves may seem contradictory, yet they are all part of our whole being.

Some of these aspects might align with societal expectations, while others might challenge them. Queering the self involves recognizing and honoring all these parts, especially those that don't fit neatly into societal norms around gender, sexuality, and relationships.

From this understanding, we can know that a person's identity and experiences cannot be reduced to a single social label like race or gender. Rather, their lived reality and identity formation emerges from the interaction of fluid, ongoing intersectional processes within overarching systems and structures of power and oppression.[33]

Here are some ways in which psychosynthesis can help us queer our sense of self:

- Recognizing the subpersonalities[34] within us can reveal how we've internalized societal expectations around gender, sexuality, and relationships. This allows us to critically examine and potentially release limiting beliefs imposed by heteronormative social norms. For instance, consider a nonbinary person assigned female at birth who recognizes several subpersonalities within themselves: a *Traditional Female* part feeling pressure to conform to feminine stereotypes, a *Gender Rebel* rejecting traditional roles, a *People Pleaser* worried about disappointing family, and an *Authentic Self* desiring to express their true nonbinary identity. By acknowledging these subpersonalities, they can critically examine these internalized beliefs, potentially releasing limiting ones like the need to conform to traditional femininity or the fear of family disapproval. Going through this process would help them disentangle their authentic identity from societal norms, leading

to greater self-acceptance and more genuine self-expression in a heteronormative society.
- Disidentifying from rigid conceptions of the self liberates us from our overidentification with certain aspects of our identity, including gender. The *Dance to Dismember the Ego* is an exemplary Work That Reconnects ritual that involves disidentification by releasing attachments to the ego through artistic creation and movement.
- Imagining and embodying new ways of being that feel authentic to us, regardless of societal expectations. This involves recognizing our fluid capability to develop any conceivable subpersonality. In other words, appreciating that we have the autonomy and personal power[35] to heal, befriend, and integrate all parts of the self, including those that may have been repressed or devalued.

To explore further, I highly suggest taking up practices explained in detail in Molly Brown's two books, *Growing Whole*[36] and *Unfolding Self*.[37]

Queering through psychosynthesis aligns our personal self with the transpersonal Self (note the capital S). Similar to the Work That Reconnects concept of the ecological self, the Self[38] refers to the understanding that our true nature extends beyond our individual identity to encompass our interconnectedness with all life.

By helping us access a deeper sense of Self beyond social roles and expectations, we can reclaim aspects of our identity that may have been suppressed. We also begin to awaken to our interbeing with all life, fostering greater compassion and inclusion for diverse gender and sexual expressions.

It is no surprise that queering the self is the act of growing whole.

Deconstructing and Reconstructing Practices

Another aspect of queering our perception involves deconstructing established practices and then reconstructing them.

The first step to doing this work is to notice and acknowledge performativity in the Work That Reconnects. In Judith Butler's *Gender*

Trouble,[39] Butler introduces the concept of gender performativity to explain how gender is not an innate essence, but a social construct that is constituted through the repetition of gendered behaviors, gestures, and speech acts over time. It doesn't mean that performativity is bad or superficial. Rather, it simply describes how concepts and mindsets are formed through repeated social acts and performances.

It is important that we constantly remind ourselves that even the core concepts of the Work are ultimately performative, whether it is enacting the Great Turning through guided group rituals and intergenerational storytelling or embodying interconnectedness in nature immersion practices. Transformation arises from rehearsed, collective action.

While the core concepts may be performative rather than universal truths, this doesn't mean that ethically anything goes. How do we honor diverse ways of being without falling into boundless relativism? Our views and actions must remain guided by the ethos of the Work That Reconnects , i.e., ecological interdependence, relational care, and collective accountability.

Here's a subtle example. The practice of identifying and separating different emotions (e.g., distinguishing between anger and grief in the Truth Mandala) may reflect a Western psychological approach that might not align with all cultural understandings of emotional experience. Alternative adaptations could be developed that honor non-Western traditions—such as incorporating Buddhist-informed approaches that explore emotions through the lens of impermanence and non-attachment.

There is nothing wrong about healing through the lens of Western psychology. The invitation here is to realize that it may not resonate and work for everyone. By viewing these practices as constructed performances rather than universal truths, we are more likely to notice when the practices implicitly center Western cultural norms and/or exclude other cultural practices.

The goal is not relativistic acceptance of all perspectives, but rather a more expansive understanding that remains ethically rooted in the contingent web of life's unfolding while transcending cultural limitations.

Being located in Malaysia, a multicultural society with remnants of British colonization, my facilitation work often involves a mix of participants who are both familiar and unfamiliar with Western cultural norms. It is through these experiences that I realize that I need to be mindful about how certain practices in the Work privilege open and spontaneous expressions of emotion that could be challenging for people from cultures that value more private or restrained emotional expression.

Through constant reflection on the performative elements of the Work, I believe we can adapt and diversify practices to be more inclusive and relevant in non-Western contexts.

Queering Ancestral and Intergenerational Work

As someone who identifies as Chinese and was raised in Chinese Malaysian culture, I've been struggling to unlearn the notion of an ancestor. Traditional Chinese ancestral altars have typically been patriarchal in nature,[40] focusing on male ancestors and the paternal lineage. This brings me a lot of sadness because I mostly grew up with elders from my mother's side. When they passed, including them in the ancestral altar in my family home was not allowed as they didn't share the same surname as my father and siblings.

Growing up with parents separated and living with my mother who still prays to her dead in-laws, I couldn't get myself to sincerely honor my ancestors. I simply couldn't feel any connection with them at all.

In spite of that, my attitude towards my ancestors changed when I encountered the Work That Reconnects. The Work has shown me a pathway to unlearn and decolonize patriarchal notions of ancestry by teaching me that these ancestral, evolutionary gifts[41] that have contributed to who I am today are not just passed down through heteronormative family structures. And that there are many diverse adaptations and strategies that have allowed life to thrive in various forms.

This renewed understanding has enabled me to stay present in my family rituals by giving me permission to honor my queer, cultural, and spiritual more-than-human ancestors, not just my familial ones.

I am also aware that this is not only a personal process but also one that can be integrated into broader frameworks of ecological and social healing.

It is therefore crucial to examine how the Work That Reconnects can be enriched and expanded through the inclusion of queer intergenerational practices. This integration not only honors the diverse experiences within the LGBTQ+ community but also contributes to the ongoing process of decolonizing and intersectionalizing the Work That Reconnects.

In ancestral practices like Strengthening Our Intentions[42] and Harvesting the Gifts of the Ancestors,[43] we can include queer ancestors who have been oppressed, silenced, and disappeared from our collective memory and history. We can explore how they have been revered and accepted before Western colonization in many cultures. From the two-spirit people in First Nation cultures[44] to the Bissu people in Bugis culture,[45] we acknowledge their esteemed positions as healers, medicine people, and visionaries.

Through exploring our historical roots, we discover that our ancestors were queer to some extent. By incorporating queer ancestral work, we can create more inclusive and transformative spaces that acknowledge the unique challenges and strengths of queer individuals throughout history.

Practices that involve future human beings like Letter from the Future,[46] Strengthening Our Intentions, and the Seventh Generation[47] invite participants to embody a future human as a queer being living in a world where people have transcended gender binaries and heteronormative social structures no longer exist.

Here are some guidelines that I have gathered for facilitating and holding space for such practices:

1. Use gender-neutral language when embodying queer ancestors and future humans. Use the term "chosen family"[48] when discussing family members and structures.

Queering the Work That Reconnects: Embracing the Wild Fluidity of Life | 173

2. Begin by explaining that the purpose is to imagine a more inclusive future, not to roleplay stereotypes.
3. Emphasize that some level of discomfort is expected and even beneficial for learning, especially when exploring new perspectives or challenging existing beliefs. Frame this discomfort as a sign of growth rather than a problem to be avoided. You may also want to introduce the window of tolerance[49] to help participants understand that there's an optimal zone where learning and growth occur, but also that it's normal to occasionally move outside this zone.
4. That said, facilitators have to also respect personal limits and provide support when needed. This can be achieved by:
   a. Emphasizing that it's okay to step back if needed
   b. Encouraging participants to monitor their own emotional state and recognize signs of moving towards hyper/hypoarousal.[50] This could include physical sensations, thought patterns, or emotional reactions.
   c. Preparing multiple options beforehand for participants to engage with the material such as individual reflection and/or small group discussions.
   d. Reminding participants of the importance of self-care practices, both during and outside of the learning session.
5. Prompt participants to consider how social, economic, and cultural systems might evolve in a post-gender binary world, rather than focusing solely on individual identities.
6. Guide participants to connect through emotions, hopes, and challenges that transcend gender, rather than fixating on gender identity.

If you have cisgender and/or heterosexual participants in the room:

1. Before the exercise, offer information on gender diversity and nonbinary identities to expand participants' understanding.
2. If they choose to embody a queer ancestor/future human, frame the exercise as "stepping into" a perspective rather than

"becoming" someone else, to avoid appropriation.[51] Remind participants that they are imagining possibilities, not claiming to know or represent actual experiences of LGBTQ+ peoples.

After the practice, facilitate a discussion on what participants learned, what challenged them, and how the experience might inform their understanding of gender and sexuality in the present. Do provide time for participants to process their experiences, share insights, and discuss strategies for managing discomfort.

What I love about these approaches is that they prompt us to exercise moral imagination, expanding our capacity to envision possibilities for a world filled with love and acceptance towards all beings.

Queering Forth

Queering is not just about challenging the status quo, opposition, and rebellion. True queering aims to align us towards what is natural and rooted in reality by inviting us to reimagine possibilities. It opens up new ways of thinking and being that aren't constrained by business-as-usual categories.

Just like decolonization and anti-oppression work, queering is an ongoing process of critical inquiry, opening avenues for constant unlearning through evaluation and relearning through integrating emerging contexts and perspectives. As Alex Johnson beautifully frames it:

> Instead of using the more-than-human world as justification for or against certain behavior and characteristics, let's use the more-than-human world as a humbling indication of the capacity and diversity of all life on Earth.[52]

There is no fixed universal blueprint for queering the Work That Reconnects. Any attempt to map or model a framework will not fully capture the actual territory.[53] This may involve even transcending human-centric understanding of sexuality and gender altogether, realizing the earthliness within us and embracing a life-centric worldview.[54]

Frameworks will eventually have to be updated as new contexts emerge. And that's expected since nature is queer, fluid, and ever-changing. As we move forward in our work towards the Great Turning, let us embrace the wisdom of Rainer Maria Rilke, who advised us to "love the questions themselves."[55] In this spirit, I invite you to live these questions:

How can we make our work queerer?

How can we challenge dominant modes of thinking?

How can we embrace fluidity in our practices and perspectives?

How can we create spaces that truly reflect the diversity of life on Earth?

Let us be patient with the process, allowing these questions to permeate our thoughts and actions. We don't need immediate answers; instead, let's approach our work with curiosity and openness, always ready to challenge our assumptions.

I must admit that this is not easy work. It requires a lot of trial and error, unlearning and relearning. Thus, appreciating the emerging, life-giving potential of failure, conflict, and contradiction is necessary.

Even if we never arrive at definitive answers—for perhaps there are none in a world as beautifully complex as ours—the very act of living these questions will transform us and our work. We are not only queering our practice but also ourselves, constantly evolving and adapting, just like the natural world we seek to protect and reconnect with.

In doing so, we're not just working towards ecological justice—we're working towards a world where all forms of life, all identities, all ways of being are recognized, honored, and celebrated. And isn't that, after all, the world we're fighting for?

PART III

Anti-Oppressive Facilitation

10

Anti-Oppressive Facilitation

By Aravinda Ananda with Kurt A. Kuhwald

Facilitating in a way that confronts and transforms systems of oppression, rather than perpetuating them, asks a lot of facilitators. It will likely take each of us quite some time to become more proficient in anti-oppressive facilitation because it requires lifelong learning (and unlearning) to better recognize and understand oppression dynamics; significant inner work to be able to shift lifelong conditioning; and building some specific skill sets.

There are some concrete steps we can take to incorporate anti-oppression approaches into group facilitation. A checklist of some recommended steps makes up the first half of this chapter. The second half explores how facilitators can address three different systems of oppression as they manifest in workshop spaces: ableism, cisheteropatriarchy, and settler colonialism.

In 2017 when I was preparing to facilitate another Earth Leadership Cohort, our co-facilitation team engaged some anti-oppression consultants. They gave us some good tips and pointers of directions to go in. If you are newer to anti-oppressive facilitation, I strongly encourage you to get mentoring from people with more experience. I'm grateful to have been able to discuss and explore approaches to anti-oppressive facilitation with my colleagues in the Anti-Oppression Resource Group over the years and highly recommend peer support spaces such as this to support your ongoing learning.

Anti-Oppression Facilitation Checklist

This checklist is divided into four sections:

1. considerations for facilitation team design and preparation
2. steps facilitators can take before the workshop begins
3. steps early on in the workshop
4. and steps to take as the workshop proceeds

The strategies offered here are not hard and fast requirements for harm-free facilitation. Rather they are approaches that some facilitators have found useful. It may take years of practice to be able to implement some of them well. This isn't about attaining perfection, simply about living into our values and commitment to a world where everyone is treated as if they matter and belong.

Consider the context of each offering and the specific groups you are working with when deciding which of these steps to implement. For example, in some cases you will not be able to communicate with participants in advance, so there will be things you will not know before the program starts. The amount of time available will determine how much and at what depth certain approaches can be incorporated. As always, some of the recommendations here may need to be adapted based on local culture, so please adapt what follows based on your context.

Facilitation Team Considerations and Preparations

- It is helpful to have co-facilitators. Different people will notice different issues and dynamics within the group, and can take on different responsibilities and bring different styles of relating into the group process.

- Whenever possible, include people on your facilitation team who are knowledgeable about oppression dynamics and have experience with addressing them. This is especially important if you are just beginning to learn how to address oppression dynamics. This can help you to cover more bases—and you can learn by observing first hand. Observing how others sense into the moment to see what is called for, based on the context and the particular circumstances at hand, can be a really helpful learning opportunity. Much of this skill is embodied, so it takes more than intention and commitment to be effective. Learning by observing helps a lot.

- As much as you are able, have your facilitation team reflect the diversity that will be present in the room. For example, some white facilitators choose to always co-facilitate with a Person of the Global Majority. A note of caution about this: if you are newer to anti-oppression work and hold lots of dominant identities, it is all too easy to replicate patterns of harm with your co-facilitators. These patterns might include tokenization (including someone only for their identity with no commitment to equitable relationships); unchecked microaggressions; or unfair expectations that those co-facilitators perform certain kinds of labor, such as educational labor or emotional labor. You may need to engage in some anti-oppression learning and do some inner work before attempting to work with people with different social identities and social locations. Sometimes it is wise to pause facilitating and do more learning before attempting to facilitate with diverse teams and to facilitate diverse groups.

- Make it explicit if your team has a shared commitment to anti-oppressive approaches.

- Discuss ahead of time some options for responding when oppressive harm occurs. This discussion can help prepare your nervous system for this possibility and offer options to draw upon in what may be a heated moment.

- Have a conversation with your co-facilitator(s) about what feelings and behavioral signs each of you exhibit if you get triggered, and what support is most helpful for you. You may want to have a plan in place in case one of you needs to temporarily tag out of a lead facilitation role.
- Prepare yourself for pushback if you dare to challenge oppression. Even well-meaning people typically have a lifetime of socialization by dominant culture, and have many unconscious defenses when the current power structure is challenged. Knowing that pushback is likely can help you meet it without the element of surprise.
- Experiment with more equitably sharing the load among facilitators.
- Have transparent conversation(s) about fair compensation and do your best to operationalize it.

Before the Workshop Begins

Workshop logistics:

- Consider accessibility factors when choosing your location. Is it accessible by public transportation? Are there only stairs to get into a building or is there a ramp or elevator? Are gender-inclusive bathrooms available? Is it located in a building that may cause some people to feel unsafe or unwelcome, such as a religious institution? Are cleaning products with artificial scents used in the building? Whenever possible, opt for more inclusive options.
- Consider regenerative pricing. If possible, offer a sliding scale or some other fee structure, such as including "no one turned away for lack of funds," in order to make the workshop available to people of different financial means while adequately compensating facilitators.

Communicating with participants in advance:

- Especially if you will be facilitating with an unfamiliar audience in an unfamiliar context, take some time to find out a little bit about

who will be in the room and what cultural and social dynamics will likely be present. If possible, obtain some information in advance about the social identities of people in your group so that you can plan your content accordingly. You can collect some of this information by including a survey or a few short questions on your registration mechanism.
- Ask participants if they have any access needs on your registration mechanism. While the venue will likely already be chosen by the time people are registering, there may be ways you can adjust logistics to provide for more needs, and having this information in advance helps you be able to plan.
- For longer programs with an explicit anti-oppression commitment, it is helpful to let people know in advance that an intention for the workshop space is for participants to lean into co-creating an anti-oppressive space. It is good practice to include a few resources that will especially support people with dominant identities to lean into this praxis together. For example, you could share some resources on whiteness with white participants in a multiracial group. It can also be helpful to define certain key concepts about oppression such as was covered in Chapter 6.
- Consider if you want to share some community agreements in advance. This gives people the option to attend only if they feel committed to striving towards these ways of relating and being.

Session Design:
- Design your content and processes to speak to and include everyone who will be in the room.
- Consider how your agenda may center certain identities and ways you can shift that dynamic for greater equity.
- Choose a variety of activities that account for different intelligences, personality types, learning styles, and neurodiversity.
- Plan your agenda to allow adequate time (including breaks) for the amount of processing people may need for the depth you are inviting them into.

- Resist the temptation to overpack your agenda. Intentionally build in extra time and space for unexpected delays, shifts in focus, or unplanned things that need to be addressed.
- Discern which community commitments can help support the kind of environment you are seeking to create. The amount of time you will have to set these up will depend on the length of your session.
- Put some forethought into whether you are including content that is likely to be particularly triggering for some of your participants, and use extra care and caution with this. When possible, prepare people in advance of the session so that they can opt in, rather than having to opt out in the moment. Sometimes content warnings when introducing a potentially sensitive topic can be helpful, but on their own may not be sufficient as it can be difficult to opt out in real time.

Towards the Beginning of a Workshop

The beginning of the workshop is an important time for the group to get to know one another, establish some social norms, and begin to build trust. Here are some steps that can be helpful in this community-forming phase:

- Sharing a diversity welcome, such as the one shared at the start of this book, or the one originally created by Training for Change,[1] can be helpful. These kinds of activities can help to set a tone of inclusion, and can make the many forms of diversity present in the room more visible. If you use such a diversity welcome, it is good to tailor it to your specific group so that it feels authentic.
- Acknowledge current realities and the social context in which you are convening in your opening comments. One way to do this in settler colonial states is with a land acknowledgment (see the section on land and labor acknowledgments later in the chapter). Publicly acknowledging dynamics of power helps to shift some of their unspoken hold on us and challenge the assumption that dominant power arrangements are just the way things are.

- Share an explicit acknowledgment of the interconnection of the struggles of people and the struggles of the Earth. This helps to overcome the false split between people and the environment and set the tone of the space for collective liberation. Please see Chapter 3 for a more in-depth exploration of how Sarah Nahar does this in the United States.
- Share an outline of the agenda early on so participants will know what to expect regarding activities and also timing throughout the workshop, particularly when breaks have been scheduled.
- Conduct a process for considering and/or creating community agreements, guidelines, or commitments. Please see Appendix B for more about community commitments or agreements that support undoing oppression.

> **Steps for using community agreements, guidelines, or commitments:**
> - Put some forethought into which group guidelines/agreements/commitments that are equity/anti-oppression focused can support your group.
> - Either have the group generate agreements (to which you as a facilitator can make additions) or suggest or request a particular set that people can review. If you suggest or request a particular set, after reviewing them, be sure to ask if there are any questions, concerns, or additions. If something is new for someone, it may require some explanation.
> - Obtain consent, such as by asking people to raise their hand if they commit to these agreements.
> - Remind people when community commitments, agreements, or guidelines are not being followed. A phrase you could use is, "That doesn't feel in alignment with X community commitment." And then if possible make a request for what could be done or said instead.
> - Have a plan for when an agreement is not being followed. Specifically address the situation when or if this arises.

- Whenever possible, make opportunities for everyone's voice in the room to be heard, such as through full group introductions. In addition to sharing names and pronouns if used, introductions can also be a valuable opportunity for making difference visible in the room. You might include a prompt such as: "Share one aspect of your identity that is important to you."
- If you were not able to ascertain access needs in advance of the workshop, ask if there are any such needs in the group. If you are aware of any access needs that require action by participants, share these with everyone. Please see the section on ableism later in this chapter for more about access needs.
- Time permitting, share some framing about nervous system regulation and tools to support it such as a grounding, centering, or other resourcing activity. See Chapter 11 on trauma awareness and approaches for group facilitation for more on this. It can be helpful to explicitly name nervous system activation states like fight, flight, freeze, appease, and dissociate, and set people up with support for self-regulation and co-regulation such as through a guided meditation that supports becoming present, centered, and grounded. Offering such a grounding or centering activity early on can help people to become more present for the group's time together.
- As time allows, include some activities that allow participants to explore their social location. See Chapter 6 for more on doing social location work with groups.
- Do activities to build trust—especially if you will be engaging with content that may feel particularly vulnerable or potentially triggering. One important approach to building trust is by having some time for sharing in small groups. This can be particularly helpful for people who struggle with speaking in large groups.

Sample agenda for the arrival and group formation phase of a workshop

(This can be shortened or lengthened depending on available time.)

8:30-9:00 Arrival period: making name tags, settling in (a half-hour window for an in-person program can be ideal; only five minutes may be feasible for online programs and background music can be a nice element).

9:00 Welcome: diversity welcome (or shorter welcome) and share the purpose for the group's time together.

9:10 Orienting to the physical space (e.g., location of exits, bathrooms, etc.) or online space (e.g., a request for cameras to be on) and addressing known access needs (e.g., please speak loudly).

9:13 Orienting to the current context including possibly a land and labor acknowledgment .

9:18 Overview agenda (present verbally and visually if possible) noting breaks.

9:22 Orienting to shared social space with community agreements. May include information about self and co-regulation.

9:30 Grounding, centering, or other becoming present activity.

9:35 Whole group introductions including name, pronouns if used, and a prompt that helps people get to know each other. If access needs were not ascertained in advance, this or another round could invite people to share if they have any particular access needs.

9:50 Small groups for reflection prompts as an opportunity for further getting to know one another or possibly exploring social location.

As you can see from the sample agenda, it can take the better part of an hour for a group that does not yet know each other to arrive in shared social space and orient for the work ahead. Setting up a strong social and psychological container provides foundational support for a group to function well together throughout their time. The next section addresses steps for maintaining the container.

As the Workshop Progresses

There are steps facilitators can take to maintain a healthy workshop environment as the workshop progresses and various issues arise. There is no one correct way to approach the varying situations that arise in groups because every situation is influenced by the multiple factors present in any given context. A crucial element of facilitation is sensing into the moment and seeing what might best support present circumstances. This requires that facilitators make room for the unplanned and practice emergent facilitation—adapting the plan in real time to address the needs that are emerging.

As Ejeris Dixon notes in *Holding Change*, "Facilitation is a practice in deep listening, noticing and engaging with words, body language, facial expressions, vocal tone, and the energy within the space. As facilitators read the room and interpersonal dynamics, it's critical to be attentive and ask questions about what people need."[2] No matter how prepared facilitators are, unknown dynamics will arise, so it is important to expect the unknown and build capacity to adapt in the moment.

- Be willing to pause the agenda, and adapt it if feedback so warrants. Not all feedback can or should be addressed in the whole group, but it is important to do so when needed.
- Build in mechanisms for receiving and responding to feedback, especially about harm.

> **Feedback Options**
>
> There are lots of ways to experiment with letting participants know that feedback is welcome, and setting facilitators up with support to be able to respond to it. A few options include:

- At the very minimum, set a tone that feedback is welcome by saying so early on in the workshop, and then be as receptive and responsive as you can to feedback that is subsequently offered. It helps to acknowledge that you have heard feedback even if you disagree with it or if it is otherwise difficult to hear.

- Have a community agreement such as "oops, ouch" whereby if someone experiences something that hurts, they can say "ouch" and the person or persons contributing to the hurt can say "oops" to acknowledge it, but otherwise not pause group process at that time. The issue at hand may or may not be followed up on at a later time.

- Have a community agreement that welcomes people to ask for a pause if someone experiences a harmful impact, and then invite the group to take three breaths together before deciding what to do next. Or, ask the group to create a community agreement together about what would feel helpful/supportive to them after someone has experienced harm.

- Do a "temperature check" by asking people how they are doing.

- Have someone in a "vibes watcher" role who is not a lead facilitator. This person, who could even be a participant, simply keeps track of the mood in the group and might watch for things like nervous system changes that can be an indication that something feels off.

- If you are able to be available during some break times, this can be an easier time for some people to approach with feedback that may have felt difficult to share in the whole group. Facilitators need break time too, so there needs to be balance with this.

- Have a feedback box or a feedback board where people can leave written feedback. A box is more private, while a board is more transparent.

- If you have co-facilitators, take time to debrief and discuss issues as the program progresses (such as during a lunch break) or after the program ends.
- Having a feedback form at the end of a workshop comes too late to adapt the workshop in real time, but it can potentially give you the opportunity to learn more about how to do things differently in the future as well as follow-up as needed.
- If you are on a learning curve about responding to feedback in real time, one approach you might try is to have a facilitator or other support person in a dedicated "feedback collector" role who the group knows they can bring sensitive feedback to. This feedback collector can then relay information to other facilitators and can help take some of the pressure off lead facilitators to register and respond to the feedback while they are sharing content or guiding group process. It can also be helpful to have a designated person to approach at a break if there are issues that feel too vulnerable to raise in the whole group.

- Don't ignore harm when it happens. Grow your muscles for naming harm and addressing the harm. Many of us have been conditioned to be quiet about harm. Speaking up can take some practice. Check out Appendix A on Giving and Receiving Feedback About Harm for more guidance about this, and also Chapter 12 on inner work, if you need some support with growing these muscles.
- After harm happens, take some time to tend to repair. Repair doesn't mean fixing, but rebuilding ruptured safety, dignity, or belonging as much as is possible. Sometimes the best thing to do is just to ask an impacted person what they need, although it is important to be sensitive to the possibility that this may make the person feel put on the spot and they may or may not be able to tell you in that moment. One of the most important

things is acknowledgment of impact by others, so the person feels seen and heard. One-on-ones during a break can be helpful when someone says or does something hurtful that doesn't get addressed in the full group.

Repair and Mending

Many Indigenous cultures have processes like council or circle where people can listen with care to other people's experience and to support mending ruptures between us as humans. Restorative circles, for example, are based on such processes. Those of us who grew up in dominator cultures have much to learn in order to more skillfully tend to the wounds between us as humans. Many of us are just beginning to learn how to do this.

Likewise, many of us have been conditioned by punitive justice systems which focus on punishing people for wrongdoing. But punishment doesn't necessarily do anything to mend what was broken, nor does it serve to transform the underlying causes giving rise to the harm in the first place. The recent upwelling of interest in restorative justice and transformative justice has begun to increase the repertoire of options for leaning in and showing up for the work of repair and mending. For those of us newer to repair and mending, some useful orienting questions include:

- Can you hold the needs of the person who experienced harm with care? You can ask: "What do you need for healing, mending, and repair?" while keeping in mind that that question may require time to answer.

- Can someone in the community hold with care the humanity and the potential learning of the person who caused the harm? This contributes to a greater possibility that learning and changed behavior can result so the harm will not happen again in the future. It cannot be emphasized enough that this

> holding does not need to be done by the person who has just been directly impacted. Offering support for learning may be the work of other people in the room/community who are less impacted and/or less activated in the moment and not needing to prioritize their own care.

- Track nervous system state changes through watching body language for cues that something may be amiss. If this is a skill that you need to develop, you can start by building a mood check (intentionally scanning the room to see people's facial expressions and body language) into your facilitation agenda. Keep in mind that sometimes people will feel upset because they are reminded of content from outside of your group space, so nervous system state changes are not always an indication of events unfolding in the room in real time.
- Offer support for nervous system regulation throughout the session as needed. Incorporate centering and grounding practices throughout your time together, and especially around content that may be activating. For more about this, see Chapter 11: Trauma Awareness and Approaches to Group Facilitation.
- Be prepared to adjust your program if an additional break is unexpectedly needed. This can be helpful not only if there is dysregulation in the group and people need some extra space and time, but also if a facilitator needs to check in with a particular participant or participants about how they are feeling or were impacted by something that happened. Sometimes things that arise can be addressed in real time in the whole group, and sometimes a more private setting is helpful. If some dynamics are addressed in a smaller group of directly impacted and implicated people, keep in mind that the dynamic may still feel unaddressed in the larger group and may need to be mentioned in some way, even if some aspects are kept private.
- Identity affinity groups can support people with similar identities to explore an issue. This could include breakout groups according

to race, gender, age, ability, or some other identity. Having spaces for people with shared identities eliminates having to navigate cross-identity dynamics and can often help to facilitate deeper conversations about the issues at play. If you use identity groups, it can be helpful to have an experienced facilitator in each group. It is also important to include some kind of process for the groups coming back together as a whole group, such as having each group share something with the larger group.

The recommendations presented here are much more than a simple checklist. Ongoing learning, unlearning, and growth are all needed to become more proficient with anti-oppressive facilitation. Growing one's competency with these steps may take a while, and may require deep inner work (please see Chapter 12 for more about this) and practice, especially if a step runs counter to one's lifelong conditioning. One tool that may aid your practice is to do roleplays of situations in order to explore more options for engaging when the unknown arises.

Practice with Roleplays

Invite co-facilitators, other colleagues, or friends to do some roleplays together. Choose a scenario you want to roleplay. Next choose who will play which roles. For example, someone plays the role of a person who has just done a microaggression, someone plays the role of the person targeted by the microaggression, and you play the role of a facilitator who considers how to intervene or otherwise respond. After you reenact the scenario, you can pause the roleplay and debrief how it felt for each person in their different role. If you like, you can re-run the roleplay to try one or more different strategies, debriefing after each roleplay to see how different approaches landed. You could also try the option of pausing the roleplay midstream if you want to slow things down and offer yourself some kind of emotional, physical, or mental support before resuming.

Practicing with roleplays can help build capacity so that action may feel more possible when we are presented with real life situations. It is important to set ourselves up with support for practicing and building our capacity over time. As adrienne maree brown advises, "Practice is the path to embodiment, which is when a way of being is not just something we believe in our minds, but something our bodies can fully hold, something that becomes a default in our behaviors, choices, and actions."[3] It can take us a while to get to embodiment, and we can take steps to support ourselves along the way. Our first steps may be clumsy; the important thing is to keep trying and learning as we go.

We turn next to some recommendations for addressing how several systems of oppression may manifest in workshop spaces. Many "isms" abound in dominant society: racism, sexism, classism, ableism, ageism, anti-semitism, Islamophobia—and the list goes on. As we have been exploring in this book, these show up in any group space that doesn't consciously interrupt and shift them. In addition to speaking up when we hear, for example, an ageist remark, there are other steps we can take to interrupt and shift how these "isms" perpetuate in group spaces.

One such step for facilitators is to take care when scheduling a program so as to avoid major holidays of different religions. A facilitation team I (Aravinda) was a part of once scheduled a program to start on a date that coincided with the first night of a major Jewish holiday. Living in a Christian-hegemonic context, at the time I was not tracking the major holidays of other religions. When this was brought to our attention, we were able to adapt the program by working with a Jewish colleague to incorporate a liberation Seder that followed the spiral of the Work That Reconnects, but it also meant that some people who would be with their families for Passover would not be able to participate in the program. I now take care to check the dates for major holidays of different religions before picking dates for a program.

While some "isms" are widespread around the globe, others are more context-specific such as ones having to do with which religion is dominant in any given context. Below are some ways to address how just three "isms" manifest in workshop spaces: ableism, cisheteropatriarchy, and settler colonialism.

Addressing Ableism So Everyone Can Participate in Meaningful Ways
This section was greatly informed by conversations with Jane Hera.

All too often, the experience of able-bodied people is considered the norm and the default priority, and the needs of people with disabilities, both visible and non-visible, are ignored or at best not adequately considered. An example of this is hosting a workshop in a building that only has stairs to get into the building and no wheelchair-accessible ramp. While this is no problem for people who can easily walk up stairs, hosting a workshop in such a venue would completely exclude people in wheelchairs who would not be able to even get into the building. While wheelchair-accessible ramps and bathrooms are more visible examples, there is a much broader spectrum of accessibility needs that must be addressed in order for people to be able to participate.

In addition to the availability of ramps, elevators, and wheelchair-accessible bathrooms, some other factors to pay attention to when choosing a venue include whether the venue can be reached by public transportation; the availability of gender-neutral bathrooms in a building; and the absence of artificial scents or other aggravations for people with chemical sensitivities.

Listing this information on one's publicity materials helps people with disabilities know if the venue will be accessible to them without having to take the added step of having to ask.

There are also various access needs for facilitators to consider for virtual venues. For example, blurring one's background can challenge some people's nervous systems in ways that decrease their ability to participate. Meeting this need may challenge other people's comfort or needs around privacy, so sometimes meeting a particular need can require some negotiation within the group. Providing closed captioning can better include people who are hard of hearing.

Facilitators can broaden their awareness of the wide spectrum of needs so they can factor that in as they are able to in their venue choice. Knowing that people with autism, PDA (pathological demand avoidance), ADHD (attention-deficit/hyperactivity disorder), environmental sensitivities, and neurodiversity (neurodivergent or non-neurotypical) have needs that will impact whether they can meaningfully participate in any given physical or social space, can help facilitators be more responsive to these needs.

If people register for the event in advance, include a question on the registration materials to get a sense of the particular needs that will be present in the space. This gives facilitators time to plan in advance how to meet these needs, or let participants know if they won't be able to meet certain needs, so they can plan accordingly. In the United States a common question to include on registration materials is "Do you have any access needs?" In England and Scotland, WTR facilitator Jane Hera has found the terminology of "access needs" to be used most typically only for wheelchair accessibility, and thus has used the language of "particular needs" to ascertain a broader spectrum of needs that will be present. So Jane would include this registration question: "Do you have any particular needs that it would be helpful for us to know about to facilitate your full participation?"

Jane finds that giving examples helps people be better able to name and claim their needs in this way, such as, "I'm hard of hearing, so I need people to speak loudly or use a microphone" or "I have a chemical sensitivity to artificial scents, so I need scent-free spaces." Obtaining this information in advance also makes it possible to communicate certain guidelines in advance to other participants, such as, "Please refrain from wearing perfume, cologne or scented products." When I (Aravinda) offer residential retreats, I provide unscented soap, shampoo, conditioner, lotion, and bug spray in case participants aren't able to procure these themselves.

While a facilitator may not be able to control all factors, the more steps we can take to be as inclusive as possible of everyone's needs in the room, the better. While some access needs or particular needs are visible and a facilitator may easily be able to see them, other needs are not visible and the only way a facilitator can be aware of them is if someone tells them about it. If a facilitator does not have an opportunity to ascertain access or particular needs in advance, they can ask the group early on if anyone has any access or particular needs. This can be a really helpful way to find out if there are participants with non-visible disabilities present such as hearing impairment, light or sound sensitivity, or environmental sensitivities.

To counter a dominant cultural trend that people with access needs or particular needs should just stay home because public spaces cater only to able-bodied people, facilitators need to expand the spectrum of needs they are able to track and provide accessibility options for. It is also important to cultivate a group culture where needs are affirmed by taking the steps to ascertain and validate needs, and then take actions to meet those needs whenever possible, or let people know if there are any needs that cannot be met.

Physical needs for one's body, as well as one's emotional and mental health, can change over the course of a program, so in addition to checking in with people early on during a program, also check in as the meeting progresses. If the program involves a lot of sitting, having a variety of chair types (cushions, backs) present to support different body needs can be helpful, or people may need freedom to get up and move and stretch. Factor in adequate breaks. Normalize that it is all right to have needs and strive to meet as many as possible.

Facilitators can take steps to meet needs with their own actions, and also by involving the rest of the group in meeting a need. For example, if someone is present who is hard of hearing, the facilitator can not only be sure to speak loudly or have a microphone, but can also invite the rest of the group to use an established signal such as cupping a hand behind one's ear if anyone senses that more volume is needed. Encouraging anyone who senses a need for more volume to use this signal, means that people who are hard of hearing don't always have to be the one speaking up to ask for their need to be addressed. Continually having to speak up about a need that is not being met can bring up so much shame and frustration that some people may not want to speak up about their need at all; self-exclusion can feel easier. So it can help for other people in the room to speak up or act to help meet these needs.

In planning and conducting activities, facilitators can factor in different options so that everyone who wants to will be able to meaningfully participate. If people with mobility constraints will be present, a facilitator may choose to either not include some activities that involve robust movement, or to have options that allow everyone present to participate. For example, in the Work That Reconnects practice called the Milling that involves fast walking around and stopping in front of different people, a facilitator could include spaces for wheelchairs or a chair option. Another example is rather than asking everyone to stand for a song, one could say "Please rise in body or spirit."

While a facilitator may or may not be able to meet all needs that are present, holding needs with care and doing one's best to meet as many as possible helps to shift the way ableism dominates in many spaces and include more people's participation in meaningful ways.

Addressing Ways Cisheteropatriarchy Manifests in Workshop Spaces

Cisheteropatriarchy is a constellation of interlocking systems of oppression that position cisgender, heterosexual males at the top of a socially constructed hierarchy; cisgender, heterosexual females below that; anyone not heterosexual below that; and transgender people at the bottom. Under cisheteropatriarchy, a gender binary is enforced in which the only legitimate genders are viewed as male and female and males are perceived to be superior to females. While the common acronym LGBTQIA+ (lesbian, gay, bisexual, trans, queer and/or questioning, intersex, asexual) combines both sexual orientation and gender categories, the two are distinct. For example a cisgender woman can be in a lesbian relationship.

> **Biological sex**: a classification based on physical characteristics including chromosomes, reproductive organs, and hormones;

> categories of male, female, or intersex are typically registered at birth.
>
> **Gender identity**: a person's internal sense of their gender.
>
> **Cisgender:** gender identity is the same as the sex registered at birth.
>
> **Transgender**: gender identity differs from the sex registered at birth.
>
> **Genderfluid:** gender identity is not fixed and may change over time.

Cisheteropatriarchy plays out in subtle and not so subtle ways in workshop spaces. Here are just a few examples of how this "ism" can show up in WTR workshops, with suggestions for what facilitators can do to address these dynamics.

1. Misgendering people
Misgendering is referring to a person with a gendered pronoun other than the one a person uses for themself.
Example: Perceiving someone else to be female and referring to the person as she, when the person uses he or they pronouns.
How facilitators can address this:
Include gender pronouns in group introductions as a way for people to learn which pronouns people use for themselves. If people do not know why this is important, consider sharing some of the information in Appendix C: Why Share Gender Pronouns.

If someone uses an incorrect pronoun for someone, you can share their correct pronoun as a way to redirect. You don't need to make a big deal about it, and it is helpful for the person who has just been misgendered to not always have to be the person speaking up about it. For those of us who have received lifelong conditioning around gender, it can take a while to retrain ourselves to use the pronouns people use for themselves rather than ones that correspond with our perceptions.

If this is you, you can try practicing with friends, and course correct when you catch yourself slipping up.

2. Using gender binary language
Gender binary language names only male and female options.
Examples: Presenting he and she as the only options; referring to only mothers and fathers, sisters and brothers. While less likely in a workshop setting, another common gender binary salutation is "Ladies and gentlemen…"
How facilitators can address this:
Use more inclusive language such as he, she, or they; parents; siblings, etc.

3. Using gendered terms to refer to everyone in the group
Example: Using gendered language such as "Hey you guys" to refer to everyone of different genders.
How facilitators can address this:
Use less-gendered or non-gendered terms such as folks, people, friends. Or, if there are two people, "Hey, you two …" instead of "Hey, you guys."

4. Promoting heteronormativity
Heteronormativity positions heterosexuality as the norm and the ideal.
Example: Speaking as if a mother and a father are the only possible parenting/family structure.
How facilitators can address this:
When speaking about families, name more possible family structures, such as two mothers or two fathers, or single parents, or just parents or grandparents with no gender suggested. Care with speaking about family structures can also extend to considering people who were raised by people other than the biological parents. You can use language such as "parents or people in the parenting role" to be more inclusive of the variety of possibilities, including people who were in foster care, were adopted, or were raised by someone other than their biological parents such as their grandparents.

Interrupting Settler Colonialism

Settler colonialism is a type of colonialism where the Indigenous people of a region are displaced by settlers who form a permanent society there—invariably claiming the land was unsettled. Some major settler colonial states include the United States, Canada, and Australia.

In settler colonial states, some groups and organizations will offer a land acknowledgment at the beginning of a group's time together to acknowledge the harm of settler colonialism and to interrupt ongoing Indigenous erasure. If you live elsewhere in the world, there may be different ongoing histories of injustice specific to the particular place where you are located that you wish to acknowledge.

If you are new to making a land acknowledgment, be careful not to refer to First Peoples only in the past, as doing so erases Indigenous peoples from the present day and is a prominent form of harm. Offering a land acknowledgment is but one step. If it is not accompanied with solidarity and an actual spiritual, mental, and material shift in relationship with the land and the First Peoples of that land, it will ring hollow. Work That Reconnects facilitator Belinda Griswold emphasizes the importance of going beyond land acknowledgments toward being in active solidarity with the area's Indigenous people and supporting their continuing efforts to rematriate the land.

In the following section, Kurt A. Kuhwald offers some framing points about offering a land and labor acknowledgment and shares one that the Thrive East Bay community offers to open its gatherings.

Land and Labor Acknowledgment, Oakland, California
Compiled by Kurt A. Kuhwald

Land Acknowledgment: Framing Points

While this Land Acknowledgment is specific to Oakland, California, USA, we hope it can serve as a model in the way that it opens specific elements of both honoring and action regarding the Indigenous people of the land where it would be offered. We believe the principles in such an acknowledgment are the same no matter what country or upon what settler-colonized land it is offered:

5. Honor the people who originally inhabited the land.
6. In some way cite the reality of their life.
7. Make clear the colonization, oppression, and genocide that was perpetrated against them and which continues in varying destructive forms today.
8. Invite action to directly support their current work to survive and flourish—citing, as well, any such actions that the presenter and/or their organization are involved in.

Labor Acknowledgment: Framing Understanding

While chattel slavery played a particularly strong role in shaping the many dimensions of the culture of the United States (economic, social, attitudinal, etc.), many countries, both in the Global North and Global South, contributed to its horrific creation and continuance. The radical exploitation of human labor, along racial and class lines, however, is endemic throughout global human history, and has contributed profoundly and inexorably to forming the modern world. Simply acknowledging the fact of that history—the history of the exploitation of human beings and their labor—is a step in keeping their stories present, their value affirmed, and the door to restorative action open.

Here is the land and labor acknowledgment:

It is an important opening practice at Thrive East Bay events here in Oakland to make two deep acknowledgment s: first a *Land Acknowledgment*, and second, a *Labor Acknowledgment*.

Whether we live an urban, suburban, rural, or mountain life, we are never separate from the land. Never. It always holds us—and it is present not only in the precious land beneath us, as the source of the food we and other beings of the land consume, but also in the very structures and tissues of our precious human bodies—we are always rooted in and embraced by the Earth.

When the land is colonized, bodies are colonized. When bodies are colonized, land is colonized. The land we are on here, now called the City of Oakland, was colonized first by Spanish military with the support of the Roman Catholic Church, and then later by others of European heritage. The colonization was brutal and riven with an abject obsession with power and toxic with fear of "The Other."

In acknowledging that the land where the event we are facilitating is taking place was the free and open home of the Lisjan (Ohlone) people, we also acknowledge that it was never ceded by them.

At Thrive East Bay we choose to lift up their struggle, in the past, and now in our current colonial, capitalist-driven society, but not just with words. It is important to financially support the Ohlone people's current efforts to rematriate land here in the Bay to which they now have legal title. The fund that supports that rematriation effort, and to which contributions can be made, is called the *Segorea Te Land Trust*, and support is made through the *Shuumi Land Tax*. You can, as we do, contribute to that fund to support their work and their home.

Along with our Land acknowledgment, we also lift up all those who labored on this continent under the horrific oppression of slavery.

Out of fierce love for all those who labored, and continue to labor, with no pay, or inadequate pay, under exploitative, immoral, and intolerable conditions—we acknowledge the fact that the systems of financial and structural wealth in which we are embedded were built on the labor of all those human beings.

We also acknowledge all immigrant labor, including voluntary, involuntary, trafficked, forced, and undocumented peoples who profoundly contributed to the building of this country and who continue to serve within this country's labor force. May we hold all immigrant people sacred and worthy of respect.

We also acknowledge all the unpaid and poorly paid care-giving labor of workers who support those in need: the injured and sick, the elderly and the indigent.

May we work for true equity, honest and relevant reparations, and an active commitment to solidarity with all workers and the Earth.

11

Trauma Awareness and Approaches for Group Facilitation

by Aravinda Ananda, Margaret Babbott, and Janna Diamond

Many of us have experienced trauma in our lives, which has left a lasting impact. Staci Haines offers a definition of trauma as "an experience, series of experiences, and/or impacts from social conditions, that break or betray our inherent need for safety, belonging and dignity."[1] Individuals may experience trauma both personally (individual life experiences) and collectively (stemming from events that impact entire populations). Systems of oppression create both individual and collective traumas, all of which can be passed down for generations as intergenerational trauma.

People experience various nervous system state changes (e.g., fight, flight, freeze, appease, or dissociate) in order to survive these traumatic experiences. If one does not have the opportunity or support to de-escalate these nervous system activations—returning to conditions of safety, dignity, and belonging—these nervous system state changes can reactively reoccur long after the initiating event, when similar stimuli are present in the environment.

While these nervous system activations may feel alarming to oneself or others, it is important to shift the ingrained cultural habit of stigmatizing them. These reactions, which happen faster than conscious thought, are life-giving when they help us to survive in traumatic situations. When these ingrained tendencies to react persist in other contexts in which they are maladaptive, we can take steps to shift them. Shifting these tendencies can be a long-term process, and requires more than just the cognitive commitment to do so. Staci Haines' book *The Politics of Trauma: Somatics, Healing and Social Justice,* the Strozzi Institute, and Generative Somatics offer some wonderful resources for embodied approaches to shifting our conditioned tendencies.

Trauma can be deeply painful and is a sensitive topic, so not using care with it in facilitated spaces can cause significant harm. It is only within the past decade that there has been a shift in the general population and among some group facilitators towards becoming more knowledgeable about the dynamics of trauma and its effects. Even with this trend, there is more room for growth in implementing trauma-informed facilitation.

It is essential for facilitators to be aware that participants will bring different trauma histories with them into the room and, depending on the degree of healing they have been able to do, will exhibit a wide range of trauma reactivity. Facilitators can take steps to reduce needless trauma activations and build resilience when trauma activations inevitably occur. Having a baseline of trauma literacy can help facilitators better be able to support groups in holding trauma activations with care and support.

The way the Work That Reconnects spiral is currently structured offers tangible support for navigating difficult content such as trauma. It begins with encouraging participants to attune to a positive resource with the Gratitude phase of the spiral, before moving into Honoring Our Pain for the World. In Honoring Our Pain for the World, people are accompanied in the pain, and *through* the pain: the spiral doesn't stop there. In the Seeing with New and Ancient Eyes portion of the spiral, people are supported to approach their pain with different perspectives, further attune to positive resources by connecting with ancestors, future beings, and the entire web of life before moving forward in engaged action. However, even with the usefulness of the spiral as it is for holding trauma with care, there are some important additional recommendations that support trauma-informed facilitation.

Trauma-Informed Facilitation

This section on trauma-informed facilitation and group formation was written by Margaret Babbott, Ph.D. and Janna Diamond, ACCEP, SEP.

Trauma-informed facilitation is the application of fundamental trauma concepts and considerations to every stage of group work. Trauma-informed facilitation offers an expanded lens on and approaches to creating a group experience that is responsive, respectful, and transformative. Its four tenets include:

1. Center harm reduction.
2. Increase awareness of the visible and invisible traumas individuals may carry and may be activated while in the group (familial, cultural, historical, ecological).
3. Expand, practice, and apply nervous system awareness for self and group regulation and resilience.
4. Recognize the facilitators' role, boundaries, and limitations regarding participants' trauma activations while simultaneously creating a frame and offering additional resources as necessary.

Understanding the Human Nervous System

A key feature of trauma-informed facilitation is to better understand the human nervous system and its activation responses with self and others. The central function of the human nervous system is survival and adaptation. The nervous system works to keep us safe by constantly assessing what to move toward and what to move away from. With this awareness, the group (facilitators and participants alike) notice, learn, and respond to individual and collective nervous systems. In the dominant culture, many people have learned to tune out or override somatic feedback, often pushing through overwhelming experiences, which can potentially contribute to burnout and fatigue.

In addition to individual life histories, it is essential to recognize and name the inherent existence of trauma that is embodied differently in each participant dependent upon their social location, cultural, communal, familial, and genetic experiences. Trauma-informed facilitation recognizes the profound impact on self, others, and the collective of ancestral and intergenerational wounds that can live in the present moment, often below the surface of awareness.

Sharing an Explicit Overview of Trauma's Impact on the Human Nervous System

Time permitting, trauma-informed facilitation can include an explicit overview of trauma's impact on the human nervous system. For some participants, this information is familiar, for others it may be new. This educational component can be presented in a multi-modal approach that includes a visual chart, auditory description, and experiential practices. One tool that can be particularly helpful is Daniel Siegel's (1999) Window of Tolerance.[2] There are many versions of this and below is a simplified model for the purposes of WTR workshops. One thing to be cautious about is using technical or jargony language without defining it. Because some of these terms about the nervous system may be new for some people, the reinforcement of having a visual graphic and an auditory explanation can be really helpful.

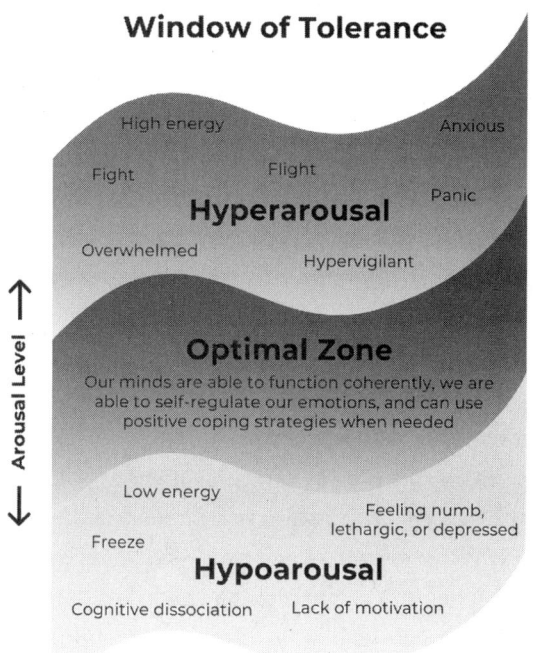

Adapted from Dan Siegel

Window of Tolerance
Credit: Design by Freida Nixdorf, adapted from Daniel J. Siegel's work by Aravinda Ananda and Margaret Babbott

We introduce the Window of Tolerance as one of the initial frames for multi-day workshops in order to create a common language, to invite a tone of embodied curiosity, and to prepare for the inevitable nervous system activations that will ensue. For some, nervous system awareness can feel like "Seeing with New Eyes" and furthers the group's capacity to hold a greater range and intensity of complex emotions.

In this model, "activation" refers to an acceleration and engagement of the human sympathetic nervous system. When activated, the sympathetic nervous system prepares the body for physical activity through increases in heart rate, blood pressure, breathing rate, and by slowing down digestive processes. Activation is not in and of itself a good or bad thing. As we will discuss in the next section on

Learning Zones, learning requires a certain degree of energetic activation. However, when we are so activated that we move into a panic response characterized by either hyperactivation (high) or hypoactivation (low), we are no longer in a window of tolerance where social engagement and responsiveness is possible, and that can make it very difficult for people to co-exist within a group.

In general, trauma tends to narrow people's windows of tolerance, while therapy and other healing modalities can help to widen it. The window of tolerance will also fluctuate for each individual depending on external demands and internal resources (e.g., sleep, nutrition, degree of stressors, social support). Because certain stressors and trauma activations can push participants out of their window of tolerance, there are things one can do to help people stay within or return to the window of tolerance. Also, we recommend that trauma-aware facilitators are sensitive to content and process that can trigger trauma memories and responses (e.g., mentioning child abuse, sexual assault).

Self-regulation and co-regulation are some commonly used terms for the process by which individuals and groups return to their window of tolerance. Some people prefer to speak of resilience, rather than regulation, when talking about returning to the window of tolerance. Resilience can be defined as a being's capacity to return to a state of equilibrium, coherence, or stabilization. After a traumatic event, we may be changed and thus not able to return to the exact same prior way of being in the world; however, we may be able to return to a new state of wellness. Trauma experts refer to Post-traumatic growth[3] when one is able to not only heal from trauma but to develop new and potentially transformative meaning, strengths, perspective, and intentions.

We like to be sure to include regulation/resilience approaches that are not breath-based because for many who panic or have high anxiety, focusing on the breath is contra-indicated because it intensifies the anxiety. For that reason, we almost always start with grounding practices such as pressing your feet into the ground and orienting to one's physical space (more about this in the section below on somatics, embodiment, grounding, and play).

Learning Zones

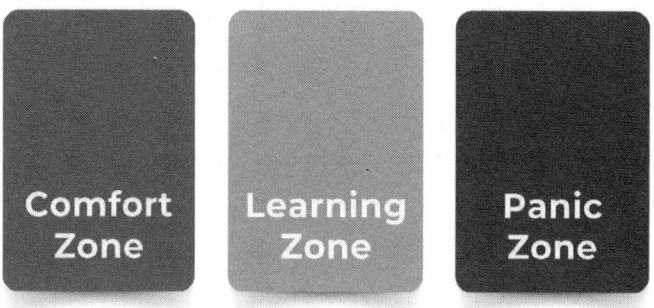

Learning Zones
Credit: Design by Freida Nixdorf, adapted from Tom Senninger's work by Aravinda Ananda and Margaret Babbott

Another simple tool is the Learning Zone or Zones of Regulation concept used by elementary school educators which offers a shared language for healthy activation and discomfort. It underscores a central workshop intention which is to be in the learning together as well as invites each participant to discern when, how, and how much to be in the stretch zone over the course of the workshop. In brief, there are three learning zones: comfort zone, learning zone (also referred to as stretch zone), panic zone. Learning does not occur when we are either too comfortable or too activated. We invite participants to be aware of how learning capacities may fluctuate over the course of the workshop and take steps to return to the learning zone if one gets too far into the panic zone.

Trauma-Informed Somatics, Embodiment, Grounding, and Play

Embodiment is the bringing of awareness to the organic intelligence of the body and the cues that the mind and body share about our environment and inner state of being. Somatics acknowledges this deep connection between mind and body and offers helpful language to understand our reactions to trauma and stress.

One form of grounding can be defined as our physical and psychological relationship to the ground beneath us. To feel grounded, we often need to have a sense of our lower body, and having a sense of our lower body, infers that we are in some form of connection with it. When we wiggle our toes or bend and straighten our knees, for example, we are reminded of this relationship.

Grounding supports us to stay present in the here and now, as well as to engage with our authentic response. Grounding orients us to our "felt sense," which locates us in time and space. This also means that information about what is safe or not isn't only coming to us in the form of thoughts.

While thoughts from the rational, thinking mind are of high importance in the dominant culture, they aren't the only way to receive information. The human experience includes images, sensations, emotions, movement, intuitions, and other voluntary and involuntary behavior. Pausing to notice if any of these other information channels can be brought to awareness offers significant insight into what is happening in the moment.

Trauma-informed facilitation invites us to check in with the felt sense of our own experience (e.g., sensations in the abdomen or chest) and track the behavior of a group (i.e., is there fidgeting, a sense of distraction), often at the same time. This widening of attention highlights what might be happening in the room for the facilitator and for participants and if something is or isn't working. The more awareness we can bring, the more capacity we have to respond versus react.

Building our capacity to respond can look like helping to hold and shift the energy in real time. It can also be discerning how to support a group to move through challenging moments, from stretch or even panic zone, and return to the safe zone.

Some practices to help shift the energy of the group:

- Move from large group to small groups or dyads.
- Move from large group to a journaling prompt.
- Move into an opportunity for receptivity with the natural world, such as inviting participants to go outside and connect with some-

thing they feel drawn to, engaging at least two of their senses, and noticing what happens in that new relationship.

Another way to support the grounding and co-regulation of a group is through movement and music. Sometimes a dance break is just what's needed. While the prompt can be optional, you might be surprised what happens when you invite people to sit or stand if they're able and move to the rhythm in any way their body wants. Starting and closing a workshop with a song, recorded or not, also encourages whole body engagement.

There are many facilitators who feel comfortable singing and leading a song and might invite participants to sing with them. If that's you, go for it! Humming also works well. This activates the vagus nerve and supports the individual and group nervous system to down-regulate and create more coherence and cohesion.

Trauma-Informed Group Formation

There are particular trauma-informed considerations for the group formation stage of a workshop, when participants are arriving into shared social space, the frame is being set for the day, and the group begins to build coherence with each other. The beginning of any workshop sets the tone and resonance field for the entire workshop and provides an opportunity to prepare for and prime the group's capacity for dynamics that will unfold.

In this stage, facilitators establish credibility, capacity, and competence so that participants can begin to assess the degree to which they may feel safe enough to take risks, contribute, and grow. One explicit intention of trauma-informed facilitation is to strengthen the collective nervous system to support group coherence, resilience, and containment.

We focus on two areas for workshops: first, nervous system awareness and activation in self and group and second, somatic or body-grounding practices. These can be adapted to online or hybrid workshops as well as to varying workshop lengths (day, weekend, week).

Recommended Practices During Group Formation

In trauma-informed approaches to group formation, we recommend welcoming activities that invite a variety of options for initial connections. Belonging is at the core of human experience, as is the need to be seen and understood, so it is to be expected that participants arrive with differing levels of anticipatory anxiety when joining a new group. Trauma-informed facilitation takes into consideration the need for agency, options, structure, and integrated activities. The options below can be adapted to setting, group size, capacities, and facilities. We have divided the recommendations into social engagement, orientation to physical space and time, orientation to each other, and connection with the natural world.

Social engagement

Some options to encourage social engagement include:
- Inviting participants to help set up chairs or finish food preparation (this fosters engagement and belonging)
- Playful and creative stations or activities (flow and options) such as name tag art-making (lanyards with name and image), collective mapping (mural paper where people draw their route to workshop or if online, current location)
- Movement games
- Music—for example, singing together, or invite contributions in advance to a collective playlist

Orientation to physical space and time

Trauma-informed facilitation recognizes that the human nervous system requires an orientation to time, place, and space in order to feel safe so participants have autonomy and don't feel trapped. Some options for helping groups orient to time, space, and place include:
- Point out physical exits in the meeting room and how to access outdoors to prevent the feeling of being trapped.
- Note program "exits" such as breaks, restrooms, and the outdoors.
- Post and review schedule to provide external frame and expectation, including planned breaks and meals.

- Invite people to pay attention to their somatic and emotional responses and encourage them to take a break as needed.
- Take 5–10 minutes to walk around or observe the surroundings, ideally outdoors, notice what you are drawn to, notice what you would like to explore further, see if any color or texture calls out to you, etc.

Orientation to each other with an opening circle or other introductions process

When time permits in new groups, it is wonderful to have everyone share their name in the whole group as a way to start to get to know each other and begin to build connections. Trauma-informed group introductions use multi-modal, multi-sensorial approaches in order to give options, access, and integration. One option for this is for the group to convene in a circle with those who are able standing, and as each participant shares their name they also make a gesture or movement and then the group repeats back the name and movement.

After introductions one option is to invite a pause to notice sensations in or on the body and perhaps compare that with when they first arrived to the space. This trauma-informed facilitation practice introduces the group to one of many forms of "checking in" throughout the workshop. If time permits, it is wonderful to have an opportunity for participants to connect with another person one-on-one or in a small group, such as with a deeper introduction or response to some other chosen prompts. Here are some open sentences that are grounded in an eco-somatic trauma-informed facilitation approach that can help people with arriving in the space and in the group, and attuning to positive resources:

As I look around this space, I am drawn to …
As my feet are on the ground, I also notice/ I'm aware of …
As I breathe in (the sky), I am filled with …
As I come into stillness, I'm surprised by …

Setting the tone and putting certain things in place at the beginning of a workshop sets people up with support for the workshop to flow better throughout the group's time together.

With gratitude for the above section from Margaret Babbott and Janna Diamond, we turn now to some other trauma-informed facilitation considerations.

Some Additional Trauma-Informed Facilitation Tips
by Aravinda Ananda

Use group agreements to introduce and encourage self-awareness and self-regulation

If you don't have time for an overview of some basic nervous system concepts such as the window of tolerance, facilitators can use group agreements or guidelines to invite self-awareness and encourage regulation. For example, Priya Parker offers a "pool rule" community agreement (you choose how deep or shallow you go) to encourage people to be choiceful in what they have capacity for and not push themselves too far beyond their limits. At a February 2024 training on cultural integrity, Work That Reconnects facilitator Lydia Violet Harutoonian offered a community agreement that invited people to pause and put their hands on their bodies and take three breaths when experiencing a moment of trigger. Saying "Pause," was an invitation to people in the group to take three breaths together, or take care of their nervous system regulation in some way before moving forward with a conversation. In these ways, facilitators can use community agreements to encourage a workshop environment where everyone is invited and encouraged to care for their nervous systems after moments of trigger.

Offer a grounding, centering, or other becoming present activity

Many facilitators are moving towards offering a grounding, centering, or other becoming present activity towards the start of a group's time together. This activity would incorporate numerous elements that Margaret and Janna covered in the group formation stage. A guided meditation or visualization may invite participants to bring their awareness to their bodies, to the breath, or to sensations such as where their body is in contact with different surfaces. Resmaa Menakem often invites people to scan their surroundings for exits, so they know how they can get out of a space if they need to. Inviting people to look around the room—allowing their eyes to linger on something that is pleasing to the eye—is a means of positive resource. Increasing body awareness, attuning to positive resources, and connecting with the present moment can all help set people up to be more regulated, resourced, and resilient.

Include as much time outside as your program allows

Connecting with the living world through spending time outside, or through reflection prompts about memories in the living world, can be a powerful way to attune to a positive resource. Ecopsychology recognizes the therapeutic and regulating/resilience-increasing possibilities of connecting with the living world. Building as many opportunities for nature connection into your program as possible can help support people's nervous system regulation.

Support a culture of consent

Explicitly establish a culture of consent—especially around touch. This can be done during a community agreements process and reinforced throughout the group's time together. Particularly important are consent for physical contact and touch; physical proximity and closeness; and confidentiality. Confidentiality includes both outside of workshop space (never share someone else's personal content outside of the workshop) and within the workshop (obtain permission before following-up with someone about something they said). Honoring consent means honoring boundaries and respecting if someone's answer is no.

Share content warnings for sensitive content

Use sensitivity when bringing up particularly traumatic content, for example graphic violence or abuse. As much as you are able, let people know in advance so that they can opt in or out. Share content warnings in the moment if bringing something up unexpectedly, and know that even doing that may not be enough as it can sometimes be difficult to opt out in real time. Having an agreement about content warnings can be useful, but you can't always have an agreement in advance about every possible harm, so you have to be willing to address issues as needed. If a general consent agreement is meant to extend to traumatic content, make this explicit.

Move at a sustainable pace

When working with traumatic content, it is useful to use "titration," wading in more slowly. It is always helpful to have warm-up activities before jumping into the deep end of the pool. The "pool rule" encourages participants to stay as shallow or go as deep as they feel willing and able to safely go. As a facilitator, use care assessing if the amount of available time is sufficient for building trust and nervous system regulation before taking participants to any great depth with potentially traumatic content. Also allow time and provide support for moving out of that space.

Special considerations for Honoring Our Pain for the World

Both participants and facilitators need support before and also after an Honoring Our Pain for the World practice or ritual where a lot of traumatic content is shared. Include a plan for this support in your agenda, whether it is offering some resourcing activities, scheduling a break or breaks, or suggesting ways to decompress. This might be a good time for movement that alternates limbs, such as walking (outside if possible); or making a butterfly tapping motion with one's hands across one's chest.

We are deeply social creatures and also co-regulate in groups. In *My Grandmother's Hands: Racialized Trauma and the Pathway to Mending Our Hearts and Bodies*, Resmaa Menakem outlines various methods of co-regulation including dancing, singing, rocking, and humming.[4] The way the Truth Mandala practice opens by people chanting the seed syllable "ahhhhh" together is a demonstration of this and can be expanded on or used elsewhere as needed. Listening to and/or participating in making music can also help regulate/calm/soothe/settle our nervous systems, supporting us to be within a wider range of social engagement and ability to respond.

Work That Reconnects facilitator Anne Goodwin has introduced support for self-regulation when moving into Honoring Our Pain for the World in this way:

I want to introduce some body practices that you can employ today as we move toward Honoring Our Pain for the World. As we witness other people's pain, we might get anxious, or an old trauma of our own might be restimulated. This can be difficult, yet it is of central importance to any solidarity work that we be able to stay present in the room with someone else's pain. Here are some somatic techniques you can try freely as we move into this work.

- **Rocking:** In *My Grandmother's Hands*, Resmaa Menakem writes that his grandmother would sometimes purposefully sit and rock to soothe and settle herself. She would rock with energy and intention, either front to back or side to side. I invite you to try that, and see how it feels. Try it with smaller or larger movements, slower or faster.

- **Rocking and Breathing:** Here's a useful breath that I learned from Buddhist teacher Deborah Eden Tull. As you breathe in, gently lean forward from the hips and imagine you are breathing in through the front of your heart. Then lean back and let the breath out through the back of your heart. Try that.

- **Breathing Through:** Joanna Macy's exercise Breathing Through is based on the Buddhist technique of *tonglen*. Let's try it. First, let images of the pain of the world arise in your mind. Then, as you breathe in, imagine the air as a ribbon. You can give the ribbon a color. Now imagine the pain as bumps along that ribbon. Let it go down into your throat, through your lungs, and into your heart. Just let it sit there for a moment. Then breathe it back out through an opening in your heart, back out into the world. You don't have to transform it in any way, but just let it pass through you and trust your heart to hold it and let it go.

Attending to co-regulation of the group

Just as our nervous systems can be positively impacted by others in a group, we can also be negatively impacted. One of the complexities with group work is that we are each affected by one another, and if one person is triggered and goes into an alarmed nervous system response, it can trigger others. Facilitators can plan regulating activities into a group's time together—for example, periodic songs, and also add in additional regulating activities if the group nervous system starts to fray.

Using care with guided meditations or visualizations

For guided meditations or visualizations, it is very important to use invitational language that allows consent around closing one's eyes. Rather than instructing people to close their eyes (which can be experienced as a command rather than an invitation with consent), you could say something like, "I invite you to close or lower your eyes as is comfortable for you."

Use extra sensitivity with practices such as the Bodhisattva Check-in/My Choices for This Life that encourage reflection on the circumstances of one's life including family life during childhood. All too many people have experienced violence in childhood, and this can leave deep wounds. In general, don't tell people that traumatic things that happened to them were gifts. Many experience this as offensive. The traumatic event or circumstances may have precipitated opportunities for healthy growth, but this can be acknowledged without ever suggesting that the traumatic event itself was a gift.

Healthy boundaries and time away from the group

While it is important not to stigmatize people for their trauma activations, it is also important to have healthy boundaries if behavior is infringing on the ability of others in the group to participate. Sometimes it may be helpful to pull someone aside at a break and check in with them one-on-one to assess if they are currently able to participate in group activities or if they need to prioritize self-care in another way. This is not to say that people need to go off alone and "fix" themselves in isolation. Because trauma often involves ruptures in belonging, being held with care by others can be particularly supportive for healing. However, there are times when what will support people most is having a break from group activities.

A final note of caution

Exploring trauma in groups of caring people can be powerful. It can enlarge an individual's window of tolerance by increasing the available nervous system capacity for metabolizing and holding the immensity of pain. That being said, while significant trauma healing can and does happen in groups, it is important to note that other kinds of support are needed for healing trauma, and not all of it can or should be done in a group setting. As Resmaa Menakem indicated in an appendix in *My Grandmother's Hands: Racialized Trauma and the Pathway to Mending Our Hearts and Bodies,* other methods are needed to support trauma healing including: internal work on one's own, talking with a trusted friend, and working with a professional therapist or body worker.

While workshops may be therapeutic in how they provide opportunities for growth and transformation, they are not psychotherapy. Group psychotherapy involves retaining professional services from a licensed professional. It is not the job of a facilitator to be a therapist and work directly with people's trauma. Taking a trauma-informed approach simply means that facilitators have greater awareness about trauma in general, are prepared for the possibility that trauma may be activated during group time, take steps to reduce needless trauma activations, and have methods to support people to stay within or return to their window of tolerance.

12

Inner Work for Collective Liberation

by Aravinda Ananda and Molly Brown

In order to embody a commitment to collective liberation, there is a tremendous amount of unlearning, inner work, and practice that many of us are asked to do. If this feels like a daunting proposition, here's good news: doing this work stands to enrich all of our relationships, improve the quality of our experience, and help build a better world through contributing to the shifts needed for the Great Turning to be possible. This is lifelong work; we don't have to complete it all overnight, nor could we. So the most important thing is one's ongoing commitment to keep working on it.

This chapter explores various facets of the needed inner work: the deep psychological, emotional, and spiritual work to unlearn oppressive conditioning and embody collective liberation. Each of us has a lifetime of conditioning including internalized superiority and/or inferiority based on our respective identities and social locations.

Taking steps to dismantle and shift these self-understandings is complex layered work. Some areas of inner work may be helpful for anyone interested in pursuing a path of collective liberation, and other areas more necessary according to social location. While some material in this chapter is applicable regardless of social location, extra emphasis is given to areas of inner work that will support dominant identity groups in learning to decrease oppressive harm.

It will take repetition (aka practice) to embody orientations different from what we are accustomed to. As Prentis Hemphill noted in *What It Takes to Heal: How Transforming Ourselves Can Change the World*, practice isn't useful only for helping us build muscles towards a desired capacity. It is also useful because with each step we take, we can learn more about our internal blockages and what we need to transform and heal along the way. Most of us, from many different social locations, likely have healing work to do to move closer to collective liberation. A commitment to collective liberation means taking our responsibility for inner work, transformation, and healing seriously.

We don't have to do it alone, nor, in truth, can we. We'll each need support, whether through friends, therapists, body workers, mindfulness teachers, or particular fields of work such as Generative Somatics or Internal Family Systems. Whatever helps you shift, heal, and grow out of patterns of oppressive conditioning and be more present and able to respond in the current moment will aid you on this path.

In this chapter we explore three areas: working with internalized oppression; developing self-awareness; and an exploration of obstacles some of us will encounter in our work for collective liberation and the inner work that will help us better navigate those challenges.

Working with Internalized Oppression
This section was written by Aravinda Ananda.

Undoing Internalized Superiority

People with dominant identities have a responsibility to do the inner and outer work required to dismantle internalized superiority. People who have been conditioned since birth to hold an internal understanding of superiority have often developed unconscious attitudes that they simply know what is best, they are right, etc. Internalized superiority has deep roots. It can take many years of concerted effort to deepen awareness, heal, and change. Support from an ongoing community can be particularly helpful in the process of learning, growth, and accountability.

While the rest of this section is tailored towards white people working to transform their own racism, it will likely be of interest to people who hold other dominant identities. There are ways that internalized superiority manifests in interpersonal interactions that hold across dominant identities. It is imperative that white people facilitating mixed-race groups do some antiracism work—both to address their own ways of acting out racism, and also to be able to notice and address when others say or do racist things. Because the internalization is deep, white facilitators will have a lot of inner work to do to shift the ways they perpetuate racism.

As explored in Chapter 6, an important place to start is with understanding one's own social location, including the advantages systemically afforded to white people based on the color of their skin, for example, the assumption of innocence until proven guilty. Beyond that is the work of actively contributing to and building more equitable relations.

White people are asked to:

- Be willing to be disturbed; get out of white comfort and sit with and feel the discomfort.
- Be accountable for their impact; seek ways to lessen defensiveness; work with patterns of collapsing in shame or guilt; and increase the capacity for centered accountability.
- Commit to long-term learning and unlearning with articles (e.g., "Habits of White Supremacy Culture" by Tema Okun), books (e.g., *How to Be an Antiracist* by Ibram Kendi, *White Fragility* by Robin DiAngelo); podcasts; and trainings (there are many

wonderful trainings out there including offerings by the Racial Equity Institute, Comrades Education [formerly White Awake], or Education for Racial Equity).

- Learn together! Form a study group or book club. White caucus spaces such as Showing Up for Racial Justice (SURJ) or the Deepening White Awareness Sangha offer valuable ongoing opportunities for learning together with others on the same path. The effectiveness of white caucus spaces is greatly enhanced by having a skilled facilitator who can help white people more clearly see dynamics of whiteness and be accountable for shifting their behavior. It takes a while to unpack and unlearn biases that are unconscious, and it can take even longer to shift the ways these biases have been embedded in our behaviors. The key is to commit to ongoing learning and just keep at it.

This work is lifelong and not just cognitive. In *My Grandmother's Hands: Racialized Trauma and the Pathway to Mending Our Hearts and Our Bodies*, Resmaa Menakem illustrates how this work also needs to happen within and through the body. It isn't about being one of the "good ones" and only reaching the performative level, and it is most certainly not about being a savior. It needs to be much deeper than that.

Internal work needs to be accompanied by (and will be supported by) a commitment to deep and honest inquiry of and challenge to racism in others. This includes both on the interpersonal level (e.g., speaking up after a racial microaggression) and on the institutional level through working to change structural conditions that reinforce racism. White people can take steps at all levels of social organization to shift racism.

> **Habits of White Supremacy Culture**
>
> "White Supremacy Culture,"[1] an essay by Tema Okun, is a useful resource for looking at habits, attitudes, and ways of

being that need shifting to get free of supremacy systems. It was originally written in 1999 to name a number of characteristics of white supremacy culture that show up in organizations. However, while it has been useful in that context and in many others as well, many of its terms have been taken out of context and misused. Okun now has a website (whitesupremacyculture.info) that emphasizes reading all the supporting materials in order to fully understand the powerful terms the essay highlights. The essay includes a list of characteristics such as perfectionism, defensiveness, paternalism, either-or thinking, fear of open conflict, individualism, and a right to comfort, as well as antidotes to these characteristics. If you haven't already engaged with this resource, it comes highly recommended as a tool to help peel back and work with shifting some of the internal conditioning of systems of oppression.

Undoing Internalized Inferiority

People from oppressed identity groups have particular work to do to dismantle and heal an internalized sense of inferiority. The work to decolonize our minds, free ourselves from the internal oppressor, and heal takes time and support. Spaces with others of the same identity group can be particularly supportive, such as Resmaa Menakem's approach of having separate spaces for Bodies of Culture (his term for People of the Global Majority) and white folks to work on dismantling racism. I appreciate Resmaa's emphatic insistence to Bodies of Culture that "you are not defective." Having internalized a sense of being wrong and bad for one's entire life, undoing this programming takes repetition to rework the ruts and grooves of the mind and body. We have to get our reps in to develop new muscles, orientations, and habits of being. Please see Appendix F: Recommended Resources for a few other suggestions for healing from internalized inferiority.

We turn next to an exploration of self-awareness, a capacity that will aid not only facilitators of anti-oppressive spaces, but all of us in our respective work for collective liberation.

Self-Awareness

The next two sections on self-awareness and subpersonalities were written by Molly Brown.

As facilitators, we need to be able to call upon our own wisdom, intuition, and inner guidance as well as past experience and book-learning as we work with each unique group of individuals within an ever-changing social and physical environment. To do so requires a high degree of self-awareness, so that we don't get lost in our own emotional reactions or those arising in the group. As facilitators it is particularly important to notice what is going on within ourselves in order to be able to make conscious choices about how we can respond rather than automatically reacting.

Self-awareness often begins with the body, noticing without judgment what is happening with my breathing, heart rate, muscle tension, sense of relative heat or cold, and impulse for movement. Self-awareness includes noticing feelings arising, those that I can name (joy, anger, confusion, fear) and those I can't yet name. Many people become aware of feelings through attention to their bodies. Feeling hot and flushed can help me realize that I am getting angry. And what are the thoughts arising with the emotion, or perhaps behind the emotion? What am I telling myself about this person or this situation? What beliefs or assumptions are taking hold in my thoughts?

Self-awareness is essential to bringing more information into the field. The beliefs or assumptions I identify may be quite accurate and helpful in the situation. My anger could be arising because of an injustice taking place. And if, as a facilitator, I am feeling or thinking something, or having a somatic reaction, it's a good clue that at least a few others in the room may be experiencing something similar.

That's when a facilitator's self-awareness can help the group as a whole become more self-aware. Simply naming the body sensations, the feelings, and even the thoughts can help the group more consciously notice what's going on. "I'm feeling a little confused right now. Let's pause and take a few breaths together, and see if things become clearer."

Facilitators need to develop their self-awareness muscles in daily life, in order to have them available in the more demanding facilitation situation. There are many approaches available today to build these muscles: mindfulness, meditation, journaling, and similar practices based in humanistic and transpersonal psychologies (e.g., Psychosynthesis, Internal Family Systems, Somatic Experiencing, Focusing), as well as individual and group psychotherapy.

The following exploration of self-awareness is adapted from my book, *Growing Whole: Self-Realization for the Great Turning*,[2] which is based in psychosynthesis, a transpersonal psychology.

Challenges to Self-Awareness

We may find it difficult to simply observe our feelings, thoughts, and body sensations, without immediately passing judgment, interpreting, or deciding to change what we observe. That tendency may be a factor in our inability to be aware. We may fear awareness because of the demands or expectations that are usually attached. Why would I want to notice tension in my shoulders if it just means I am doing something wrong or that I may have some disease process going on? Why would I want to feel my feelings if they are labeled "crazy" or seen as inappropriate? So our first task may be to learn to observe without making any judgment or analysis—not an easy undertaking.

Observing with Detachment

We can begin by trying to simply observe the judgments, analyses, or expectations. "Oh, now I am judging those feelings ... Now I am thinking about what I should do about my tight shoulders ... Now I am trying to figure out why I feel this way." By observing a process, we may be able to step away from it—to detach somewhat from that perspective. The possibility arises of a more neutral compassionate Observer of all that is going on within—or, when facilitating, what is going on in the group.

Uncomfortable Feelings

Another difficulty arises when I do notice what I am feeling and I don't like it. I feel depression and pain, or anger. Isn't it better to just ignore such feelings and go on about my business instead of paying attention to them and maybe making them worse?

The problem is that feelings we ignore still affect us. They sink beneath the level of our awareness and nibble away at our well-being. They pop out at inappropriate times or get dumped on people we don't really want to hurt. Or they may lower our levels of energy and joy so that we operate out of a narrow band of blandness and mediocrity.

Respect the Feelings

Noticing feelings does not necessarily mean plunging into them, although on occasion we might choose to do so. Noticing feelings does mean giving them respectful attention, being ready to learn from them about ourselves or our situation. If I notice that I am feeling depressed, I can take a look at what might be provoking my depression. Maybe I am neglecting my basic needs in some way or maybe my communication in an important relationship is off the track, so we are not really connecting. By being present with the emotions and the messages they carry, I may be able to address root causes.

Sometimes it is important to just feel the hard feelings, to go into them and through them. Feelings are natural and may guide us through a necessary process of change. When we are grieving over a loss, for example, allowing ourselves to feel our feelings, express them, trust them, and follow them through, may help us to arrive at a place of acceptance and peace. Similarly, allowing ourselves to go through anger in a safe setting can put us in touch with our deepest values, giving us a sense of commitment and power.

Ah, So!

Spiritual teacher Ram Dass often spoke of an attitude of calm acceptance exemplified by the monk who greeted each event, pleasant or unpleasant, with the gentle exclamation, "Ah, so!" I often think of that phrase when observing some life event from a more accepting perspective: "The clutch went out on the car today. Ah, so!" "I received an invitation to speak at an important conference. Ah, so!" "I am frustrated and scared about my financial situation. Ah, so!"

Of course, this phrase could easily become a slogan for shutting down feelings and becoming numbly detached from life, but that is not the purpose. Our purpose is to allow ourselves the full range of emotions, from elation and celebration to despondency and despair. Paradoxically, this may be far more possible as we learn to maintain a compassionate Observer who serves as an anchor for our emotional and mental health, an anchor for awareness of ourselves and our world. As we become more accustomed to observing our responses to our personal lives, we can more readily observe our responses to events in the larger world around us. We build our capacity to notice and respond compassionately and effectively to whatever arises in our facilitation spaces.

> **The Further Reaches of Self-Observation** (by Kurt Kuhwald)
>
> Many contemplative practices and modern consciousness research take self-observation to another wider and deeper opening, which is further enriched when woven with embodied justice seeking. Engaged Buddhism and teachers of mindfulness and nonduality, teach that self-observation can become more expansive, and more deeply grounded in reality, by observing the observer. According to this teaching, that step opens to the field of "awareness of awareness"—an expanded consciousness, a liberated Love. From that place, our actions are realized in a flow that moves with an embodied presence free of negative judgements, restrictive identities, disabling and demeaning projections, and effortlessly engages the world with creativity, compassion, intelligence, and an open heart.

Subpersonalities: The Many Faces of Everyone

Our various ways of being and acting are often crystallized into behavioral patterns, called "subpersonalities" in psychosynthesis, or "parts" in Internal Family Systems.[3] Self-awareness often helps us recognize that we have more than one personality, more than one way to respond to life's challenges. It really is okay to be more ways than one; it is not a sign of mental instability that we act and feel radically different ways at different times. If anything, it is a sign of health. We may even hold two seemingly conflicting points of view at the same time. We can be both frightened and assertive; both angry and caring. This can give us a sense of flexibility, freeing us from the struggle to conform to how we are supposed to be.

Subpersonalities are habitual ways of reacting to various events and demands in a person's life. People learn these habits from others as well as creating them for themselves. Unfortunately, these habits can create problems for people as their life circumstances change.

Self-observation can help us become aware of our subpersonalities. Once we are aware of them, however, our first impulse may be to try to deny or get rid of a troublesome part, as if that was even possible. The qualities and skills of every subpersonality are too much a part of us to be abandoned and are of too much value to be scorned. Instead, we need to embrace and reintegrate these vital parts of ourselves, with love, compassion, and clarity.

Facilitators may discover that they have one or more subpersonalities that come into play when they are facilitating, such as Charismatic Leader, or Benevolent Parent, or Enlightened Antiracist. These subpersonalities could be quite useful in some situations, but we need to be aware of when they are useful and when not. We need flexibility and freedom to respond creatively to each situation; over-identifying with one subpersonality can severely limit our options. When we disidentify and observe a subpersonality from a centered place, we can choose to bring forth its characteristics and qualities as needed.

Obviously, we need to become acquainted with our subpersonalities outside of our facilitation work, so we have that self-knowledge to draw upon when needed. This probably means finding and actively working with one or more of the personal growth approaches mentioned above. Working with one or more of these approaches can bring more joy and freedom into our lives as a whole, as well as greatly enhance facilitation.[4]

Working with Internal Obstacles

The remaining sections in this chapter were primarily written by Aravinda Ananda.

As we dig into the work of collective liberation, each of us will face different internal obstacles. This next section explores some challenges frequently encountered in the work to get free of systems of oppression, and the kinds of inner work that can help us to move through these challenges.

Internal Obstacles to Responding After Witnessing Oppressive Harm as a Bystander

In Chapter 8, we explored the additional harm that arises when bystanders—people not directly targeted—do not act to interrupt oppressive harm in interpersonal interactions. Knowing that it is important to respond when we witness oppressive harm, doesn't mean we will immediately be able to do so in a helpful way. Based on our particular social identities and life experiences (including our trauma histories), each of us may face some different internal obstacles to responding after witnessing oppressive harm. Here are examples from our author/editor team showing how these obstacles may differ.

Molly: When needing to address harm as an older white woman, I have to overcome a lifelong conditioning to "make nice" and not upset anyone by rocking the boat—especially people in positions of power or leadership. I have to confront a lifelong tendency to gloss over harm by telling myself internally, "He didn't mean that," or "Maybe it isn't so bad," or "Maybe (I hope) no one else noticed." I believe that is part of another pattern that I have recently become aware of: I take in plenty of information about oppression and violence inflicted on other people, but that's not enough. I don't allow myself to really experience their suffering, emotionally and viscerally. It's happening "out there." My challenge is to really let it into my body and soul. I am asking myself, "What am I afraid will happen if I do?"

Aravinda: One internal obstacle I have faced when addressing harm is a lifelong tendency to freeze when I witness harm. When contemplating speaking up about it, fear of annihilation comes up, and it is tricky for me to sort out how much of this is ancestrally inherited fear from my Black ancestors for whom challenging the status quo could be deadly, and how much is from my white ancestors' "white polite" conditioning to make nice and not rock the boat. The freezing response combines with a slow processing speed in which I may not understand until hours later what was going on in a given situation, making it difficult to speak up in the moment. Many times after witnessing harm, I have felt immobilized and turned inward with racing thoughts, anxiety about not knowing what to say or do, and a spiral of self-blame about personal inadequacy for not meeting the needs of the moment. I have been working for years to heal this default freeze response, and still have more work to do in order to be able to speak up when my conscience compels me to.

Kurt: While, as a white male, I would like to be able to point to the usual patterns of white privilege in myself that have kept genuine openheartedness locked down—a lockdown that results in the severance of feeling, and blunting of care and sensitivity for others (particularly people whose skin color is darker than mine)—the truth is deeper than that. What I have very slowly understood, after years of inner transformational work, is that as a childhood victim of traumatic abuse, and the devastating effects of unbridled drug usage (including amphetamines) in my very early adulthood, my neural system was damaged and my psycho-spiritual resources, that fill out my personhood, had to deeply fortify against pain and dysfunction. While it all worked quite well, well enough, in fact, for me to outwardly succeed in three difficult and demanding professions, the inner healing has been very, very slow. That long lag in my inner world has required special attention when it comes to racial issues and to my unearned privilege. Working on this book, with a talented and sensitive team, has helped enormously for me to dare to face into the patterns so well illustrated in Okun's work on white consciousness (see the section earlier in this chapter) at a level deep enough to make real change, rather than performative posturing, begin to happen. My thanks are big.

> **Self-Reflection**
>
> These questions can help you reflect on what comes up for you when you witness oppressive harm as a bystander:
>
> *Are you aware of any internal obstacles you face in responding after witnessing harm? If yes, what are they?*
>
> *In what ways do you see these obstacles as connected with your social identities, social locations, or other life experience?*
>
> *Has the way you have reacted or responded after witnessing oppressive harm changed over time? Are you even aware of automatic reactions you may have? Have you already done a lot of work with shifting automatic reactions and building capacity to choose a response in the moment? Do you have more work to do?*

Trauma Healing

In *What It Takes to Heal: How Transforming Ourselves Can Change the World*, Prentis Hemphill makes a compelling case for the important role of healing ourselves in ending oppression. The healing needed is multifaceted and complex. Each of us will bring our particular trauma patterning to this work of getting free of systems of oppression and will have particular healing work to do. In this section we look more specifically at how trauma healing can help us better be able to respond to oppression happening in the moment.

As Prentis writes, "Unprocessed trauma or conditioning by our families or social expectations can cause our protective body to become our predominant way of meeting not only potentially traumatic moments, but any moment in which we perceive stress, even when there's no real threat to our lives or bodily integrity."[5] We can find ourselves going into an automatic fight, flight, freeze, fawn, or dissociative reactions—nervous system mobilizations that originally arose to protect us in a particular traumatic experience. When these activations become our generalized reactions to threats or any form of stress, they can project the past onto the present, and rob us of the ability to respond to the reality of the present moment.

Triggers and Triggering

Triggering happens when we experience a stimulus in the present moment and are automatically brought to a situation from our past. We move into re-action (reenacting a strategy of the past) before conscious thought, and therefore choice, are activated. In life-threatening situations, it can be a life-saving action to act instantaneously. However, because our nervous systems can interpret a wide variety of threat levels as threats to our lives, our reactions can become overgeneralized.

Building the capacity to allow more space between stimulus and action in situations that are not actually life threatening helps us be able to move from reactivity to responsiveness. It takes healing to create space around a stimulus that triggers a conditioned reaction so that we can respond to the present moment rather than react with a past strategy. As Molly mentioned earlier in this chapter, in the section on self-awareness, there are numerous modalities that can help with this such as meditation, mindfulness, or other spiritual practices. Therapy can also help.

It takes time to transform triggered reactions to grounded responses, both in the moment of trigger, as well as over the course of time. If you have never been taught how to shift triggered reactions to grounded responses, you will likely need some support.

Any steps we can take to grow our capacity to center—to return to a place within ourselves of stabilization/groundedness/settledness where we are able to make intentional choices about how we act—will aid us in our work for collective liberation.

> **A few facilitation tips/options for working with triggers**
>
> - If you have co-facilitators, talk in advance about what it looks like when each of you is in trigger. Come up with a plan that can support each of you in those times; for example, a facilitator could tag out if they need to and another facilitator could be prepared to tag in.
>
> - When talking with the group about workshop culture, or community agreements or guidelines, encourage people to lean into greater self-responsibility with triggers, for example by drawing on self-regulation techniques that support settling in the present moment.
>
> - Use self-regulation tactics as needed to help settle your own activated nervous system.
>
> - Build regular opportunities for co-regulation into your program agenda, such as using music or song, especially after content or activities that may be particularly triggering.
>
> - Sense into what additional participant support may be needed in moments of trigger: perhaps a break is needed, or another group co-regulation practice.

When a present-day stimulus triggers the same reaction as a previous traumatic incident, we can get stuck in the past and be unable to see the present situation clearly. Triggering can sometimes cause us to misidentify responsibility when we think someone providing a stimulus in the present is inflicting the same harm we experienced in the past, which may not be the case. Based on a lifetime of experience with frequent threats to one's safety, some people live in a constant state of alert and experience frequent triggering. While we may need to have some healthy boundaries with the behavior of people who are in high states of reactivity, we can simultaneously increase our compassion for the circumstances of their lives that created the need to behave in this way as an act of defense/survival.

Shifting Defensiveness

Defense is an important protective move that in many situations can be life preserving. However, when trauma and/or conditioning causes defensiveness to become our automatic, default way of meeting the world, it can be maladaptive in contexts in which that behavior is not life affirming. It can cause us to miss significant opportunities to grow, learn, heal, change, and respond to what is actually needed in the moment for the greatest good of all.

Many of us, regardless of our social location, have real work to do to shift automatic patterns of defensiveness so that we can remain open when situations call for learning and growing rather than closing, constricting, and defending an existing position. Dominant identity groups have some particular automatic defensive reactions when challenged that shut down honest exploration (see the discussion of accountability deflection in Chapter 8). People with dominant identities often need to do critical inner work in order to shift their defensiveness that serves to dodge accountability. Education for Racial Equity is one organization that has done work with white people drawing on both Resmaa Menakem's work on somatic abolitionism and Robin DiAngelo's work on white fragility[6] to help white people work with and shift ingrained defensiveness.

> *What might support you in shifting patterns of automatic defensiveness so that you can show up differently in situations that call for learning, growing, healing, and changing?*

Sometimes, however, it can be genuinely difficult to sort out what is our responsibility. People may project things onto us that we are not actually doing; or, in another example, historical pain is triggered that engenders a reaction far exceeding what you are responsible for having done in that particular moment. In the latter instance, beginning with genuinely empathizing and acknowledging the hurt, rather than only delineating where your responsibility lies, can help to serve healing from wider systemic harms. This empathy and acknowledgment does not mean you have to own more responsibility than is yours to take. See the section on building healthy accountability in Chapter 8 for more discussion of "centered accountability"—taking responsibility for what is yours, not more or less.

Strengthening the Capacity to Hold BOTH/AND

Moving from "either/or" (binary) towards "both/and" (multiple things can be simultaneously possible) ways of relating will greatly support us in our work for collective liberation.

An important both/and to hold in work for collective liberation is this: we can simultaneously be accountable for harmful impact and can also retain inherent worth and dignity. Acknowledging our responsibility for harmful impact does not cancel out our inherent dignity and worth. To the contrary, acknowledging impact and taking steps toward repair only increases our alignment with a commitment to care for all.

Internal Family Systems' understanding of "parts" (or subpersonalities in psychosynthesis) can help with liberating us from false binaries by strengthening our capacity to acknowledge multiplicities. This can be particularly helpful with collective liberation work in that it can help free us from the false binary that we cannot do "bad" things if we are "good" people. Rather than getting tied up in a defense of our essential goodness, we can allow and know the truth of our inherent worth and dignity while at the same time acknowledging harmful impact.

Here's an example: "A part of me was conditioned to be racist: racism was deeply ingrained in me from the moment of my birth (in truth before my birth throughout many of my ancestors' lives). *And* it is not all of who I am: there is also a part of me that accesses a deeper caring about justice and is willing to be accountable and work to change the parts of me that have racist conditioning."

Mistakes, Shaming, Inherent Dignity, and Conditions for Learning

Collective liberation necessitates learning. And for learning to be possible, we have to find ways to be okay with ourselves when we make mistakes.

Our conditioning is deep, and as Joanna Macy has said, the mind gets stuck in ruts and grooves. It takes time for each of us to learn, grow, and shift into new ways of doing and being. That reality does not absolve us of responsibility for the impact of our missteps, but it can help to know that we will make many missteps along the way, and the important thing is to be open to what we can learn from them and to keep trying.

It can be helpful if someone extends some compassion and grace to us when we mess up, because if making a mistake renders us as *being* a failure, the odds are we may stop trying and learning, needing to hide our shame and assumed lack of dignity. So, it is important to build beloved communities where people are committed to both compassion and rigor—where a mistake does not make us unloveable (compassion), but rather can point the way to further work (rigor) if we are willing to rise to the challenge.

How, then, can we create cultures where compassion and grace are extended to us and learning is possible? What if our mistakes are greeted with curiosity: How can this situation support moving closer to liberation? Is learning or unlearning needed? Is acknowledgment of harm and redress needed? With everything that happens, ask the question—what is the opportunity here for further liberation?

Of course, people who have just been impacted by harm may or may not be able or want to extend curiosity, compassion, or grace. Someone who was just harmed by you is not responsible for extending grace and compassion to you unless they are willing to, because they may need to prioritize their own healing in the moment. So, a path to liberation especially entails building the capacity within oneself and within the wider community to hold mistakes we may make in this way.

Self-Reflection Questions

How we have been treated when we made mistakes, especially at a young age, can be a vulnerable topic. The questions in this activity may bring up some deeply painful experiences. Allow yourself to pause and lightly feel into how making mistakes feels for you. Check in if you want to proceed.

> *What were you taught about mistakes during your early childhood?*
>
> *How were you treated after you made a mistake?*
>
> *How did you see others treated?*

If you have been taught that you *are* a mistake if you *make* a mistake, it can bring up deep shame when being confronted with mistakes you have made. The trouble with shaming other people after they make mistakes is that while shaming can sometimes create short-term behavioral changes, it often does not support the long-term growth and transformation needed for collective liberation. As a form of control, shaming can sometimes temporarily stop an action. However, it is usually counterproductive to sustained change because it tends to cause us to retreat from social engagement and curiosity.

Shaming (being told you *are* bad, as distinguished from guilting, being told you *did* a bad thing) is often experienced as an attack on our inherent worth and dignity, and often activates our nervous systems to be in a closed, defensive, and protective position. Conversely, settled nervous systems allow us more capacity to be open to learning. Safety and belonging support settled nervous systems and thereby the ability to be curious. This helps set up better conditions for learning to be able to happen. The more we can create spaces of belonging rather than exile, the more we support one another in our learning. The more we can build capacity so that mistakes can be learning opportunities, the better our chances are of moving toward collective liberation.

One complexity here is that people (especially people with dominant identities, e.g., white people) can *feel* shame when called out, in, on, or up (see Appendix A for the distinction between these), regardless of whether or not shaming tactics were used. This highlights the need for more inner work with shifting the above-mentioned conditioning that conflates *doing* a "bad" thing with *being* "bad."

For those of us accustomed to comfort, a different but related struggle is working with conditioning that makes other people into "bad" people if they challenge our comfort. This dynamic is seen prominently in white supremacy with an assumed right to comfort for the dominant group, and white people engage all kinds of defenses (aka white fragility) when their comfort is challenged. These defenses impede being open to feedback and the conditions for learning and growing. One space-creating question people with dominant identities can ask is, "Is it my safety that is actually at risk, or just my desire for comfort?"

Relationship and Skill with Conflict and Confrontation

Different cultures have different ways of approaching conflict and confrontation, as do individuals according to their life experience. Some are more comfortable with it than others. White supremacy culture has a prominent fear of open conflict, and especially conditions white people to be conflict avoidant. For those of us who have been conditioned to be conflict avoidant, speaking up in times of conflict and confrontation can require a lot of inner work to shift this lifelong conditioning. While harm is distinctly different from conflict (a difference of opinion), the dilemma of confrontation often arises after harm has happened, so we explore conflict and confrontation more here for that reason.

Whether you have conditioning towards conflict avoidance or not, many of us have grown up in a culture that does not demonstrate how to generatively engage with conflict. Depending on what we saw at home, school, etc., we may never have had healthy conflict engagement and transformation modeled for us.

> **Self-Reflection and Assessment**
>
> *How was conflict handled in your family when you were young? What was modeled to you in the larger society (e.g., at school, in the media)?*
>
> *What is your current relationship with conflict and confrontation? Does it feel difficult or easy for you? Does it bring up fear or avoidance? Or does it seem like no big deal?*

> *Do you notice ways you habitually react when faced with confrontation?*

As Prentis Hemphill explains in their book, *What It Takes to Heal: How Transforming Ourselves Can Change the World*, all too often we come into conflict wanting to defend our own position and innocence, and prove others' guilt, rather than being open to what needs more understanding and attention. Lacking the competence to engage skillfully with conflict, some of us may lash out and demonize the other party, setting up a polarization that does not support moving through the conflict or confrontation in a generative way. To be able to more generatively move through conflict, we need to grow our ability to simultaneously hold the truth of our own experience along with another's truth. Conflict can be generative and a way to bring us closer to our true needs and desires if we are able to keep our minds open to learning.

The depth and breadth of inner work needed to realize collective liberation is considerable.

Confronting and shifting our inner conditioning will at times require courage. Courage isn't some tough muscling up and soldiering on in a way that attempts to banish or ignore our fear; rather, it is a summoning of our deep commitment to something greater. We can root in our commitment to us all getting free.

As we conclude this chapter, here's one last self-assessment to help you orient to the work ahead.

> **Self-Assessment**
>
> *What areas of inner work are a priority for you to address?*
>
> *Who and what can support you to do that inner work?*

PART IV

Cultural Contexts

13

Culture and the Work That Reconnects

Portions of this chapter were written by Aravinda Ananda and Molly Brown, with a section by Rukmini Iyer and Mayuree.

The developers of the Work That Reconnects, principally Joanna Macy but also many others who have contributed to this body of work, have drawn on numerous cultural wells. The Work has also been profoundly informed by a Western context. It is important for facilitators of this Work, from both within and outside of the Western context, to understand the sources on which this work has historically drawn, and to be in right relationship with how cultural elements are engaged with. This chapter offers some initial suggestions for respectfully engaging with culture.

While people may be more familiar with external expressions of culture such as language, music, food, dance, dress, etc., Patricia St. Onge shares that, similar to an iceberg where only the tip is visible, culture too has deeper invisible elements such as "ordering of time, conversation patterns in various social contexts, patterns of handling emotions, eye contact, notions of leadership and approaches to problem solving."[1] In the 2014 edition of *Coming Back to Life*, St. Onge offered this definition of culture: "Culture is the behaviors, norms, attitudes and assumptions that inform a group of people who are joined by common myths, life ways, values and worldviews. It forms the group's context based on shared knowledge, understandings and experience, both above and below the surface of consciousness."[2]

The ability to interact with people from different cultures in a respectful way is a critical skill set for facilitators of culturally diverse groups. This includes being curious and learning about other cultures so as to be aware of appropriate language, taboos, sensitive topics, etc. There is no way you can be an expert on every culture, but you can be open and curious about cultures other than your own. An important foundation is knowing your own culture, including its worldviews, beliefs, and behaviors, and knowing that your culture is only one of many. From there, an attitude of curiosity can help you learn about and be more inclusive of other cultures. When drawing on cultural elements outside of your own heritage, there are important considerations for how to do so respectfully.

Cultural Roots of the Work That Reconnects

The Work That Reconnects has historically drawn on three main wells: engaged Buddhism, systems theory, and deep ecology. (See Chapter 4 for Marc Decitre's exploration of how deep ecology came into this work). While many people have contributed to the creation of the Work That Reconnects, and it draws on many cultural traditions, Joanna Macy's scholarship on Buddhism and systems theory was central in her development of Work That Reconnects theory and practices. We offer here some further context and cautions for the role of Buddhism and systems thinking in present-day Work That Reconnects.

Buddhism

The body of teachings of the Buddha, often called the Dharma, has been transmitted with care through many lifetimes and has taken root in different places around the globe. As it has traveled, it has been shaped by the cultural and political dynamics of each place. While essential Dharma teachings remain the same, different interpretations and variations arise by location and community.

Buddhism greatly influenced Joanna Macy in her construction of the theory, teachings, and practices shared in the Work That Reconnects. In her autobiography, *Widening Circles: A Memoir*,[3] Joanna shares about encountering Tibetan Buddhism when she lived in Northern India and worked and studied in a Tibetan refugee community. She further explored Buddhism in her doctoral work, receiving instruction in Vipassana (insight meditation) and studying early Buddhist texts. Her PhD dissertation, entitled "Mutual Causality in Buddhism and General Systems Theory: The Dharma of Natural Systems,"[4] explores some of the convergence in insights between Buddhism and systems thinking.

After living in Northern India, Joanna became more deeply involved with Engaged Buddhism. This more recent form of Buddhism emerged beginning in the 1960s from the teachings of Vietnamese Zen monk Thich Nhat Hanh. Engaged Buddhism applies Buddhist ethics, insights from meditation practice, and the teachings of the Buddhadharma to contemporary situations of social, political, environmental, and economic suffering and injustice. In 1966, Thich Nhat Hanh established a new order, the Order of Interbeing. Exiled from Vietnam for his antiwar activism, he continued to teach, lecture, and publish around the world, including in Europe and North America. In 1982, he founded his monastery, Plum Village, in southwest France. In his lifetime and beyond, Thich Nhat Hanh widely shared Buddhist teachings through his talks and over a hundred books on various Buddhist themes. Anyone who has participated in the Work That Reconnects has benefited from the perspective and teachings of Engaged Buddhism.

Joanna Macy has brilliantly translated Buddhist philosophy into a Western ecological and social justice framework, thereby making it more accessible for many people. Joanna weaves perspectives from the Buddhadharma throughout her teaching and writing, and into the Work That Reconnects. These perspectives challenge many of the linear, mechanistic assumptions of Western thought, recognizing the fluid, changing nature of the self, a "mutual co-arising" understanding of causality, and power as "intrinsic to the self-organizing nature of the phenomenal world itself."[5]

Facilitators of the Work can understand more about the Buddha-dharma by studying directly with a Dharma teacher as well as reading some of the many written resources available today. (See Recommended Resources at the back of this book.) Some Dharma teachers emphasize the importance of reading the Buddha's teachings directly in order to come into deeper relationship with them and be able to draw one's own conclusions.

Because anyone who experiences the Work That Reconnects benefits from the philosophy of the Dharma which has been woven throughout the work, facilitators may want to seek out ways to reciprocate with the people who have given so much to ensure that these teachings continue. For example, Tibetan Buddhists have tended the Buddhadharma with great care and sacrificed much in order to preserve their teachings. Tithing to Tibetan Dharma teachers when studying directly with a Tibetan Dharma teacher is one way to support this community.

Take care when sharing Buddhist practices or teachings to give appropriate credit to their origins and context, as they arise in many places in the Work That Reconnects. For example, facilitators often quote Thich Nhat Hanh: "What we most need to do is to hear within us the sounds of the earth crying," when exploring the Honoring Our Pain for the World phase of the spiral. The practice Bowing to Our Adversaries comes from the Order of Interbeing and Thich Naht Hahn's teachings. The inspiration for the practice of the Five Vows came to Joanna when teaching in a Buddhist setting, where the taking of vows is traditional. An exercise originally called by Joanna the Bodhisattva Check-in (but that has now been renamed My Choices for This Life) draws on the deeply sacred figure of the Bodhisattva in Buddhism. Giving appropriate credit when using any of these elements is only a starting place. Facilitators do well to understand the context, come into deeper relationship, and reciprocate for what has been received.

There are some teachings and practices facilitators may choose not to share at all. A significant example is with the Shambhala Warrior prophecy that Joanna received as an oral teaching from Tibetan Buddhist Rinpoche Choegyal Tulku. Having received permission and blessing to share it with others, Joanna has retold this teaching many times. Some facilitators who did not receive this teaching orally from a Tibetan Buddhist are choosing not to reshare it, while others are putting great care into their framing of this teaching.

The Buddhadharma has many gifts to contribute to the transformation needed in the world in these times, and those of us who use the Dharma can take steps to be in respectful relationship.

Systems Thinking and Indigenous Understandings of Interconnectedness

Systems thinking is a major body of work that has informed the Work That Reconnects and offers meaningful insights that help overcome the false separation inherent in a mechanistic worldview. If you want to offer systems theory in your WTR facilitation, it is recommended that you study more deeply on the topic. However, the field of systems theory that arose in the Western world in the mid-20th century with the work of Ludwig von Bertalanffy, Gregory Bateson, and others is only one source of teachings on interconnectedness. Many wisdom traditions have known for millennia that the life of the "natural world" is organized in interconnected organic processes rather than mechanistic ones.

Enclosure of common lands and the development of a mechanistic worldview in the 1700s catapulted many Europeans, along with people of European descent and people influenced by European colonization around the world, into a profound loss of the sense of the essential interconnectedness of all life and the embeddedness of humans within the web of life. Systems thinking and deep ecology present a rediscovery of this more ancient knowing by Western science and philosophy. It is important for Western facilitators to acknowledge and honor those non-Western traditions while being mindful of appropriation. Western facilitators can also acknowledge Indigenous wisdom in the Gratitude stage of the Spiral by pointing out that wisdom traditions have been inviting and teaching people to begin with gratitude for thousands of years; this custom did not begin with the Work That Reconnects.

The third phase of the Spiral of the Work That Reconnects was historically called "Seeing with New Eyes." As Patricia St. Onge—who is of Haudenosaunee (Mohawk) and Quebecois descent—shared in *Coming Back to Life*, the essence of many systems thinking and deep ecology teachings is only *new* for people who have become disconnected from cultural traditions that are based in interconnectedness. For St. Onge and her Indigenous family members, returning to our interconnectedness with the living Earth and the beings of all times is "seeing with *ancient* eyes." People enter this work differently and expanding the name of the third phase of the Spiral (into Seeing with New and Ancient Eyes) expands who is included, and can remind everyone present that the truths we wish to embody are as ancient as life itself.

All too often, Work That Reconnects facilitators have over-relied on Western cultural icons, including poets, philosophers, cosmologists, and teachers, in their facilitation. As you offer "brain food" in the Seeing with New and Ancient Eyes phase of the Spiral, reference more diverse sources about the insights of the interconnectedness of existence, rather than primarily citing European or European-descended systems thinkers. If you hold dominant identities, take extra care that you do so in a respectful way. Greater presence of voices of people from cultures and areas of the world where People of the Global Majority is the best descriptor, deepens the power of this Work. The movement in this direction expands understanding of equity grounded in unity and integrity of all peoples.

Avoiding Cultural Appropriation

Referencing with credit is an important step to take when borrowing from another culture, such as when sharing a song from another cultural tradition, but one's responsibility does not end there.

Cultural sharing between different groups can and does happen all the time, and greatly enriches our lives. Several factors distinguish cultural sharing from cultural appropriation including consent, relationship, and power differentials. Cultural appropriation happens when someone takes a cultural element from another culture without permission, without accountable relationship to the culture from which it is taken, and especially across power differentials.

Historical and ongoing colonization have greatly impacted cultures in many places around the world. Some groups have experienced a more long-term severance from their Indigenous cultural traditions. For example, some people with European ancestry may feel that Indigenous cultural, land-based traditions are lost to them. People who have assimilated into whiteness, capitalism, or other dominant systems have often given up a lot of connection with their cultural roots as a price of admission. This absence can lead people to grasp at others' cultures for the depth they long for, especially from cultures indigenous to the Americas, Africa, and Asia, and can often result in appropriation with harmful impacts.

For people who have more recently faced colonization and other causes of cultural erasure through systems of human domination, their cultural work may lie much less with avoiding appropriation, and more with reclamation and resurgence of their Indigenous cultural ways. For example, in India where Indigenous populations are working to decolonize from British colonial rule, some important work is embracing and reviving suppressed cultural practices, as Mayuree and Rukmini describe below. Many people around the globe who have faced more recent colonization and severance from Indigenous cultural understandings are working to reclaim and strengthen their Indigenous traditions that colonization sought to wipe out.

Cultural appropriation can feel particularly sensitive for groups who have been targeted by cultural erasure, that is, attempts to wipe out their culture. Erasure happens in both overt and more subtle ways. For example, many Indigenous children in the United States and Canada were taken from their parents and communities and put in residential schools in order to erase their cultural heritage and assimilate them into the dominant culture (albeit without the power and privilege given to people of European ancestry). After generations of attempts at cultural erasure, it can feel particularly sensitive to Indigenous people who have survived for remaining elements from their cultures to be appropriated by white settlers. Contemporary white people in the United States—by dint of their social, economic, political, and judicial power—are the current settlers. It adds insult to injury when they are able to be paid or receive accolades for sharing these Indigenous cultural elements in ways that are not accessible to Indigenous people themselves.

Myke Johnson's essay entitled "Wanting To Be Indian: When Spiritual Searching Turns Into Cultural Theft," written in 1995 and updated in 2008 and 2023, is a wonderful source for learning more about cultural appropriation. It is available on Johnson's website at findingourwayhome.blog.

> *For readers around the world, what ways do you see dominant groups where you are located taking cultural elements from oppressed groups without their permission, and without being in active solidarity relationships?*

Moving Towards Right Relationship

These questions can be a compass for moving towards right relationship with the use of elements from another culture:

- Do you know both who the people are from which the element comes, and also the context in which it originated?
- Is there a power differential with the culture you are seeking to borrow from?
- Was consent given for this cultural element to be used in other contexts by other people?
- Do you give credit and acknowledgment for the source of a cultural practice, teaching, or element?
- Do you have any relationships with people from the culture you are wanting to borrow from? Can you have conversations with members of those groups about use of their practices and what feels respectful and what doesn't, while keeping in mind that each

member of a group is an individual and not a representative of their entire group?

- If someone from the culture you wish to borrow from says, "You shouldn't do or say that," are you willing to pause?
- Are you in active solidarity in any ways with people from the culture you are seeking to borrow from? Do you have ways to be in reciprocal relationship—giving as much as you take?
- Are you benefitting from using or sharing the practice in a way that is not even accessible to members of the group from which you are borrowing? An example is being paid to share a ceremony when that opportunity is not available to people from the original culture.

Many of these questions are informed by Lydia Violet Harutoonian's February 2024 workshop on cultural integrity for Work That Reconnects facilitators[6] and Myke Johnson's essay mentioned above. As Harutoonian cautions, these questions can offer a compass, not a destination. It is possible you could have asked and received permission to use a practice, given credit, are in active solidarity with people from the original culture, and still people may feel upset about your use of the practice. Even if you are acting in integrity with the use of a cultural practice, it may open up deep pain for impacted people. Pain that is triggered may or may not be from the present moment. "Are you willing to be sensitive about this pain?" is an important question to add to the above list.

Drawing On Your Own Cultural Heritage

Whoever you are and regardless of your social identity and locations, you are encouraged to bring in your own cultural roots when facilitating the Work. You especially don't need to appropriate others' culture or assimilate into dominant cultures. Following some of the guiding questions for being in right relationship with different cultural practices can help meet the conditions for cultural sharing. While cultural sharing has many benefits and can deeply enrich our lives, our work is made more authentic by first drawing on our own cultural heritage, especially when done without centering it.

For people who have long been severed from their Indigenous cultural traditions (e.g., some Europeans and people of European descent), drawing on one's own cultural heritage may feel daunting and take effort. Many people are working on different approaches to recovery, such as Hilary Giovale with her recent book *Becoming a Good Relative: Calling White Settlers Toward Truth, Healing and Repair*.[7] Eleanor Hancock and Chris Crass, through the organization that began as White Awake and is now called Comrades Education, offer a course called "Before We Were White: Ancestral Recovery for Collective Liberation."[8]

If you are someone who has experienced severance from the cultures indigenous to your lineages, seek out support for this reconnection. There are others on this path, and you don't have to do it alone.

Cultural Relevance for Participants

Drawing first on your own culture heritage in a non-centering way (see Chapter 7 for more on centering), can and should be balanced with a commitment to cultural relevance and inclusion for all participants. Ascertaining in advance the cultural heritage of participants can help you to design your workshop to be relevant for all. Because you may not be able to obtain this information in advance, one way to be more inclusive is to share from your own culture (acknowledging it as such) and ask participants how their cultural experience is similar or different.

In the People of Color cohorts that happened in Oakland, California, in 2012, 2013, and 2014, many participants noticed that no one from their cultural heritage was quoted in the Seeing with New Eyes phase of the spiral. Primarily people of European ancestry were referenced when exploring systems theory and deep ecology. A 2024 participant in the Spiral Journey Facilitation Development Program from Botswana noted a similar dynamic when reading about Seeing with New Eyes in the most recently published edition of the manual on Work That Reconnects facilitation, *Coming Back to Life*.[9]

If you are sharing the Work That Reconnects outside of a Western context, there is no need to draw on Western philosophies unless you want to. Wherever you are, the encouragement is to draw first on your own cultural traditions as Priyal Shah, a Hindu facilitator of the Work That Reconnects who lives in England, does with the Hindu Vedas in the Seeing with New and Ancient Eyes and Going Forth phases of the Spiral. That being said, especially when working with different cultural groups, you can take care to avoid centering your own culture as if it were the only one, and respectfully include content that is culturally inclusive of who is present.

One Work That Reconnects practice that has been revisited in particular for cultural relevance is Harvesting the Gifts of the Ancestors.[10] In this practice, participants are invited through a narrated script to journey back in time, harvesting the gifts of what their ancestors went through. If you go back far enough in time, all humans share a similar ancestral journey, but in more recent generations, experience can vary greatly. An earlier version of the script spoke much more to the experience of European-descended peoples and as such was not inclusive of all people's experiences. Anne Marie Davis, a Person of the Global Majority living in California, rewrote the script for this practice, adapting it to work better for her experience and the communities she is a part of.

Davis's revised version is available on the Work That Reconnects Network website, in the Resource section, under "Practices," as well as in the 2017 special edition of the *Deep Times* journal on the impact of race and culture on the Work That Reconnects.[11] If you would like to offer this practice, check out how Davis has revised and adapted it, and then see how you can do the same for the groups you wish to share this practice with. Whenever making statements about shared history, consider what is relevant to your local context and members of your group.

The next section explores the authors' efforts to make the Work more widely accessible, sensitive and relevant across India's diverse cultural landscapes.

The Work That Reconnects in India

By Rukmini Iyer and Mayuree

In the vast and vibrant tapestry of India—a land of profound ecological diversity, deep cultural heritage, and complex historical and intergenerational ruptures—the Work That Reconnects (WTR) finds a fertile ground for seeding its transformative philosophies and practices.

India's Ecological and Cultural Mosaic

India's ecological expanse, from the Himalayan ranges in the north to the coastal plains in the south, encapsulates diverse biomes that have sustained ancient civilizations and modern settlements alike. This land has witnessed the ebb and flow of numerous cultures, each leaving behind a legacy of harmony and exploitation, wisdom and mindlessness.

The historical onslaught of waves of colonization, followed by rapid industrialization, has scarred India's landscape and psyche, leading to deep ecological and social rifts. The British rule is one example of the numerous ways in which not only the natural resources of this land were exploited but also divisive social structures were instigated that persist to this day. This epoch is layered over older wounds of assimilation of Indigenous cultures by mainstream religions and caste discrimination,[12] poverty, and gender inequality. Modern challenges such as deforestation, industrial pollution, and urban sprawl exacerbate these issues, manifesting in crises like air and water pollution, which are visible across all major cities of the country.

The complex web created by these environmental challenges and social issues requires a multifaceted and sensitive approach to healing and restoration. The Work That Reconnects methodologies, which emphasize interconnectedness and resilience, offer tools for addressing these crises in a holistic manner.

In contemporary India, the pressures of Business as Usual are palpable, with economic aspirations and urbanization often driving unsustainable practices. The environmental and social unraveling in India is not hidden; it is seen in the stark disparities between the wealthy urban centers and the struggling rural areas, and in the environmental crises that affect both the poor and the affluent. Cities like Delhi face severe air pollution, with Air Quality Index (AQI) levels often reaching hazardous levels. Rivers like the Ganga and Yamuna are heavily polluted, affecting the health and livelihoods of millions. The agrarian crisis, marked by farmer suicides due to debt and crop failures, underscores the vulnerability of rural communities to environmental and economic shocks.

There is a growing awareness and critique of this model, alongside a rising interest in sustainable alternatives that align with the principles of the Great Turning. Burgeoning movements, many unsung change makers, and community initiatives seek to reclaim and revitalize sustainable practices, ranging from organic farming to solar energy adoption through Indigenous knowledge systems. Grassroots movements, led by the Indigenous Adivasi communities and joined by city folks, are fighting deforestation and mining. These movements demonstrate how traditional ecological knowledge can inform and guide modern conservation efforts. The environmental activism of the Chipko Movement in 1973, where villagers hugged trees to prevent them from being cut down, continues to inspire contemporary movements such as the Save Aarey movement[13] started in 2014 in Mumbai.

Looking forward, the challenge lies in making the Work That Reconnects widely accessible and relevant across India's diverse cultural landscapes.

Creative Constraints for Adapting the Work That Reconnects in India

India's diversity means that there is no one-size-fits-all solution; instead, we must embrace a plurality of approaches and be open to continuous learning and adaptation. For instance, holding a circle with groups from different religious, political, or geographical backgrounds requires being open and curious to identify rituals and narratives that are matched to their worldviews and ways of life. Since it is not always possible to go with textbook knowledge or pre-researched data on different aspects of demographics and identities before meeting the group, the facilitators need to be open and engaged.

Holding space for this work requires a willingness to engage with the messiness and unpredictability of real-world situations, and to find ways to navigate through them with flexibility and resilience. It also involves recognizing that change is often nonlinear and that progress may be slow and incremental.

In India, caste operates as a deeply entrenched structure that shapes social, economic, and cultural realities in ways that are both overt and subtle. While historically rooted in religion, caste has extended its reach across secular and institutional domains, often reinforced by conversions and the assimilation of communities for survival, inclusion, or social mobility. Facilitators working with diverse groups in India must recognize that caste is always present, whether overtly or implicitly, influencing power dynamics and social interactions.[14]

The intersectionality of caste with class, geography, religion, and gender adds further complexity. For instance, caste-based hierarchies may manifest in group settings through language dominance or making marginalized voices invisible. Facilitators need to create opportunities to name and address these dynamics, fostering dialogue that challenges entrenched patterns of exclusion.

It is equally important to avoid specific religious symbols or rituals unless explicitly contextualized. Such symbols, while meaningful in certain traditions, may inadvertently reinforce hierarchies or alienate participants from other backgrounds. This demands cultural sensitivity, active listening, and the co-creation of inclusive practices that honor the diverse identities present in the room.

Decolonizing Mindsets and Embracing Indigenous Wisdom

The need for a decolonial approach in adapting Work That Reconnects to India cannot be overstressed. This involves recognizing, valuing, and reintegrating the Indigenous practices and approach of interconnected living rooted in cyclical time, interdependence, decentralized local governance, community-based resource management, and spiritual ecology. These approaches have been overshadowed by the imposition of linear, extractive models of development by a series of colonizers. This is combined with the aspirations of a large section of society to join the bandwagon of modernity, the industrial complex, and technological addiction, thus falling prey to widespread disconnection and a pathologizing of our emotions.

There is a need to distinguish the valuable re-membering and rekindling of Indigenous wisdom from its co-option into narratives of cultural superiority or nationalist pride. Reclaiming positive aspects of heritage must be undertaken alongside a conscious recovery from both unhealthy shame and inflated pride, each of which, in different ways, deepens disconnection. In this context, reflective practices and dialogue from the Work That Reconnects need to be thoughtfully adapted to integrate local and Indigenous ethos with discernment and cultural sensitivity. For example, chanting or singing devotional songs has historically served as a shared, unifying practice across many faiths and communities in India. However, in today's polarized socio-political climate, the public performance of such chants, especially those tied to dominant religious traditions (particularly Hinduism and Islam), can evoke unintended responses. Depending on the context, they may trigger resistance, evoke memories of exclusion or violence, or inadvertently reinforce religious supremacy, despite the chants themselves carrying universal and life-affirming messages

Creating Inclusive and Brave Spaces

In order to make the Work That Reconnects truly inclusive in a diverse land such as India, the design of WTR workshops and initiatives needs to ensure that all voices can be heard, especially those from marginalized and vulnerable communities and that all different perspectives are valued and respected, taking into account intersectionality of caste, class, ethnicity, gender, age, language, and region. One practice that has helped is to invite sharing in multimodal formats. When participants are invited to engage with the process through various forms of expression—including visuals, movement, sound, talking in mother tongue, or gibberish along with words—it creates a form of inclusion that mitigates some of the impact of privilege among participants.

Cultural sensitivity is crucial in this process. Adapting Work That Reconnects practices to the local context involves understanding and respecting the cultural norms, values, and traditions of the communities we work with. This includes using accessible spaces, local languages, incorporating traditional stories and metaphors, and being mindful of cultural practices and taboos. When the local people take ownership and participate in designing the process, it helps facilitators adapt to the cultural ethos of the specific groups. For instance, although growing up in the Indian context, we are aware that lighting a candle for Christians can be as sacred as lighting a lamp to mark the commencement of a journey is for Hindus. It was only while holding a circle in Kashmir that we learned to adapt the practice of burning seeds of the *isband (Peganum harmala)* shrub that has been part of rites for centuries in the Kashmiri tradition.

Diverse forms of collective singing and storytelling have been important ways of sharing knowledge and building community in many cultures in the subcontinent. Incorporating universal elements of sounds and narratives into WTR workshops have made the practices more relatable and engaging for participants.

The Role of Storytelling and Ritual

Storytelling and ritual play a significant role in the Work That Reconnects, helping to bridge the gap between the personal and the collective, the past and the present. In India, these practices are deeply embedded in the cultural fabric and can be powerful tools for reconnection and healing.

This land is steeped in diverse traditional narratives, such as folktales, myths, and legends, that offer rich resources for the Work That Reconnects. These stories often carry deep ecological and ethical wisdom, reflecting the interconnectedness of life and the importance of living in harmony with nature. By drawing from these narratives, WTR can tap into a collective reservoir of knowledge and inspiration that resonates with participants at a deep level.

For example, in the Hindu as well as Indic Indigenous traditions, there is a story of the Earth Goddess Bhoomi Devi that emphasizes the sacredness of the Earth and the responsibility of humans to care for it. Such stories can be used in WTR workshops to inspire a sense of reverence for nature and to encourage participants to reflect on their relationship with the Earth. Depending on the group composition, stories from different traditions will need to be sourced.

Rituals such as communal meals, nature walks, and meditation practices, can also enhance the Work That Reconnects by providing a structured way for participants to connect with themselves, each other, and the natural world. These rituals can be adapted to reflect local traditions and customs, making them more meaningful and relevant for participants. For instance, a simple ritual of making a mandala, honoring the five elements, offering flowers, lighting a lamp or burning incense can be a powerful way to start a WTR workshop, grounding participants in a sense of shared purpose and reverence for the work ahead.

The ritual elements of the Truth Mandala, for example, have worked better with fewer instructions among some groups in India. There is a cultural resonance and memory to rituals that are invoked by certain ways of setting up space such as the presence of an earthy centerpiece, or a feet-wash station at the entrance, incense, a certain kind of music and the like. Fewer instructions at such a moment lead to a higher chance that people will stay with the immersion and the emergence. Going through the entire list of instructions would bring people from certain backgrounds into a head space and make it harder to access their emotions.

This exploration into the Work That Reconnects within the Indian context is both a reflection and an invitation. It calls for a deep engagement with the land and its people, to learn from the past and to collaboratively envision a future that honors all forms of life. As we stand at this critical juncture, the insights and practices from India can offer valuable lessons for global sustainability and peace, reminding us of our intrinsic connectivity and shared destiny on this planet.

Through this work, we have the opportunity to not only address the pressing ecological and social issues of our times but also to rediscover and rejuvenate the ancient wisdom that has sustained communities for generations. Let us embrace this journey with open hearts and minds, willing to learn, unlearn, and co-create a more just and harmonious world.

Reflections and Questions for Further Exploration

Experiences of facilitating WTR in different contexts in India can serve as examples of how to adapt the Work to enhance resonance and receptivity. Some of these approaches could be rich learning ground for WTR facilitators across the globe, to consider if any of the approaches, practices or their adaptations may be useful in their local contexts. Similarly, facilitators from other locations may need to consider which instructions are important in their own context.

As we conclude this exploration of the Work That Reconnects in the Indian context, it is important to gestate some questions for further reflection and exploration that might embrace the wider cultural and social context in which the WTR is offered across the globe. These questions can serve as prompts for deeper inquiry and ongoing dialogue about how we can collectively navigate the challenges and opportunities of our times.

- How can we honor and integrate Indigenous wisdom and practices in our efforts to reconnect with the Earth and each other?
- In what ways can we decolonize our mindsets and challenge the dominant narratives that drive unsustainable and oppressive practices?
- How can we create more inclusive and equitable spaces for dialogue and action, ensuring that all voices are heard and valued, and challenging the deep patterns of caste, class, gender, ethnicity, religion, and region?

- What roles can storytelling and ritual play in fostering a sense of interconnectedness, liberatory awareness, and resilience in our communities?
- How can we balance the need for immediate action with the understanding that true transformation requires time, patience, and persistence?

14

Re-Conectando: Weaving the Mycelium of the Soul for Peace in Colombia

By Helena ter Ellen, Héctor Aristizábal, Liliana Moreno
(final editing: Helena ter Ellen)

The Mycelium of the Soul: A Guiding Metaphor

The soul's mycelium is a metaphor that embodies what we in Re-Conectando have experienced with our work in Colombia as the essence of the human spirit: resilient, interconnected, and continually evolving on the journey of healing and self-discovery.

Like the mycelium in the dark soil, it represents the intricate invisible network of experiences, emotions, beliefs, and spiritual connections within and between us. Just as mycelium extracts nutrients from decomposing matter, the soul's mycelium extracts meaning and growth from life's traumas and challenges. It embodies the nonlinear journey of healing, where diverse pathways lead to personal and collective transformation, empowering participants to move forward, supported by a shared sense of Active Hope. This metaphor celebrates diversity, fluidity, and adaptability, highlighting our ability as humans to thrive and evolve despite adversity.

From the Ashes of War: Re-Conectando's Origins

In 2012, the Colombian government under President Juan Manuel Santos and the FARC, the world's oldest and largest guerrilla group, initiated peace negotiations in Cuba, aiming to end a war that had raged for five decades. The four-year peace process that ensued was a period marked by tense calm, imbued with both hope and uncertainty, following numerous failed attempts in the past.

Amidst this backdrop, Helena ter Ellen, a Dutch facilitator of the Work That Reconnects with a deep commitment to the peace process in Colombia teamed up with a young Colombian peace activist, Felipe Medina, and started offering workshops in 2014 titled "Deep Ecology and Peace Construction," rooted in the Work That Reconnects methodology.[1] Although relatively unknown in Colombia, this team believed the approach could resonate deeply with the country's ancestral wisdom, helping grassroots leaders foster resilience, renew alliances, and inspire creative visions in the world's second-most biodiverse nation. Our goal was to support the peace process by bringing together people from diverse backgrounds, including many victims, and creating safe spaces where the pain of human suffering, war, and environmental destruction could be interwoven and transformed. In Colombia, areas of significant violence coincide with the presence of legal and illegal megaprojects, such as oil fields, mining, monocultures, livestock farming, and illicit coca crops, making it one of the most dangerous places in the world for environmental leaders.[2]

When peace negotiations concluded in 2016, President Santos, feeling optimistic, decided to put the internationally acclaimed peace agreement to a public vote. This agreement aimed to end decades of atrocities committed by paramilitaries, the army, and guerrillas, which had resulted in up to 800,000 deaths (with 80% being civilians), over 120,000 missing persons, the forced displacement of nearly nine million people, and widespread environmental devastation.[3]

However, the plebiscite held on October 2, 2016, saw 50.21% of voters rejecting the peace agreement. This outcome raised questions: Did Colombians desire to prolong the war indefinitely?

A revised peace agreement was eventually signed in November 2016, but the plebiscite revealed deep polarization within the country. Even among those who supported the peace process, many viewed the agreement merely as a procedure for disarmament, neglecting the beliefs and identities forged during the war and embedded in the collective and individual psyche, including those who had not taken up arms. Recognizing the tremendous need for broad-based accompaniment of this process, it became clear that the peace agreement provided an opportunity to create spaces for what we would later describe as "regenerating the soul's mycelium," harnessing its transformative power to transition from a nation perpetually at war to one beginning to imagine peace.

Reality obliges us to say that despite the peace agreement and all of the efforts to transform the country, Colombia still struggles with persistent violence from armed groups, slow implementation of key provisions of the agreement, the drug trade, political polarization, social inequality, human rights violations, economic instability, and displacement crises, making peace seem far away as of July 2024.

Accompanying the Truth Commission

One of the commitments established by the 2016 peace agreement was the creation of a Truth Commission (hereafter "the Commission") as an entirely autonomous state institution. Formed in 2018, the Commission included members from various sectors of civil society and was led by Francisco de Roux, a well-known Jesuit peaceworker. The Commission was given a four-year mandate (2018–2022) to address three ethical challenges: 1) clarifying the truth, 2) recognizing the victims and the individual and collective responsibilities, and 3) promoting coexistence, "Buen Vivir," and non-repetition.[4]

By the end of 2017 we had conducted twelve workshops, and Francisco de Roux, who had participated in our first workshop in 2014 and was convinced of the transformational power of our work, invited us—among many other allies—to support the Commission's challenging mission. To our knowledge, this was the first time the Work That Reconnects methodology was implemented and funded at an international institutional level. It was also the first time a Truth Commission incorporated a non-anthropocentric approach, recognizing nature as a victim of conflict.[5]

Our team had grown to include several Colombian colleagues from the fields of theater for reconciliation and audiovisual arts. Given the depths of personal and collective traumas throughout all sectors of Colombia, our intention was to continually alternate the Work That Reconnects—with its collective and transcendental approach—alongside theater, rituals, and more personal, nature-based healing and regenerative soul work. We recognized that these elements were inextricably interwoven, much like the mycelium network, to foster a holistic healing process.

A few months later, our deep ecology initiatives were rebranded as "Re-Conectando: Laboratories of Truth and Reconciliation in the Womb of Mother Earth." From its inception, Re-Conectando was viewed as a crucial ally in enriching the soil for the Commission's work in the regions and preparing participants for the process of truth telling and encounters with their perpetrators in subsequent events organized by the Commission.

Unlikely Dialogues in the Womb of Mother Earth

During the work of the Commission and in spreading its legacy thereafter, Re-Conectando traveled extensively across the country.[6] It was crucial for our team to find in each region a "womb of Mother Earth" that provided a safe space for our healing work, allowing participants to express long-silenced truths without fear.[7] We sought nature reserves not just as picturesque settings adorned with jungles, caves, waterfalls, and mountains, but as territories that had been stigmatized by violence and were now healing themselves and their communities through meaningful ecological and social initiatives.

Selecting participants from these polarized and fragmented regions was equally vital to the process's success. This selection took up to six to eight weeks, involving research, patient conversations with potential candidates—often initially suspicious and exhausted from decades of war and peace work—and careful collaboration with civil society and state organizations, particularly the Houses of Truth established in 28 territories. Many participants were direct or indirect victims of unimaginable violence, including forced displacement, massacres, assassinations, kidnappings, torture, and rape. Some were ex-combatants from various sides of the conflict seeking reintegration into society through restorative justice. Depending on the region, these might be local leaders from Indigenous, Afro and rural and urban communities, scholars and journalists, activists and artists, LGBTI-people, ex-combatants from all sides (guerrilla, paramilitary, armed forces), and sometimes even local entrepreneurs or politicians. In our invitations, we acknowledged the violence inflicted on Mother Nature by the capitalist paradigm and our lifestyles, driven by a schizophrenic sense of separation from nature for many of us living in the Industrial Growth Society, even in Colombia, the most biodiverse country per square meter on the planet.

Our extensive, sensitive, and respectful approach created ideal scenarios for the "Unlikely Dialogues" the Commission hoped for, inspired by the pioneering work of John Paul Lederach, an American professor internationally recognized for his groundbreaking work in the fields of peacebuilding and conflict transformation.[8] These dialogues, especially when set amidst the untamed beauty of nature and enriched with "wild conversations" with other-than-human beings,[9] gave deeper significance to the concept of the soul's mycelium.

Colombia's diversity is reflected not only in its vast ecosystems and species but also in its rich tapestry of ethnic cultural expressions. Just as mycelium thrives on diversity, interactions among individuals from various backgrounds brought a multitude of perspectives, insights, and experiences to the group dynamic. This diversity enhanced our discussions, sparked creativity, and fostered critical thinking, leading to deeper understanding and personal growth for each participant and the communities they represented. And it especially enabled significant experiences in building relationships across former dangerous boundaries.

A Rite of Passage: Reweaving the Social Fabric

We understand that a peace process involves much more than laying down arms. The hearts and minds of former combatants—and all participants—need to be disarmed, and these broken individuals must be rewoven into the fabric of the community. For this to happen, Re-Conectando introduces the power of ritual in most of her dynamics, as it allows participants to engage in a structured, symbolic act that fosters healing, reflection, and renewal.

Participants begin their journey with Re-Conectando by physically leaving their everyday environments and entering the nature reserve. This departure symbolizes leaving behind former roles, identities, and conflicts. Guided by our activities, they engage in rituals that mark the start of their transformative journey, entering a liminal space—a threshold between their old lives and the potential for new growth and healing. This liminal phase is characterized by uncertainty, vulnerability, and openness to change. Drawing on the concept of sacred time and space and propelled by the Work That Reconnects spiral, the rituals conducted in often breathtaking natural settings evoke a sense of sacredness and reverence. Victims, activists, and ex-combatants see a lush forest with new eyes, a place where they can feel safe and be received without judgment, allowing themselves to be touched by its healing beauty.

Participants of the Sierra Nevada de Santa Marta, leaving behind former identities and roles. Nature Reserve "La Helenita," Pueblo Bello. March 2022.
Credit: Maria Milena Zuluaga

In a country where nature has often been the backdrop for hiding enemies, assaults, bombings, torture, detaining hostages, and mass graves, and where gorgeous rivers have carried poisonous mercury or dismembered bodies, these rituals open up a mutual process of healing and care. Men and women who previously carried weapons and faced the harsh choices of killing or risking being killed for their ideology now learn with humility to make offerings of gratitude or ask permission before entering a wild sanctuary. It all invites participants to transcend their individual concerns and connect with something larger than themselves. Pablo, included as a child soldier in the FARC guerrillas, shared his experience:

> I was kidnapped by the guerrillas when I was 11, but then I decided to stay. I lived in the jungle for 35 years and didn't come out until the peace agreement. When we arrived and you told us to ask permission to the river before crossing it I wondered where the hell I was? But now, after this whole experience with Re-Conectando, I realize that even though I lived in the jungle and never cut down a tree or killed an animal unless I needed food or shelter, I never saw nature as I do now. I feel more respect and see it as a living being with the same rights as we humans have. (Laboratory in Caquetá, July 2019)

Identity Unknown

When participants first arrive at the laboratories, they are unaware of each other's backgrounds. This is intentional, ensuring that interactions are not influenced by identity positions that could spur enmities or hinder genuine encounters. The initial phase of the Work That Reconnects spiral, Coming from Gratitude, helps create a safe container, what we call "the membrane of trust," for the new ecosystem we're building together. Delegates from the House of Truth explain the immense task and opportunity the country faces with the peace agreement. Theatrical games are introduced to encourage creativity and free expression, creating a level playing field amidst mistakes and laughter.[10]

An essential part of building trust is the Market of Care for Life "farmers' market," where everyone brings their "homemade products"—or, in this case, projects. This activity allows everyone—even those who have committed atrocities—to share how they are working towards peace, restorative justice, and "Buen Vivir" in their communities. We are often astonished by the love, care, courage, and creativity hidden within these individuals. This process gives everyone a dignified place and role in our village.

Some participants exemplify the Re-Conectando principle "the medicine is next to the wound,"[11] like Virgelina, a former high-placed

FARC commander and participant in our Laboratory in Caquetá. She tells us how she and her former guerrilla comrades founded "Caguan Expeditions" after the peace agreement was signed. Their unique tour operation offers rafting adventures called "Rowing for Peace" on the turbulent El Pato River in Caquetá, a river they had often crossed during the war. Using their deep knowledge and strength, they now invite Colombians from all backgrounds, including victims and ex-combatants, to join ex-guerrilla guides in this daring meeting space in order to begin to break down the barriers of stigma and exclusion.

> Sitting down and rowing alongside someone who was once my enemy, or someone I harmed, and now having to row in unison, team up, and overcome obstacles together to avoid being swept away by the strong currents, is far more powerful than merely distributing peace agreements and talking about peace. Our commitment is to keep rowing for peace. Because rowing for peace is not just about reaching a river and going downstream. It's about helping each other to strengthen and build retaining walls that, at this moment, are creating bridges so that peace can flow.

Fostering Trust for Truth Telling

The Commission has emphasized the importance of fostering trust as a fundamental condition for truth telling, addressing one of the main losses left by war. This trust is crucial for revealing not just a mechanical truth, often repeated by victimized people or perpetrators who have given testimony countless times, but a healing truth, welling up from the deep waters of their wounded souls.[12]

Francisco de Roux, president of the Truth Commission, states: "We do not want a truth that deepens hatred and feelings of revenge, but a truth that opens us to compassion for what happened to us as a country, with our nine million victims. We need a truth that can help build a new country together."

During our laboratory, the mission of the Commission comes alive when we share a 40-minute recording of a personal message from Father

Francisco, who recounts the suffering of many victims he witnessed during the peace negotiations in Cuba. His straightforward yet compassionate stories awaken painful memories in most of us. Following the viewing of the video, we engage in the Museum of the Unspeakable, an image theater exercise inspired by Augusto Boal's Theater of the Oppressed. Statues and frozen scenes represent the horrors of war locked within our bodies. As we "visit" the museum and project our own memories onto the statues, we uncover the many faces of suffering and begin to embrace the complexity of Colombia's history. The images are polysemic, allowing us all to project our own experiences with the war onto them. This ocean of projections creates a deeply embodied way to enter the Truth Mandala.

Among the various practices of the Work That Reconnects offered, we have discovered—not surprisingly—that the Truth Mandala takes on essential meaning for the work of the Commission. It begins with the truth of participants' deep traumas and pain, which have rarely been addressed. It seems only normal that we put our shields up to protect ourselves from feeling the pain, especially the warriors. Vulnerability is often seen as weakness and can hold us back from opening up, or shame inhibits us from doing so. But the sense of containment produced by the group, the ancestral Mother holding us, and the metaphor of interdependence carefully woven through every moment of the process, all contribute to the practice of care as an embodied principle that upholds trust among the group. And then we discover that vulnerability is an extraordinary source of power and strength. Because it shows our heart, and we accept that rather than hiding our pain or shame, we can offer it as a gift.

It is often at this moment that participants learn about the groups to which others were associated. Former guerrilla members, paramilitaries, and soldiers face both their victims' truths and their own sorrowful and regrettable actions. Likewise, victims learn about and are exposed to the vulnerabilities of their perpetrators, creating a horizontal relational ground and fostering connection.[13] These transformative moments of deep understanding can only occur when participants feel safe.

Opening the Wounds to Find the Medicine

In a laboratory held in the Magdalena Medio region of Colombia, two victims expressed distrust toward a former paramilitary member's sharing in the Truth Mandala. "I felt that he did not speak the truth. Something stopped him from opening up to us and he just told us what we wanted to hear," Diana, one of these victims, said after the Truth Mandala had taken place. The facilitators formed a new circle for the two women to speak directly with the ex-combatant.

After hearing their fears and concerns, he responded: "It is very difficult to know that one is sitting here practically as a representative, because at the beginning I said: I come in representation of a group of ex-combatants, but I never said what group it was. Why? Because of fear. Right now you see me as an ordinary person. I was no longer the man with the armband, the rifle, who was looking at you and you had to lower your gaze because uh huh. No, not anymore." He explained that he felt ashamed, because, as he recalled: "Eighty percent of the atrocities that you just narrated has to do with the paramilitary."

After him being able to explicitly say who he had been, the group showed a renewed willingness to listen to stories of his present life, his processes, and the challenges he faces in reintegrating into civil society.

Although Re-Conectando presents itself as *Laboratories for Truth and Reconciliation in the Womb of Mother Earth*, we do not offer any incentives for asking forgiveness or working toward reconciliation. We understand that these actions are meaningful only when they come from the heart and are born out of the empathy created through deep listening in a nonjudgmental and safe space, free from pressure or expectations.

Laura Cifuentes, an officer from one of the Houses of Truth in our Sumapaz laboratory, noted in an interview:

> What struck me about Re-Conectando is that participants are not told what to do or what to believe. They aren't given instructions on what is good or bad, what should be, or the only way to do things. Instead, they are presented with doors

that open and pathways to explore. This approach sparked a significant reflection on the possibility of choice and responsibility, which I believe is fundamental to the spiritual dimension of peacebuilding.

In our laboratory in the Urabá region in 2019, several high-level ex-combatants from opposing sides of the conflict—guerrilla and paramilitary—participated, creating a space for deep listening and unlikely dialogues amidst the nurturing embrace of nature, on this occasion the Caribbean sea. Through shared experiences of awe, wonder, play, and interconnectedness, participants developed a greater sense of empathy for each other's suffering and a deeper appreciation for the sanctity of all life. This environment naturally fosters the need for sincere forgiveness, as seen between ex-paramilitary commander Dario and ex-guerrillero soldier Eduardo:

> Eduardo, my words are not going to give you back the parents and family that you lost as a child and that those same circumstances led you to make mistakes in life; but, today I want to ask for your forgiveness from the bottom of my heart and invite you to be that light for those who do not have light, because who else than you and I can tell the world that we can, Eduardo? And I will say it again, forgive me, forgive me a thousand times for the damage we caused.

After several days the former high level FARC commander Francisco was taken by surprise by what unfolded in the village between "us and them":

> I think this village, what we call Re-Conectando, is what I needed to heal my wounds. I never imagined I would be able to hug a paramilitary, someone from a group that killed my family. But look, where is the revenge? It's in smiles, in eating together, like brothers. I wish for all of us to reconnect, for all of us to belong to this village, to all of Colombia.

At the end of the gathering, Francisco invited Dario to join forces for peace:

With this PEACE that we will achieve, with these rifles we consign to oblivion—rifles that took away mothers and children—with this peace and harmony, we will help the communities that have suffered and heal their wounds. Let's join forces and build this peace together!

Dario responded while lifting Francisco in his arms:

That's how it is, brother. God bless us, and I will visit you soon!

Former paramilitary commander Dario and former FARC commander Francisco promising to work for peace together. Re-Conectando Laboratory in Necoclí, Urabá. August 2019.
Credit: Maria Milena Zuluaga

In an interview afterwards Dario concluded:

I do not believe in the kind of forgiveness that a judge orders you to do: "Go ask the victim for forgiveness," because that is a mechanical forgiveness, people are not even prepared for that. Real forgiveness is what we did this week, that came from the heart, that is the true reconciliation that this country needs.

We observe that proposing care for our shared natural world and ancestral Mother transforms into a powerful source of inspiration on the path to peace and reconciliation, not only among humans but also with the living body of Earth, as many ancestral communities in Colombia have long practiced. In the same laboratory in Urabá, beside the Caribbean Sea with its unique and healing energy, after cleansing their "inner beaches" in the Truth Mandala the group was spontaneously drawn to a collective act of material and symbolic restoration—gathering all kinds of debris from the beach. Standing proudly behind many filled garbage bags, facing the sea turning orange with the setting sun, the participants burst into singing Re-Conectando's anthem: "*Está pasando, nos estamos Re-Conectando!*"

The Game of the Elastics: Experiencing Interbeing

An impactful practice we have developed to experience interbeing and the theory of living systems[14] is what we currently call the Game of the Elastics. Each participant receives a closed elastic band, long enough to form various shapes by stretching it with different body postures. The elastic represents qualities or "medicines" that each of us carries within. Gradually, participants are invited to join their bands with others to create increasingly complex shapes until all the bands are intertwined into a single network. At this point, we ask them to describe what they see. Common responses include words like "brain," "community," "entanglement," "spider web," "ecosystem," and "mycelium." This sets the stage for a reflection on what might happen to the human and natural ecosystem if current trends continue.

Then the facilitator begins to separate parts, unlinking the participants one by one. At this point, they no longer represent themselves but are seen as parts of an ecosystem being devastated. Having researched the specific socio-environmental conflicts of the territory beforehand, the facilitator makes cynical, harsh comments during the disconnection process: "This is a river contaminated with mercury from gold mining, now lifeless, but who cares!" "This is a mountain being decapitated for its mineral wealth, but who cares! There are thousands of mountains in this country!" "This is an Indigenous community driven to extinction, taking with it a unique cosmogony, language, and art, but who cares? They're just obstacles to progress!" "These are orchids no one has ever seen, now vanished, but it doesn't matter." "And you, the social leader making a fuss about all this, we'll disappear you too. You're just a troublemaker, always arguing and complaining, doing nothing useful ... and nothing happens, because we are all afraid."

As the unraveling progresses, some participants start to resist the dismemberment, reflecting the real-life struggles in Colombia. The facilitator responds with increased determination to make them disappear, cruelly mirroring the harsh reality they face. Eventually, the network is almost completely detached, leaving only a few participants loosely connected by their elastics, while the rest lie disconnected on the floor.

At that point, we ask the participants how they feel about what has happened. They usually express feelings of desolation, hopelessness, and pain for everything that has been lost, realizing the deep impact it has on them. We sometimes comment on what remains, sharing facts such as only 17% of animals left on Earth are wild, 75% of birds are chickens, and almost 60% of mammals are cows. This prompts reflection on what these changes mean for the planet and humanity. Next, we invite participants to consider what they can do or contribute to prevent the remaining parts from disappearing and to regenerate life. As they name the qualities they bring to the ecosystem (e.g., "protect the rivers," "reforest," "raise awareness through art", they reconnect their elastics with the surviving network. This process continues until the network is fully restored, giving rise to a new, interconnected system.

This dynamic is rather painful, yet clarifying, serving as a perfect introduction to seeing our interconnectedness in the web of life through new (or ancestral) eyes, regardless of the role or place you occupy in this web. Often, we proceed by reconnecting participants to the causes they defend through the beautiful Work That Reconnects practice, Widening Circles. This involves working on their ecological self, cultivating passion and compassion, and opening up to new identities.

The Game of the Elastics—Laboratory in Escuela Gelva, Bochalema, Norte Santander, 2019.
Credit: Maria Milena Zuluaga

We invite participants to create small theater scenes in evocative natural settings, which themselves become actors in the performance. This exercise helps to strengthen the muscle of imagination and allows participants to fully embody the experience. Amidst liberating laughter or while holding their breath, the audience witnesses scenes where a victim takes the place of a perpetrator, a former combatant embodies a child of the future, or an Indigenous leader represents the CEO of the mining company destroying his land. This approach creates a transformative space for participants to confront past traumas, articulate emotions, and reconnect with their inner selves and a larger, collective purpose. Through Forum Theater, participants also practice agency by intervening as "spect-actors," exploring new, alternative approaches to these complex issues.

El Acuerdo de Paz: A Walk Towards Peace

Throughout all our activities—whether in heartfelt "wild conversations" amidst nature, during moments of playful interaction, or in the profound silence of our Gaia refuge—we recognize that the soul's mycelium is weaving together our past experiences, emotions, and beliefs. This intricate process shapes our present and future selves, integrating these elements to foster a sense of wholeness across our life journey. To deepen our experience of integration and interbeing, both personally and collectively, we have developed another ritual in our laboratories: the Peace Walk. This walk is inspired by the Peace Agreement, *el Acuerdo de Paz* in Spanish. "*Acuerdo*" comes from the latin verb *accordare*, meaning "to unite hearts" and it reminds us also of "*cuerda*", the cord that can guide us along the arduous path toward peace. Symbolically, our cord is represented by a fragile woolen thread.

The Peace Walk has emerged as a pivotal activity, symbolizing various facets of our national journey from conflict to harmony with ourselves and the natural world. Participants are guided to a rugged, untamed natural environment, brimming with challenging terrain—rivers to cross, towering rocks to scale, dense bushes, precipices, dark caves, mountains, diverse vegetation, and fallen trees. In silence and blindfolded, participants traverse this terrain, one hand resting on the shoulder of the person ahead, the other holding the thread symbolizing the *Acuerdo de Paz* concluded in 2016. Intuitively, each person decides where to grip the cord, leading the way upfront, amidst the group, or following behind, sensing the movement of the thread guided by those ahead. Guides assist when paths grow too perilous, facilitating a journey into the unknown. This collective endeavor serves to bring the unconscious into consciousness and reveal the unseen barriers within our spirit, heart, and body. It navigates uncertainty toward the horizon of peace and reconciliation—with oneself, others, and the Earth. Questions arise: What do I need for healing? What must I release? Can I trust those beside me, those leading me? Am I myself trustworthy?

The blindfolded Peace Walk, crossing the Arenal river in the Nature Reserve of Zafra. Re-Conectando Laboratory, San Rafael, Antioquia, January 2020.
Credit: Maria Milena Zuluaga

The Misak people of northern Cauca have imparted a profound teaching that inspires us to deepen our understanding about interdependence and deep time: *The past is not behind us, but ahead of us. We move forward by tracing the footsteps of our ancestors.* Moving forward does not mean forgetting the past or the ongoing challenges, but rather, learning from those experiences to prevent their repetition and honoring the pain endured by humanity and all living beings. Moving forward entails reconnecting with the ancestral wisdom of Indigenous peoples, listening to the Elders who have always understood the deep interconnection among all beings on Earth. As we walk, one hand rests on the shoulder of the Elder before us, while on our other shoulder, we feel the hand of what could be a child from the future. Together, we hold onto the delicate cord of peace, which at times breaks when someone stumbles or when the tension becomes overwhelming, prompting us to pause, reconnect, and then continue our journey towards peace.

We often share traditional tales as rich forests of symbols, embedding ourselves in collective rites of passage. The Borneo story of "The Half Boy" has been a guiding narrative for us on many occasions. This traditional initiation tale illustrates the journey from childhood (incompleteness) to adulthood (wholeness), culminating in the community's joyous celebration upon the return of the fully initiated boy to the village. During our Peace Walks, we immerse ourselves in the boy's trials of initiation from this timeless story. Each participant confronts their fears, pains, feelings of abandonment, vulnerability, fear, and the necessity to trust others for survival. At one point, we invite participants to pick up heavy rocks symbolizing the emotions or narratives that hinder their personal growth. Uphill, we carry our traumas, pain, resentment, desires for revenge, fears of authenticity, and more.

On other occasions, we pause by the river, using colored clay to mark our bodies with the stories and wounds life has inflicted upon us: feelings of inadequacy, shame, regret, fear, violence, illness, and destructive addictions. Each person engages in a self-generated ceremony, adorning their body with these marks. Then, with this marked skin, we proceed towards a waterfall or flowing river. When ready, we immerse ourselves, asking the waters to wash away the old skin we wish to shed, allowing us to emerge renewed, cleansed, and ready for a fresh start—a rebirth of self. Emerging from the waters purified and rejuvenated, as if reborn, we are welcomed into a new village where we sing and celebrate one another. We commit to embracing a new life and nurturing a country at peace with itself and in harmony with nature.

In our laboratory in Sumapaz, something extraordinary unfolded. Former FARC combatants and individuals who had suffered violence at the hands of the FARC as well as the national army (which was notorious for their atrocities in this region), came together. Among them was Mario Calle, a retired member of the army, now wheelchair-bound due to an anti-personnel mine planted by the FARC. Initially, over the first two days, many harbored resistance, distrust, and even anger toward Mario, who symbolized what many considered "the enemy." However, as they listened to his profound suffering and learned how he now dedicated himself to making wheelchairs for victims of anti-personnel mines regardless of their affiliation, a process of humanization began to unfold. As we prepared as a team for the Peace Walk, the challenge arose of how Mario could participate, given the wheelchair-accessibility issues on the path. To everyone's surprise, three participants—among them a victim of the army and a former FARC commander—stepped forward. They took turns carrying Mario on their shoulders, becoming his legs and enabling him to partake in this symbolic gesture of peace. This act became a powerful manifestation of mutual care that naturally emerged, fostering healing not only for Mario and his "carriers" but for the entire group.

Icela Durán, an officer from the House of Truth in the Magdalena Medio region, expressed in an interview after the laboratory in which she took part: "If we had established a Ministry of Re-Conectando in our country and given every Colombian the opportunity to undergo this transformational experience, we would all be much better equipped to collectively build peace—and it would have cost significantly less!"

The Truth Telling of the Living Earth

One of the significant contributions Re-Conectando has made to the Truth Commission is the recognition of our deep ecological connection, our innate belonging to Earth's living body. Miguel Grijalba, an officer of the local House of Truth in Norte Santander, shared after his experience in 2019: "We were really touched by Re-Conectando's ability to reconnect us with Earth as a living, suffering, sentient, wise, and healing entity."

According to Miguel, the Commission needed to include nature as an active participant capable of narrating the war's effects, the pain it has inflicted, and pathways to collective healing inspired by nature's resilience. As Mamo Evangelio, one of the spiritual leaders of the Arhuaco community in Sierra Nevada de Santa Marta, states in the final report of the Truth Commission:

> We as Indigenous people consider violence to be the reflection of our disconnection with nature. What we call violence today is the detachment from the umbilical thread with Mother Earth and the loss of knowledge of her codes. If we also consider Mother Earth as a suffering body, we should ask ourselves where her pain can be located. How can we hear it? Who can give testimony: a river, a tree, a spirit, a cricket?[15]

The truth of the living nature and the ancestral wisdom of what are called the "ethnic communities" will indeed be acknowledged as an important source for understanding the human tragedies experienced by different regions. It is interwoven into several chapters of the Commission's final report, notably in the chapter "Nature wounded by violence," in the Ethnic chapter focusing on Colombia's Indigenous peoples' resilience: "Resistance does not mean mere endurance", and in the chapter named "When the birds did not sing."[16] It is gratifying to know that Re-Conectando has been able to contribute, modestly yet profoundly, to fostering this awareness.

In the Final Declaration of the Commission titled *Convocatoria a la Paz Grande*, the metaphor of Colombia's wounded body[17] is employed, emphasizing that to heal the body of the nation, all of its parts must be healed. This shows how the Commission has integrated the principles of interdependence and interconnectedness—here at the level of its human trauma.

> We call for the healing
> of the physical and symbolic body,
> pluricultural and multiethnic,
> that we form as citizens of this nation.
> A body that cannot survive
> with a heart infarcted in Chocó,
> arms gangrenous in Arauca,
> legs destroyed in Mapiripán,
> a head severed in El Salado,
> a violated vagina in Tierralta,
> empty eye sockets in Cauca,
> a ruptured stomach in Tumaco,
> crushed vertebrae in Guaviare,
> shredded shoulders in Urabá,
> a neck slit in Catatumbo,
> a face burned in Machuca,
> lungs pierced in the mountains of Antioquia
> and the indigenous soul ravaged in Vaupés.

288 | COMING TOGETHER IN THE GREAT TURNING

The Colombian President-elect Gustavo Petro receiving the final report of the Truth Commission, elaborated by its president, Francisco de Roux and his team of Commissioners. Bogotá, June 28, 2022.
Credit: Maria Milena Zuluaga

Navigating Colonial Legacies

Colombia is a country with a strong religiosity associated with various branches of Christianity (mostly Catholic), especially in rural areas. However, beyond the Christian context, it is also a profoundly multicultural country, where numerous Indigenous groups and Afro-Colombian communities, descendants of people enslaved by the Spanish during colonial times, (representing respectively 3.4% and almost 10% of the total population) coexist. These communities maintain strong cultural identities and rituals, honoring a deep and sacred connection to the living Earth, that have been pivotal in their resistance against historical marginalization.

Re-Conectando is a cross-cultural proposal, so creating inclusive ritual spaces entails multiple challenges related to this past—and in the perspective of deep time, also this present—colonial context of Colombia. Our practices could be viewed with suspicion or even as a threat if the necessary care is not taken to always present them as invitations for participants to perform them from their own sovereignty.

Practices offered by Animas Valley and The School of the Lost Borders are really helpful in this context. Their proposals of self-generated ceremonies in nature are being woven into the tapestry of Re-Conectando, alternating collective dynamics such as the Work That Reconnects and the Theatre of the Oppressed with these soulful personal practices experienced in solitude. We observed that invitations like an immersion in their "Gaia Refuge," "wild conversations" with other-than-human-beings, offerings of thanksgiving, aligned with individual paths and intentions, foster self-awareness and personal growth. These ceremonies offer opportunities to confront shadows, fears and weaknesses, gaining clarity on life paths free from judgment or conformity.

All of these practices highlight the incredible opportunity contemporary societies have to transform themselves by drawing from different traditions and streams of symbolic content, allowing participants to craft rituals tailored to their life transitions and spiritual beliefs. We recognize that not everyone may fully engage due to personal convictions or challenges in connecting with the ritual's energy. Rather than criticize non-participation or judge it as resistance, we validate this as a way to explore one's own cultural and spiritual awareness and personal boundaries. Integrating post-ritual reflections encourages participants to independently evolve their understandings, supported by community resonance and personal storytelling. In this integration process, no one on the team dictates the meaning of the experiences or symbols discovered; instead, we echo the experiences, encouraging participants to interpret and redefine them as time passes. Sharing our personal stories is crucial, as it fosters mutual understanding and connection.

> Our goal is for participants to reclaim tools such as ritual and mythical language, which have been lost in the modern world. When appropriate, we invite participants from ethnic minorities who still practice these traditions to lead the way. We've noticed that many from urban contexts, with few or no traditions, feel relieved and blessed being guided by those rooted in Earth-based spirituality. This approach fosters our "unlikely dialogues" and mutual healing in a country where these communities often face invisibility and racism. Despite challenges, these have spurred meaningful dialogue on the enduring impact of colonialism and the imperative of integrating local wisdom and ancestral practices into Re-Conectando's work.
>
> Carlos Rodriguez—also known as "El Diablo," the Devil—is the Afrocolombian director of the House of Truth in Tumaco, on the Pacific coast. At the end of the laboratory in Buenaventura in 2019 he reassured us, stating:
>
>> Re-Conectando allows us to be reborn, reminding us of our own roots. It proposes a reconnection with life, with nature, as a vital source. We know that for us blacks, afros, indigenous people, for ethnic communities, the territory represents Life. (...) Re-Conectando helps us to reconstruct the truth and above all to contribute to peace inspired by our deep belonging to nature.

Weaving the Mycelium of a Soulful Society

The years of collaboration with the Truth Commission have yielded another potent harvest: the "Seeds of Re-Conectando." From the start in 2018 our intention was to identify community leaders, scholars, and artists from different origins who would strongly resonate with our vision and values and could champion our methods in their regions, integrating their own practices and ancestral wisdom. With dedication, methodological workshops, and mentorship, we've been weaving a network that already includes more than 50 people. In our online community of practice, ongoing training is offered and open source knowledge sharing is promoted. We've been empowering several leaders to start co-facilitating in teams under the guidance and mentoring of senior Re-Conectando members and some are now part of the coordination team.

Gathering of some of the "Seeds of Re-Conectando" in Casa Sumapaz, during a farewell ritual for cofounder Helena ter Ellen. Arbeláez, Colombia. July 2023.
Credit: Maria Milena Zuluaga

The vision of Re-Conectando Foundation, established in 2023 with the aid of a new donor, is clear: to sustain a flourishing network of people connected to their souls and the soul of the Earth, embodying empathy and interconnectedness. Together they can weave a tapestry of transformation, enhancing the healing of the pluricultural and multiethnic body of Colombia, holistic peace education, and environmental stewardship. Alliances are in the making to accompany efforts for climate adaptation[18] and internationals can now participate in some of our laboratories and connect with our mycelial network.

Our approach is intended to adapt and thrive in diverse environments, mirroring the resilience of mycelium in nature. The soul's mycelium, once planted, has the potential to transform Colombia's society, one connection at a time.

RECONECTANDO

You know you're dying
you feel burst
your insides
You bleed

/ lost in delirium
and the memory/

Life
at the end of the day
always achieves
break through

And you end up vomiting
/thank heaven/
the corpse
that you were dragging
/stubbornly/
in the deepest
of your tired belly

You stop clinging to the void
and that's how you manage to find yourself
In the boiling bed
of a sulfur river

Like the caterpillar that bursts
giving birth to colored wings
You break the shell
that clung to fear
and you start groping
but with sure step
around the world

/Without more light
May the light of your soul
Your old scabby skin
finally comes off
to pieces of your face

You will never be again
the terrified girl
that hides
Of her self
behind the mask
of her own hatred.

—Diana Forero,
poetess, former FARC combatant from the region of Meta

A healing poem that sprouted in the crystalline waters of the Güejar River, during our Laboratory in Lejanías in the region of Meta (February 2023).

Swings for the Children

I saw the waters of the Arenal River running calm,
And heard the birds sing with joy among the leaves.
I sensed the scent of freshly born flowers ...
But the misery of Colombia weighs heavy on me.
I long to carry a flower in my hands instead of a rifle,
For I know the horrors of war upon humanity.
I am a man who fought, believing in planting love,
And I am an ex-combatant because I cherish peace.
Last night, I dreamed of a land without evil or resentment
How sad it was to wake from such a beautiful dream,
Where there were no oppressors, nor the oppressed.
We joined our rifles to make swings for the children.
Let the breeze blow and wrap yourself in it and take with you

the echo of this poem,
Spread this message of peace to every village,
Let it be known that against injustice, we shall not retreat,
For I desire peace, not war, as the path forward.

—Ludwin Gomez,
former FARC commander and poet from the region of
Magdalena Medio

A poem written one week after the Laboratory in the nature reserve "Zafra," with the people from the Magdalena Medio region (April 2021).

www.reconectando.org
Check out our video of the powerful Laboratory in the region of Urabá (2019) and others:
https://reconectando.org/fotos-y-video.html

PART V

Going Forth in Today's World

15

Up Against the Limits: *Shifting* Towards a New Human Compact with Mother Earth

By Gopal Dayaneni and Brooke Anderson of Movement Generation

Introduction

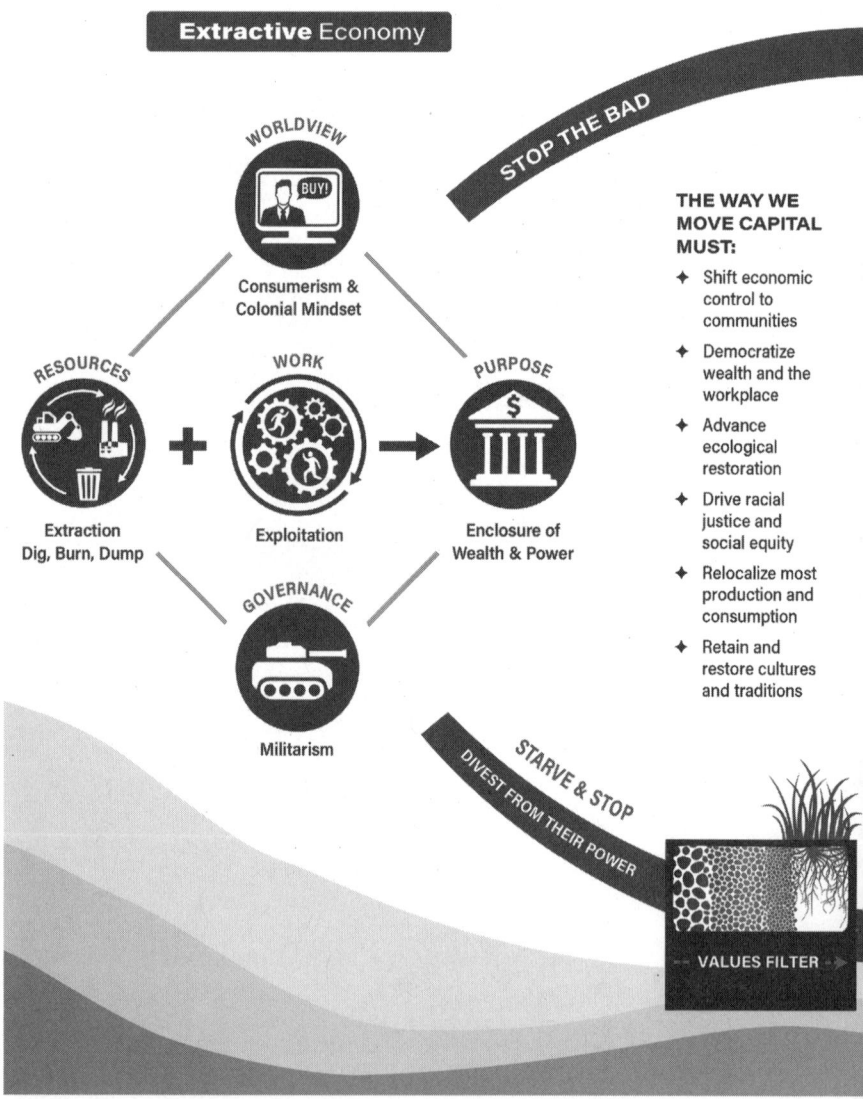

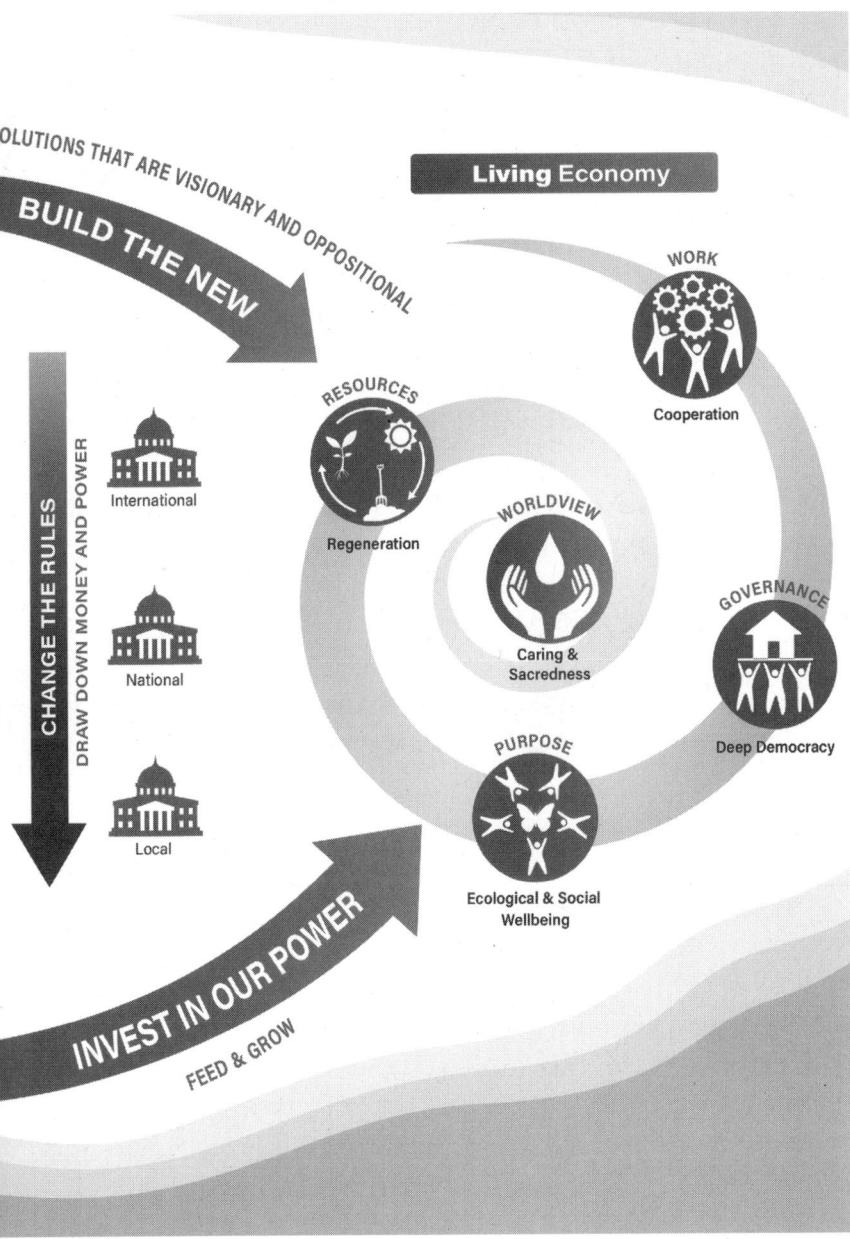

A Strategy Framework for a Just Transition
Credit: Design by Micah Bazant

When the author/editors of this book began to imagine who we would ask to contribute to its pages, I (Kurt A. Kuhwald) knew immediately that I wanted to ask Gopal Dayaneni, a cofounder of the Movement Generation Justice & Ecology Project (MG), to write a chapter. When he agreed, he reached out to Brooke Anderson, MG staff member, to team up on the writing. Movement Generation's work on the frontlines of climate justice is a legend among on-the-ground activist and frontline communities fighting for survival and for ecological justice in the United States and beyond.

Movement Generation's revolutionary Just Transition framework, shown above, reflects a comprehensive grasp of the profound shift in understanding about what it will take to reconnect humans to the more than human world as well as to one another, so that humanity's and the planet's future are truly free of oppression and exploitation and in deep sync with Earth's sacred processes.

MG's work[1] to "inspire and engage in transformative action towards the liberation and restoration of land, labor and culture" is a vital part of the transformative work that is, in truth, an essential dynamic of a global ecosystem of organizations and individuals dedicated to bringing transformative justice on many levels and in multiple global communities, for restoration and liberation of people and planet.

That important work, then, is part of a global engagement of frontline organizations that builds the kind of essential solidarity the editor/authors of this book recognize as "work that reconnects" writ large. It is mirrored by the work of the Work That Reconnects itself which *draws on foundational teachings,[2] including systems thinking, deep ecology and deep time, spiritual traditions, transforming the relationship with power and undoing oppression (summarized from the WTR network website).*[3]

On a more granular level, MG and the WTR share elements of analysis, understanding, and engagement that are deeply complementary. For instance, there is a specific convergence of analyses of global unraveling with MG and the WTR about what the WTR calls the *Great Unraveling*. The Great Unraveling produces multiple slides and shocks, and the WTR's claim that they can be used as opportunities for systems change rather than reinforcing *Business as Usual*, fits well with MG's vision about the effective actions necessary to achieve a Just Transition.

Lastly, though what is described above does not exhaust the similarities, complementarities, and mutually supportive dynamics between the two, the deep, active and courageous action both take on behalf of all life inspired our team to have a chapter from MG take its place as one of the two chapters closing this book. We saw this as a way to underscore the WTR's commitment to utilize the power of its processes and its work to contribute to collective liberation for all peoples, for all Earth's living systems, and for a global future that is profoundly liberative, safe, equitable, regenerative, and grounded in love.

Please note that, as is true within much of MG's work itself, this article focuses on and primarily uses examples that are drawn from organizations located within the United States. MG is a U.S.-based organization.

It is also important to note that the ubiquitous "we" the editor/authors have worked hard to unpack and dismantle in this book, is not how that first person plural pronoun is used by MG in this chapter. Rather, located rigorously and actively within the collective of Frontline organizations and communities, "We" becomes a reflection of their active commitment to shift the planet's social/economic oppressive design into a Just Transition from the vantage point of those who know the effects of oppression best.

Transition Is Inevitable. Injustice Is Not

The unfolding planetary ecological regime shift propagates impacts through all dimensions of life, from the biotic to the economic to the cultural and spiritual.

While there are aspects of this transition that humanity cannot change,[4] we can absolutely change how we experience them. The tendency towards climate or ecological catastrophism can lead us to imagine the future will only play out in the world as it is organized today. Even though social movements are committed to a better world, we tend to project into the future not just the ecological changes but also the unjust relationships of power in the world that both brought it into being and make its consequences acutely unfair.

At Movement Generation we say, "Social inequity is a form of ecological imbalance that inherently results in greater ecological erosion." If you accept this premise, then every action we take to transform our relationships from extractive, exploitative, abusive, and unjust toward cooperation, care, compassion, and consent changes not only what will unfold but *how it will unfold*. Yes, it is true that transition is inevitable. But the injustice, most certainly, is not.

This "Just Transition" or "Just Transformation," aligns with what the Work That Reconnects, and Joanna Macy have called the Great Turning. So how do we make this Great Turn? How do we not just *turn* but *return* to what is deep in our souls, stories, seeds, soils, and seas? How do we remember our way forward towards reciprocal relationships that do not perpetuate the false distinction between social and ecological well-being?

> We must remember that if "Ecosystems" are literally the relationships of home; and "Ecology" is literally, "knowledge of home"; and "Economy" is literally the stewardship and care of home—then Ecological Justice is the applied knowledge of our relationships of home towards Justice, which the Rev. Dr. Cornel West teaches us is, "what love looks like in public." This, of course, begs the question: What is love? To this we lean on our beloved ancestor, bell hooks, who reminds us that "Love is a combination of six ingredients: care, commitment, knowledge, responsibility, respect and trust." To this we will add, as bell hooks did throughout her work, consent.

There is often an assertion that humanity needs to have less of an impact on the world. But the Great Turning we need is not about "shrinking our footprint" or "minimizing our impact." Instead, we must have a much greater impact on the world in the next hundred years than we have had over the past five hundred—but it must be in a different direction, guided by a collective moral compass with new cardinal directions of cooperation, care, commons, and consent.

Navigating these questions with clarity may be the biggest and boldest challenge that needs to be faced. An organized, visionary, and strategically aligned push—*by thousands of social movements across the globe*—is the task at hand. While many social movements, from food sovereignty to disability justice to queer liberation, invite us to engage with complexity and diversity—and approach injustice and ecological erosion as entangled—we are often still unprepared for the ongoing shifts in the landscape of struggle. We need to expose the crisis for what it is and generate profound proactive transformations.

The following are some important strategic frameworks that we think will empower us to deliberately face the crises, and to recognize and navigate the rapidly shifting conditions that will help bring into being the *Great Turning* we know we need.

Harnessing *Shocks* and Directing *Slides*

Instability has become a defining feature of our times. In many ways, this instability is the new landscape of social struggle. It is useful to recognize that the different ways this "new normal" of instability manifests requires different organizing, mobilizing, and movement responses. It is also important to learn to read and forecast the differing conditions that confront us. One tool we use to name how instability is presenting itself is called "shocks, slides, and shifts."

Shocks present themselves as acute moments of disruption. These are, for example, market crashes, huge environmental or "natural" disasters,[5] and social uprisings.

Slides, on the other hand, are incremental by nature. They can be catastrophic, but they are not experienced as acute. Sea level rise is a slide. Increased unemployment is a slide. The soaring cost of food and energy is a slide that consists of multiple mini-shocks. Mass incarceration, erosion of democratic governance, and collapse of biocultural diversity are all examples of large scale changes, that while often experienced as personal shocks, on the macro level constitute slides.

While they share a set of root causes, the scale, pace, and implications of shocks and slides differ and, therefore, require different responses by social movements. One of our key roles, as social movements, must be to harness the shocks and direct the slides—*all towards achieving the systemic, cultural, and psychic **shifts*** we need to navigate the changes with the greatest ecological resilience, biocultural diversity, deeply democratic governance, and justice possible.

Shocks

As just stated, shocks come as acute moments of disruption. In the U.S. context they are the Deep Water Horizon oil spills, Hurricane Katrinas, or 9/11s. While they may be decades or centuries in the making, they explode onto our consciousness in a short, sudden burst, often dominating the 24-hour news cycle or social media. They can stun, hurt, and even outrage us. Different social forces typically jockey to frame what meaning[6] people make of these moments in order to advance their particular interest. Too often, progressive social movements are caught off guard by the shocks, without the infrastructure or access to shape a public response, let alone an organizing and mobilizing response. Meanwhile, regressive and dominant social forces seize the space and use the shock to advance their profit-based interests—what Naomi Klein has dubbed "Disaster Capitalism." In her book, *The Shock Doctrine*, she quotes artist and activist Harry Belafonte reflecting on Hurricane Katrina in the U.S.: "Katrina was not unforeseeable. It was the result of a political structure that subcontracts its responsibility to private contractors and abdicates its responsibility altogether."[7]

In the aftermath of the 2011 earthquake, tsunami, and Fukushima-Daiichi nuclear disaster in Japan, there was fairly widespread shock and horror, but little organizing to reveal the true cost of extreme energy.[8]

The moment could have opened up new space to rise up against nuclear power, but it instead was framed effectively in the mainstream by elites as a "natural disaster," "unpredictable," and "unique." Further, information of the disaster and impacts was vented to the public much the same way as the radiation was vented; slowly, so as to make the catastrophe appear less acute and easier to absorb. We are still not aware of the full impact of that ongoing disaster.

That said, the disaster was completely predictable. While their timing is often a surprise, most shocks are actually quite predictable, as inevitable consequences of our (mis)management of home. Japan is the Western edge of the Pacific Ring of Fire—the tectonic belt of land masses formed through volcanic activity and earthquakes. As such, Japan is home to 90% of all earthquakes and 80% of all severe earthquakes on the planet. *Tsunami* itself is a Japanese word that means "harbor wave." There are even "warning stones," as old as 600 years, cautioning future generations of where it is not safe to build along coastal Japan. But ancient wisdom and place-based knowledge are routinely forgotten or ignored in the interests of extractive-industrial development. There was some forward momentum in Japan to question nuclear energy and some changes in the European Union as well, but these attempts were not able to draw into question the larger problem of industrial development, the growth economy, or extreme energy.

Shocks and slides are of course related and often accompany each other. Shocks can trigger slides, and slides can have their shocks. For example, in 2023, there was the shock of the wildfires in Lahaina, Maui, which unfolded from a series of shocks and slides. The shock of the colonization of the kingdom of Hawaii (from 1798 onward) later led to a slide of increased tourism, corporate developments, and unsustainable agriculture on Lahaina resulting in the present-day devastating fires, leading to a slide of more land grabs, and a decrease in affordable housing for local Indigenous peoples.

To spring into action, social movements must first anticipate the coming shocks and proactively prepare for them. Shocks are, in a sense, easy to predict; but they are hard to organize around. While the timing of shocks is hard to know, they are certain to occur. Despite the dominant framing of shocks as unpredictable, anomalous, or "out of our control," they are actually inevitable consequences of the political economy. There is no drilling without spilling. There is no empire without blowback. There are no economic bubbles that do not burst.

Yet it is not enough for us to point to shocks as inevitable. Knowing about and even feeling the intensity of shocks does not automatically spark social action. Rather, our social movements need to be asking questions like: *"What kinds of leadership, organizing, infrastructure, skills, and planning are required to prepare for and harness these shock moments as key opportunities to articulate both the nature and scale of the crisis; as well as our transformative solutions?"* And, *"What are the material and cultural shifts needed to address the root cause of the problem?"* We believe that networking communities to identify and proactively build the infrastructure to mount a peoples' response to the shocks is needed. This includes rapid-response, mutual aid, and disaster collectivist infrastructure.

We know, for example, that the weather has become more extreme and predictably unpredictable, which means there will continue to be stronger, more frequent storms, floods, droughts, and fires. We also know that neither corporations nor federal or state governments have the capacity or interest to respond to these disasters in a just way.

We have seen more and more of this practice over the past several years. We've seen how, since Hurricane Katrina in New Orleans in 2005, mutual aid, disaster collectivism, and peoples' relief efforts have gotten better organized and more effective. During Superstorm Sandy in New York in 2012, we saw organizations such as Communities Against Anti-Asian Violence (CAAAV) and Occupy Sandy (born out of the Occupy Wall Street Movement) offer massive, direct, and well-organized relief to the most vulnerable communities—the ones FEMA and the Red Cross chose to ignore—and did so while bluntly stating that Sandy was not a "natural" disaster, but the obvious consequence of an economy based entirely on the exploitation of the labor of the living world.

We know that there is no drilling without spilling, no refining without fires, but when oil spills, refineries catch fire and mines collapse, each event is treated as if it is an anomaly—something we could never see coming. To create permanently organized communities, we must plan and prepare for these events so that our responses live into a better way forward.

Further, the shifts we need don't miraculously come from predicting shocks and slides. Rather, they come from a vision that guides us to anticipate how we're going to navigate the constantly shifting conditions. Creating a vision of the world is not new to our social movements. And we often use that vision to guide a multi-year plan (five-year plans, ten-year plans). But these road maps often are not equipped to respond to how rapidly conditions are changing under the weight of accelerating social and ecological erosion.

Shocks—Acute Moments of Disruption

- industrial environmental disasters (e.g, Fukushima and Deep Water Horizon)
- climate-induced extreme weather (e.g., Hurricanes Katrina and Maria, and the 2022 floods in Pakistan caused by heavy monsoon and accelerated melting glaciers)
- price spikes in food and energy
- pandemics and epidemics (e.g., COVID-19 pandemic)
- market crashes and bursting bubbles (e.g., 2008 housing market crash)
- military actions, coups, and covert operations (e.g., the invasion of Ukraine, genocide in Gaza, assassinations of prominent political leaders)

CASE STUDY: The Shock of Hurricane María and Puerto Rico's Fight for a Just Recovery

Arturo Massol Deyá of Casa Pueblo talks about his organization's work to build an "energy insurrection" in Puerto Rico in the aftermath of Hurricane María.
Credit: Brooke Anderson

Hurricane María's landfall on Puerto Rican soil on September 20th, 2017, was a shock—an acute moment of disruption—to the archipelago. Over 4,000 people were killed, three million people were left without power for several months, and 80% of the bioregion's agriculture was lost.

The hurricane was also the beginning of a battle between disaster capitalism and just recovery forces to shape how Puerto Rico would rebuild.

Of course, shocks can trigger slides, slides can trigger shocks, and shocks can build on each other. Such is the case with Puerto Rico—or Borikén, the Indigenous Taíno name for Puerto Rico. The first shocks to Borikén were Christopher Columbus's invasion in 1492, Spain's colonization of the island the following year, the ensuing enslavement of West Africans and Indigenous peoples of Puerto Rico, and the arrival of deadly smallpox and measles. The shock of colonization gave way to the slides of toxic pollution from U.S. military practice, the takeover of public fertile land by large agribusiness, the destruction of coastal ecosystems by luxury/tourist development, and of colonial, neoliberal policies that privatized Puerto Rico's natural resources and industries and plunged the archipelago into debt and austerity. All of these slides prepared the way for the shock of Hurricane María, but especially the loss of coastal habitat that otherwise would have slowed winds and flooding, protecting Puerto Rico from the worst impacts of the hurricane, and the centralization and privatization of Puerto Rico's energy grid, which made it vulnerable to long-term outages.

Puerto Rican social movements provide us with powerful examples of how to use shocks not to reconstruct what was, but to radically remake governance toward real resilience.[9] In contrast to disaster capitalism, Just Recovery is a framework that climate justice activists have used to build permanently organized communities to both weather the storms and build regenerative economies (or ways of managing home). Just Recovery requires a redistribution of resources and power, such that frontline communities are in positions of leadership to determine their futures and to build visionary economies for life.

Jesus Vasquez of Organización Boricuá explains that, in a Puerto Rican context, "We use 'Just Recovery' as a long-term process where we practice mutual support for the empowerment of communities through the relationships and local organizing efforts that have kept us together in the past, make us stronger in the present, and that will guarantee us a future together."

In Puerto Rico, forces of disaster capitalism (developers, bankers, corporate CEOs, corrupt politicians, and other architects of the extractive economy) used the shock of the hurricane to push their neoliberal agenda. They were attempting to liquidate Puerto Rico's assets to maximize debt repayments, implement drastic downsizing, deregulation, privatization of public services, and austerity measures like deep cuts in pensions, health care, and education, while shuttering public schools, displacing communities, and changing laws to allow for a massive transfer of agricultural land and commons to wealthy foreign interests. Their agenda was one that would have intensified the impacts of climate change and social inequity even as they sought to profit from the shocks that resulted from these injustices.

At the same time, social movements advanced a Just Recovery agenda, building and strengthening resistance, while working hard to create regenerative systems based on collective self-management, such as food sovereignty, solidarity economies, and mutual aid projects. Organizers on the ground in Puerto Rico repeatedly told us, "The problem is not the hurricane. The problem is the system. The problem is colonialism." If colonialism is the problem, then Just Recovery must inherently be a decolonial project.

In addition to demanding an end to *la junta* (the fiscal control board), and the cancellation of $74B of illegitimate debt, Puerto Rican social movements built hundreds of local projects that centered and advanced sovereignty—from community-governed micro-solar grids to people's forests, and from social kitchens to occupying abandoned schools. Here are a few examples:

- **Casa Pueblo's** community-controlled microgrid allowed people all over Adjuntas to store refrigerated medicine, plug in their respiratory equipment, charge their cell phones, and send messages to family through their solar-powered radio station.
- **Organización Boricuá's** peasant farmer members rebuilt each other's farms, shared ecologically appropriate seeds, and mitigated the impacts of climate chaos on small farmers.
- **Cocina Rebelde and Comedores Sociales** worked to feed the people in the aftermath of the hurricane and again at protests outside the governor's mansion.
- **Centros de Apoyo Mutuo** occupied vacant buildings for housing, created community kitchens, generated electricity through solar energy, and provided resources for trauma and healing.

Slides

In contrast to shocks, slides are incremental by nature. They are not experienced as acute even though they can be or become catastrophic.

Once set in motion, they are hard (sometimes impossible) to stop. Slides may be slower, but this does not mean they are less serious.

Take sea level, for example. We will not wake up one morning to find we are all washed away. Because of the sheer mass of the ocean (and the planet), the amount of energy it takes to increase the temperature and volume of the oceans is enormous and this process takes time.

Yet once set in motion *it will continue for hundreds of years*. So we will not likely *experience* significant impacts of sea level rise in California till closer to mid-century. Yet every day we delay in changing course seriously magnifies the future problem. The "landing" (or collapse) down the line for vulnerable communities in coastal areas around the world will become more difficult and dramatic if we don't effectively address the slide *now*. More importantly, the time scale for ecological recovery (reaching some new level of balance in the system) will take much longer—on the order of millennia.

Another slide, the predicted "collapse of California's agriculture," as it is often called, will not happen in a single, swift moment, but over time as well. This collapse refers to the economic disruption that will result from the degrading productivity and viability of large-scale mono-cropped industrial agriculture, as seen in the Central Valley of California. This is an agricultural system that is over-consuming water and fossil fuel, destroying topsoil, addicted to toxic chemical inputs, and dependent on the exploitation of immigrant labor and surrounding communities. Key components that drive these trends in food production are fairly certain: rising energy and farm-system input costs, increased instability of weather due to climate change, and dramatic reductions in available water supply. These realities form a slide that will change what food we can grow, where we can grow it, how much we can grow, and how we process and distribute what we grow.

How we manage that slide, where it lands, and the path it takes are not at all certain. Will California agriculture transition to smaller-scale farming methods based on perennial crops, polyculture management, drought-resistant tree crops, and long-term sustenance? Or will larger public subsidies and more violent water grabs continue to temporarily prop up the destructive, death-dependent industrial agriculture? Will we be able to transition "wine-country" into "food-country" in order to strengthen regional food security, or will we import ever more canned, GMO, irradiated, and processed food from far away? With the central role of California agriculture in the United States' food system and the economy, the stakes are high on local, national, and even international levels. Setting the agenda for the outcome of this slide will continue to be a key political struggle in the coming 20 years. It cannot be the sole responsibility of sustainable agriculture activists, small farmers, and farmworkers to lead on this front of struggle. Nor will we resolve the problem with small-scale urban food production (though it is important). We will need a new rural-urban political, cultural, and economic alliance to direct this slide toward regional sustainability and ecological justice.

Slides—Incremental by Nature
- sea level rise
- desertification
- deforestation
- rising costs of food and energy
- collapse of industrial agriculture
- rising unemployment

CASE STUDY: The North Bay Jobs With Justice Farmworkers-Turned-Landworkers Story

NBJWJ member Sandra de Leon adds branches to a burn pile in Santa Rosa, California, on December 18, 2022.
Credit: Brooke Anderson

In 2017, the North Bay (the communities north of the San Francisco Bay) experienced the shock of successive, massive wildfires. In some ways, this *shock* was an inevitable result of the *slide* of the desertification of land by big agriculture—specifically, the billion-dollar wine industry in the North Bay. Though depicted as small and idyllic, these vineyards are anything but. The wine industry has eroded local ecological balance and accelerated climate destabilization through planting monoculture crops, intensive water use, soil erosion, and applying toxic pesticides and herbicides.

Meanwhile, many farmworkers working for these vineyards, who are indigenous to Oaxaca but working in the North Bay, were escorted by vineyard managers through mandatory evacuation zones to harvest grapes while breathing in toxic fumes from nearby blazes. They report having worked up to eight hours per day in these conditions for as little as $20/hour.

Farmworker Sandra de Leon described it this way: "When we arrived at work, there were patrol cars because it was an evacuation zone, but they waved us through to harvest. The skies were red and heavy smoke was in the air. They didn't give us any protective equipment. No masks. There was so much ash on the grapes that when you'd cut the grape, it would get on your face. Our faces were black."

The shock of back-to-back devastating wildfires in California in the last five to ten years has created two possible paths: the disaster capitalism path in which farmworkers toil under increasing heat and smoke for low wages and no benefits while their labor further erodes over-extended ecosystems, or the path of Just Recovery in which immigrant and Indigenous farmworkers lead the way toward drawing down state and federal funding to apply the traditional ecological knowledge from their homelands to do controlled burns and vegetation management to bring depleted ecosystems back into ecological balance, along with good wages and collectively-governed work.

Through North Bay Jobs With Justice, many of these farmworkers are reclaiming their labor, previously used to erode the life system of the planet, to now restore ecological balance and to heal a fire-ravaged landscape and people. They know that the current wine industry will eventually collapse, so they are getting ahead of the impending transition, assuring that this transition happens justly.

Calling themselves *trabajadores de la tierra* (land workers), these farmworkers-turned-land-healers have drawn down hundreds of thousands of dollars of state and federal money to do fuels reduction work. With that funding they're able to apply their labor *not* toward the ecological devastation of the wine industry but instead to clearing wildfire-prone fuel-ladder brush and conducting controlled burns. Many of these farmworkers have now received their wildlands fire certifications, all while earning $35/hour wages—significantly more than what they made in the vineyards—and organizing their labor through worker-governed collectives. This fuels reduction work is of critical importance in reducing California's wildfire risk, which is worsening every day due to climate change.

Despite the physically grueling nature of clearing brush, workers say that while in the vineyards their labor is wielded against land, water, and soil, here it is used to heal such harm. Whereas the vineyard bosses treat farmworkers as disposable labor, here workers are well paid, safe, self-governed, and respected for the deep wisdom and relationships with the land they bring to the work. Together, they are growing an immigrant- and Indigenous-governed fire mitigation and ecological resilience workforce.[10]

No More Status Quo

It is worth restating that this new era of increasing instability signifies that there is no longer a status quo. This means that all social forces—left and right, progressive and repressive, are attempting to create shifts that solidify or improve their position. For the dominant forces, the pretense of stability and the predominance of "there is no alternative" are key to enabling large numbers of people to accommodate the disruptions we experience. If a disruption cannot be explained as "normal" then it is dismissed as an aberration. Economic downturns are talked about as "natural" cycles or the result of "a few bad apples."

In addition to this maneuvering in the cultural and public discourse, dominant forces are looking for structural ways to take advantage of the unforeseen and unplanned changes. For example, as the ecological means of production continue to erode, new speculative finance models are emerging to commodify nature. Couched as the "green economy" or "climate action,"[11] we are seeing further moves to capture and control nature via financialization—from the privatization of fresh water sources to the creation of markets that measure the carbon capacity of forests. More and more components of the natural world are being given a price at which to be bought, sold, and traded.

So our challenge is to both: 1) Clearly name the shifts we want and work towards achieving them, while also 2) Anticipating and exposing the false solution shifts being promoted by corporate profiteers and their political allies.

Shifts: Obtaining What We Truly Need

We define a shift as social, political, economic, and/or cultural transformation. From our perspective, we want, as an imperative, shifts in the direction of ecological resilience and social equity. We believe that shifts can emerge from collective "aha" moments when social movements awaken the popular imagination to new possibilities and spark social action. The coming *shocks* and *slides*—if we anticipate and prepare for them properly—can be key opportunities to spark these "aha" moments.

The Occupy Wall Street moment in 2011 is a strong example of a collective "aha" moment in which social action opened up new cultural space—most notably, a significant change in how wealth and corporate concentration and power are talked about in the mainstream. The early actions of Occupy, as manifested in the camps, attempted to model a better way to meet people's needs. Occupy then evolved into diverse expressions of community resilience, resistance, and self-governance.

Shifts also result from well-organized communities creating new institutions that meet people's needs in response to the shocks and slides *better than the dominant systems can*, such as food sovereignty projects, collectivized housing systems, cooperative economics (time banks, worker co-ops, food shares, community-based restorative justice projects, etc.).

The shock[12] of the SARS-CoV2 (COVID-19) pandemic shifted the political and economic landscapes in ways that created new contested space for shifts. The possibility that there might be a moment of collective reflection and visioning for a more care-full and just future were beautifully articulated by author and activist Arundhati Roy in her piece, "The Pandemic as a Portal." The pandemic created the conditions in which we could imagine massive shifts. Unfortunately, most social movements across the world were not prepared for the moment. While there were many expressions of mutual aid and collective care, our organizing efforts were unable to codify any significant transformations. While we hoped it might be a portal to a post-capitalist world; it turned out to be a pothole in the capitalist road.

Covid Activist.
Credit: Brooke Anderson

CASE STUDY: Rojava (Northern Syria)

Another example of people harnessing the shocks and directing the slides toward the shifts we need comes from Rojava. Following the outbreak of the Syrian Civil War in 2012, northeastern Syria experienced a power vacuum. Instead of seizing on the opportunity to create new nationalist borders and a new nation state of Kurdish people (the Indigenous peoples whose lands had been divided between the modern states of Turkey, Syria, Iraq, and Iran), Kurdish social movement forces created a democratic, autonomous region which is now home to five million people, including a multiplicity of ethnic and religious groups.

In place of borders and nation states, the revolution in Rojava opted to implement direct democracy at the level of the bioregion. Residents participate in public decision making in a system of democratic confederalism beginning with delegates elected by neighborhood assemblies, called communes. With women's liberation at the center of their direct democracy, all institutions have one woman and one man as co-chairs and require 50% women members, with women's committees having veto power over any decisions specifically impacting women. The communes also drive a cooperative economy, grounded in principles of ecology and sustainability. Despite persistent drought, attacks on the region's water supply, and pervasive pollution from military attacks, ecologists are working to reforest the land and diversify agricultural production.

For more information about Rojava, visit the Emergency Committee on Rojava at defendrojava.org.

Getting There from Here: New Approaches for Shocks and Slides

For reasons of ecological resilience, social equity, and movement strategy, we believe that we need to:

1. Remake governance to maximize direct participation by people in the decisions that affect their daily lives in the places where they live.
2. Remap the geography of governance by rejecting arbitrary, rigid, political borders and embracing ecologically informed, permeable, fluid, and interdependent boundaries relevant to the particular arena to be governed. For example, the governance maps for watersheds and trade-sheds and energy-sheds are all different for different places and they overlap in different ways creating sets of interdependent relationships.
3. Innovate on our existing movement strategies to more effectively respond to shocks and slides while simultaneously implementing a Just Transition out of the existing economy.

In all probability, future shocks will get more frequent and intense, and the slides will get steeper. Given this, we must move quickly to develop shared goals, narratives, and strategies to help us make sense of, respond to, and be resilient in the face of change. We must be grounded in a common vision while also naming and exposing the minefield of well-resourced false solutions that currently predominate the popular imagination.

We believe that this work of responding to shocks and slides while cultivating shifts will best be done at the local and regional levels. Of course, state, national, and international struggle will remain necessary as we seek to solve different problems at various scales, redistribute resources to communities, and act in solidarity with other peoples and places.

Yet, when transforming our relationships to food and water, for example, the most strategic boundaries for organizing (and, ultimately, for governance) must be drawn at an appropriate bioregional scale (i.e., foodsheds and watersheds). The scale and scope of the reach of any strategy—whether at the neighborhood, city, county, or multi-county level—will be different depending on the place and the objective.

Said another way: the scale of the problem does not dictate the scale of the solutions. Climate disruption is a planetary problem, but the necessary solutions are at the ecosystems scale.

That said, for our solutions to be effective we must understand how they relate to larger economic and environmental systems and must create enough counterpressure to stop false solutions moved at the state, national, and international levels. For example, when addressing food insecurity in a local community, real solutions depend on understanding global food supply chains, and industrial agriculture systems. Otherwise, false solutions, such as big-box retailers in poor communities, become the easy solutions. If we want to lower energy consumption at the local level, we have to understand and confront private utilities that rig the systems to ensure that centralized, dirty, costly energy is privileged over local, clean, community-controlled energy. If we are committed to restoring local creeks to bring the salmon home, we have to also understand their relationship to the whole of the watershed, from the headwaters to the ocean. We have to understand how disruptions at various stages affect the soil, water, and fish.

Once we start to think at regional scales and begin imagining resilient, democratic governance of our primary resources, our conceptions of community and place also need to change. When working to transform a foodshed or watershed towards bioregional equity and resilience, rural small farmers are suddenly part of the same impacted community as poor and working-class food-insecure urban communities.

The current shocks and slides of peak water, energy, and food create opportunities to build new bioregionally-based relationships. These alliances will not be easy to build or comfortable culturally, but they are necessary if we actually intend to govern. Currently, political borders and market-based economies separate rural communities from urban communities, though they are fundamentally interdependent. This false separation has allowed us to imagine cities as independent, self-reliant spaces, when, in fact they are not. Further, cultural isolation has been created between urban and rural residents; something that integrated, short-chain food systems and interdependent economic activity break down. Corporate intrusion into the food system on every level, from seed and soil to tongue and table, is made easier by the lack of bioregional organizing. Building these urban-rural relationships and alliances will benefit both communities.

In addition to being strategic, we know that the ecologically and socially responsible way to re-organize governance and economy must be bioregional. At the bioregional scale, the tendency to over-exploit, over-produce, and over-consume resources has more immediate checks and balances. The actual ability for a people to assess the consequences of their activity—and to govern their own solutions—is greater (and the impact more visible) at scales defined by resources and relationships. Without the concentration of these resources by power hoarders who are able to use their concentrated power to both externalize consequences on to communities and ecosystems *and* insulate themselves (temporarily, of course) from those consequences, we would not be experiencing planetary-level changes. This is one of the key reasons that we must re-localize primary production and consumption: doing so places us in a much more direct relationship with the consequences of our actions, particularly those that are ecologically and socially destructive.

A shift to relocalization and bioregional economics and governance does not mean that we must become isolated or that trade will end. Quite the contrary, trade and migration will continue—and become even more valuable—as constraint is applied in what is produced and how many people can live where in any given regional resource base. As an example, in the Western United States, trade up and down the Pacific Coast will continue, as it has for thousands of years; but over the next several decades trade *across* the Pacific, which is incredibly resource intensive and unsustainable, will need to contract. Trade over the Sierras will diminish some, and trade over the Rockies even more so. At the same time, the populations of the Southwest, such as Phoenix and Tuscon, living off of rapidly depleting water resources that depend on huge amounts of energy to divert and push them uphill for thousands of miles to desert cities (e.g., Las Vegas, as well as semi-arid Los Angeles) will have to move.

Of course, *local* does not inherently mean *democratic*. We are already seeing the rise of eco-fascism throughout the South and Southwest of the U.S., most visibly in repressive immigration politics and increased privatization of formerly public services, resulting in fewer and fewer services for those in greatest need. The intended result is a contraction of the population and a consolidation of control over resources by white nativists. Re-localization must be constrained by equity and democracy for it to be truly ecologically resilient.

In closing, we want to offer that our framework is not intended as a method simply for recognizing what is coming (as shocks and slides), as if that in and of itself helps us win the transformations we need. Instead, we think that understanding critical moments in this way can help us embody organizing praxis that transforms our relationships to each other and the whole of the living world.

Just Recovery, Disaster Collectivism, Mutual Aid, and the many examples used in this chapter, are all examples of the praxis of people reclaiming their labor to meet their needs in moments of shock in ways that also help them transform larger relationships of power. This transformation doesn't happen spontaneously; rather, it happens because communities prepare themselves for these moments by cultivating the relationships and capacities necessary to act.

Organizing in this way is work that reconnects.

16

Whose World Is Ending? Resisting the Climate Apocalypse Narrative

By AJ Hudson

Adapted from an article originally published in Deep Times: A Journal of the Work That Reconnects, *V. 7, #1, March 2022.*

With the horrific disasters our planet and this country (the United States) have been confronted with this year, and every year lately it seems, it is almost easy to forget that the world is supposed to be ending sometime soon due to climate change. According to the UN, we have 10 years to get our act together. 9 years. 8 years. 7 years. 6 ... How many years are even left? A few years for us to change nearly everything about our society. I know I can't be the only person fearful that they have lost count, that everyone seems to have forgotten. Add to this that the pandemic seemed to change how time flows, creating the paradox of feeling we are both travelling at breakneck speed towards the chasm, while also lurching snail-like forward lethargically and helplessly. Can both be true? When I think of climate change, I can already feel the time left for us to right the ship escaping me, like sand falling between my fingers. I know that for many folks, when they think of the immense responsibility we have before us to "fix" what is so deeply broken, they are transfixed with terror, paralyzed by a fear of loss, or frozen by the enormity of the crisis.

I am not here to tell you that it will be OK. If it was ever my job to console you, it is certainly and especially not my job in this moment or for this crisis. As a Queer Black man confronting colonialism, racism, and environmental injustice in the heart of the American Empire, as an intersectional marginalized activist with nearly everything to lose, my job is not to comfort you. It is to challenge. I am actually here to confirm that the apocalypse *is* coming. To let you know that the world is indeed ending. Nothing will ever be the same. But I am also here to question whether that ending is even a bad thing. If it is a bad thing, then who is this ending a bad thing for? Whose world is ending?

Truly, on this planet, there are many people for whom the world is already over. Who have very little to lose. Where are you right now? Some of them live a world away; some of them live a mile away; some of them live even closer. They will never see the nature that so many environmentalists are fighting to protect, they continue to have very little if any access to the resources that the climate change advocates are asking them to conserve, and they are not a respected part of the climate change conversation. Our society fears a coming climate apocalypse, but so many people in our society have already faced their own personal apocalypse, and at the hands of the same reckless and greedy powers which have caused this current catastrophe. When will their suffering hold meaning for the rest of us? When will that suffering become our priority?

This is why climate change cannot be fixed with a simple chart depicting emissions reductions, creative blockchain mechanisms, carbon taxation schemes, or other forms of various magical accounting that allow us to cancel out local emissions through trees planted (allegedly) entire continents away. Fundamentally there is no feasible technology real or imagined that can save us from ourselves, and if we can't see the incredible opportunity before us to change the problems that lead us to this very precipice in the first place, if we can't embrace that challenge to become something more ... then who are we? If we don't want to face that reality of the billions of apocalypses both gone and current, and instead choose half measures that will take carbon from the air but leave the world a shattered and unequal place ... then do we even deserve this precious planet?

For many fearing climate change apocalypses, they fear their lives changing forever, diminished from the privileges they now hold. They fear their access to natural wonders canceled, their children's economic futures made bleak and obscure, their sacrifices of comfort and convenience made in vain due to petty partisan politics. It is *their* world that is ending. Not mine. For so many others, the apocalypse has already happened. The world has already ended. In fact, the world has already ended countless times. It ended the moment Columbus landed on the islands of the Caribbean. It ended for the kidnapped villagers in Western Africa—my ancestors—when they were stuffed into the wicked belly of a slave ship and cast into slavery in a strange land with a strange new climate. It ended with the first blanket covered in smallpox. It ended on Thanksgiving Day. It ended with the Trail of Tears. Agent Orange. Hiroshima. The Holocaust. It ended with Hurricane Katrina, Maria, Kenneth, Harvey, and Dorian. It ended for George Floyd and Breonna Taylor. It ended in an ICE camp on the U.S. border. It ended with the Maui wildfire. It ended for the 20 million or so people killed by COVID-19.

So many people have already faced the ends of their own civilization. So many people have already faced the ending of their personal worlds. Most of these shattered worlds never truly recovered. None of them have ever been given what they, as sacrifice zones sanctioned to enable the perpetual motion of our economy, are owed. So many forgotten apocalypses lay heaped below the engine of the world we fear losing, sacrificed and discarded for the sake of its continuity and status quo. These sacrificed people have never even had a real slice of *this* world-at-risk, to begin with. This was not their world. These people and their ancestors know better than anyone how to tackle what's coming, and what forces have allowed it to come. They know the extent of the problem beyond its surface-level symptoms, fatally familiar with its cancerous rot. Even as the dispossessed descendants of these broken worlds face the new onslaught of climate change impacts which they have so little responsibility for causing, they still stubbornly fight for change. They fight against the very same systems that sacrificed their ancestors.

To be clear: our global civilization, the one that everyone reading this chapter is benefitting from, was built on the literal ashes of other civilizations. Meanwhile, a few white men from a few white nations have made nearly all of the decisions that have led our planet to this present point. To this present danger. Ending any inconvenient worlds that fell into their path along the way. Justifying their revolting actions with caste and class. In many ways, this looming climate chaos is nothing more than the culmination of those generations and generations of colonial recklessness. In many other ways, the terror of this oncoming apocalypse only reminds those with broken worlds of how forgotten they truly are and have always been. My family, and my colleagues in the BIPOC-led climate justice movement, have grown up out of these shattered post-apocalyptic worlds, they are our story and our education, they are our burden and our strength, and to be frank, the world that so many of you fear losing … is not a world that we have ever had full access to. It is not a world that we could ever truthfully call ours.

This is not to mean I am hopeless or bitter. I find great strength in honoring the generations of pain and suffering that have allowed me to exist and have given me my own small chance to change this story. It is in fact these billions of broken worlds that allow me to access a stream of radical imagination and audacious hope, to see a future that many mainstream climate activists, academics, and policymakers can scarcely picture. One way or another climate change will end our world. But not all endings are bleak. Not every end carries with it tones of Ragnarök or Armageddon. The future could hold the end of human life *as we know it* … but are you really certain that has to be a bad thing? Sure, this coming age could be the end of life on our planet.

Alternatively, it could be the end of all the ugly things that caused our environmental problems in the first place.

We are offered an unprecedented opportunity to change the very worst things about our society. To redistribute the power which has been continuously abused to lead us to this point. We are also offered an unprecedented opportunity to see our doom looming before us and to do nothing in response but try to suck carbon out of the air and spray aerosols. These are apolitical ahistorical solutions for a political problem that bleeds history. Like taking a mild decongestant when you have a critical case of pneumonia. In approaching climate change, we have a unique chance to change the scale of our society. To right centuries of wrongdoing. See, we have a choice: ignoring the social implications of climate change is also ignoring human suffering, the reckless extravagant greed and the global inequality that allowed climate change to happen. Honoring that suffering, and centering it, working to alleviate it, may be our only hope. For so many of us, the world is already over! Protecting this spent shell, that a few live on prosperously, does not inspire us.

Imagine a world without inequality. A world that doesn't depend on resources reaped through modern-day imperialism. An economy that doesn't depend on environmental degradation, or take homelessness, illness, and starvation as givens. A world without first-worlds or third-worlds. Without poverty and endless war. A world where nature itself has indisputable rights, and people of all colors have indubitable entitlements to access that nature safely without harm from police violence, pollution, and corporate exploitation. A world where a society's wealth distribution matters far more to us than its GDP. A world where we don't even need vacations because we have redefined and reclaimed labor as a source of joy, fulfillment, and healing. Is it hard to imagine? OK, that's fair. But how difficult? More difficult to imagine than a world-ending cataclysm like a megadrought? More difficult than the end of humanity itself? Perhaps that is a large part of the problem at hand: we need to learn how to radically reimagine the world that's possible.

Yet those voices who could teach this radical envisioning of the future, those voices who have already survived apocalypses, are too often excluded from this conversation. Their pain and suffering and broken worlds are not a part of the discussion. When you find yourself in rooms of privilege and power, with apolitical solutions to climate change that do not address social responsibility being poured into your ear, ask yourself who is not sitting at the table, and who is missing? Call attention to whose voice is not being heard. Who is not a part of the climate change dialogue?

So, let me also ask: Who has the most to teach our society about triumphing over unbelievable odds and hardship? Who is already faced with apocalyptic conditions on a daily basis? Who has already witnessed the end of the world? When do we let them speak? When do we honor their pain?

For those of us still feeling the urgency of our survival, and the fear of loss in the face of climate change, perhaps we need to reexamine the entire premise. My ancestors and my tradition frame this problem entirely differently. Human society will persist. The real question is: what will survive of who we are now? The best of our world ... or the very worst? It's our job, our privilege, to decide that, and as environmental practitioners, as activists, as academics, as concerned human beings, we will need more than carbon offsets to do our part. We will need outspoken bravery, a commitment to justice, and audacious levels of radical hope. We will need to know ourselves, and we will need to know history: that hideous stream of imperialism and colonialism that led us to this most current apocalypse and ended so many beautiful worlds on our way here.

This radical hope, this fearless acknowledgment of the horrors of the past, this bold imagination aimed towards the future is a key difference between the mainstream climate change movement and the climate justice movement that I have joined: we know that a world with less carbon in the air isn't necessarily a better world. Yet in fighting to keep carbon in the ground, not with technology, but by changing who we are and what we stand for, we can build a world that is better for everyone. A world that is more just, more kind, and so much less precarious than what we have right now. A world where pandemics and hurricanes and government-sanctioned killings don't shockingly "reveal" what so many of us have known as truth for generations. A world that finally begins to do justice to the countless worlds sacrificed in the name of this one.

Truly, the world is ending, and honestly, it's about time. Not all endings are bad. Far from it. The end of sexism, racism, corporate corruption, inequality, and apartheid in all its hideous forms. The real thing here is hope and the audacity, the bold daring spirit, to imagine a future that is so much better than what we have right now. Look inwards and ask: have you given yourself permission to see this future? I can see it. You can too.

Building this necessary audacity begins with realizing that the world we have now simply isn't worth preserving, and for so many people—the world's global majority, in fact—it never actually has been. This audacity is endowed to many of us whose ancestors were never a part of this world, who proudly and enduringly carry the ends of shattered civilizations on our shoulders. With a radical shift of perspective, this audacity, this fearless hope, can be yours too. Put more simply, it's not our world that's ending, and by letting go of it we are left with an incredible freedom. We are freed from those half-measure solutions that attempt to preserve the status quo. We reject those mere slivers of prosperity that we have guaranteed a few. We refuse to gamble with our survival rate like the quarterly profit margins for some Dow Jones corporation. This is the gift of shattered worlds and the wisdom of the sacrifice zones which is embedded in the climate justice movement: an audacious hope that challenges the conventional despair and denial that so often stands in the way of real climate action. We take another path. Instead of simply fighting to protect the world that we already have, a lie that we could never afford to believe in, we struggle to create the world that we don't have.

So, I ask you again, whose world is ending? Is it your world?
It doesn't have to be.

Afterword

By Kurt A. Kuhwald

In this Afterword, I offer a further necessary take on the intent and work of this book.

To begin, I gratefully take a note from the Preface of *When No Thing Works*, by Zen Roshi Norma Ryūkō Kawelokū Wong. As she wrote about her book, this Afterword (as well as this entire book) is:

> … a concentrate to which your own water should be added. Unlike deep sea diving, this inquiry benefits from coming up for air from time to time. You may even be disoriented by the words strung together seemingly making sense for which no logic can be made. It is part of the secret sauce of navigating the in-between spaces as you move from the one worldview that you and I intimately know yet are no longer served by, and at first observe and then slip into an emergent worldview.

Navigating from there …

As this book began to take shape—and its chapters emerged from the enormously creative labor of writing and editing by our team and its many contributors, as well as our complex, passionate, and sometimes difficult team dynamics—we three author/editors sought to figure out where my poem and its critical epigraphs could find a place. My teammates were gracious enough to accept that I was convinced it had one, but *where* was the question.

It was a bit of a conundrum.

I hope that conundrum is brought to a genuine solution by the fact that what I have written is a single piece, from its title, through the short introduction and prayer, through the epigraph, and on, landing finally in the poem's three-line conclusion—a single piece, like a single human being, complex and multifaceted, who has finally come home. Further, may what I have written bring both rest and resolve for you because you find here a large and embracing sensibility, a sensibility that I know as love: love for our beleaguered Eaarth,* and deeply for each other—we two-leggeds (of all ages), located precisely as Rumi's stunning words declared, in *the glory and the indignity of being alive in a human body*.

And may this book, in the profound work that is its body, even if in a very small way, bring us to a greater skillfulness of heart that we may keep close a wide knowing and embrace of sacredness—the sacredness of honoring more than one truth at the same time.

And may this book, as well, assist you, and the wider circle of its readers, to circle round and ground in a commitment to liberation and to bring your skills and gifts to liberation's profound and challenging work in this long dark of planetary crisis.

And, finally, may this book and this Afterword, as we, as you, turn to go forth from its pages, enliven your vision, deepen your courage, and open wide your heart to be a force for change and for good.

As a Lakota brother once instructed me to say
Mitakuye Oyasin …. We are all related

Elder Poem
Kurt A. Kuhwald

A Thatch of Epigraphs and a Signal to Remember

The poem that I offer here is a signal to remember that aging in Late-Stage Capitalism, that is, at the very least, the psycho-socio-economic rebar of Modernity, is both gift and unbridled vulnerability.

As Hollywood actor, Jack Nicholson, once excoriatingly said, "The older you get, the stronger the wind is. And it's always in your face." Human oppression is an equal opportunity barbarity. This book is devoted to opening, analyzing, and functionally strategizing how to understand and counter its effects within the Work That Reconnects spaces and beyond. Yet further still, it seeks to co-foster building the grounded possibility of human Beloved Community across the entire Eaarth—a community as diverse as the varied ecosystems that thrive across Its gorgeous and endangered vitality.

At 81 years of age, however, I was unable to imagine this book without a deep look, however briefly, into what it expressly means for Elders who know their longevity as a gift of psycho-spiritual power and who courageously face into the storm that is ever more voraciously engulfing the planet and all its systems, and for whom ageism emerges as a *far enemy*.**

Ageism emerges as a *far enemy* of the veneration that once had a greater purchase on public consciousness, but which has been literally drowned in the calculated and toxic flood of global corporate hype selling the corrosive, sunshine image of an eternal youthfulness where aging and death are banished.

That look for me, therefore, had to carry the full weight of our mortality and our innate morality. That look, then, had to come in a poem.

To lay a poem down into these pages—to prepare a way that it might offer "a measure of tenderness and grace" with which to exist, and return us "to the scope of our mortal lives" in these perilous times—I offer a preface in the form of a thatch of epigraphs harvested from the living archives of current-day world poetry and literature.

May they, and the poem itself, do their work in your heart, mind, body, and spirit. And may you enter them, as I have, held firm in the prayer offered by Joy Harjo, Muscogee Nation American poet:

With praise for the Breathmaker, by whose intent
We arrive here, and by whose grace we leave.

Thank you for reading this offering.
Kurt A. Kuhwald
Oakland, California, USA

Epigraphs

The West in me wants the mansion to last. The African knows it cannot.
    —nicole sealey, *Ordinary Beast*

My life is created as I narrate, and my memory grows stronger with writing.
    —Isabel Allende, *Paula* (quoted in *Trace: Memory, History, Race, and the American Landscape,* by Lauret Savoy)

Faith, like love, cannot be measured, but they will both be tested.
    —Amina Wadud, African-American Muslim scholar and activist

The poem is an invention that exists in spite of history ... In a time of violence, the task of poetry is in some way to reconcile us to our world and to allow us a measure of tenderness and grace with which to exist ... Poetry's task is to reconcile us to the world—not to accept it at face value or to assent to things that are wrong, but to reconcile one in a

larger sense, to return us in love, the province of the imagination, to the scope of our mortal lives.
—Meena Alexandra, Address to Yale Political Union

What happens when we claim the dark as a presence with weight and substance, rather than an absence of? What happens when we understand the dark as a location of the ultimate? Allow that change to be our guide, our goodness. What happens then? How might we see this moment differently?

Maybe we can use the darkness right now to steady our hands, to soften our spirit, to level our gaze, to ground our inside. We might be afraid, but there is wisdom for us right now.
—Malkia Devich Cyril, Talk at Thrive Sunday Event, January, 2025

All Law-breaking comes from that first evil thought, that original sin of placing yourself above the land or above other people.
...
I stand in this gully and see the Rainbow Serpent in one place; you stand on the hill and see him in another, and he gives us different messages that we are supposed to share with one another.
—Tyson Yunkaporta, *Sand Talk: How Indigenous Thinking Can Save the World*

"To decolonize" in Lakȟóta is *KhiLakȟóta*: *Khi* means "return to our own" and *Lakȟóta* " the people/the humans." To Tipiziwin, the *Lakȟóta* language revivalist, this translates to "a return to ourselves, our true selves." And that is the radical promise of decolonizing. It is to become humble once more in the face of life's greater intelligence.
—Rupa Marya and Raj Patel, *Inflamed: Deep Medicine and the Anatomy of Injustice*

Human speciesism (men over animals and nature), and supremacist politics (alpha-male over other human beings) draw the line of separation and hierarchy on which instrumentalization resides. But not everything can be instrumentalized. Poetry escapes from the

instrumental rationality that disdains the inner adventure of being. Poetry is a journal of existence and experience that unfolds like the branches of a living forest.
—Jesús Sepúlveda, *Poetic Reason in the Age of Digital Control*

I believe that the spiritual/ethical mandate at this moment is to go beyond the understandable.
—Rabbi David Cooper, Emeritus, Kehila Synagogue, Oakland, California

For the last 400 years, we have been told who we are by the wrong people.
—Fuse, Ghanaian-English rapper and educational entrepreneur

And why not a *black* unicorn?
—Dudley Randall, 1981 video interview

The poem is a plank laid over the lion's den.
—James K. Baxter, Christchurch, New Zealand

Every person, but maybe every ancestor (most specifically my grandfather) who has made a song not out of a desire to please or entertain or seduce a listener but because their sorrow or longing or happiness could not remain held only within.
—Joan Kane, Interview response about her poem *Hyperboreal*

Poem

Blade of Certainty

Not one is not given to ecstasy's lions.
Not one does not grieve.
Not one is not held in the arms of the rest, to blossom.
—Lines (reordered) from *The Lives of the Heart,* Jane Hirshfield

I
It is one thing
to take up residence
in the decades of our elder years
in a time when time

when time was believed to be flowing
into a vast and at the very least
if not welcoming then benign future

It is quite another
at every turn of vision
of imagining and hope
to face reality
now trapped
in a terrible and growing wound:

Violently riven through humankind
the grip of a deadly ignorance
betrays the earth
and the single heart of our human family.

II
It is one thing
to feel the nourished accretions
of a life lived long and deep
ripened in awareness
in skill of mind and heart and soul

mind and heart and soul
growing in maturity
if not fully
then surely enough

It is quite another
to face into the wind
stunned that no matter
where you turn
it is driven with a cold
so deep we may never
heal

III
It is one thing
to feel balance regained
innocence fully freed at last
these Elder years dripping
with unexpected sweetness
as blessing and gift

It is quite another
to feel everything
slipping over the edge
of a catastrophic precipice
propelled by an unhinged ferocity
so unrelenting
in its ignorance and greed
    its deep self-absorption
    its deeper fear

life-giving impermanence itself
is turned against us.

IV
Yet it is here
that the heart in its sacred musculature
its rich intelligence
its depth of feeling intellection

> grounded in silence beyond time
> embracing tenderly personal infinite
>
> cuts through
> as a fearless blade of certainty:
>
> Love has never
> will never
> abandon us

---

* In his 2011 groundbreaking book, *Eaarth: Making a Life on a Tough New Planet*, Bill McKibben purposefully renamed our planet Eaarth. His intention was to signify that the assault on our Planet's ecosystems had already caused irreversible damage. He added the extra "a" so that the catastrophic changes would be memorialized.

** In the canon of Buddhist literature, as well as practice, there are often references to *Near* and *Far Enemy*. A simple example: The *far enemy* of *loving kindness* is seen as ... hatred, ill will. The *near enemy* is ... sentimentality. In the prefacing of my poem, "Blade of Certainty," as well as in the poem itself, I was impelled to lift up the dynamic, centered in the heart, of *near* and *far*, which has become seductively and harmfully woven through the innate inequity of capitalism.

The *Far Enemy*, then, of *authentic veneration* for Elders is ... *ageism*.

Appendix A: Giving and Receiving Feedback About Harm

Credits: Aravinda Ananda compiled these suggestions drawing on many sources including but not limited to: work with Sarah Pirtle;[1] the blog on norasamaran.com; conversations with Naava Smolash; Sandra Kim's "Healing from Internalized Whiteness" and "Compassionate Activism" approaches;[2] Patricia St. Onge;[3] Nonviolent Communication;[4] Mia Mingus's work on The Four Parts of Accountability;[5] Loan Tran and Loretta J. Ross's work on Calling in the Calling Out Culture;[6] and Cynthia Ganote, Floyd Cheung, and Tasha Souza's technique called "opening the front door."[7]

Feedback is essential if systems of oppression are to be transformed. However, giving and receiving feedback about harmful impact can be particularly challenging. Many of us could use practice with more generative ways of giving and receiving feedback about harm than dominant culture has taught.

When harm happens, dominant conditioning is often to ignore what just happened, or if it is acknowledged, to attack by shaming the person who has just caused harm. While it is understandable to cry out when in pain, abrasive naming on its own and shaming don't typically lead to changed behavior for the person who caused the harm or healing for the person who experienced the harm. If the goal is collective liberation, it is helpful to take steps for everyone's dignity to be held with care.

What follows is an exploration of different options for naming harmful impact, and then some suggestions and steps to try for more generative ways of giving and receiving feedback about harmful impact.

Calling out involves public naming of the harmful behavior and sometimes a "call out" is most appropriate if there is a gross power imbalance, if the person causing harm is unresponsive to feedback, or if it is the only thing you have capacity for in the moment. Unfortunately, call outs do not always produce the most generative outcomes for changed behavior as they can tend to cause people to retreat and hide or to lash out in bewildered confusion or defensiveness. If we want to give feedback that supports healing, growth, and learning—conditions which support collective liberation and the shifting of root causes—we have a number of options for "calling in," "calling on," or "calling up."

Calling in entails naming a harmful behavior in a way that holds with respect the humanity of the person who caused the harm. A person who has just been harmed is under no obligation to do this holding, so it can often be much better for bystanders (people not directly targeted by the harm in the moment) to do the emotional and educational labor of calling in. For more about calling in approaches, see Loretta J. Ross's work.[8]

Calling on (a term from Sonya Renee Taylor) also names a harmful behavior, and holds with respect the humanity of the person who caused the harm, but doesn't include expending other emotional labor (e.g., offering empathy), or educational labor. Calling on asks the person who caused the harm to do the needed learning on their own or seek help for this learning from others whose identities are not targeted by the harm.

Calling up describes a way of engaging whereby your vibration and words are "calling the person up to a higher place" of deeper alignment with equity. Sometimes standing in our integrity and commitment to equity in a nonjudgmental way can be a welcoming invitation for others to join us there. One caution with this approach is to take care not to use it as a means to spiritually bypass the material conditions of oppression, because that would leave root causes unaddressed. It is also important not to call up from an attitude of superiority.

Note: When harm happens it is often important to center the healing and needs of the person who just experienced harm. This counters a longstanding trend towards the contrary. At the same time, if the person who has just caused harm is to have an opportunity to learn and grow, and thereby not do the same oppressive harm in the future, they can often use help. In many cases, without explanation they will not know why their words or actions caused harm.

However, expecting a person recovering from harm to support this learning may be much too tall an ask, and may reenact another pattern of harm involving default expectations of labor along certain identity lines. So, whenever possible, it is helpful for other people in the community to support this learning. To have robust communities where oppressive harms are acknowledged and addressed, we need many team players. Sometimes this need may be met within a single community, and sometimes we will need to meet it by connecting with other communities, such as an accountability group or an anti-oppressive learning space.

Giving Feedback

If you have witnessed harm as a bystander (you are not being directly targeted):

First check in with yourself: what is your emotional capacity and nervous system state? Is there anything you can do in the moment to feel more resourced? If you feel up for proceeding, here is a menu of possible options for naming harm.

1. Saying a quick "ouch" can register it aloud to the person who caused the harm but not otherwise interrupt group process. It signals to the person that they have further learning to do about the impact that just happened. If you feel willing, you could also offer some learning support, e.g., "Ouch. What you just said seems to have some painful assumptions embedded in it. Could we unpack this later together?"
2. Ask for a pause and check in with a facilitator: "I'm not sure if this is a time to pause and process what just happened or carry on with the next planned part of the agenda." Someone

in the group may say, "Please pause and process," or someone else might say, "Please carry on." One size doesn't fit all, so you need to build the muscles of assessing in the moment. And any given choice may not work well for everyone.
3. If it seems like the situation could serve group learning and cohesion if addressed in the moment, you could offer the feedback in the whole group. Another option is to have the group get into pairs with a prompt such as, "What is coming up for you right now?" while one facilitator pairs with the person who just caused the harm, and another facilitator pairs with the person or person(s) directly targeted. After the pair sharings, facilitators can assess whether or not to bring up more in the whole group, depending on their sense of whether or not there is consent from the people directly involved.
4. Speak with the person privately afterward, or request a co-facilitator or another trusted person to speak with the person afterward—either with or without you, depending on your capacity.

If you don't have the capacity to name the harm directly, you can at least privately note it to yourself and commit to do processing later on your own or with someone else. If the latter, you could even try doing some roleplays of the situation to help you work through possible options should a similar situation occur again in the future. With this preparation, you may feel more equipped to respond in the moment. Or, this may be a topic you want to work through in therapy or with a trusted friend if there are internal blockages keeping you from speaking up.

If you have experienced or witnessed harm (either to yourself or others) and want to call the person in for learning and growth, possible steps could include:
1. Assess if you feel you have the capacity to hold space for someone by calling them in at that moment, or want to attempt later. You may want to seek help. If you do not have

the capacity for these steps, trust your inner limits! Either stop entirely or try a resourcing technique to see if that changes your capacity. If you find you do have the capacity,

2. briefly recap specifically what someone said or did,
3. share why and how it was hurtful (if you are a witness, this may be sharing a guess about the impact), and
4. make a request for how you would like them to change their behavior or speech.

Steps 2–4, which echo Ganote, Cheung, and Souza's technique called "opening the front door" as well as the Nonviolent Communication (NVC) process of sharing observations, feelings, needs, and requests can support people in learning and changing behavior. If you have experienced harm, know that you do not have to be responsible for someone else's learning in that (or any) moment.

Receiving and Responding to Feedback About Harm

Once someone has named harm they have experienced through your words or actions, some steps you can take include:

1. **Pause.** As needed, **ground and center** using techniques that work for you. It can often be destabilizing to discover that you have caused harmful impact, and so it can be helpful to re-ground in the moment. You may have many habituated reactions to being confronted in this way. Taking a deep breath, pressing your feet on the floor, or using another technique you prefer can be a helpful way to create a little more space from your conditioned tendencies so that something else—responding rather than reacting— may become possible. This is typically an internal or at least a nonverbal step.
2. **Hear the feedback and really take it in** and allow it to register. Having an ability to hold both/and can really help you with this. You don't have to dismiss your experience, but you

can open with curiosity to the experience of another. At this point, this is also likely an internal or nonverbal step.
3. While it is not necessary (and can often cause further harm) to defend your actions or intentions aloud to the person who has named harm, it is good to internally **show yourself empathy and compassion**. This can also be done internally and nonverbally.
4. One way to **invite spaciousness and move toward curiosity** is to allow the possibility that your behavior was likely part of a larger system of social conditioning. Taking this collective, historical, systemic lens can help circumvent the default responses of hyperindividualism, namely shame and defensiveness. Rather than being a flawed "bad apple," you are a human being who has been conditioned in some toxic ways. You can affirm this for yourself without having to declare or explain it to the person who named harm.

    Lifting up to a structural or systemic lens can help with realizing that a single individual cannot take responsibility for an entire system of oppression, but they can attend to their own role and begin to address that. If the systemic connections are not immediately evident, sometimes it can help to process later with friends. Remember, if we have systemic privilege, it is often not easy to see the systems of oppression in operation until we have engaged in learning on the topic.

    Once again, this is typically an internal and likely nonverbal step to support oneself. These are quite a few steps! Without practice, you are not likely to be able to do all of these things in an instant, so you may need to say you need a little time before proceeding with the next step.
5. **Acknowledge the feedback**, either internally or aloud depending on what feels right. It may be helpful simply to reflect back what you heard. If you feel grateful for having been given this information, you might say thank you, knowing that there is a good chance it may have been vulnerable for the person to name the harm.

6. Depending on the circumstance, and if you feel called to, you may want to **offer a quick apology**. This does not need to be long and drawn out. It should center the person who experienced harm, not yourself. A common pitfall is for people to get bogged down in explaining their intentions or something else about their experience, and give little or no attention to an apology.
7. **Commit to repair.** You can inquire if there are any actions that the person who has named the harm would like for repair. If yes, try your best to follow through.
8. **Commit to future changed behavior.** It is also important to take steps toward not causing the same kind of harm again in the future. This may require learning more about the system of oppression you were consciously or unconsciously acting out, so you can grow in understanding of harm and complicity. Changing behavior can sometimes take a long time and require support. Committing to learning and changing behavior is an important first step.

To summarize more succinctly: hold yourself with compassion *and* own/acknowledge the feedback about harmful impact, apologize if appropriate, and commit to whatever repair may be possible. There are four suggested steps (steps 1–4) to take before you verbalize anything! It may take some time before you are able to do all of these—both in the moment, and also over time. It may require changing lifelong tendencies in order to be able to do these steps. If you aren't able to get to a place of groundedness or remorse that would authentically allow you to do steps 6–8, you could simply do the step of acknowledging the feedback (step 5) and commit to reflect on your role and responsibility in causing the impact.

If you do want to make an apology, it is only meaningful if it is genuine. Mia Mingus, a disability activist and transformative justice practitioner, wrote a useful guide on the four parts of accountability and how to make a genuine apology.[9] This can be used with people you know for lesser-magnitude harms. This is not necessarily applicable with more extreme forms of violence and abuse, nor when there is a gross power differential. The four parts include:

1. **Self-reflection** is about getting to a place of understanding the impact of your actions, knowing you have done something hurtful or harmful, and wanting to make amends or address it genuinely.
2. **Apologizing** is a chance to acknowledge and take responsibility for the hurt or harm you caused or were complicit in. This is an important opportunity to demonstrate to those you have harmed that you understand what you did and regret what the impact was.
3. Committing to **repair** is offering amends and rebuilding broken trust, and must be done in relationship. This can take a long time and does not proceed on the timeline of the person offering the apology.
4. **Behavior change** can take time for many reasons. For one thing, much of our behavior is deeply ingrained and often not even conscious. The important thing is making the commitment, and then setting yourself up with whatever support you need to address the underlying conditions giving rise to the behavior in the first place.

Once you have done whatever internal work you need to do to get to a place of healthy remorse, you could try including these components in your apology:

1. **Acknowledge the impact:** For example, "I want to acknowledge X impact on you when I did Y."
2. **Apologize:** For example, "I am sorry, I don't want to have that impact on you and I regret it."
3. **Offer repair:** For example, "When you feel ready, will you let me know if there is anything I can do that could help to address the impact on you, if there is anything I can do that would help you to heal from this, if there is anything that can help to rebuild broken trust?"

4. **Commit to behavior change:** For example, "I am committed to not causing this hurt or harm again and will work to change my behavior." Or, "I will do X, Y, or Z to support my learning on this topic."

Appendix B: Community Agreements

By Aravinda Ananda

Distinct from rules that are established and then enforced by an authority (a coercive model), community agreements are one tool facilitators can use to help shift the group culture towards collective liberation. They can help groups to learn and practice ways of being together that are different from what dominant culture teaches. As Sage Crump wrote in *Holding Change,* facilitation spaces can be "... a location of practice for learning and strengthening culture. Community agreements are the first moments in a gathering where you invite folks into a collective practice of culture building."[1]

I have moved towards calling community agreements or guidelines a "Community Container" because these behaviors collectively set up certain ways of being in community together. Most often, I will generate a set that I share with the group and ask if there are any questions or needed additions so that I offer a starting point—but not an ending point—if there are things participants need that I have not already covered.

I always like to tailor my community agreements according to assessments about the capacity of the group (e.g., level of awareness of systems of oppression and degree of inner work that supports self-responsibility), the purpose for gathering, and the amount of time available. For shorter gatherings, less time is available for setting up some shared social norms and agreements. For longer gatherings, facilitators can choose to spend more time with it.

For shorter programs, here are a few common community agreements or guidelines that can support undoing oppression:

Use I statements and speak from personal experience
Make space, take space
Obtain and honor consent

Another important guideline to explore is the difference between intent vs. impact and to emphasize the importance of acknowledging impact.

It is also good to have an agreement that supports naming and acknowledging harm such as "ouch, oops." See below for more about an expanded "ouch, whoa, oops."

It's important to take the time to explain when someone does not understand an agreement as well as take the time to address it, if people are not following the agreements.

Visions Inc. has put together a set of "8 Guidelines for Equity and Inclusion"[2] that I also find particularly useful and will sometimes incorporate into my programs with proper credit.

I also appreciate Parker J. Palmer's suggestion from his Circle of Trust approach which is, "When the going gets rough, turn to wonder" as a way to encourage openness and curiosity when we inevitably encounter challenges.

For longer programs, you can take more time with the culture-building aspect of setting up a community container as well as maintaining that container. Here's what I offered to begin a longer program (five days) for a group of people experienced in the Work That Reconnects and who already had some undoing oppression experience.

2022 Interdependence JAM: Community Container

care for the self, care for the group and care for the earth

We invite you to lean in with us to build Beloved Community and transform oppressive conditioning and behavior as it arises among us during our time together. To help support us in this intention, here are some ways of being we are asking you to commit to:

Presence. When in group session together, be as present as you are able to be, bringing your caring attention.

Self responsibility. Take a good deal of responsibility for yourself including your triggers and reactions; attend to what you need for self care; and ask for support when you need it.

Mutual support and care of the whole. As you are able to, have each others' backs and extend care to others. Part of this commitment is balancing some of your personal needs with other needs in the group. One way this could look is showing up on time for shared sessions, or if you need to be late for a session, letting someone know so the group is not waiting for you.

Brave space. This is a space where we invite you to be in learning, and take risks with dismantling oppressive conditioning and behavior. We want to be, as Sandra Kim says, "soft on the person, hard on the system." If you feel or see an "ouch," this is encouragement to speak up about it as soon as you are able to, holding as best you can the principle of mutual support. This space is also meant to be a place where you can practice how you offer feedback when "ouches" happen, leaning towards ways that hold all of our humanity.

Compassion. Turn towards compassion for yourself and for one another. We are each learning how to be better humans each day. It isn't about perfection, but about holding each other's humanity as we live and work to get free of systems of oppression. As adrienne maree brown encourages us to do, we will strive to move at "the speed of trust."

Accountability. If you contribute to an "ouch," practice turning towards acknowledgment, listening, and exploring if there is any repair you can offer. This may take some time.

An equity lens. Lean in to developing an equity lens—in each decision you face, increasingly consider what can serve equity. One way this could look is if you tend to talk a lot in groups, hold back sometimes to ensure there is space for less heard voices.

Consent. Practice asking for and honoring consent. This is for all beings, including yourself.

Confidentiality. Given that some of what we will be sharing will be personal in nature, please don't share any content with identifying characteristics outside of our time together. Double confidentiality means that if someone shares something personal, you wouldn't approach them later and bring it up without first asking for and honoring their consent.

"Ouch, Whoa, Oops"

Many of you may be more familiar with "Ouch, Oops" as a model for acknowledging and interrupting harm. I was excited to encounter an expansion of this with "Ouch, Whoa, Oops" as explained by the North Pacific Yearly Meeting.[3] Groups can agree that people are welcomed and encouraged to say:

- **"Ouch"** when you want to publicly acknowledge that you just experienced a harmful impact. (Keep in mind that feeling uncomfortable is different than being harmed.)
- **"Whoa"** when you witness something that reinforces some type of systemic oppression or dehumanization and you want to draw everyone's attention to it.
- **"Oops"** when you want to acknowledge that you have done something that was experienced as harm or that reinforced systemic oppression.

This offers a tool to publicly acknowledge impacts, even if everyone present does not fully understand what happened, and offers an important opportunity for the group to interrupt the normalization of oppressive harm.

Most often, the oppressive harm we cause is because of unconscious bias, so we won't even know that we said or did something harmful until it is pointed out to us, and we may not be able to understand how or why what we said or did was oppressive without further learning. Sometimes a group may choose to explore why or how something was harmful in the moment, and other times this learning is better done outside of group time. "Ouch," "whoa," and "oops" are primarily a means of public acknowledgment, but depending on the depth of harm experienced, more may be needed beyond just acknowledgment.

The person who experienced the "ouch" or witnessed the "whoa" may not have the energy or willingness in the moment to explain how or why something was harmful, so it can be helpful to have opportunities to debrief later.

After someone says "ouch" or "whoa," the next invitation is to **pause and take a few breaths.** Take a moment to **sense into: "What is a caring response to this expression of pain?"** and then **choose a response based on that**. Sometimes it will just be acknowledgment such as with saying "oops," and sometimes it will entail more, such as offering an apology or other amends.

As most of us do not want to cause harm, it can be a bit destabilizing to learn that we have just caused or contributed to harm, and may bring up a lot of painful conditioning for us about making a mistake, our inherent worth and dignity, etc. Because we likely did not intend to cause harm, we may feel the urge to explain our intentions. That is not the purpose of "oops." "Oops" places the emphasis on simply acknowledging harmful impact. So, if we have just committed an "ouch" and it has been named, the three breaths can also help us to settle the nervous system so we may better proceed with acknowledging impact.

Appendix C:
Why Share Gender Pronouns

The Interhelp Network[1] offers the following explanation of why sharing pronouns is important when introducing oneself.

Pronouns are words that are used to replace names, such as she/her/hers, he/him/his, they/them/theirs, or per/pem/pers. Example—Edward parked *his* bike over there.

Because a person's gender identity, and another person's perception of their gender based on appearance do not always match, it is important to learn from a person which gender pronouns they identify with and would like to have used to refer to them.

Gender can be very important to a person's sense of self, so to misgender someone by using pronouns other than the ones they choose for themselves can feel disrespectful, alienating, and invalidating.

Thus, including gender pronouns with name introductions and on nametags helps everyone be clear from the very beginning how a person wishes to be referred to.

In the dominant gender binary conditioning of Western civilization, people are labeled either male or female. However, gender exists on a spectrum. Many people historically and today do not identify as male or female. For example, two-spirit people exist in many Indigenous cultures. People may identify as nonbinary, gender fluid, or transgender (meaning their gender identity is different from the sex registered for them at birth).

In dominant culture, cisgender identity (meaning a person's gender identity is the same as their sex registered at birth) has been normalized and carries a privilege, while people who do not conform to the gender binary often face a lot of discrimination.

When everyone shares gender pronouns during introductions, this shifts the burden of responsibility from already marginalized people, for whom identifying themselves can be quite vulnerable. For this reason, everyone sharing gender pronouns can be an important act of solidarity. It may also be too vulnerable to share one's gender pronouns, so it is good to use invitational language in introduction prompts such as "Share your name, pronouns if you use them, or however you would like people to refer to you."

Some people prefer that no gender pronouns be used for them, and that only their name be used. Example: Edward parked *Edward's* bike over there.

If you use gender pronouns for yourself, we ask you to join this community in identifying which gender pronouns you would like people to use when referring to you. Knowing and accurately using someone's gender pronouns is a demonstration of respect, inclusion, and validation in our community.

Appendix D:
Reconsidering the Practice Called "Reporting to Chief Seattle"

By Aravinda Ananda and Kurt A. Kuhwald

Many facilitators are choosing not to share the Work That Reconnects practice called "Reporting to Chief Seattle" that appears in the 2014 edition of *Coming Back to Life: The Updated Guide to the Work That Reconnects*. Rather than simply recommending that you no longer share this practice, let's unpack what some of the concerns are.

In *Coming Back to Life*, Joanna Macy and Molly Brown wrote that the practice was intended to illuminate the contrast between "Industrial Growth Society and our indigenous ancestors' reverence for the natural world. ... Reminding us that respect for the web of life is our birthright, it evokes both sorrow for its loss and a yearning for its return." While it is true that if you go back far enough in any of our ancestral lines you will get to earth-honoring ancestors, and for many of us there is important work to be done uncovering and reclaiming this birthright, there are other ways to do so that don't reinforce harm as this practice currently does.

In the practice, participants read a rendition of a famous interpretation by a white man of one of Chief Seattle's speeches made in 1854 (Seattle was an Indigenous chief from the Pacific Northwest United States). The interpretation begins, *How can you buy or sell the sky, the warmth of the land. This idea is strange to us ...* It later continues, *The earth does not belong to man; man belongs to the earth ... All things are connected. Whatever befalls the earth befalls the sons of the earth. Man does not weave the web of life; he is merely a strand in it. Whatever he does to the web, he does to himself.* The practice then invites participants to "imagine that Chief Seattle's spirit is present at the center of the circle" and then people share what has happened to the land and its inhabitants since the speech was made.

Some of the harm that arises with this practice is embedded in the practice itself—in how it amplifies white interpretation and stereotypes of Indigenous peoples. Portraying only an essentialized, romanticized version of Indigenous peoples reduces them to a stereotype rather than allowing them their full complexity as real people. It is similar to the harm caused by the use of mascots which portray Native Americans as caricatures of their full selves.

This practice can also unwittingly reinforce Indigenous erasure by placing Indigenous people only in the past. Speaking of them only in the past, with no attention to current realities, and no solidarity with current struggles, can be quite painful and carries similarities with cultural appropriation where something desirable such as a teaching is taken by people with more positional power without any accompanying relationship of solidarity with current struggles.

If settler participants partake in this practice, invoking an essentialized, romanticized Indigenous ancestor without an accompanying awareness of and commitment to present-day Indigenous struggles, the situation amplifies harm to Indigenous participants who continue to experience ongoing erasure on a daily basis.

All the Real Indians Died Off: And 20 Other Myths about Native Americans by Roxanne Dunbar-Ortiz and Dina Gilio-Whitaker[1] offers a useful resource for learning more about some of the harmful dynamics at play in this practice. As facilitators we can learn more to avoid falling out of alignment with a commitment to collective liberation.

Appendix E: Facilitator Assessment Guide

Assess where you are and continue to grow

In 2018, Joanna Macy, Molly Brown, Chris Johnstone, and Constance Washburn created a "Facilitator Competency Framework" in response to a question they asked themselves, "What does someone need to know or be able to do in order to facilitate the Work That Reconnects well?" Our team has revised it and retitled it for this book, including more anti-oppression approaches.

The statements below are *aspirational* about the understanding, skills, and capacities that could improve our facilitation skills *over time*. They represent a journey, not an end point. It's likely that very few experienced facilitators would rate themselves with a 4 on even a majority of these statements. Moreover, some of the statements refer to facilitating complete Spirals of the Work That Reconnects, not facilitating stand-alone practices and short introductory workshops. So let this guide be just that—a guide to growing your capacities over time.

For each statement, ask yourself "how true is this for me?" and answer on a scale of 0–4 where:

0 = not true at all

1 = true in some small ways, I've made a start

2 = about half-way

3 = mostly there

4 = this is totally true for me

We invite you to use this scale to identify your strengths and (if repeated) track your progress in cultivating capacities that are less developed.

Starting Points

1. I have experienced the Work That Reconnects (WTR) as a participant in a variety of workshop settings and lengths. 0 1 2 3 4
2. I have thoroughly studied *Active Hope* and *Coming Back to Life*. 0 1 2 3 4
3. I have experience leading some WTR practices. 0 1 2 3 4
4. I have participated in diversity/anti-oppression/decolonization trainings or courses. 0 1 2 3 4

Workshop Design and Facilitation

1. I am confident in my ability to structure a workshop that guides participants successfully through the transformational processes of the WTR in:

   A. moving from individual self to a sense of Self connected to the whole living Earth 0 1 2 3 4
   B. moving from fear of feelings to courageous open heart 0 1 2 3 4
   C. moving from disempowerment to empowerment 0 1 2 3 4
   D. moving from a colonized mindset to a liberated consciousness 0 1 2 3 4

2. I am confident in my ability to design a workshop that:

   A. flows well 0 1 2 3 4
   B. connects with and respects participants with a variety of learning styles 0 1 2 3 4
   C. connects with and respects participants from different cultural and racial backgrounds and lifestyles 0 1 2 3 4
   D. is sensitive to the potential for activating trauma responses across a wide spectrum of workshop activities 0 1 2 3 4

3. I am sensitive to the needs of the group and responsive to feedback and nonverbal cues, adjusting or varying my

approach and the agenda where needed to maintain energy and engagement. 0 1 2 3 4
4. I cultivate safety and trust in a group, so that people feel comfortable sharing at a deep level. 0 1 2 3 4
5. I can create a safe environment and respond honestly and sensitively to statements or actions that might cause harm to a group member. 0 1 2 3 4
6. I listen deeply and actively to participants' ideas and feelings, even if they are divergent from my own. 0 1 2 3 4
7. I am resilient when challenges come up while facilitating, so that I can recover from setbacks as well as learn from them. 0 1 2 3 4
8. I can work within time constraints in a manner that does not rush or drag things out. 0 1 2 3 4

WTR Concepts, Worldviews, and Philosophies

1. I can explain, with current real-life examples, the Three Stories: Business as Usual, the Great Unraveling, and the Great Turning, acknowledging their roots in colonization and supremacy systems historically and today (while aware of their over-simplification). 0 1 2 3 4
2. I can explain the nature and problems of the Industrial Growth Society or modernity—including institutionalized racism, sexism, economic inequality, mass extinctions, and climate disruption—with examples and personal stories. 0 1 2 3 4
3. I can explain and provide examples of the four dimensions of the Great Turning: Holding Actions, Transforming Social and Economic Systems, Shifts in Perception and Values, and Nurturing Life. 0 1 2 3 4
4. I pay attention to trends in society, social injustice, the economy, politics, cultural-artistic domains, and environment so I can speak to what is currently happening in our world. 0 1 2 3 4

5. I can envision a Life-Sustaining Society and what would be required to create it, and can support others to explore their own vision. 0 1 2 3 4
6. I can articulate basic concepts of Systems Thinking, the Ecological Self, Gaia Theory, Deep Ecology, and Deep Time in enlivening ways. 0 1 2 3 4
7. I have an understanding of and relationship with Buddhism that supports my respectful use of Buddhist concepts and related practices. 0 1 2 3 4
8. I can articulate basic concepts of systemic racism, anti-oppression, white privilege and supremacy, decolonization, and collective liberation. 0 1 2 3 4
9. I value and validate both pain for the world and joy for the world as healthy expressions of interconnectedness within the web of life—and foundations for a grounded integrity. 0 1 2 3 4
10. I recognize the difference between optimism and active hope; lack of optimism does not stop me from acting to support my hopes for the future. 0 1 2 3 4
11. I understand and can convey the value of "positive disintegration." 0 1 2 3 4
12. I can compare the paradigms of "power over" and "power with," and illustrate their consequences. 0 1 2 3 4

WTR Framework and Practices

1. I can describe the Work That Reconnects and why it is valuable at this time, in language that is meaningful to a variety of audiences. 0 1 2 3 4
2. I can articulate the importance and value of each stage of the WTR Spiral and the progression from one to another. 0 1 2 3 4
3. I am confident in leading:
   A. Gratitude practices that open people's hearts and minds to their love for life on Earth. 0 1 2 3 4
   B. Practices for Honoring Our Pain for the World that help people tell the truth about what they see, know, and feel is

happening to their world, including their grief, anger, fear, and despair. 0 1 2 3 4

C. Seeing with New/Ancient Eyes and Deep Time practices that shift people's perceptions toward understanding themselves as interconnected beings through time and space. 0 1 2 3 4

D. Going Forth practices that help people clarify their focus, mobilize their energies, and identify next steps needed to move forward. 0 1 2 3 4

4. I am confident in leading:

   A. Practices and conversations that help people explore and share their social location and ancestry. 0 1 2 3 4

   B. Practices and conversations to help people become more aware of differences in privilege, oppression, and life experience in the group and in the world. 0 1 2 3 4

   C. Practices and conversations that help people identify steps they can take to further their own liberation from classism, racism, sexism, patriarchy, ableism, ageism, and other systemic oppressions. 0 1 2 3 4

5. I am able to be alongside my own and other people's pain for the world, including despair, without needing to fix it. 0 1 2 3 4

6. I can help people calm their nervous systems by sharing simple self-regulation techniques and group co-regulation practices. 0 1 2 3 4

Living the Great Turning

1. I engage in practices that help keep me nourished, connected, and resourced, so that I may maintain my effectiveness as a facilitator. 0 1 2 3 4

2. In my everyday life, I comfortably integrate people from different cultures and lifestyles into my circle of friends whenever possible. 0 1 2 3 4

3. I recognize the deep uncertainties of this global moment, and ways we can be strengthened by them. 0 1 2 3 4

4. I allow and express my pain for the world, including fears, anger, grief, and hopelessness—and acknowledge the ways I might avoid or distract myself from these feelings. 0 1 2 3 4
5. I allow and express my love and joy for the world and also acknowledge ways I might block these feelings. 0 1 2 3 4
6. I live my life as nonviolently as possible in the food, products, and energy I consume. 0 1 2 3 4
7. I am proactive in addressing racism, classism, ageism, ableism, and other forms of oppression and continue to educate myself on these issues. 0 1 2 3 4
8. I use my time, money, and other resources in ways that support the Great Turning. 0 1 2 3 4
9. I actively support others in their work for the Great Turning and I ask for help when I need it, since no one can do this work alone. 0 1 2 3 4
10. I engage in spiritual practices—particularly those that clarify my mind, strengthen my resolve, and open my heart to all beings, human and nonhuman. 0 1 2 3 4
11. I spend time in nature to renew my soul, and receive guidance from the living Earth and all its beings. 0 1 2 3 4
12. I inhabit a larger timescape that connects me to beings past, present, and future, to experience their support. 0 1 2 3 4

Appendix F: Recommended Resources

There is a vast wealth of existing resources to support collective liberation. Here are just a few select resources for deeper learning that we recommend or come recommended to us.

Ableism

Disability Visibility: First-Person Stories from the Twenty-First Century by Alice Wong

Antiracism

How to Be an Antiracist by Ibram X. Kendi
My Grandmother's Hands: Racialized Trauma and the Pathway to Mending our Hearts and Bodies by Resmaa Menakem
How to Have Antiracist Conversations by Roxy Manning
Me and White Supremacy by Layla Saad
White Fragility by Robin DiAngelo
What Does It Mean to Be White? by Robin DiAngelo

Buddhism

  Engaged Buddhism

  Peace Is Every Step by Thich Nhat Hahn
  The Heart of Buddha's Teaching by Thich Nhat Hahn
  The Path of Compassion, Writings on Socially Engaged Buddhism, edited by Fred Eppsteiner
  Engaged Buddhhist Reader, edited by Arnold Kotler
  Buddhist Peace Fellowship: https://www.bpf.org/

  Buddhism in the West

  World as Lover, World As Self by Joanna Macy

Buddhism and Whiteness: Critical Reflections, edited by George
   Yancy and Emily McRae
Books by Jack Kornfield, Joseph Goldstein, Pema Chodron
East Bay Meditation Center: https://eastbaymeditation.org

Tibetan Buddhism
The Myth of Freedom and the Way of Meditation by
   Chogyam Trungpa
Meditation in Action by Chogyam Trungpa
Cutting Through Spiritual Materialism by Chogyam Trungpa

Zen Buddhism
When No Thing Works by Norma Kawelokū Wong
A Fire Runs Through All Things by Susan Murphy
Bring Me the Rhinoceros by John Tarrant
Zen Mind, Beginner's Mind by Shunryu Suzuki
Being Black: Zen and the Art of Living With Fearlessness and Grace
   by angel Kyodo williams

Community, Education, Engagement, and Activism
Cultural Emergence: A Toolkit for Transforming Ourselves & the World
   by Looby MacNamara
Elders Action Network: eldersaction.org
Movement Generation: movementgeneration.org
Showing up for Racial Justice: surj.org
Sociocracy for All: sociocracyforall.org
Third Act: thirdact.org
*Who Decides Who Decides: How to start a group so everyone can have
   a voice!* by Ted J. Rau

Decolonization and Decoloniality
"Decolonization is not a metaphor" by Eve Tuck and K.Wayne Yang,
   appearing in Vol. 1 of *Decolonization: Indigeneity, Education &
   Society* (2012) pp 1–40
*Hospicing Modernity: Facing Humanity's Wrongs and the Implications
   for Social Activism* by Vanessa Machado de Oliveira
Website of Resources: Decoloniality, First Nations Thinkers and

Thought and Practices from the Global South: omeka.cloud.unimelb.edu.au/decoloniality-and-thinkers-from-the-global-south/

Becoming a Good Relative: Calling White Settlers Toward Truth, Healing and Repair by Hilary Giovale

Inherited Silence: Listening to the Land, Healing the Colonizer Mind by Louise Dunlap

Facilitation

Holding Change: The Way of Emergent Strategy Facilitation and Mediation by adrienne maree brown

Healing from Internalized Inferiority

How We Get Free by Keeanga-Yamahtta Taylor

Interior Beauty Salon by Nicolás Dumit Estévez Raful Espejo Ovalles www.interiorbeautysalon.com/

My Grandmother's Hands: Racialized Trauma and the Pathway to Mending our Hearts and Bodies by Resmaa Menakem

"10 Signs of Internalized Racism and Gaslighting" by Preston Ni, *Psychology Today* website

Indigenous Wisdom

Sand Talk: How Indigenous Thinking Can Save the World by Tyson Yunkaporta

The Dreaming Path by Paul Callaghan with Uncle Paul Gordon

Braiding Sweetgrass by Robin Wall Kimmerer

The Story is in Our Bones: How Worldviews and Climate Justice Can Remake a World in Crisis by Osprey Orielle Lake, Foreword by Casey Camp-Horinek

Non-Punitive Responses to Harm

Fumbling Towards Repair: A Workbook for Community Accountability Facilitators by Mariame Kaba and Shira Hassan

Healing Resistance: A Radically Different Response to Harm by Kazu Haga

"The Four Parts of Accountability & How to Give a Genuine Apology" by Mia Mingus https://leavingevidence.wordpress.com/2019/12/18/

how-to-give-a-good-apology-part-1-the-four-parts-of-accountability/
We Do This 'Til We Free Us: Abolitionist Organizing and Transforming Justice by Mariame Kaba
We Will Not Cancel Us: And Other Dreams of Transformative Justice by adrienne maree brown

Trauma Healing
The Politics of Trauma: Somatics, Healing and Social Justice by Staci K. Haines
Fierce Vulnerability: Healing from Trauma, Emerging through Collapse by Kazu Haga
What It Takes to Heal: How Transforming Ourselves Can Change the World by Prentis Hemphill
Your Resonant Self: Guided Meditations and Exercises to Engage Your Brain's Capacity for Healing by Sarah Peyton

Educational Programs
Comrades Education (formerly White Awake): www.comrades.education/
Education for Racial Equity: educationforracialequity.com
Racism in Real Time –Workshop: kokorotherapy.co.uk/racism-in-real-time
Rooted Global Village: rootedglobalvillage.com
Cultural Somatics Training Institute: courses.culturalsomaticsinstitute.com
Unraveling Whiteness—Embodied Anti-racist Practices following the Work That Reconnects Spiral: nicolebauman.com/unravelingwhiteness
White People Confronting Racism: whitepeopleconfrontingracism.org

Podcasts, Videos, and Blogs
Arab Women & Feminist Visions for Equity and Belonging (Part 1/3)—Rights, Equity, Dignity & Social Justice: https://belonging.berkeley.edu/arab-women-series-part-1
"In Conversation with Nova Reid & Resmaa Menakem" youtube.com/watch?v=dph_N6FuTng Nova Reid (Black British

woman, antiracist liberator, and author of *The Good Ally*) in live conversation with Resmaa Menakem.

Miki Kashtan's blog "The Fearless Heart," e.g. thefearlessheart.org/liberation-for-all-how-we-can-talk-differently-about-power-and-privilege/

Acknowledgments

Collectively our author/editor team would like to extend our gratitude to the immense number of people who made this book possible, especially:

- Joanna Macy and all of the many people who have contributed to the creation of the Work That Reconnects for the immense gifts this Work offers.
- All of the people and communities who have worked for collective liberation and contributed to our understanding, growth, and accountability.
- All our generous and inspiring contributors: Sarah Nahar, Marc Decitre, Ian Goh, Carmen Rumbaut, Margaret Babbott, Janna Diamond, Rukmini Iyer, Mayuree, Helena ter Ellen, Héctor Aristizábal, Liliana Moreno, Brooke Anderson, Gopal Dayeneni, and AJ Hudson.
- People who wrote potential sections that were not included in the final manuscript: thanks you for your time, work, and inspiration.
- Pat McCabe for graciously agreeing to write a Foreword.
- The colleagues who previously looked at a project of this nature with us, including Tzy-Ping Chen, Mutima Imani, and Rachel Marco-Havens.
- Members of the Anti-Oppression Resource Group (AORG) who have been particularly active at different times over the years and helped shape the content in this book, especially Belinda Grisworld who was one of the co-founders of AORG and offered a deeply insightful workshop at the WTR Network's 2023 Gaian Gathering, Sarah Nahar, Carmen Rumbaut, Mutima Imani, Rachel Marco-Havens, Tzy-Ping Chen, Paula Hendrick, Jane

Hera, Kara Bender, Constance Washburn, Joseph Rotella, Gwen Gordon, and Aryeh Shell.

- Belinda Griswold, BJ Star, Jade Begay, Sarah Nahar, and all who contributed to a gathering of WTR facilitators on Whidbey Island in 2016 where many of the topics that gave rise to this book were explicitly explored.
- Christopher and LuAnne Hormel, the Firemonkey Fund, RSF Social Finance, Barbara Ford, and Sitka Fund for financial support.
- Interhelp Network for fiscally sponsoring this project, and the Interhelp Board including Carol Harley, Margaret Babbott, Joseph Rotella, Aravinda Ananda, and Janna Diamond for their support of this project.
- Jane Hera for consultations on ableism.
- Paula Hendrick for editorial assistance.
- Kara Bender for her collaboration on an anti-oppression foundations curriculum which informed certain sections of this book, especially the development of the social location mapping wheel.
- Carmen Rumbaut for her original work on the "de-escalating patterns of harm in white dominant spaces" document that so greatly informed the chapters on seeing and addressing patterns of harm.
- Rachel Marco Havens for the insights she offered on several topics and for pushing our editorial team towards deeper integrity.
- Lydia Violet Harutoonian's work on cultural integrity.
- Mary McClintock for manuscript preparation.
- And lastly, by no means least, we owe gracious and heartfelt thanks to Rob West, our acquisitions editor, for his enthusiasm and spirit and his patient, helpful responses to our many queries and delays. We thank Murray Reiss for his thorough and thoughtful copy editing. And we are grateful to the team at New Society Publishers who welcomed and supported this book.

Aravinda:

I offer special thanks to my life partner Joseph Rotella for supporting me so much in general but especially for supporting me to direct countless hours towards this project, no small thing when we have a child under the age of two and a half. I thank all of the people who helped with childcare, especially Sorell Sitton and my dad, John Moran. To my child, Raphael, thank you for your patience with me as I labored on this project during some of the earliest moments of your life.

I offer gratitude to all of my ancestors, known and unknown, who went through so much so that I can be alive today. Thank you to my mother Satyena Ananda and my sisters Ishael and Tiphareth Ananda for your love. Thank you to my grandmothers Beth Brennan and Regina Anderson for offering such powerful examples of how to be strong loving humans.

I offer express thanks to Paula Hendrick in particular for editing and emotional support.

I give thanks for all of the friends, colleagues, and mentors along the way whom it has been an honor to learn from and with, including members of the Anti-Oppression Resource Group; members of the Interhelp Tending and Mending the Social Web Action Circle—Sarah Pirtle, Paula Hendrick, and Carol Harley; Patricia St. Onge and Anne Marie Davis in our work together as guest editors of the 2017 special issue of *Deep Times* journal on the impact of race and culture on the Work That Reconnects ; all of the people who have been part of the Earth Leadership Cohort (ELC) including co-facilitators Margaret Babbott and Joseph Rotella, ELC assistant facilitators and ELC participants from whom I have learned so much; Mutima Imani, Tzy-Ping Chen, Jo Hamilton, and Jane Hera for collaborations on De-escalating Patterns of Harm practice sessions; members of the 2018 Regenerative Culture Learning Laboratory; and Nora Samaran for inviting me to do a dialogue in *Turn This World Inside Out: The Emergence of Nurturance Culture*. I have learned so much from each of you and I am grateful.

I offer particular thanks to Tamir Notovny for working with me for over a year on a 70-page document entitled "From Harm to Care:

De-escalating Patterns of Harm in Group Facilitation." Our work together deeply informed the content of Chapters 7 and 8 in this book.

I thank all of the people who have been teachers to me, especially Louise Dunlap and her work on healing the colonizer mind, Lucien Demaris and Cedar Landman of Relational Culture, Sarah Peyton's work with accompaniment and unconscious contracts, and Myke Johnson's work on cultural appropriation. I offer thanks to all who have contributed to Generative Somatics, and in particular Staci K. Haines, Prentis Hemphill, and adrienne maree brown for their teachings. I am grateful to Aryeh Shell for the parts of my learning journey that we traveled together and for being a friend and colleague in this work.

Special thanks to Mutima Imani, for all of the support offered on my learning journey including but not limited to support for attending Lee Mun Wah's program on the Art of Mindful Facilitation; collaborating on the "de-escalating patterns of harm in white dominant spaces" practice sessions and collaborating on an anti-oppression foundations curriculum for Work That Reconnects facilitators.

Special thanks to Sarah Nahar for holding so much over the years with the Anti-Oppression Resource Group.

To all of the many wonderful people who have come into my life through the Work That Reconnects, many of whom have supported this book—thank you. You have been a deeply important community in my life.

To the land at Starseed Healing Sanctuary which has been a spiritual home for me, the living Earth that sustains me daily and especially the food plants, dairy cows, and chickens for nourishment and energy—thank you.

Thank you to the land that I now call home, and the original stewards of this place—the Pequosette band of the Massachusett tribe—for caretaking this land for many generations. I pledge to work to become a better neighbor.

Thank you to Molly Brown for continually showing up for AORG meetings and this work for years, for taking on so many pieces with this book project and for persevering. Thank you to Kurt A. Kuhwald for believing in this project, sticking with it, and especially for a commitment to ensure that contributor offerings in this book made it out into the world. What each of us has committed to birth this project has been considerable, and I am grateful that none of us gave up even when the going got rough, and the going was quite rough indeed at numerous times.

I thank all of the people who helped share elder care responsibilities so as to free up some of my time for this project including my sisters, Minda Sanchez and Emma Schoenberg.

Thank you to Jane Hera for accountability and support calls and cards.

To all of the people who believed in and supported the immense labor of love that is this book, thank you.

And last but not least, I thank the universe for building within me strength and fortitude, such that I was able to persevere through trying circumstances that were the opposite of support.

Molly:
My deep gratitude also goes out to my teachers and guides over the years, too many to name. Among them, Joanna Macy stands out for developing and sharing the Work That Reconnects, and giving me the honor and creative delight of co-authoring with her the two editions of *Coming Back to Life*.

My gratitude goes out to my beloved life partner Jim Brown, whose presence uplifts and gladdens my days. To Greg and Cassidy, adult sons who have become my advisors and guides. I send love and gratitude to my grandchildren Ben and Summer, as they make their way into a very troubled world. My gratitude goes out to Jen Rousseau and Rami Margron for the years of love and support we have shared—and continue to share.

I am grateful for my partners and colleagues in the Spiral Journey Facilitator Development Program, Mutima Imani, Constance Washburn, and Yulia Smagornisky, for their collaboration and creative contributions, and willingness to work through the challenges together. I am grateful to Jo delAmor and Silvia DiBlasio for providing administrative and moral support in the early years of the program. I honor the participants in the program over the years, many of whom are now offering the Work That Reconnects in their communities around the world.

I send thanks to many other colleagues in the Work That Reconnects: past and present Weavers, the amazing collaborative team at *Deep Times* journal, and the many people who have participated in the Anti-Oppression Resource Group over the years. I have learned so much from you and have thoroughly enjoyed our work together. Special thanks to Kathleen Rude who stepped up to help me offer an online workshop series called Roots of Resilience after my beloved colleague Jolie Elan, suddenly passed away.

And to my colleagues and collaborators on this book project, Aravinda Ananda and Kurt A. Kuwald, I send big gratitude; I honor their insightful contributions and the sacrifices they made to keep writing and editing during months of unanticipated life challenges.

Kurt:
Sitting down to offer my thanks to the people and powers that supported and empowered this person called Kurt A. Kuhwald, "I" am filled with deep tenderness. How clear it is that no effort to do good, to be of genuine service, to authentically join the collective stream flowing toward a just transition and liberation for the human family is ever accomplished alone.

For my mother, Isabelle Russell Godfrey Kuhwald, tenacious, vivacious, courageous warrior for healing, and my father, Arthur Andreas Hans Von Hindenburg Kuhwald, sensitive beyond his capacity to endure the demands placed on men, whose namesake was more a curse than a gift—I owe a complexity of love and gratitude.

Special thanks to Aravinda and Molly for their tenacity, sensitivity, courage, dedication to this project, and good ol' chutzpah and for contributing by far the largest amount of time and energy, at no small cost, to this project. Thanks to Rob West, at NSP, for the ease he brought to the process, and for his consistent availability—also to the other fine NSP staff I had the privilege to engage along the way.

Since this is my first professionally published volume, I'm feeling some crazy flow of like and love toward all the literary folx I have read, and whose work has mentored me from childhood to my ninth decade as a person who knows his psycho-social-spiritual persona needs to write. (Some who come to mind/heart are: Janette Sebring Lowry, Antoine de Saint-Exupéry, William Blake, Jane Hirshfield, Keeanga-Yahmahtta Taylor, Thomas Wolfe, Lauret Savoy, Tony Hoagland, Rashid Khalidi, Walt Whitman—with all his flaws—Octavia Butler, Ernest Hemingway, James Baldwin, Rupa Marya, and Raj Patel ... Ohmygodwhataninadequatelist!!! Of course, it's one hundred times longer.)

Another list is family and friends: my darling daughter, Caitlin; my wonderful grandson, Llewyn, and son-in-law, Martin; my dear ex-wife, Jodie and her partner Cherie; the Many Morses; the incredible Orchard family; the loves of the Thrive Family; my primary and beloved Conscious Elder community, SEEDs (Bing, Rika, Rabon, Trymon, and Virginia); the Thrive Elder Council and Circle and my co-conspirators in the Circle Keepers (Connie, Dee, Drew); my dear spiritual companion, Virginia (and Misha and Ylena); my buddy, Ralph; my father's mother Techla and his father, Arthur—and the many ancestors extending through England to the mainland and into the primal forests of what is now Germany and Austria.

Finally, and not last, the therapists and teachers, professors, ministers, and craftspersons whose care and support and mentoring have shaped and saved my life. Among them: Helen Craw, Mary Oulette, Rev. Dave Sammons, Rev. Susan Suchocki-Brown, Dr. Leon Spencer, Drs. Norm Chambers and Robert Lee, Carl Rogers (The Center for Studies of the Person, and CRI), professors Carnavale and Bruce, Judith Greer, Lysa Castro, Leanne Whitney, Loch Kelly, and Veronika Appleford Divoncova, IFS therapist *par excellence.*

Blessings and love to you all, I would not have made it this far without you.

Endnotes

Welcome

1. Training for Change, accessed May 3, 2015. www.trainingforchange.org/training_tools/diversity-welcome

Chapter 1

1. In adrienne maree brown, *Holding Change: The Way of Emergent Strategy Facilitation and Mediation* (AK Press, 2021).
2. brown, *Holding Change: The Way of Emergent Strategy Facilitation and Mediation*, 117.
3. "Core Assumptions of the Work That Reconnects," n.d., https://workthatreconnects.org/resources/core-assumptions-of-the-work-that-reconnects/.

Chapter 2

1. From Resources in "Work That Reconnects," Work That Reconnects Network, accessed January 22, 2025, https://workthatreconnects.org/ and Joanna Macy and Molly Young Brown, *Coming Back to Life: The Updated Guide to the Work That Reconnects* (New Society Publishers, 2014).
2. Lebogang Seitshiro, private communication, November 2024.
3. Craig Schindler and Gary Lapid, *The Great Turning: Personal Peace, Global Victory* (Bear & Co., 1989).
4. Raoul Peck, "Exterminate All the Brutes" (HBO, 2021), https://www.hbo.com/exterminate-all-the-brutes.
5. Term suggested by Jo delAmor in *Raising Children in the Midst of Global Crisis: A Compassionate Guidebook to New Paradigm Parenting* (Radiant Balance, 2023).
6. Vanessa Machado de Oliveira, *Hospicing Modernity: Facing Humanity's Wrongs and the Implications for Social Activism* (North Atlantic Books, 2021), 16.
7. Machado de Oliveira, *Hospicing Modernity*, 92.

(sidenotes)

1. Naomi Klein, *Doppelganger: A Trip Into the Mirror World* (Farrar, Straus and Giroux, 2023), 228.
2. Naomi Klein, *Doppelganger: A Trip Into the Mirror World* (Farrar, Straus and Giroux, 2023), 228.
3. bell hooks, *All About Love: New Visions* (William Morrow, 1999).
4. Jo delAmor, "Nurturing Life," *Deep Times* journal 9, no. 2 (September 2024).

Chapter 3

1. Patricia Hill Collins, *Black Feminist Thought, 30th Anniversary Edition: Knowledge, Consciousness, and the Politics of Empowerment* (Routledge, 2022).
2. Kimberlé Crenshaw, "Demarginalizing the Intersection of Race and Sex: A Black Feminist Critique of Antidiscrimination Doctrine, Feminist Theory and Antiracist Politics," in *Feminist Legal Theories* (Routledge, 2013), 23–51.
3. Moya Bailey, "Misogynoir Transformed: Black Women's Digital Resistance," in *Misogynoir Transformed: Black Women's Digital Resistance* (New York University Press, 2021).
4. Sally Roesch Wagner, *Matilda Joslyn Gage: She Who Holds the Sky* (Sky Carrier Press, 2002). Gage was an intersectional feminist in the face of an increasingly conservative white women's suffrage movement. Gage advocated for Indigenous rights, abolition of slavery, and against Christian supremacy. She was deliberately sidelined by Susan B. Anthony and others.
5. Amanda Lannan and Nicholas Lamar Wright, "Making Access a Priority in Hiring," *Inside Higher Ed*, March 29, 2024, https://www.insidehighered.com/opinion/career-advice/2024/03/29/improving-hiring-processes-those-disabilities-opinion.
6. Rachel G. McKane, David N. Pellow, and Patrick Trent Greiner, "Envisioning Disabled and Just Futures: Mutual Aid as an Adaptive Strategy for Environmental Change and Ecological Disablement," *Environmental Justice* 17, no. 3 (2023), https://doi.org/10.1089/env.2022.0104.
7. Ibid.
8. Ibid.
9. "Anti-Oppression Resource Group," accessed January 8, 2025, https://workthatreconnects.org/anti-oppression-resource-group/. This is part of the broader efforts at Undoing Oppression in the WTR. https://workthatreconnects.org/undoing-oppression-in-the-work/.
10. Sarah Nahar, "Group Agreements: Seeding the Field," *Blog From The Belly* (blog), August 29, 2024, https://blogfromthebelly.com/2024/08/29/group-agreements-some-seeds/.
11. Mariame Kaba, *We Do This 'Til We Free Us: Abolitionist Organizing and Transforming Justice* (Haymarket Books, 2021).
12. "Museum of People Power in Beautiful Action Training Modules," Beautiful Trouble, accessed November 5, 2024, https://beautifultrouble.org/training/for-trainers.
13. "Weaving Togetherness Lab on What We Offer," Nonviolent Global Liberation, accessed November 5, 2024, https://nglcommunity.org/what-we-offer/.
14. Joshua Michael Schrei, "The Emerald Podcast," accessed November 5, 2024, https://www.patreon.com/theemeraldpodcast.
15. Jade Begay, personal interview, February 4, 2018.

16. Kelly Hayes, "How to Talk about #NoDAPL: A Native Perspective," Transformative Spaces, October 27, 2016, https://transformativespaces.org/2016/10/27/how-to-talk-about-nodapl-a-native-perspective/.

17. "The Climate Clock," Climate Clock, n.d., https://climateclock.world/.

18. A listing of these bulls includes Papal Bull Dum Diversas, 18 June 1452, The Bull Romanus Pontifex (Nicholas V), January 8, 1454, and The Bull Inter Caetera (Alexander VI), May 4, 1493. Later expansions of these bulls include the Treaty of Tordesillas, June 7, 1494, the Patent Granted by King Henry VII to John Cabot and his Sons, March 5, 1496, The Requerimiento, 1514. https://doctrineofdiscovery.org/.

19. "An Expanded Analysis of Johnson v. McIntosh by Steven Newcomb," Indigenous Values Initiative, August 25, 2020, https://www.youtube.com/watch?v=Wo8LpsfIr-4. 2020.

20. Dana Lloyd, "City of Sherrill v. Oneida Indian Nation of New York," Doctrine of Discovery Project, October 19, 2022, https://doctrineofdiscovery.org/sherrill-v-oneida-opinion-of-the-court/.

21. "Dum Diversas," Doctrine of Discovery, June 18, 1452, https://doctrineofdiscovery.org/papal-bulls/.

22. Daniel Quinn, *Ishmael: A Novel* (Random House Publishing Group, 2009).

23. Bayo Akomolafe, "A Slower Urgency," The Emergence Network, n.d., https://www.bayoakomolafe.net/post/a-slower-urgency.

24. Sarah Nahar, "Intersectionalization of the Work That Reconnects," *Deep Times* journal, August 2017, https://journal.workthatreconnects.org/2017/08/29/intersectionalization-of-the-work-that-reconnects/.

25. Sarah Jolena Wolcott, "ReMembering the Story of the Anthropocene Age: Papal Bulls of Domination, Private Property, and an Ecotheology That (Re) Members Towards Creating the Beloved Community," Columbia Academic Commons, March 2020, https://doi.org/10.7916/d8-zgp1-6446.

26. Jodi A. Byrd, *The Transit of Empire: Indigenous Critiques of Colonialism* (University of Minnesota Press, 2011).

27. Paula Hendrick, "Miki Kashtan's Work of Reconnecting," *Deep Times* journal, March 2024, https://journal.workthatreconnects.org/2022/03/24/miki-kashtans-work-of-reconnecting.

28. Joanna Macy and Molly Young Brown, "Basic Assumptions of the Work," in *Coming Back to Life: The Updated Guide to the Work That Reconnects* (New Society Publishers, 2014), 65, and Core Assumptions of the Work That Reconnects. https://workthatreconnects.org/resources/core-assumptions-of-the-work-that-reconnects/.

29. Anti-Oppression Resource Group, Zoom Meeting of the Anti-Oppression Resource Group, December 2024.

30. Melissa K. Nelson, ed., *Original Instructions: Indigenous Teachings for a Sustainable Future* (Simon and Schuster, 2008).

31   Gabriel Pietrorazio, "Land, Life, and Language: The Thanksgiving Address," *Central Current*, November 24, 2022, https://centralcurrent.org/land-life-and-language-the-haudenosaunee-thanksgiving-address-is-a-greeting-of-gratitude-to-honor-all-thats-left/. Though there are numerous resources on the Address, I chose this article because there are pictures of so many Onondaga comrades that I know and work alongside, and a few that would have been here when Joanna Macy was in the area as well. *Central Current* is also a progressive press in the area that covers uplifting news. The adjacent articles demonstrate both the impact of the interlocking systems of oppression on communities, and the power of responses in service of collective liberation.

32   Rich Meyer, personal interview, August 2014.

33   "Anti-Oppression Resource Group Context and History Document," n.d., https://docs.google.com/document/d/1gsNiKIcaqCScV7f5V3Wt5Ey8CqYwSosgsHylVkJxJw8/edit#heading=h.1fwrs439ndap.

34   Ibid.

Chapter 4

1   For a more detailed dive into this part of the story, see my article in the *Deep Times* journal, March 2024 issue. The article includes links to pieces on the broader peace and ecofeminist movement. Marc Decitre, "An Early History of the Work That Reconnects," *Deep Times* journal 9, no. 1, accessed January 8, 2025, https://journal.workthatreconnects.org/2024/03/19/an-early-history-of-the-work-that-reconnects/.

2   This story has been told many times, including in chapters 16 and 17 of Joanna's biography (*Widening Circles*), as well as the "Thunderclap" story that opens Part II of *A Wild Love for the World*. Joanna Macy, *Widening Circles: A Memoir* (New Catalyst Books, 2007); Stephanie Kaza, ed., *A Wild Love for the World: Joanna Macy and the Work of Our Time* (Shambhala Publications, 2020).

3   In addition to the classic *Thinking Like a Mountain*, this part draws from three main sources. Vanessa Bible's book *Terania Creek and the Forging of Modern Environmental Activism* (2018) offers a useful backdrop to the region's history as well as a historical reconstruction of the mobilization. Bobbi Allan's chapter ("The Rainforest Protecting Itself: Australia Rising") in *A Wild Love for the World* and the article she co-wrote with Karina Shields for the *Deep Times* journal ("Activism Inside the Tiger's Mouth") offer rich first-person narratives. John Seed et al., *Thinking Like a Mountain: Towards a Council of All Beings* (New Society Publishers, 1988; Vanessa Bible, *Terania Creek and the Forging of Modern Environmental Activism* (Palgrave Pivot Cham, 2018), https://doi.org/10.1007/978-3-319-70470-8; Bobbi Allan, "The Rainforest Protecting Itself: Australia Rising," in *A Wild Love for the World: Joanna Macy and the Work of Our Time*, ed. Stephanie Kaza (Shambhala Publications, 2020).

4   Quote from Vanessa Bible, *Terania Creek and the Forging of Modern Environmental Activism*.

5 Laid out in books like *Alternatives to Economic Globalization: A Better World Is Possible* edited by John Cavanagh and Jerry Mander, *The Great Turning: From Empire to Earth Community* by David Korten, *Earth Democracy: Justice, Sustainability, and Peace* by Vandana Shiva, or *Local is Our Future* by Helena Norberg-Hodge. John Cavanagh and Jerry Mander, eds., *Alternatives to Economic Globalization: A Better World Is Possible* (Berrett-Koehler Publishers, 2004); David C. Korten, *The Great Turning: From Empire to Earth Community* (Berrett-Koehler Publishers, 2007); Vandana Shiva, *Earth Democracy: Justice, Sustainability, and Peace* (North Atlantic Books, 2015); Helena Norberg-Hodge, *Local Is Our Future: Steps to an Economics of Happiness* (Local Futures, 2019).

6 The question had been largely articulated around classism within the peace movement, with the Summer 1985 issue of Interhelp's journal dedicated to the topic. The issue includes a poignant article by Rosa Lane. Rosa Lane, "From Lower Class American to Peace Activist," *Interhelp Journal*, Summer 1985.

7 Barbara Jeanne Fields's article "Slavery, Race and Ideology in the United States of America" offers a good historical introduction. Barbara Jeanne Fields, "Slavery, Race and Ideology in the United States of America," *New Left Review*, no. 181 (June 1990): 95–118.

8 See Keeanga-Yamahtta Taylor's book *From #BlackLivesMatter to Black Liberation* for a synthetic overview of these developments. Keeanga-Yamahtta Taylor, *From #BlackLivesMatter to Black Liberation* (Haymarket Books, 2016), 1.

9 Michael Rothberg, *The Implicated Subject: Beyond Victims and Perpetrators* (Stanford University Press, 2019).

10 Sarah Nahar, "Intersectionalization of the Work That Reconnects," *Deep Times* journal, August 2017, https://journal.workthatreconnects.org/2017/08/29/intersectionalization-of-the-work-that-reconnects/.

11 The links to these resources are centralized on the "Undoing Oppression" page of the WTR Network's website: "Undoing Oppression in the Work," accessed January 8, 2025, https://workthatreconnects.org/undoing-oppression-in-the-work/.

The Evolving Edge directory in *Deep Times* journal includes further articles by members of the Work That Reconnects community: "Evolving Edge Directory in *Deep Times* Journal," accessed January 8, 2025, https://journal.workthatreconnects.org/evolving-edges/. You can also find a more detailed history of the Anti-Oppression Resource Group and a list of its projects on their page on the WTR Network's Website: "Anti-Oppression Resource Group," accessed January 8, 2025, https://workthatreconnects.org/anti-oppression-resource-group/.

Chapter 5

1 Sarah Nahar, "Intersectionalization of the Work That Reconnects," *Deep Times* journal, August 2017, https://journal.workthatreconnects.org/2017/08/29/intersectionalization-of-the-work-that-reconnects/.

2 Teasing out the full implications of this statement goes beyond the goals of

this chapter. For a rich and elegant study of the evolution of this political culture, see Patricia Applebaum, *Kingdom to Commune: Protestant Pacifist Culture between World War I and the Vietnam Era* (University of North Carolina Press, 2009).

3   See Andrew Cornell, *Oppose and Propose: Lessons from Movement for a New Society* (AK Press / Institute for Anarchist Studies, 2011).

4   Chellis Glendinning, "Telling Our Nuclear Stories," *New Age Journal*, 1981.

5   The quote is from historian Quincy Wright in his *Study of War*, discussed in Perrin Selcer, *The Postwar Origins of the Global Environment: How the United Nations Built Spaceship Earth* (Columbia University Press, 2018).

6   We may add, in the U.S. context, that the legacies of 40 years of "colorblind" racism that sought to invisibilize the continued oppression faced by racialized people have meant that movements like BlackLivesMatter and others needed to re-emphasize difference, to challenge naive appeals to harmony and unity, in order to address these particular injustices.

7   Rob Nixon, *Slow Violence and the Environmentalism of the Poor* (Harvard University Press, 2013).

8   Dahr Jamail and Stan Rushworth, eds., *We Are the Middle of Forever: Indigenous Voices from Turtle Island on the Changing Earth* (The New Press, 2024).

9   See Andreas Smith's essay "Heteropatriarchy and the Three Pillars of White Supremacy" for a useful breakdown of the different forms racial violence can take. Andrea Smith, "Heteropatriarchy and the Three Pillars of White Supremacy: Rethinking Women of Color Organizing," in *Color of Violence: The INCITE! Anthology*, ed. INCITE! Women of Color Against Violence (Duke University Press, 2016).

10 Murray Bookchin and Dave Foreman, *Defending the Earth: A Dialogue Between Murray Bookchin and Dave Foreman* (South End Press, 1991), 65.

11 See Greta Gaard, *Ecological Politics: Ecofeminists and the Greens* (Temple University Press, 1998).

12 There are a number of rich works on this historical process, but James C. Scott's *Seeing Like a State*, Karl Polyani's *The Great Transformation*, Silvia Federici's *Caliban and the Witch*, and Carolyn Merchant's *Death of Nature* remain important references for the way this process unfolded within rising European nations. *The Nutmeg's Curse* by Amitav Ghosh extends this analysis to colonial relations. James C. Scott, *Seeing Like a State: How Certain Schemes to Improve the Human Condition Have Failed* (Yale University Press, 2008); Karl Polyani, *The Great Transformation: The Political and Economic Origins of Our Time (2nd Beacon Paperback Ed)* (Beacon Press, 2001); Sylvia Federici, *Caliban and the Witch: Women, the Body and Primitive Accumulation* (Penguin Publishing Group, 2021); Carolyn Merchant, *The Death of Nature: Women, Ecology, and the Scientific Revolution* (Harper & Row, 1989); Amitav Ghosh, *The Nutmeg's Curse: Parables for a Planet in Crisis* (University of Chicago Press, 2022).

13 The *Shock of the Anthropocene* by Jean Baptiste Fressoz and Christophe Bonneuil highlights how contestation to industrialization, on proto-environ-

mental grounds, has existed from its very beginning. Jean Baptiste Fressoz and Christophe Bonneuil, *The Shock of the Anthropocene: The Earth, History, and Us*, trans. David Fernbach (Verso, 2016).

Chapter 6

1. The clearest example is the Black feminist Combahee River Collective from the 1970s. See the re-edition of their work in Keeanga-Yamahtta Taylor, ed., *How We Get Free: Black Feminism and the Combahee River Collective* (Haymarket Books, 2017).

2. Jack P. Manno, *Privileged Goods: Commoditization and Its Impact on Environment and Society (1st Ed.)* (CRC Press, 2000), https://doi.org/10.1201/9780429104398.

3. Maria Mies, *Patriarchy and Accumulation on a World Scale: Women in the International Division of Labour* (Palgrave Macmillan, 1998).

4. Barbara Fields, "Slavery, Race and Ideology in the United States of America," *New Left Review*, no. 181 (May 1990).

5. Jason Hickel, *The Divide: A Brief Guide to Global Inequality and Its Solutions* (Penguin Random House, 2018).

6. Isabel Wilkerson, *Caste: The Origin of Our Discontents* (Penguin Random House, 2020).

7. The Four I's of Oppression framework is generally credited to John Bell. John Bell, "The Four I's of Oppression," accessed February 10, 2025, https://www.joliet86.org/assets/1/6/Four_Is_of_Oppression.pdf.

8. "Implicit Bias," American Psychological Association, accessed February 9, 2025, https://www.apa.org/topics/implicit-bias.

9. Bobbi Harro, "The Cycle of Socialization," in *Readings for Diversity and Social Justice, 2nd Ed.*, ed. Maurianne Adams (Routledge, 2010), https://www.nea.org/sites/default/files/2021-02/Cycle%20of%20Socialization%20HARRO.pdf.

10. Tessa Watkins, "Wheel of Privilege and Power | Intersectionality," *Just 1 Voice* (blog), November 21, 2021, https://just1voice.com/advocacy/wheel-of-privilege/.

11. "Social Location Mapping Wheel," Interhelp Network, n.d., https://interhelpnetwork.org/wp-content/uploads/2024/12/Social-Location-Mapping-Wheel-for-IH-Website-12.2-final.pdf.

12. Aysu Erdoğdu Miskbay, "A Study for Power Analysis (Güç Analizi İçin Bir Çalışma)," 2024, https://catlakzemin.com/guc-analizi-icin-bir-calisma/.

13. Amy Tan, "Power and Privilege in Canada," accessed February 10, 2025, https://learn.cupe.ca/wp-content/uploads/sites/149/2022/09/power-privilege-in-canada-graphic-dr-amy-tan-md-1.pdf.

14. adrienne maree brown, *Holding Change: The Way of Emergent Strategy Facilitation and Mediation* (AK Press, 2021), 166.

15. Ibid., 166.

Chapter 7

1. Joanna Macy and Molly Young Brown, *Coming Back to Life: The Updated Guide to the Work That Reconnects* (New Society Publishers, 2014), 34.
2. Patricia St. Onge, et al., *Embracing Cultural Competency: A Roadmap for Nonprofit Capacity Builders* (Fieldstone Alliance, 2009).
3. "Diversity Welcome," Training for Change, accessed February 2, 2025, https://www.trainingforchange.org/training_tools/diversity-welcome/.
4. Sarah Nahar, "Intersectionalization of the Work That Reconnects," *Deep Times* journal, August 2017, https://journal.workthatreconnects.org/2017/08/29/intersectionalization-of-the-work-that-reconnects/.
5. adrienne maree brown, *Emergent Strategy: Shaping Change, Changing Worlds* (AK Press, 2017).
6. adrienne maree brown, *Holding Change: The Way of Emergent Strategy Facilitation and Mediation* (AK Press, 2021), 172.

Chapter 8

1. Derald Wing Sue et al., "Racial Microaggressions in Everyday Life: Implications for Clinical Practice," *American Psychologist* 62, no. 4 (2007): 271–86, https://doi.org/10.1037/0003-066X.62.4.271.
2. Sue et al., "Racial Microaggressions in Everyday Life," 274.
3. Ibid, 274.
4. Mia Mingus, "The Four Parts of Accountability & How to Give a Genuine Apology," *Leaving Evidence* (blog), December 18, 2019, https://leavingevidence.wordpress.com/2019/12/18/how-to-give-a-good-apology-part-1-the-four-parts-of-accountability/.
5. Prentis Hemphill, *What It Takes to Heal: How Transforming Ourselves Can Change the World* (Random House, 2024).
6. Staci K. Haines, *The Politics of Trauma: Somatics, Healing, and Social Justice* (North Atlantic Books, 2019).
7. Kazu Haga, *Healing Resistance: A Radically Different Approach to Harm* (Parallax Press, 2020).

Chapter 9

1. Atmos, "Queering Nature | Twenty Summers Gathering, 11:08 to 11:28," July 20, 2023, https://www.youtube.com/watch?v=20iOiuX21PE.
2. "Cambridge Dictionary: Queer," Cambridge Dictionary, accessed July 15, 2024, https://dictionary.cambridge.org/dictionary/english/queer.
3. Candace West and Don H. Zimmerman, "Doing Gender," *Gender and Society* 1, no. 2 (June 1987): 125–51.
4. Michael Mikulewicz, Martina Angela Caretta, and Neil J. W. Crawford, "Intersectionality & Climate Justice: A Call for Synergy in Climate Change

Scholarship," *Environmental Politics* 32, no. 7 (n.d.): 1275–86, https://doi.org/doi:10.1080/09644016.2023.2172869.

5   Sean G. Massey, Meredith G. F. Worthen, and Kimberly A. Drews, "Prejudice and Discrimination against LGBTQ+ People," in *Introduction to LGBTQ+ Studies: A Cross-Disciplinary Approach*, ed. Deborah P. Amory et al. (Milne Publishing, 2022), https://milnepublishing.geneseo.edu/introlgbtqstudies/chapter/prejudice-and-discrimination-against-lgbtq-people/.

6   Centers for Disease Control and Prevention, "The National Intimate Partner and Sexual Violence Survey: 2010 Findings on Victimization by Sexual Orientation" (Centers for Disease Control and Prevention, 2013).

7   National Coalition of Anti-Violence Programs (NCAVP), "Lesbian, Gay, Bisexual, Transgender, Queer, and HIV-Affected Intimate Partner Violence in 2015" (New York City Anti-Violence Project, 2016), http://avp.org/wp-content/uploads/2017/04/2015_ncavp_lgbtqipvreport.pdf.

8   Hanne Blank, "Straight: The Surprisingly Short History of Heterosexuality," OutHistory, accessed July 19, 2024, https://outhistory.org/items/show/1296.

9   Intersex Human Rights Australia, "Intersex Population Figures," Intersex Human Rights Australia, accessed July 15, 2024, https://ihra.org.au/16601/intersex-numbers/.

10 Adrienne Rich, "Compulsory Heterosexuality and Lesbian Existence," *Signs* 5, no. 4 (1980): 631–60.

11 Jennifer Mullan, *Decolonizing Therapy: Oppression, Historical Trauma, and Politicizing Your Practice* (W.W. Norton & Co., 2023).

12 "Welcome to the Work That Reconnects Network," Work That Reconnects Network, accessed July 16, 2024, https://workthatreconnects.org.

13 Caroline Medina et al., "Improving the Lives and Rights of LGBTQ People in America," Center for American Progress, January 12, 2021, https://www.americanprogress.org/article/improving-lives-rights-lgbtq-people-america/.

14 Joanna Macy and Molly Young Brown, *Coming Back to Life: The Updated Guide to the Work That Reconnects* (New Society Publishers, 2014).

15 Queer Nature, "Nature-Intimacy, Naturalist Studies, Place-Based Skills for LGBTQIA+, Two-Spirit, & Non-Binary People and Allies," Queer Nature, accessed July 16, 2024, https://www.queernature.org.

16 José M. Gómez, A. Gónzalez-Megías, and M. Verdú, "The Evolution of Same-Sex Sexual Behaviour in Mammals," *Nature Communications* 14, no. 1 (2023): 5719, https://doi.org/doi.org/10.1038/s41467-023-41290-x.

17 Frans B. M. de Waal, "Bonobo Sex and Society," *Scientific American*, June 1, 2006, https://www.scientificamerican.com/article/bonobo-sex-and-society-2006-06/.

18 Taylor Evans et al., "Lifetime Stability of Social Traits in Bottlenose Dolphins," *Communications Biology* 4, no. 1 (2021): 759, https://doi.org/doi.org/10.1038/s42003-021-02292-x.

19 Gwénaëlle Pincemy, F. Stephen Dobson, and Pierre Jouventin, "Homosexual Mating Displays in Penguins," *Ethology* 116, no. 12 (2010): 1210–16, https://doi.org/doi.org/10.1111/j.1439-0310.2010.01835.x.

20 Lindsay C. Young, Brenda J. Zaun, and Eric A. VanderWerf, "Successful Same-Sex Pairing in Laysan Albatross," *Biology Letters* 4, no. 4 (2008): 323–25, https://doi.org/doi.org/10.1098/rsbl.2008.0191.

21 Paul E. Rose and Darren P. Croft, "Evaluating the Social Networks of Four Flocks of Captive Flamingos over a Five-Year Period: Temporal, Environmental, Group and Health Influences on Assortment," *Behavioural Processes* 175 (June 1, 2020): 104118, https://doi.org/10.1016/j.beproc.2020.104118.

22 Laura Casas et al., "Sex Change in Clownfish: Molecular Insights from Transcriptome Analysis," *Scientific Reports* 6, no. 1 (October 17, 2016): 35461, https://doi.org/10.1038/srep35461.

23 Michael Le Page, "Bluehead Wrasse Fish Switch from Female to Male in Just 20 Days," *New Scientist*, July 10, 2019, https://www.newscientist.com/article/2209254-bluehead-wrasse-fish-switch-from-female-to-male-in-just-20-days/.

24 Jessica L. Hoskins, Michael G. Ritchie, and Nathan W. Bailey, "A Test of Genetic Models for the Evolutionary Maintenance of Same-Sex Sexual Behaviour," *Proceedings of the Royal Society B: Biological Sciences* 282, no. 1809 (2015): 20150429, https://doi.org/doi.org/10.1098/rspb.2015.0429.

25 Bruce Bagemihl, *Biological Exuberance: Animal Homosexuality and Natural Diversity*, 33–34 (St. Martin's Press, 1999).

26 Ella Saltmarshe, "Chapter 3: The Narrative of Separation," Stories For Life, accessed July 20, 2024, https://stories.life/chapter/the-narrative-of-interbeing/.

27 Kate Raworth, "Chapter 4: The Narrative of Interbeing," Stories For Life, accessed July 20, 2024, https://stories.life/chapter/the-narrative-of-interbeing/.

28 Diana Pamela Urbina, "Mother Earth Day in the Andes," August 1, 2018, https://ieu.greenclimate.fund/blog/mother-earth-day-andes/.

29 Sarah Epstein, "What Is Both/And Thinking?," *Psychology Today* (blog), February 23, 2021, https://www.psychologytoday.com/us/blog/between-the-generations/202102/what-is-bothand-thinking.

30 Wendy K. Smith, "Shifting to Both/And Assumptions," in *Both/And Thinking: Embracing Creative Tensions to Solve Your Toughest Problems* (Harvard Business Review Press, 2022).

31 Henri Lipmanowicz and Keith McCandless, "Wicked Questions," Liberating Structures, accessed July 18, 2024, https://www.liberatingstructures.com/4-wicked-questions/.

32 Chimamanda Ngozi Adichie, "The Danger of a Single Story (18:49)" (TEDGlobal, Oxford, UK, July 2009), https://www.ted.com/talks/chimamanda_ngozi_adichie_the_danger_of_a_single_story.

33 Samuel D. Jackson, Jonathan J. Mohr, and Alison M. Kindahl, "Intersectional Experiences: A Mixed Methods Experience Sampling Approach to Studying

an Elusive Phenomenon," *Journal of Counseling Psychology* 68, no. 3 (2021): 299–315, https://doi.org/doi.org/10.1037/cou0000537.

34   Kenneth Sørensen, "Subpersonalities, According to Roberto Assagioli," Kenneth Sørensen, June 18, 2022, https://kennethsorensen.dk/en/subpersonalities-according-to-roberto-assagioli/.

35   Cedar Barstow and Amanda Aguilera, "Types of Power Handout," Right Use of Power Institute, September 2022, https://www.rightuseofpower.org/.

36   Molly Young Brown, *Growing Whole: Self-Realization for the Great Turning* (Psychosynthesis Press, 2009).

37   Molly Young Brown, *Unfolding Self: The Practice of Psychosynthesis* (Helios Press, 2004).

38   Catherine Ann Lombard, "Psychosynthesis: A Foundational Bridge Between Psychology and Spirituality," *Pastoral Psychology* 66, no. 4 (August 1, 2017): 461–85, https://doi.org/10.1007/s11089-017-0753-5.

39   Judith Butler, *Gender Trouble: Feminism and the Subversion of Identity* (Routledge, 2006).

40   Nancy Riley, "Patriarchies Old and New in Chinese Society," in *Routledge Handbook of Chinese Culture and Society*, ed. Kevin Latham (Routledge, 2020).

41   Joanna Macy and Molly Brown, "The Evolutionary Gifts of the Animals," Work That Reconnects, January 1, 2014, https://workthatreconnects.org/resources/the-evolutionary-gifts-of-the-animals/.

42   Joanna Macy and Molly Brown, "Strengthening Our Intentions (or Corbett)," Work That Reconnects, January 1, 2014, https://workthatreconnects.org/resources/strengthening-our-intentions-or-corbett/.

43   Joanna Macy and Molly Brown, "Harvesting the Gifts of the Ancestors (Original)," Work That Reconnects, January 1, 2014, https://workthatreconnects.org/resources/harvesting-the-gifts-of-the-ancestors-original/.

44   Michelle Filice, "Two-Spirit," The Canadian Encyclopedia, June 21, 2023, https://www.thecanadianencyclopedia.ca/en/article/two-spirit/.

45   Ayu Arman, "The Bissu From Segiri: The Guardian of the Ancient Bugis Tradition," Our Islands, January 15, 2021, https://ourislands.id/en/stories/the-bissu-from-segiri-the-guardian-of-the-ancient-bugis-tradition/.

46   Joanna Macy and Molly Brown, "Letter from the Future," Work That Reconnects, January 1, 2014, https://workthatreconnects.org/resources/letter-from-the-future/.

47   Joanna Macy and Molly Brown, "Seventh Generation," Work That Reconnects, January 1, 2014, https://workthatreconnects.org/resources/seventh-generation/.

48   Rina Sawayama, "Chosen Family," Genius, accessed July 16, 2024, https://genius.com/Rina-sawayama-chosen-family-lyrics/.

49   Annie Wright, "What Is the Window of Tolerance, and Why Is It So Import-

ant?," *Psychology Today* (blog), May 23, 2022, https://www.psychologytoday.com/intl/blog/making-the-whole-beautiful/202205/what-is-the-window-tolerance-and-why-is-it-so-important/.

50   David A. Treleaven, "Stay Within the Window of Tolerance: The Role of Arousal," in *Trauma-Sensitive Mindfulness: Practices for Safe and Transformative Healing* (W.W. Norton & Co., 2018).

51   Alliant International University Center for Teaching Excellence, "Gender Inclusive Teaching," accessed July 17, 2024, https://cte.alliant.edu/dei/gender-inclusive-teaching/.

52   Alex Carr Johnson, "How to Queer Ecology: One Goose at a Time," *Orion Magazine*, March 24, 2011, https://orionmagazine.org/article/how-to-queer-ecology-once-goose-at-a-time/.

53   Shane Parrish and Rhiannon Beaubien, "The Map Is Not the Territory," in *The Great Mental Models, Volume 1: General Thinking Concepts, 1st Ed.* (Penguin Publishing Group, 2024).

54   Joseph R. DesJardins, "Biocentrism," Encyclopedia Britannica, April 4, 2023, https://www.britannica.com/topic/biocentrism.

55   Rainer Maria Rilke, *Letters to a Young Poet*, trans. Anita Barrows and Joanna Macy (Shambhala Publications, 2021).

Chapter 10

1   "Diversity Welcome," Training for Change, accessed February 2, 2025, https://www.trainingforchange.org/training_tools/diversity-welcome/.

2   Ejeris Dixon, "We Keep Us Safe: Facilitating Safer Spaces," in adrienne maree brown, *Holding Change: The Way of Emergent Strategy Facilitation and Mediation* (AK Press, 2021), 85–86.

3   brown, *Holding Change*, 108.

Chapter 11

1   Staci K. Haines, *The Politics of Trauma: Somatics, Healing and Social Justice* (North Atlantic Books, 2019).

2   Daniel J. Siegel, *The Developing Mind: How Relationships and Brain Interact to Shape Who We Are* (New York: Guilford Press, 1999).

3   Richard G. Tedeschi, Jane Shakespeare-Finch, and Kanako Taku, *Posttraumatic Growth: Theory, Research, and Applications* (Routledge, 2018).

4   Resmaa Menakem, *My Grandmother's Hands: Racialized Trauma and the Pathway to Mending Our Hearts and Bodies* (Central Recovery Press, 2017).

Chapter 12

1   Tema Okun, "White Supremacy Culture," n.d., https://www.whitesupremacyculture.info/uploads/4/3/5/7/43579015/okun_-_white_sup_culture_2020.pdf.

2   Molly Young Brown, *Growing Whole: Self-Realization for the Great Turning* (Psychosynthesis Press, 2009).

3   Richard C. Schwartz, *No Bad Parts: Healing Trauma & Restoring Wholeness with the Internal Family Systems Model* (Boulder, CO: Sounds True, 2021).

4   To learn more about psychosynthesis, see Molly Brown's book, *Growing Whole: Self-Realization for the Great Turning*. Additional sources for application of subpersonalities in healing and transformational work can be found in Loch Kelly's *Effortless Mindfulness* and also at the Internal Family Systems Institute.

5   Prentis Hemphill, *What It Takes to Heal: How Transforming Ourselves Can Change the World* (Random House, 2024), 60.

6   See Robin DiAngelo, *White Fragility: Why It's So Hard For White People to Talk About Racism* (Beacon Press, 2018).

Chapter 13

1   Joanna Macy and Molly Young Brown, *Coming Back to Life: The Updated Guide to the Work That Reconnects* (New Society Publishers, 2014), 258.

2   Ibid., 258.

3   Joanna Macy, *Widening Circles* (New Society Publishers, 2000).

4   Joanna Macy, *Mutual Causality in Buddhism and General Systems Theory: The Dharma of Natural Systems* (State University of New York Press, 1991), https://doi.org/10.2307/jj.18254717.

5   Macy, *Mutual Causality in Buddhism and General Systems Theory*, xiii.

6   Through her School for The Great Turning, Lydia Violet Harutoonian offered a workshop in February 2024 on Cultural Integrity for Work That Reconnects Facilitators, Lydia Violet Harutoonian, "School for The Great Turning," accessed February 10, 2025, https://lydiafiddle.com/school-for-the-great-turning.

7   Hilary Giovale, *Becoming a Good Relative: Calling White Settlers Toward Truth, Healing, and Repair* (Green Writers Press, 2024), https://greenwriterspress.com/book/becoming-a-good-relative/.

8   "Comrades Education," Comrades Education, accessed February 10, 2025, https://www.comrades.education.

9   Macy and Brown, *Coming Back to Life*.

10 Original version in Macy and Brown, *Coming Back to Life*, 175.

11 Ann Marie Davis, "Re-Imagining Harvesting the Gifts of the Ancestors," *Deep Times* journal 2, no. 5 (Summer 2017), https://journal.workthatreconnects.org/2017/08/29/re-imagining-harvesting-the-gifts-of-the-ancestors/. See also Ann Marie Davis, "Harvesting the Gifts of the Ancestors (Decolonial Adaptation) - Work That Reconnects Network," January 1, 2017. https://workthatreconnects.org/resources/harvesting-the-gifts-of-the-ancestors-decolonial-adaptation/.

12 For more information about the history and effects of the caste system in India, see Dhirendra Nath Majumdar, *Races and Cultures of India* (Universal Publishers Ltd, 1951).

13. Hepzi Anthony, "Nine Years of 'Save Aarey': The Unique Citizens' Movement Lives on in Mumbai," Citizen Matters, December 27, 2023, https://citizenmatters.in/mumbai-aarey-movement-nine-years/.

14. As co-authors, we, Mayuree and Rukmini, acknowledge our Brahmin identities and the privilege these afford within the Indian socio-cultural context. This privilege has historically shaped our access to resources, education, and platforms, including the ability to engage with the Work That Reconnects. We recognize that our perspectives are shaped by our social location, lived experiences, and professional engagements. And they are not exhaustive. We encourage readers to explore and integrate insights from diverse social, cultural, and historical contexts.

Chapter 14

1. For the history of this endeavor see the article written by the initiator of these workshops: Helena ter Ellen, "Re-Conectando in the Wounded Land of Colombia," in *A Wild Love for the World: Joanna Macy and the Work of Our Time*, ed. Stephanie Kaza (Shambhala Publications, 2020), 134–43. The young Colombian peace activist was Felipe Medina.

2. Global Witness, "Almost 2,000 Land and Environmental Defenders Killed Between 2012 and 2022 for Protecting the Planet" (Global Witness, September 13, 2023), https://www.globalwitness.org/en/press-releases/almost-2000-land-and-environmental-defenders-killed-between-2012-and-2022-protecting-planet/.

3. Numbers presented together with the Final Report of the Truth Commission. Comisión de la Verdad, "Hay Futuro Si Hay Verdad" (Bogotá, Colombia: Comisión de la Verdad, 2022), https://web.comisiondelaverdad.co/actualidad/noticias/principales-cifras-comision-de-la-verdad-informe-final

4. Official website of the Truth Commission: Comisión de la Verdad, "Official Website of the Truth Commission," Comisión de la Verdad, accessed November 14, 2024, https://www.comisiondelaverdad.co/

5. Various chapters contain references to nature as a victim of conflict: Comisión de la Verdad, "Cuando Los Pajaros No Cantaban (Chapter of Hay Futuro Si Hay Verdad)" (Bogotá, Colombia: Comisión de la Verdad, 2022), https://www.comisiondelaverdad.co/cuando-los-pajaros-no-cantaban and Comisión de la Verdad, "Naturaleza Herida Por La Violencia (Chapter in Hay Futuro Si Hay Verdad)" (Bogotá, Colombia: Comisión de la Verdad, 2022), https://www.comisiondelaverdad.co/impactos-afrontamientos-y-resistencias/la-naturaleza-herida-por-la-violencia, and Comisión de la Verdad, "The Ethnic Chapter (Chapter of Hay Futuro Si Hay Verdad)" (Bogotá, Colombia: Comisión de la Verdad, 2022), https://www.comisiondelaverdad.co/resistir-no-es-aguantar.

6. Throughout the 4.5 years of the Commission's mandate, and amid the challenges caused by the pandemic, the national strike, and the resurgence of violence, Re-Conectando carried out 15 laboratories in 12 different territories.

7. Many participants, including ex-FARC combatants who support the peace

agreement, face life-threatening risks and often require escorts for protection. To understand the mandates of the three institutions established by the peace agreement—the Truth Commission, the Special Jurisdiction for Peace, and the Search Unit for Missing Persons— visit: https://en.wikipedia.org/wiki/Colombian_peace_process#

8   These dialogues are—paraphrasing Lederach—conversations between people from different contexts in many cases of great polarization that help to create bridges and contribute to the construction of peace—a process that goes way beyond negotiation or the signing of a peace agreement.

9   Based on the practice proposed by Bill Plotkin in his book *Wild Mind*, we foster an interspecies conversation for which we ask participants to go alone into the wilderness until they feel called by an other-than-human being. Drawing on the wisdom of the natural world, participants come to a deeper understanding of themselves and their interconnectedness with all life. They learn to honor and respect the intrinsic value of all beings and acquire knowledge that helps them on their personal and collective path toward healing and reconciliation. Bill Plotkin, *Wild Mind: A Field Guide to the Human Psyche* (New World Library, 2013).

10 Laura Vargas and Mariana Prandini Assis, "Buen Vivir in the Aftermath of Armed Conflict: A Critical Examination of a Community-Level Reconciliation Experience in Colombia" (Narrating Transitional Justice: History, Memory, Poetics and Politics Conference, McMaster University, Hamilton, Canada, 2021). Confronting Atrocity Project at McMaster's Centre for Human Rights and Restorative Justice, in partnership with Illinois State University and the Social Sciences and Humanities Research Council of Canada.

11 Héctor Aristizábal and Diane Lefer, *The Blessing Next to the Wound: A Story of Art, Activism, and Transformation* (Brooklyn: Lantern Books, 2010).

12 Transitional justice research indicates the need to examine informal, community-level reconciliation activities alongside formal mechanisms like truth commissions: Vargas and Assis, "Buen Vivir in the Aftermath of Armed Conflict: A Critical Examination of a Community-Level Reconciliation Experience in Colombia."

13 Vargas and Assis, "Buen Vivir in the Aftermath of Armed Conflict."

14 This exercise was inspired by other experiential practices described in the book *Coming Back to Life*: Joanna Macy and Molly Young Brown, *Coming Back to Life: The Updated Guide to the Work That Reconnects* (New Society Publishers, 2014).

15 Mamo Evangelio of the Arhuaco community, Sierra Nevada de Santa Marta in Comisión de la Verdad, "Cuando Los Pajaros No Cantaban (Chapter of Hay Futuro Si Hay Verdad)" (Bogotá, Colombia: Comisión de la Verdad, 2022), https://www.comisiondelaverdad.co/cuando-los-pajaros-no-cantaban, p. 185.

16 Comisión de la Verdad, "Cuando Los Pajaros No Cantaban (Chapter of Hay Futuro Si Hay Verdad)" and Comisión de la Verdad, "Naturaleza Herida

Por La Violencia (Chapter in Hay Futuro Si Hay Verdad)," Comisión de la Verdad, "The Ethnic Chapter (Chapter of Hay Futuro Si Hay Verdad)."

17 Comisión de la Verdad, "Opening Chapter of the Final Report of the Truth Commission" (Bogotá, Colombia: Comisión de la Verdad, 2022), https://www.comisiondelaverdad.co/convocatoria-la-paz-grande, 10.

18 An alliance is in the making with the Foundation Mundo Común: "Foundation Mundo Común," Foundation Mundo Común, accessed November 14, 2024, www.mundocomun.org/.

Chapter 15

1 Search Movement Generation's website for a full description of its work. "Movement Generation," accessed January 22, 2025, https://movementgeneration.org/.

2 The Foundational Teachings has a page on the website of the Work That Reconnects. "Foundational Teachings," Work That Reconnects Network, accessed January 22, 2025, https://workthatreconnects.org/foundational-teachings/.

3 "Work That Reconnects," Work That Reconnects Network, accessed January 22, 2025, https://workthatreconnects.org/.

4 Many within the mainstream of the climate movement have relied so heavily on the "time is running out" frame to suggest that if we "don't act now, climate change will be irreversible." There are some aspects of this which are true—for example, sea levels will continue to rise, even if we cease all emissions tomorrow. Similarly, we may have breached some climate tipping points (or will in the near future). But our argument is that we should not simply throw our hands in the air and declare, "it's too late," since the changes in the climate system are only half the story. How we will navigate those changes is the other half.

5 We assert that there is no such thing as a natural disaster. There are natural occurrences, like earthquakes or tsunamis, but what makes them a disaster is how they travel through the economy. An earthquake doesn't discriminate, but the economy does; and an unjust economy will unjustly distribute the consequences, and that's what makes it a disaster.

6 For more on Narrative Power, check out Center for Story-based Strategy www.storybasedstrategy.org

7 From *The Shock Doctrine* by Naomi Klein. Naomi Klein, *The Shock Doctrine: The Rise of Disaster Capitalism* (Metropolitan Books, 2008).

8 Extreme Energy: We define Extreme Energy based not on a particular set of technologies, but upon the risks and impacts of energy development on communities. Extreme energy goes beyond "unconventional" energy, such as Tar Sands, deepwater drilling, or gas fracking; it includes all ecologically destructive, centralized, and undemocratic forms of energy extraction. Conventional oil and coal are extreme forms of energy if you live in Occupied Iraq or Appalachia; just as mega-dams are for river-dependent peoples.

9   To dive deeper into Just Recovery in Puerto Rico, download "Protesta y Propuesta: Lessons from Just Transformation, Ecological Justice, and the Fight for Self-Determination in Puerto Rico" by Movement Generation (primary author Brooke Anderson) and Grassroots International (primary author Jovana García Soto), on which the above is heavily based. Brooke Anderson and Jovana García Soto, "Protesta y Propuesta: Lessons from Just Transformation, Ecological Justice, and the Fight for Self-Determination in Puerto Rico" (Grassroots International and Movement Generation, February 2020), https://grassrootsonline.org/wp-content/uploads/2024/03/Grassroots-MG-Puerto-Rico-Report-web-Feb2020.pdf.

10 To dive deeper into farmworker organizing in the North Bay in the wake of wildfires there, read Brooke Anderson, "From Farmworkers to Land Healers," *YES! Magazine*, April 25, 2023, https://www.yesmagazine.org/environment/2023/04/25/california-farmworkers-immigrant-indigenous and Brooke Anderson, "Indigenous Farmworkers Can Show How to Heal Our Burning Planet," *In These Times*, January 26, 2022, https://inthesetimes.com/article/indigenous-farmers-ecological-knowledge-climate-change-global-warming-winery-wineries both by Brooke Anderson at Movement Generation, on which the above is heavily based.

11 Terms like "green economy" are a narrative pretense to cover up the attempt to resolve the ecological contradictions of capitalism in order to maintain extractive relationships of power.

12 COVID-19 is a great example of the "predictability" of shocks. While we experienced it as a major shock, there have been many predictions of global pandemics as a result of ecological erosion and zoonotic spill-over from industrial agriculture and urban encroachment. *Big Farm Makes Big Flu* by Rob Wallace, for example, was written in 2016. Rob Wallace, *Big Farms Make Big Flu: Dispatches on Influenza, Agribusiness, and the Nature of Science* (Monthly Review Press, 2016).

Appendix A

1   "Sarah Pirtle and The Discovery Center," accessed January 23, 2025, https://sarahpirtle.com/.

2   "Everyday Feminism," accessed January 23, 2025, https://everydayfeminism.com/.

3   Patricia St. Onge is the lead author of Patricia St. Onge et al., *Embracing Cultural Competency: A Roadmap for Nonprofit Capacity Builders* (Fieldstone Alliance, 2009).

4   Marshall B. Rosenberg, *Nonviolent Communication: A Language of Life, 3rd Edition* (PuddleDancer Press, 2015).

5   Mia Mingus, "The Four Parts of Accountability & How to Give a Genuine Apology," *Leaving Evidence* (blog), December 18, 2019, https://leavingevidence.wordpress.com/2019/12/18/how-to-give-a-good-apology-part-1-the-four-parts-of-accountability/.

6   Loretta J. Ross, "Join the Calling In Movement!," accessed January 23, 2025, https://lorettajross.com/callingin-online.

7   Floyd Cheung, Cynthia Ganote, and Tasha Souza, "Microaggressions and Microresistance: Supporting and Empowering Students," Faculty Focus, April 1, 2016, https://www.facultyfocus.com/articles/equality-inclusion-and-diversity/microaggressions-and-microresistance-supporting-and-empowering-students/.

8   "Loretta J. Ross," accessed January 23, 2025, https://lorettajross.com/.

9   Mia Mingus, "The Four Parts of Accountability & How to Give a Genuine Apology."

Appendix B

1   Cited in adrienne maree brown, *Holding Change: The Way of Emergent Strategy Facilitation and Mediation* (AK Press, 2021), 54.

2   "The 8 Guidelines for Equity and Inclusion – Visions, Inc.," accessed February 12, 2025, https://www.edomi.org/wp-content/uploads/2020/02/8-Guidelines-for-Equity-and-Inclusion.pdf.

3   "Ouch, Whoa, Oops: How to Acknowledge and Respond to Harm in the Moment" North Pacific Yearly Meeting, accessed on June 4, 2025, https://quakerinstitute.org/wp-content/uploads/Ouch-Whoa-Oops-Handout.pdf

Appendix C

1   "Interhelp Network," accessed January 31, 2025, https://interhelpnetwork.org.

Appendix D

1   Roxanne Dunbar-Ortiz and Dina Gilio-Whitaker, *All the Real Indians Died Off: And 20 Other Myths about Native Americans* (Beacon Press, 2016).

The Bibliography for this work is availabe online at:

https://newsociety.com/book-resource/
coming-together-in-the-great-turning-bibliography/

Index

A

ableism, 15, 24, 38, 41, 42, 49, 64, 100, 131, 158, 179, 194–198. *See also* disability justice
Abya Yala/Turtle Island, 59
accountability, 84, 117, 119, 140–143, 346, 351
   avoidance, 145–148
   building healthy accountability, 148–151, 238–239
   centered, 149, 225, 239
   collective, 170
   deflection of, 146–148
   and dominant identities, 238
   and healthy remorse, 147
   peer accountability spaces, 152
active hope, 238, 268, 361
Active Hope (Joanna Macy and Chris Johnstone), 79–81
ageism, 57, 100, 194, 333, 339
Akomolafe, Bayo, 39
Alexandra, Meena, 334–335
Allen, Bobbi, 75, 77, 107, 379n3
Allende, Isabel, 334
All the Real Indians Died Off (Roxanne Dunbar-Ortiz and Dina Gilio-Whitaker), 357
alter-globalization, 72, 78–81
Ananda, Aravinda, 12–13, 85–86, 122, 402
ancestors, 6, 7, 28, 42, 71, 159, 207, 234, 239, 284, 302, 336, 356
   Harvesting the Gifts of the Ancestors, 13, 44, 124, 172, 257
   and queer identity, 171–173
Angelou, Maya, 47
anthropocentrism, 5, 150, 270
anti-oppression, 8, 81, 129, 145, 152, 174. *See also* anti-oppressive facilitation
   anti-oppressive spaces, 118, 183, 227
   awareness of, 127–129
   definition of, 18
Anti-Oppression Resource Group, 13, 15, 26, 50–51, 66–69, 85–86, 121, 180
anti-oppressive facilitation, 179–204
   and ableism, 195–198
   addressing issues, 188–191
   body language awareness, 192
   checklist, 180–195
   and cisheteropatriarchy, 198–200
   co-facilitation, 180–182
   Facilitator Assessment Guide, 358–363
   and interrupting settler colonialism, 201–204
   nervous system regulation during, 192
   "Ouch, Whoa, Oops," 189, 342, 350, 352–353
   religious holiday awareness, 194
   repair and mending, 181–192
   roleplay, 193
   workshop beginnings, 184–188
   workshop preparations, 182–184
antiracism, 84, 88–89, 93, 139, 225, 232
   resources, 364
APEC, 80
Australia, 31, 71, 74–76, 201
   "Rainbow Region," 75
   Terania Creek, 75

B

Babbott, Margaret, 404
Baxter, James K., 336
Becoming a Good Relative (Hilary Giovale), 256
Begay, Jade, 58–59, 85
Bell, John, 106
belonging, 6, 7, 20, 41, 99, 137, 149, 190, 214, 241, 286, 290
   and changes in nervous system state, 205–206
   mutual, 22, 25
   and trauma, 220–221
Beloved Community, 20, 22, 118, 333, 350
Bender, Kara, 110
bioregional relationships, 319–321
Black Lives Matter, 37, 81–86
Bookchin, Murray, 93, 94
Borikén. *See* Puerto Rico / Borikén

brown, adrienne maree, 8, 150, 194, 351
  Emergent Strategy: Shaping Change, Changing Worlds, 133–134
  Holding Change, 119
Brown, Molly, 7, 13–15, 66, 77, 79, 161, 233, 356
  Growing Whole: Self-Realization for the Great Turning, 169, 229
  Unfolding Self, 169
Buddhism, 24, 68, 74–75, 165, 170, 219, 231, 248–251, 339
  dharma, 248–251
  resources, 364–365
Buddhist Peace Fellowship, 34
Business As Usual, 11, 29–31, 36–39, 59, 62, 66, 79–80, 159, 174, 258, 301. *See also* capitalism; neoliberalism
Butler, Judith, 169–170

C
California
  agriculture, 311–312
  Land and Labor Acknowledgment, Oakland, 201–204
  wildfires, 313–315
  wine industry, 312–315
capitalism, 30, 39, 57, 78, 87, 89, 94, 102–103, 151, 156, 203, 253, 271, 316, 333, 339, 392n11
  corporate globalization, 76–78, 80
  disaster capitalism, 62, 304, 308–310, 314
  green, 62
  racial, 66, 102
carbon, 59, 62, 315, 324–328
Casa Pueblo, 308, 310
Caste (Isabel Wilkerson), 104
Central Current, 379n31
Centros de Apoyo Mutuo, 310
Cifuentes, Laura, 277–278
Circle of Trust, 350
cisgender, 156, 199
  assumptions, 156
  bias, 157–158, 198
cisheteropatriarchy, 198–200
climate apocalypse narrative, 323–329
climate catastrophe/crisis, 6, 62, 80
climate clock, 59–65

climate justice movement, 81, 300, 309, 326–329
Cocina Rebelde, 310
collective liberation, 3–11, 19–21, 26, 58–59, 67, 145, 148, 154, 301
  and ancestral recovery, 256
  committing to, 117–119
  definition, 54
  and embracing queerness, 160
  and feedback on harm, 340–341
  inner work and, 223–243
collectivity. *See also* collective liberation
  collective action, 5, 36, 103, 160, 170
Collins, Patricia Hill, 48
Colombia, 267–294. *See also* Re-Conectando
  colonial legacies in, 288–290
  FARC, 268–269
  Truth Commission, 269–272, 275, 286–288
colonialism, 40, 87, 102, 179, 195, 209, 310, 328. *See also* decolonialism, decolonization; slavery
  Doctrine of Discovery and Domination, 60–65
  interrupting settler colonialism, 201–204
colonization, 35, 59, 61–63, 171–172, 203, 251–253, 258
Columbus, Christopher, 63, 308, 325
Comedores Sociales, 310
Coming Back to Life (Joanna Macy and Molly Brown), 7, 14–16, 24, 29, 44, 55, 66, 85, 124, 161, 248, 252, 255, 356
commons, 37, 63, 102, 303, 309
community, 7–8, 14, 16
  community action, 35–36
  community/group agreements, 53, 130–131, 349–353
  resources on, 365
Comrades Education, 256
Cooper, David, 336
corporate globalization, 76–78, 80
Council of All Beings, 27, 76, 78

and queer wisdom, 163–163
Thinking Like a Mountain: Towards a Council of All Beings, 76
Crass, Chris, 256
Craw, Helen, 17
Crenshaw, Kimberlé, 48
Crump, Sage, 7, 349
cultural appropriation, 151, 252–255, 357
cultural awareness, 127–128
and right relationship, 254–256
Cyril, Malkia Devich, 335

D
Dass, Ram, 230
Davis, Anne Marie, 257
Dayaneni, Gopal, 300
Decitre, Mark, 403
decolonialism, decolonization, 7, 86, 159. *See also* colonialism
and Just Recovery, 310
resources on, 365–366
Decolonizing Therapy (Jennifer Mullan), 159
Deep Ecology, 28, 48, 71–80, 92–95, 248, 251, 252, 256, 300. *See also* Re-Conectando
Deep Ecology Work, 71, 74–76, 79
Foundation for Deep Ecology, 80
and social ecology, 92–95
Deep Time, 28–29, 42, 55–56, 64, 284, 288, 300
Deep Time Work, 77, 78
Dwelling in Deep Time, 55–56
Deep Times (journal), 13, 81, 84–86, 133, 257
defensiveness, 9, 69, 142, 147, 150, 225, 227, 341, 345. *See also* feedback about harm
shifting, 238–239
de Leon, Sandra, 313–314
de Oliveira, Vanessa Machado, 39–40
de Roux, Francisco, 269–270, 275–276
Despair and Empowerment Work, 71–78, 89
Despair and Personal Power in the Nuclear Age (Joanna Macy), 73–74
Deyá, Arturo Massol, 308
Diamond, Janna, 207

DiAngelo, Robin, 238
disability justice, 50, 303. *See also* ableism
disaster capitalism, 62, 304, 308–310, 314
Disaster Collectivism, 306, 321. *See also* shocks
Doctrine of Discovery and Domination, 60–65
Dunbar-Ortiz, Roxanne, 357

E
Eaarth, 333, 339
EarthFirst!, 94
Earth Leadership Cohort, 12–13, 179
ecocide, 60, 92
eco-fascism, 50, 321
ecofeminism, 92
ecopsychology, 217
Education for Racial Equity, 226, 238
education resources, 367
Elan, Jolie, 34
emergence, 27–28, 263
Emergent Strategy: Shaping Change, Changing Worlds (adrienne maree brown), 133
empathy gaps, 9, 114–115, 126
environmental justice movement, 81, 90–92, 163
ethnocide, 64
Exterminate All the Brutes (docuseries), 32
extraction, 150–154
educational labor, 152
emotional labor, 151–152
shifting the patterns of, 152–154
Extreme Energy, 391n8

F
facilitators, facilitation, 49–59, 64–68. *See also* anti-oppressive facilitation; group spaces; workshops
addressing microaggressions, 140–145
and body language, 141, 144
co-facilitation, 180–182
and cultural awareness, 248–257
and decentering dominant identities, 127–134

Facilitator Assessment Guide, 358–363
feedback about harm, 142, 147, 340–348
queer-affirming language, 162
resource on, 366
self-awareness, 228–233
and social location, 113–117
and trauma awareness, 205–222
and triggers, 237
feedback about harm, 142, 147, 340–348. *See also* defensiveness
femicide, 63–66. *See also* witches
feudalism, 102
Fleming, Pat, 75–76
Foreman, Dave, 94
Forero, Diana, 293
Foundation for Deep Ecology, 80
Fukushima–Daiichi disaster, 304–305
Fuse, 336

G

Gage, Matilda Joslyn, 377n4
Gaia. *See also* Re-Conectando
 Gaian mandate, 3
 Gaian structures, 33–34, 36–37
 Gaian unraveling, 17
 Gaia refuge, 283, 289
gender. *See also* cisgender; cisheteropatriarchy; queering
 gender binary language, 200
 gender terms, 199–200
Gender Trouble (Judith Butler), 169–170
genocide, 24, 31, 39, 59, 60, 64, 92, 202, 307
Gilio-Whitaker, Dina, 357
Ginsburg, Ruth Bader, 61
Giovale, Hilary, 256
Glendinning, Chellis, 91
global polycrisis, 4, 15, 19, 23–24, 27, 37
 and transformation, 23–24
Gomez, Ludwin, 294
Goodwin, Anne, 219
Great Turning, 4–5, 15, 21, 24, 26, 32–33, 36–37. *See also* collective liberation; Three Stories of Our Time

"Be," 37–38
"Block," 35–36
"Build," 36–37
and collective liberation, 54
dimensions of, 33–34
Nurturing Life, 34–35
origins of the phrase, 29
queering of, 157–174
and repair of kinship structures, 56
Shift in Perception and Consciousness, 37–38
transformational resistance, 35–36
Great Unraveling, 14, 29, 31–32, 66, 79, 92, 124, 300
Green, Tova, 77
green capitalism, 62
green economy, 315, 392n11
Griswold, Belinda, 69, 85, 201
group spaces, 6–7. *See also* workshops
 addressing harm in, 131–132
 affinity or identity caucuses within, 133
 and cultural awareness, 127–128
 and decentering dominant identities, 127–134
 group/community agreements in, 53, 150, 153, 349–353
 systems of violence in, 20
group work, 7, 207, 220. *See also* facilitators, facilitation; group spaces; workshops
 and empathy gaps, 114–115
 participant introductions, 115–116, 130, 186–187, 199, 215, 354–355
 and social location, 114–117
Growing Whole: Self-Realization for the Great Turning (Molly Brown), 169, 229

H

Haga, Kazu, 149
Haines, Staci K., 149, 205–206
Hancock, Eleanor, 256
Harjo, Joy, 334
harm, 340–348. *See also* oppression
 calling (out, in, on, up), 341–342
 giving feedback on, 340–344
 misgendering, 139, 199–200, 354

398 | Index

non-punitive responses to, 20, 118–119, 150, 366–367
receiving and responding to feedback on, 344–348
Harro, Bobbi, 107
Harutoonian, Lydia Violet, 216, 255
Hassan, Shira, 150
Haudenosaunee, 68, 252
Havel, Vaclav, 4
Havens, Joseph, 89
Healing Resistance: A Radically Different Approach to Harm (Kazu Haga), 149
Helms, Janet E., 118–119
Hemphill, Prentis, 4, 150
  What It Takes to Heal, 147–148, 224, 235, 243
Hera, Jane, 41, 195, 196
heteronormativity, 57, 156–172, 200. *See also* cisheteropatriarchy
  and patriarchy, 159
Hirshfield, Jane, 336
Holding Change (adrienne maree brown), 7, 119
hooks, bell, 33, 57, 302
Horney, Karen, 17
Hospicing Modernity (Vanessa Machado de Oliveira), 39–40
Hurricane Katrina, 304, 306
Hurricane María, 304, 306, 308–310

I

identity fear, 101
I Know Why the Caged Bird Sings (Maya Angelou), 47
Imani, Mutima, 42–43
imperialism, 30, 35–36, 56, 59, 64, 87, 89, 92, 102–103, 327, 328. *See also* colonialism; colonization
implicated subjects, 83–84
India
  Business as Usual in, 258–259
  caste in, 104, 260
  and decolonialization, 253, 260–261
  religion in, 260
  storytelling and ritual in, 262–263
  Work That Reconnects in, 258–265
Indigenous wisdom, 251, 260–261, 264

resources on, 366
Industrial Acceleration, 60, 66
Industrial Growth Society, 25–26, 30, 38–39, 57, 67, 92, 95, 271, 356
Industrial Revolution, 31, 59–60
inner work, 133–134, 142, 150, 153, 179, 181, 190, 193, 223–243
  conflict and confrontation responses, 242–243
  defensiveness, 238–239
  false binaries, 239
  internal obstacles, 233–243
  mistakes and shaming, 239–242
  responding after witnessing oppressive harm, 233–235
  self-awareness, 228–233
  self-observation, 229–232
  subpersonalities, 231–233
  trauma healing, 235–239
  triggers and triggering, 236–237
  undoing internalized inferiority, 227, 366
  working with internalized oppression, 224–227
interconnected systems of support, 7, 48–69
Interhelp Network, 71–76, 82, 89–90, 93, 110, 354
Internal Family Systems, 17, 224, 229, 232, 239
internalized inferiority, 227, 366
International Forum on Globalization, 80
intersectionality, intersectionalization, 48–49, 72, 81–88, 101–103
  in India, 260–261
  Intersectionality Wheel of Privilege, 110
  and queering, 162–163, 167–168, 172
  and the Work That Reconnects, 133
Iroquois Confederacy. *See* Haudenosaunee

J

Japan, 304–305
Johnson, Alex, 174
Johnson, Myke, 254, 255
Johnstone, Chris, 79

Jung, C.G., 17
Just Recovery, 309–310, 314–315, 321

K

Kaba, Mariame, 150
Kane, Joan, 336
Kashtan, Miki, 55
King, Martin Luther, Jr., 15
kinship networks, 55–57
Klein, Naomi, 30, 31, 304
Kuhwald, Kurt A., 201–204

L

labor acknowledgements, 202–204
land acknowledgements, 201–204
Lapin, Gary, 29
liberation, 49, 54, 67, 157, 240, 300, 332.
  See also collective liberation
  of all beings, 159
  Black liberation, 83 (See also Black Lives Matter)
  definition of, 18–19
  human liberation, 17–19, 30, 87
  queer, 159, 303
  from white supremacy, 37

M

Macy, Joanna, 7, 8–9, 12–16, 23, 27–28, 38, 63, 79, 89, 240
  Active Hope, 79, 80
  and Buddhism, 68, 219, 248–251
  Coming Back to Life: The Updated Guide to the Work That Reconnects, 7, 14–16, 24, 29, 44, 55, 66, 85, 124, 161, 248, 252, 255, 356
  and deep ecology, 94
  Despair and Personal Power in the Nuclear Age, 73–74
  "How to Deal with Despair," 72
  and John Seed, 75–76
  positionality of, 65
  Widening Circles: A Memoir, 249
Malleus Maleficarum (Heinrich Kramer), 60, 63–65
Martin, Trayvon, 82, 83
Marxism, 93, 101–103
Marya, Rupa, 335
materialism, 101–103
McKibben, Bill, 336

Medina, Felipe, 268
Menakem, Resmaa, 216–217, 227, 238
  My Grandmother's Hands, 218, 219, 221, 226
microaggressions, 9, 51, 105, 136–145, 181, 193, 226
  addressing, 140–145
  microinsults, 138
  microinvalidations, 138–139
Mies, Maria, 102
Mingus, Mia, 142, 150
misgendering, 139, 199–200, 354
Miskbay, Aysu, 111
misogynoir, 49
moral imagination, 27–28, 174
more-than-humans, 56, 61, 94, 164, 166, 171, 174
Movement for a New Society, 89
Movement Generation Justice & Ecology Project, 300–307
  Just Recovery, 309–310, 314–315, 321
  Just Transition, 298–302, 318–319
  Just Transition Framework, 298–300
  shifts, 316–318
  shocks, 303–310, 318–321
  slides, 303–304, 310–315, 318–321
Mullan, Jennifer, 159
Mutual Aid, 321
My Grandmother's Hands (Resmaa Menakem), 218, 219, 221, 226

N

Naess, Arne, 76
Nahar, Sarah, 84, 85, 133, 185, 402–403
natural disasters, 303, 305, 306, 391n5.
  See also Fukushima disaster; Hurricane Katrina; Hurricane María; shocks
neoliberalism, 62, 78, 80, 309
Nixdorf, Frieda, 34, 41, 106, 209, 211
North Bay Jobs With Justice, 313–315
Notovny, Tamir, 122
nuclear accidents. See Fukushima disaster; Three Mile Island
Nuclear Freeze Campaign, 73, 90
nuclear threat, 73, 77, 90–92

O

Oaxaca, 313
Obama, Barack, 83
Occupy Wall Street, 306, 316
Okun, Tema, 226–227
Open Sentences, 26, 28, 31–33, 35, 37, 38, 43
oppression. *See also* anti-oppression; systems of oppression
    and avoiding accountability, 145–150
    and decentering dominant identities, 126–134
    dynamics of, 121–154
    in Work That Reconnects spaces, 121–126
    extraction, 150–154
    Four I's of Oppression, 105–106
    harm, giving and receiving feedback on, 340–348, 352–353
    ideological, 105–106, 105–107
    and implicit bias, 107
    institutional, 105–106
    interlocking systems of, 48–69
    internalized, 105–106
    interpersonal, 105–106
    microaggressions, 136–145
    reinforcing oppressive harm, 135–145
    systemic, 18–19
    undoing, definition of, 18
Organización Boricuá, 310

P

pacificism, 74, 88–90
Palmer, Parker J., 350
Papal Bulls, 60–63, 378n18. *See also* Doctrine of Discovery and Domination
Dum Diversas, 61–63
Parker, Priya, 216
Patel, Raj, 335
patriarchy, 14, 30, 38, 39, 63, 87, 100, 102, 158
    cisheteropatriarchy, 198–200
    and heteronormativity, 159
    and queering, 162
    and undervaluation of women's work, 151

patterns of harm, 7, 51–52, 85, 122–129, 181, 342. *See also* oppression; systems of oppression
    centering, 123–126
    feedback about harm, 142, 147, 340–348
Peavey, Fran, 77, 89
Peck, Raoul, 32
Pellow, David Naguib, 50
People of the Global Majority, 15, 18, 32–33, 100, 129, 152, 227, 252, 329
Plotkin, Bill, 390n9
police violence, 36, 83, 327
praxis of indispensability, 50
prejudice, 14, 24, 101–105, 109–112
psychosynthesis, 229, 231, 388n4
Puerto Rico / Borikén, 308–310
    and colonialism, 310
punishment, 147–148, 191
    cycle of, 119
    non-punitive responses to harm, 20, 118–119, 150, 366–367

Q

Quakerism, 74
queer ecology, 157, 163
queering, 155–175
    and actions in defense of life, 157–161
    of ancestral and intergenerational work, 171–174
    of binaries, 166–167
    and capitalism, 156
    of language, 166
    of perceptions and values, 165–174
    of practices, 170–171
    and psychosynthesis, 168–169
    of self, 167–169

R

race, 81–86, 89, 103, 105, 112, 113, 138–139, 225–226
racial justice, 72, 83, 226
racism, 14, 89, 94, 100, 104–105, 133, 158, 194, 225–227, 232, 239, 290, 324, 329. *See also* antiracism
    "colorblind" racism, 83, 86, 381n6
Randall, Dudley, 336
Reagan, Ronald, 62, 73, 77, 78

Re-Conectando, 267–294
  and Colombia's colonial legacies, 288–290
  Game of the Elastics, 280–282
  Houses of Truth, 274, 276
  Market of Care for Life, 274
  Museum of the Unspeakable, 276
  mycelium metaphor, 267–272, 283, 290–291
  nature in, 270–274, 278, 280, 282, 286–287
  origins of, 268–269
  Peace Walk, 282–286
  Seeds of Re-Conectando, 288–291
  Truth Mandala, 276–277, 280
re-localization, 320–321
rewilding, 62
Rilke, Rainer Maria, 175
Rinpoche Choegyal Tulku, 251
Rio Earth Summit, 80
Rojava, 317–318
Rosenberg, Marshall, 55
Rothberg, Michael, 83–84
Roy, Arundhati, 316
Rumbaut, Carmen, 122, 137

S
sealey, nicole, 334
Seed, John, 75–76, 78
Seitshiro, Lebogang, 27
self-awareness, 42, 52, 115–117, 216–217, 223–233, 236, 289
Sepúlveda, Jesús, 335–336
Seventh Generation practice, 27, 172
Shah, Priyal, 257
Shields, Karina, 77
shifts, 316–318
Shindler, Craig, 29
shocks, 303–310, 318–321
Siegel, Daniel, 208–209
Simon, Adelaja, 55
slavery, 14, 31–32, 37, 39, 56, 60–62, 65–66, 94, 105, 151, 202, 203, 288, 308, 325
slides, 303–304, 310–315, 318–321
Social Change Training & Resource Centre, 77
social ecology, 90, 92–95

social identities, 8, 18, 146, 181, 183, 233, 235
  and social location, 8, 109–117, 129
socialization, 107–109
  Cycle of Socialization, 107–109
social justice, 72, 77, 86, 149, 159, 163, 249
  and Work That Reconnects, 87–95
social location, 8, 9, 42–43, 81, 84, 91–92, 109–117, 129, 152, 186–187, 208, 223–225
  and (de)centering, 129–134
  and empathy gaps, 114–115
  in group settings, 113–117
  and historical process, 101–103
  Power and Privilege Graphic Tool, 112
  Simplified Social Location Mapping Wheel, 110–112
  and social identities, 8, 109–117, 129
Spiral of the Work That Reconnects, 40–43, 53, 68, 73, 194, 206–207, 250–252, 256–257
  Decolonized Expanded Spiral, 42–43
  Deep Time, 28–29, 42, 55–56, 64, 77–78, 284, 288, 300
  Dwelling in Deep Time, 55–56
  Go Forth, 42
  (Coming from) Gratitude, 40, 42, 206, 251, 274
  Honoring Our Pain for the World, 40–41, 73, 114–115, 206–207, 218–219, 250
  Seeing with New/Ancient Eyes, 40–43, 73, 207, 209, 252, 256–257, 272, 274
St. Onge, Patricia, 29, 55, 85, 247–248, 252
Strategy Framework for a Just Transition, 298–299
structural violence, 52, 87. See also police violence
Sue, Derald Wing, 136, 140
Symens-Bucher, Anne, 55, 84
Syria, 317–318
systems of oppression, 13, 15, 22,

99–119. See also social identities; social location
  freeing ourselves from, 99–119
  interlocking, 47–69
  materialist understanding of, 101–103
systems theory/thinking, 27–28, 33, 38, 68, 87, 102, 165, 248–249, 251–252, 256, 300

T

Tan, Amy, 112
Taylor, Keeanga-Yamahtta, 83
ter Ellen, Helena, 268
Thatcher, Margaret, 78
The Politics of Trauma: Somatics, Healing and Social Justice (Staci K. Haines), 149, 206
Thinking Like a Mountain: Towards a Council of All Beings, 76
Three Mile Island, 72
Three Stories of Our Time, 29–33, 65, 79, 124. See also Business As Usual; Great Turning; Great Unraveling
tokenization, 129, 181
Transformative Justice, 119, 191, 300, 346
transitional justice, 390n12
trauma
  healing resources, 367
  intergenerational, 205
  and nervous system changes, 205–206
trauma awareness, 205–222
trauma-informed facilitation, 207–221
  and confidentiality, 217
  and consent, 217
  content warnings, 217–218
  co-regulation, 187, 210, 213, 218, 220, 237
  embodiment, somatics, grounding, 211–213, 215–217, 219
  group formation, 213–216
  introduction processes, 215
  nervous system awareness, 207–211, 216–221
  and physical contact, 217
  self-regulation, 216, 219, 237
  Window of Tolerance, 173, 208–210, 216, 221
  Zones of Regulation, 211
truth and reconciliation
  in Colombia, 269–272
  commissions, 37
Truth Mandala, 170, 218, 263, 276–277, 280
Turtle Island/Abya Yala, 59

U

uncertainty, 27–28
Unfolding Self (Molly Brown), 169
United States. See also California; capitalism; centering; disaster capitalism; Hurricane Katrina; police violence; racism; slavery; white fragility; white supremacy
  Civil Rights Movement, 82
  and colonialism, 31, 82
  DEI programs in, 6
  green capitalism, 62
  hierarchies in, 100
  and racial ideology, 82–86
  and right-wing ideologues, 5–6
  Texas, 6

W

Wadud, Amina, 334
web of life, 5–7, 12, 19, 22, 24, 25, 43, 54, 59, 60, 64, 66–69, 95, 170, 207, 251, 281
West, Cornel, 4
What It Takes to Heal (Prentis Hemphill), 147–148, 224, 235, 243
white fragility, 225, 238, 242
White Fragility (Robin DiAngelo), 225
white nativists, 321
white supremacy, 5, 9, 14, 24, 30, 37, 39, 147, 226–227, 242
Wild Mind: A Field Guide to the Human Psyche (Bill Plotkin), 390n9
Wilkerson, Isabel, 104
Window of Tolerance, 173, 208–210, 216, 221
witches, 60, 63–65. See also femicide
Wolcott, Sara Jolena, 63–64

workshops, 15, 49–69. *See also* facilitators, facilitation; group spaces; group work
diversity welcomes, 130
group/community agreements in, 53, 130–131, 349–353
and the hegemony of dominant culture, 7
participant introductions, 115–116, 130, 186–187, 199, 215, 354–355
versus psychotherapy, 221
reinforcing oppressive harm in, 135–145
Work That Reconnects. *See also* Brown, Molly; Great Turning; Macy, Joanna; Open Sentences; Spiral of the Work That Reconnects
Accepting the Challenges and Gifts of This Lifetime, 44
Bodhisattva Check-in, 44, 220, 250
and Buddhism, 24, 248–251
core assumptions of, 24–26
and cultural awareness, 252–257
cultural roots of, 248–252
Dance to Dismember the Ego, 169
decolonial approaches within, 7
and Deep Ecology, 28, 48, 71–80, 92–95, 248, 251, 252, 256, 300
and Deep Time, 28–29, 42, 55–56, 64, 77, 78, 284, 288, 300
Harvesting the Gifts of the Ancestors, 13, 44, 124, 172, 257
history of, 71–86
in India, 258–265
and intersectionalization, 81–86
Milling, 27, 44, 198
and the Movement Generation Justice & Ecology Project, 300–307
and pacifism, 88–90
politicizing practice, 159–161
practices of, 43–45 (*See also* specific practices)
queering of, 155–175
Reporting to Chief Seattle, 355–356
and self-awareness, 42, 52, 115–117, 216–217, 223–233, 236, 289
and social justice, 87–95
and systems thinking/theory, 27, 28, 33, 38, 68, 87, 102, 165, 248–249, 251–252, 256, 300
and trauma awareness, 205–222
Widening Circles, 281
Work That Reconnects Network, 24, 43–44, 66, 81, 257
World Trade Organization, 80

Y

Yunkaporta, Tyson, 335

Z

Zen Roshi Norma Ryūkō Kawelokū Wong, 331

About the Authors and Contributors

The Author/Editor Team

Aravinda Ananda is a social ecologist living on Massachusetts land with her partner and child. She enjoys living a rEvolution in relationship in her daily life and work. Website: Living rEvolution.net

Molly Brown lives in Mount Shasta, California, with her life partner Jim. Eco-philosopher, writer, and workshop facilitator, she co-authored *Coming Back to Life* with Joanna Macy and edits *Deep Times: A Journal of the Work That Reconnects*. Website: MollyYoungBrown.com. Substack: mollyybrown.substack.com/

Kurt Kuhwald was educated, trained, and is committed to learning and contributing, in many transformational, anti-oppressive lifeways. He is a grandfather living on Ohlone land in Oakland, California.

Contributors

Chapter 3:
From Interlocking Systems of Oppression to Interconnected System of Support

Sarah Nahar, MDiv, PhD, is a nonviolent action trainer and Work That Reconnects facilitator. Her doctoral work centers on discard studies: how worldviews impact community environmental decision making in relation to human excreta. She was a Rotary Peace Fellow, and worked at the Martin Luther King, Jr. Center. She founded a climate justice organization EFERT) in her hometown of Elkhart, Indiana, (traditional Potawatomi land) and is the coordinator of Anticolonial Arrivants, an Indigenous solidarity initiative of People of the Global Majority living on Turtle Island. She became the Executive Director of Community Peacemaker Teams after living abroad and graduating from Spelman College and Anabaptist Mennonite Biblical Seminary.

Chapter 4:
A Critical History of the Work That Reconnects
—Phases of Development

Chapter 5:
The Work That Reconnects' Evolving Commitment to Social Justice Over Time

Marc Decitre is a Brussels-based playwright, academic, and activist, who situates his work at the intersection of social ecology and eco-spirituality. He is currently working on a PhD in environmental philosophy and a play that revisits the Tower of Babel story through an ecological lens.

Chapter 8:
Seeing and Addressing Oppression Dynamics: Part 2

Carmen Rumbaut is a retired lawyer and social worker with a focus on social justice. She was a child immigrant to the USA, and is now a seeker of universal truths. She has facilitated and supported the Work That Reconnects and trained in Al Gore's Climate Project. Carmen currently lives as a mystic hermit in San Marcos, Texas, where she focuses on the arts and her four young granddaughters. She has published two books of poetry, over 100 articles on medium.com, and is now working on a series of adult coloring books to help people explore their inner worlds.

Chapter 9:
Queering the Work That Reconnects—Embracing the Wild Fluidity of Life

Ian Goh (he/they) is a contributing editor of The Everyday Philosopher's Guide, dedicated to offering free philosophical tools for daily

life. A facilitator at heart, Ian began by hosting philosophical dialogues with diverse audiences in Malaysia. Driven to integrate somatic and ecological dimensions into his work, he pursued the Spiral Journey Facilitator program. Ian is committed to queering and decolonizing these practices to align with Malaysian contexts, enriching his philosophical practice in the process. His work aims to help others build resilience in times where chaos and possibility intertwine within the Three Stories of Our Time.

Chapter 11:
Trauma Awareness and Approaches for Group Facilitation

Margaret (Markie) Babbott is a psychologist in western Massachusetts. Over the past decade, she has increasingly focused on ecopsychology and helped facilitate the Earth Leadership Cohorts through Interhelp. In addition to spending time with her two adult children and fabulous four-leggeds, she loves hiking, art in every form, and tending her community garden plot.

Janna Diamond (she/her) is a somatic therapy practitioner and the founder of Evolutionary Somatic Practice, where she guides people to heal trauma, embody their truth, and cultivate new skills for an evolving world. For over a decade, Janna has been a leader on climate change resiliency, developing programs for organizations and universities across the U.S. She serves as a Regional Coordinator for the Climate Psychology Alliance of North America, works with frontline activists, and lives in the foothills of the Appalachian Mountains. Learn more at www.jannadiamond.com.

Chapter 13:
Culture and the Work That Reconnects

Rukmini Iyer is the Founder of Exult! Solutions, a consulting practice blending leadership development, organizational transformation, and peacebuilding. With over 24 years of global experience, she integrates ecocentrism, conscious leadership, and dialogic processes into her work. A practitioner of the Work That Reconnects, Rukmini brings her expertise in decolonization, trauma-informed practices, and intersectionality to facilitate collective healing and ecological resilience. She serves on international boards, teaches mediation and conflict resolution, and has led transformative initiatives across corporate, educational, and community contexts. Her work embodies a commitment to bridging systemic inequities while fostering sustainable and inclusive futures.

Mayuree is a facilitator, community nurturer, and practitioner of the Work That Reconnects with over two decades of experience in social change, community-building, arts-based facilitation, and peace creation. She co-creates spaces that address collective grief, foster dialogue across divides, and integrate ancestral wisdom, ecological awareness, and embodied practices. A co-initiator of Collective Healing Circles and active in local and international peacebuilding movements, she supports transformative processes that nurture well-being, leadership, and community resilience. Her dedication to shared liberation and holistic practices reflects a deep commitment to fostering connection with self, community, and the Earth.

Chapter 14:
Re-Conectando: Weaving the Mycelium of the Soul for Peace in Colombia

Helena ter Ellen is from Dutch origins and has studied languages, international politics, and intercultural and interfaith dialogue. A WTR-facilitator since 2009, she co-founded the Belgium association Terr'Eveille. She has been a peace activist in Palestine and especially in Colombia since 2001. She brought WTR to this South American country from 2014 on and later co-created Re-Conectando, a unique process accompanying the Truth Commission, bringing together people from all sides of the conflict around deep ecology and ancestral perspectives. During all these years she took great care in weaving together a "Mycelium of the Soul," reaching out to and training promising leaders in the territories. In 2024, she returned to living in l'Echappée, her cohousing project in Brussels.

Héctor Aristizábal is the Director of the Re-Conectando Foundation and an internationally recognized leader in social theatre. He has dedicated more than 30 years to processes of personal, social, and nature reconciliation through art, deep ecology, and healing rituals. A victim of violence in Colombia, he went into exile in 1989 and founded ImaginAction, working in war and post-conflict zones for 25 years. He returned to his country during the peace process to co-create Re-Conectando with Helena ter Ellen, supporting the Truth Commission with their laboratories in the womb of Mother Earth, and giving rise to the Mycelium of the Soul in the territories.

Liliana Moreno is a Colombian anthropologist, master in rural development, and specialist in narrative creation. In one of her past lives, she worked in the evaluation of social impacts of mining-energy projects, where she realized the need to work on a change of consciousness to face the current ecological and civilizational crisis. In 2022, after experiencing her first Re-Conectando laboratory, she felt the call to bring together the paths traveled in the service of the Earth. Since then, she planted herself as a seed and is currently a facilitator and coordinator of Re-Conectando.

Chapter 15:
Up Against the Limits: *Shifting* **Towards a New Human Compact with Mother Earth**

Brooke Anderson is a former Movement Generation Core Collective member. As a movement photojournalist, her work has been featured in many San Francisco Bay Area exhibits, including Yerba Buena Center for the Arts, East Side Arts Alliance, and Survival Media Agency. She guest-lectures on photography and photojournalism in high schools and universities, and teaches digital photography and visual storytelling for community organizations. Brooke fell in love with photography while documenting the struggles of the low-wage workers (hotel housekeepers, port truckdrivers, recycling workers) she worked with as a union and community organizer. She's a proud union member of Pacific Media Workers Guild CWA 39521 AFL-CIO http://mediaworkers.org/.

Gopal Dayaneni (he/him) has worked for social, economic, environmental, and racial justice through organizing, campaigning, teaching, writing, speaking, and direct action since the 1980s. He co-founded several activist organizations, including Movement Generation: Justice and Ecology Project, which inspires and engages in transformative action towards the liberation and restoration of land, labor, and culture. Currently, Gopal supports movement building with numerous frontline organizations at the intersection of ecology, economy, ending extractivism and empire, and creating commons and community. He teaches at two California universities. Most importantly, Gopal parents two amazing rabble-rousers. He lives in Huichin/Oakland in an intentional, multigenerational social justice community.

Chapter 16:
Whose World Is Ending?
Resisting the Climate Apocalypse Narrative

AJ Hudson is an environmental educator and climate justice activist. Before becoming a professor, AJ spent five years teaching in Brooklyn's low-income and still-segregated public schools. He remains a public school teacher at heart and a profound commitment to education and youth empowerment grounds his nonprofit work, scholarship, and climate activism. His service agenda seeks to design frameworks that redirect environmental policy and the resources of conservation towards human rights, the just transition, and the needs of marginalized climate justice communities. AJ is a published expert on climate change adaptation and a contributor to the recent Routledge Environmental Justice in North America textbook.

ABOUT NEW SOCIETY PUBLISHERS

New Society Publishers is an activist, solutions-oriented publisher focused on publishing books to build a more just and sustainable future. Our books offer tips, tools, and insights from leading experts in a wide range of areas.

We're proud to hold to the highest environmental and social standards of any publisher in North America. When you buy New Society books, you are part of the solution!

At New Society Publishers, we care deeply about *what* we publish—but also about *how* we do business.

- This book is printed on 100% **post-consumer recycled paper**, processed chlorine-free, with low-VOC vegetable-based inks (since 2002)
- Our corporate structure is an innovative employee shareholder agreement, so we're one-third employee-owned (since 2015)
- We've created a Statement of Ethics (2021). The intent of this Statement is to act as a framework to guide our actions and facilitate feedback for continuous improvement of our work
- We're carbon-neutral (since 2006)
- We're certified as a B Corporation (since 2016)
- We're Signatories to the UN's Sustainable Development Goals (SDG) Publishers Compact (2020–2030, the Decade of Action)

To download our full catalog, sign up for our quarterly newsletter, and to learn more about New Society Publishers, please visit newsociety.com.

ENVIRONMENTAL BENEFITS STATEMENT

New Society Publishers saved the following resources by printing the pages of this book on chlorine free paper made with 100% post-consumer waste.

TREES	WATER	ENERGY	SOLID WASTE	GREENHOUSE GASES
30	2,400	13	100	12,900
FULLY GROWN	GALLONS	MILLION BTUs	POUNDS	POUNDS

 Environmental impact estimates were made using the Environmental Paper Network Paper Calculator 4.0. For more information visit www.papercalculator.org